JAMES E. ANDERSON
University of Houston

Politics and Economic Policy-Making
Selected Readings

ADDISON-WESLEY PUBLISHING COMPANY
Reading, Massachusetts
Menlo Park, California • London • Don Mills, Ontario

Preface

This collection of readings is based on a policy approach to the study of American politics and is especially intended for courses dealing with policy formation and government-economy relationships. In contrast to the more standard process approach with its focus on institutions and institutional processes, such as the legislative process and the administrative process, the policy approach is concerned with the analysis of policy problems and the formation and administration of policies relating to them. The policy approach, like the process approach, is also concerned with studying the interaction of political variables in decision-making, but it puts more stress on understanding policy problems and policy substance and on the in-depth analysis of particular policy areas.

The policy approach should not be confused with the "great issues" approach, as one might call it, to public policy. This type of treatment of public policy has a strong normative element, involving consideration of such matters as the proper role of government in the economy and the "case" for and/or against actual or proposed policies, such as minimum wage legislation or agricultural price supports. Description, analysis, and explanation of existing problems and policies are the burden, and a substantial one it is, of the policy approach.

The policy approach has several merits. First, the focus on policy permits us to apply our knowledge of the various elements (political attitudes, voting behavior, pressure groups) and processes of politics to the study and understanding of something substantive, of what government actually does and why it does it in seeking to resolve public problems. Second, the policy approach focuses attention on the interaction of institutions, processes, and policy substance—on how the nature and structure of political processes may shape policy and, in turn, how policy may affect the operation of the political process. Third, the policy approach should sharpen and deepen the study of political processes and make resulting generalizations more meaningful and more rooted in the realities of political life. Fourth, the policy approach should help satisfy the demands of those who want politics courses to be more "relevant," more attentive to the needs, problems, and conditions of modern life and the relationships of government thereto. (To add a caveat, the policy approach is not of course a panacea, a one-shot cure-all, for the study of politics. It supplements but does not supplant the other approaches to political study.)

No attempt has been made to include in this anthology selections dealing with all the areas of economic policy. Limitations of space plus the desire to include fairly lengthy and thorough items made selectivity necessary. Apart from the introductory chapter on the policy environment, the decision was made to concentrate on a few policy areas which are rather standard for courses on economic policy, such as business regulation and labor-management relations, and a couple which represent fairly new or neglected policy areas, namely, antipoverty activity and natural resources. Within each chapter, one or two relatively broad policy problems are treated. The organization of the material along substantive policy lines reflects the policy approach and the notion that, when all is considered, the policy-making process is a pluralistic phenomenon, varying from one substantive area to another as problems, participants, and procedures vary.

Hopefully, these readings will help provide the student with both a systematic understanding and an "intuitive feel" for the policy-making process, its complexity and diversity, and its relation to policy substance. If it stimulates further interest in the study of public policy, I will be especially pleased. Political scientists have too long neglected this aspect of politics, although a reversal of this trend is now underway. May continue.

I wish to thank the various authors and publishers who have given their permission to reprint the various selections in this book. Without their cooperation there of course would have been no book.

Houston, Texas   J. E. A.
January 1970

Contents

chapter one

The Policy Environment

Public policy can be usefully defined as the course of action followed by government in dealing with some matter, such as poverty, industrial monopoly, or agricultural prices. Viewed as a course of action, policy involves both decisions to take action, as by the enactment of statutes, and whatever is done to implement or enforce such decisions. Thus, antitrust policy consists not only of statutes such as the Sherman and Federal Trade Commission Acts but also of the administrative, judicial, and other activity relating to their enforcement (or nonenforcement). It should be noted also that policy may be either positive or negative in nature, involving decisions to act or not to act, as the case may be, on some matter. For example, when Congress refuses to regulate the wages of some farm workers, it is making policy (i.e., deciding the course of governmental action) just as it is when it decides that the prices of some farm commodities should be supported.

The formation of public policy does not take place in a political vacuum. Rather, a variety of political, institutional, ideological, and other factors operate to influence and shape decisions and policies. The readings in this section are intended to acquaint the reader with some of the major components of this "policy environment." Among these components are pressure groups, political parties, governmental structure, and political beliefs. Although their operation and impact will vary from one time and situation to another, each will affect most if not all major policy decisions.

Private organized interest groups (or to be less clinical, pressure groups) are a major source of demands for action, or as is quite frequently the case, inaction, by those officials in policy-making positions. In order to influence governmental action in ways favorable to their interests, these groups need access to policy makers, that is, the opportunity to express and advocate their interests. However, Professor Gable states, access does not by itself guarantee effective influence. Cultural factors, such as group status and symbols, importantly affect the influence which particular groups will have on policy makers. Gable goes on to discuss the techniques used by pressure groups in seeking to influence policy and their role in the democratic political process. His discussion of the Federal Power Commission points up the role administrative agencies may play in the formation of policy.

In the American political system, political power is fragmented and dispersed by such institutional arrangements as federalism and the separation of powers. These create a variety of policy-making arenas and, additionally, often necessitate bargaining and compromise among official and nonofficial participants in two or more of these arenas (for instance, Congress and the Presidency) to secure final decisions on policy issues. Harmon Zeigler's discussion of how federalism and the separation of powers affect the activities and success of pressure groups illustrates these generalizations. Some groups will have more access and influence at the national level, others at the state level; some will have more access to the legislature, others to the chief executive or judiciary. Generally groups will seek to have policy decisions made at those points where they believe they have the most likelihood of obtaining action favorable to their interests. Thus, as Zeigler relates, the oil companies wanted development of the "tidelands" to be controlled by the state governments rather than the national government, believing they could more successfully influence decisions on oil development policy made by state legislatures and agencies. Again, groups opposed to legalization of the basing-point system (a device for reducing industrial price competition) were unable to prevent congressional passage of a bill to this effect, but were successful in securing a presidential veto of it because of the President's agreement with their position. Policy can thus be made at a great many points in the American political system, and the point at which a particular decision is made often substantially affects who prevails in the struggle for advantage.

Many commentators have suggested that the major political parties in the United States are simply a case of Tweedledee and Tweedledum or, as a recent presidential candidate put it, "there's not a dime's worth of difference between them." Clearly the major parties are not, to use Sir Edmund Burke's definition, bodies "of men united, for promulgating by their joint endeavors the national interest, upon some particular principle in which they are all agreed." Nor do the parties appear to have a significant role in the *origination* of policy proposals. However, these comments should not be taken to mean that political parties are of no consequence in policy-making. The findings reported by Keefe and Ogul indicate that in Congress the Republican and Democratic parties have an important impact on voting on many policy issues, especially in the general area of social welfare and labor legislation. (See the selection from the *Congressional Quarterly* in Chapter Five for a discussion of the effect of political parties on agricultural price support legislation.) Although the parties are not by any means completely unified in voting, there are substantial differences between them in such areas as social welfare, agricultural prices, and public power legislation, differences which outweigh their internal divergencies. Party affiliation has been found to be the best *single* indicator as to how congressmen will vote on policy issues. Keefe and Ogul provide support for this generalization.

Professor Emmette S. Redford argues that patterns of beliefs are a significant factor shaping social action and, in point here, the formation of economic policy. He supports his position by discussing a number of political, economic, and legal beliefs which have been instrumental in the development of regulatory policy for domestic commercial air transportation. In his view, to be feasible or practical, policy proposals must fit within existing belief patterns, or else these patterns must be modified. Policy proposals designed to promote the interests of particular groups are often rationalized and made more publicly acceptable by being expressed in the terms and symbols of widely-held beliefs, such as those relating to private property, equality of opportunity, due process, and individual freedom. Conversely, some proposals have been defeated by being depicted as contrary to existing belief patterns, as when the American Medical Association successfully stigmatized the Truman Administration's health insurance proposal as "socialized medicine." Widely-shared beliefs help both to shape and to limit the nature of public policy.

INTEREST GROUPS AS POLICY SHAPERS
Richard W. Gable

The heart of government is public policy and its life blood is the policy-making process. A public policy is a decision or set of decisions that establishes a purpose, creates a precedent, or lays down a course of action. The decision itself is a conclusion drawn from a set of premises.

Policy originates and results from the actions of interested groups inside or outside of government which desire to influence the basic premises underlying policy decisions or the conclusions drawn from those premises. The interested group may be a legislative group, political party, administrative agency, foreign government, or private interest group. However, policy almost never originates solely within the legislature, and political parties have largely ceased to be centers of policy creation. Foreign governments assume importance in policy making only in very special cases. Administrative agencies and private interest groups have come to be the principal originators of policy, while legislative groups, along with administrative and private groups, are the major shapers of public policy.

Contrary to a common myth, public policy does not result from any generalized feeling or opinion that exists in the "public." There is, in fact, no single public in the community. What is often referred to as the "public" consists of a number of publics which, on specific issues, have particular opinions but which, on other issues, may have no opinion or divergent opinions. This is not to say that the opinions of the various publics are unimportant. Moreover, since interest groups cannot always identify the publics which are relevant to their interests, they may direct their campaigns to manipulate public opinion at the public in general.

The role of private groups in shaping public policy depends upon the cultural setting within which they operate and the nature of the policy-making process. Brief attention will be given to these topics

Reprinted from the *Annals of the American Academy of Political and Social Science,* Vol. 319 (September, 1958), 84–93, by permission of the author and publisher. Copyright 1958 by the American Academy of Political and Social Science.

before analyzing the general role of private groups in the formulation of public policy. No effort will be made to catalogue all of the points at which private groups might exert pressure or to describe the myriad of techniques which have been employed. The intention is to sketch a generalized picture of pressure group functioning and to indicate some of the factors which contribute to a group's success in shaping public policy.

The Cultural Environment

Government is an aspect of society. The political process in which political interest groups figure most directly is but an aspect of the broader social processes in which general interest groups play a role. Interest groups originate whenever an identity of interests is recognized by a group of people who are willing to organize or act in concert to promote and defend their interests; they become political interest groups when their objectives are sought by attempting to shape public policy.

The nature and functioning of political interest groups are dependent upon the social and political environment within which they operate. Properly the entire cultural milieu should be understood to appreciate fully the role and influence of interest groups in society. As cultural factors such as attitudes, status, and symbols vary, the nature and function of pressure groups may vary. Social attitudes establish expectations about the role of pressure groups in society. Some groups, like the doctors and lawyers in the United States, may have more status than others. The predominant cultural symbols may favor some groups over others also. Since ours is a business civilization, groups which utilize the symbols of private property, free enterprise, and the like enjoy an advantage.

Any analysis of the role and influence of political interest groups in shaping public policy must take into account the cultural environment within which they operate. It would be impossible to indicate here all of the factors which might have to be considered to present a realistic picture. A random listing suggests some of the more important cultural elements which condition the political activity of interest groups: the history of a people, the predominant values and myths of the culture, the structure of society, the class system, the nature of the educational system, the influence of religion, the media of communications, the nature of the economy and the state of economic development, the role of government in relation to the economy, the constitutional separation and distribution of powers of government, the electoral system, the party system, the nature of the civil service—its organization and control—and the level of efficiency in the management of the affairs of government.

The Policy-making Process

Almost never does a public policy serve the interests of or result from the action of a single group. The more complex and controversial the decision, the more likely that a great number and variety of contending groups have participated in some way in the shaping of the policy.

The formulation of public policy pervades government in all its branches and at all its levels. It is a continuous process which intersects and overlaps the three branches of government and includes the activities of political parties and political interest groups. Public policy is made by all the processes and procedures which operate in government. It may be a legislative enactment which takes the form of law, or it may be a high level executive decision. Policy determination also occurs in the process of administration quite as much as does policy execution. An administrative rule or regulation, internal in effect, highly specific and limited in scope, is still an aspect of public policy. Furthermore, the decisions of the courts constitute policy and have consequences for other centers of policy making.

In order to assert their will, political interest groups seek access to the key points where decisions are made. An important characteristic of the process in the United States is the multiplicity of points of decision and hence points of access. To be successful a pressure group must conduct its campaign along a series of fronts—individual legislators, legislative committees, legislative leaders, party leaders, the executive, the bureaucracy, the courts, opinion leaders in the community, and so forth.

A brief, oversimplified description of the process by which public policy in the field of natural gas regulation has evolved may be helpful in illustrating the number of contact points at which interest groups, in this case oil and gas interests and consumer groups, may direct pressure. It also dramatizes the continuous nature of the political process as a policy question gravitates between the courts, Congress, the President, and the bureaucracy.[1]

A series of Supreme Court decisions over a period of twenty-five years left a broad segment of the natural gas industry unregulated. At the production end of the industry the states imposed controls to conserve natural resources. At the other end, retail sales were subject to state regulation because the business of serving the consumer was held to be affected with a public interest. However, the rates charged by interstate pipe-line companies were found to be beyond the jurisdiction of the states because of the constitutional restraints which prevent state regulation from burdening interstate commerce.

Congress enacted the Natural Gas Act in 1938 to fill this gap. The jurisdiction of the Federal Power Commission was specified as applying to the transportation of natural gas in interstate commerce and to the sale of natural gas in interstate commerce. Production and gathering of natural gas and local distribution were specifically exempted from FPC jurisdiction. Unfortunately, the law did not make clear whether the prices charged by the producers and gatherers of natural gas, so-called field prices, were sales in interstate commerce and hence subject to FPC regulation, or whether they were a part of production and gathering and hence exempt. A review of the legislative history of the law provided no help.

In several cases the FPC denied that it had jurisdiction. Then, in 1943, the Commission handed down a ruling sustained by the courts which was interpreted as implying that the FPC did have jurisdiction over field prices. This decision triggered a campaign in Congress to amend the Natural Gas Act exempting field prices from federal regulation. When Congress failed to pass any amendatory legislation the FPC issued an order in which it announced that field prices were not subject to Commission jurisdiction.

In the next session of Congress a renewed effort to exempt field prices was successful although the FPC, with the addition of a new member, now opposed the amendment. Congressional hostility to the members of the Commission who opposed the exemption reached such a pitch that when the reappointment of Leland Olds, the Chairman of the FPC, was submitted to the Senate for confirmation, Olds was denied the reappointment.[2] Nevertheless, Olds' replacement joined the majority of the Commission in urging a Presidential veto which was forthcoming. The Commission immediately rescinded its rule exempting field prices. Then, just a year later in the most important in a long series of cases, the FPC refused to assume jurisdiction over the field prices of the Phillips Petroleum Company. The Supreme Court reversed the Commission, asserting it did have jurisdiction over field prices under the original law. (As an aftermath of the Phillips case, the Senate refused to confirm the reappointment of another Commissioner, who was the sole dissenter to the Commission's denial of jurisdiction in the Phillips case.)

Again, another campaign was launched to amend the Act. It was successful in Congress and would have undoubtedly received Presidential approval if some of the pressure exerted on certain Congressmen had not been so blatant. When it was made public that money had been passed in an attempt to gain support, the President vetoed the measure.

The "Washington Symphony of Natural Gas" was played in counterpoint. The theme was set by Congress. Contrapuntal melodies were devised in the hearing rooms of the Federal Power Commission and the courts, but the harmony was sometimes discordant. Congress responded with efforts to introduce variations on the original theme, while the musicians whose brass notes were too loud were dropped from the orchestra. E. Pendleton Herring's comment on our political system is appropriate here although the metaphor becomes mixed. We believe, he said, that "power must be handled like a loving cup and passed around lest one of the company grow drunk."

Role and Influence of Political Interest Groups

Political interest groups constantly endeavor to shape public policy. An interest group may succeed in shaping public policy when it is able to identify its conception of the needs of the moment with the prevailing or predominant attitudes of a number of prominent publics and when it has access to the major centers of policy decision in government.

Attention is usually given to the amount of access which an interest group has, whereas access may be the least important way by which a group gains its end. Certainly, access does not mean influence. Many groups have had extensive access, but have had little influence. After the Wagner Act was passed the National Association of Manufacturers and other employers' associations had access to Congress and its committees, but the law was not amended for twelve years, not until there was a significant shift in the climate of opinion in the nation. Labor has had almost continual access to Congress since the Taft-Hartley Act was enacted, but it has failed to have the law repealed or modified.

The degree to which a group is able to associate itself and its objectives with relevant publics is often the crucial factor. Any decision involves the selection of certain values or premises over others. The choice of one set of values over another would result in entirely different public policy. The values or premises must be made acceptable at the place where a policy decision will be made before access can be exploited.

Identification of the interests of a group with those of relevant publics may be accomplished in several ways. A group may manipulate public attitudes so that they approximate those of the interest group or, at least, so that the relevant publics are neutral or indifferent to the group's objectives. On the other hand, the group might adjust its attitudes so that they more closely conform to public attitudes. More commonly the group will attempt to manipulate public attitudes at the same time that it modifies or adjusts its own attitudes.

For example, the NAM carried on intensive and expensive public-relations and propaganda programs designed to influence Congress to modify the Wagner Act. These programs had both strategic and tactical objectives. The strategic goal was the creation of a climate of opinion within which the NAM's conception of individualism, free enterprise, and laissez-faire would be habitually accepted as values of positive good and alternatives to it would be rejected. The tactical campaign sought a favorable response to the particular proposals the Association submitted as solutions to current labor problems.

At the same time the NAM adjusted its policies somewhat to conform to public attitudes. Between 1933 and 1945 the NAM's conception of social needs did not keep pace with rapidly changing conditions. Rather than rely any longer on the futile attempt solely to manipulate public attitudes to conform to its values, the NAM underwent a metamorphosis. Prior to 1937 the NAM strenuously opposed government guarantee of the rights to organize, bargain collectively, and engage in concerted action. Not immediately, but gradually after the Jones-Laughlin decision upheld the constitutionality of the Wagner Act, the NAM came to the conclusion that these rights actually contributed to the welfare of both industry and labor—if circumscribed by certain regulations. Thus, the NAM accepted the necessity of government action and intervention in labor relations in place of industrial self-rule and laissez-faire; but it demanded that the intervention be on behalf of employers. After modifying its basic system of values the NAM had considerably more success in its public-relations and propaganda efforts.[3]

Propaganda: degree of success.   Much money and effort are spent by political interest groups in their unending campaigns to maintain the friendship of their supporters, woo the potentially sympathetic, sway the neutral and the indifferent, and convert the actively hostile. However, it is a mistake to assume that wide use of the various media of communications, broad coverage of the various audiences, and ingeniously prepared material are indicators of sure success. The propaganda effort might fail for any of several reasons. The target population might not perceive the group's message at the time and in the way the interest group intended it to be perceived, the group's message might fail to arouse the expected attitudes, or the propaganda might not produce the particular action sought.[4]

Furthermore, many factors involved in manipulating attitudes are external to the group and to a large extent are not subject to its control regardless of how well prepared the campaign. Generally, these factors are basic aspects of the culture which condition or limit the influence of particular interest groups in the political process. For example, the ability of a group to create a favorable climate of opinion depends upon the current political and economic conditions in the community and the values and expectations which are predominant at the time, the status and prestige of the group and its members in society and of competitive groups, and so forth. Professional groups, like doctors or lawyers, or business groups in general, as examples, enjoy a propaganda advantage because of the prestige and status factor.

Even if the group succeeds in bringing about the desired alignment of attitudes, the desired public policy might not result. The NAM was successful in convincing a number of employer publics of the need to change the Wagner Act, but these groups were unable to exert sufficient influence at key points in policy determination to gain their ends. In other words, the propaganda campaign may have been successful, but the publics who responded to it were not able to gain access to centers of policy formulation or to exploit that access to their advantage.

Ultimately, to gain its end a political interest group must gain access to the centers of policy making in government while at the same time it attempts to prevent or limit competing groups from gaining a similar advantage.[5] The ability of a group to gain or exploit access is limited by certain factors external to the group which, to a large extent, are not subject to its control. It is dependent upon the structure of government, the organization and procedures of the legislature and administrative offices, the party structure and degree of party responsibility, as well as the status of the group under the existing values of society.

Access involves not only the act of communicating with legislators and administrators, but the skill with which the position of accessibility is exploited and the willingness, for various reasons, of a legislator or administrator to make decisions that accord with the proposals of the group. Again, a group does not enjoy complete control over these activities. The skill with which a group can exploit its position is dependent upon the structure of government, legislative organization and procedures, party structure and responsibility, and so forth. The willingness of a legislator or administrator to decide in a way that suits an interest group may result from no action of the group itself.

In the past some political interest groups gained access to government using the techniques of what E. Pendleton Herring called the "old lobby." The stains of political corruption, underhanded methods, and payment of election expenses characterized the "old lobby." In contrast, the "new lobbies" have learned to work in the open; they have nothing to hide; they know what they want and how to get it. The "new lobbyist" offers advice, assistance, and his services to willing legislators and administrators. Modern interest groups often have access to more facts than do legislators or administrators. They have extensive staffs of highly qualified persons and the financial resources with which to do research. They can open new channels of communication between government and private groups. Legislators and administrators have actually come to rely upon them.

Areas of influence.   Political interest groups exert influence on the policy-making process along several fronts. They attempt to elect government officials favorable to their position and defeat those unfavorable, influence party platforms and other policy utterances of the political parties, and influence the legislative and administrative process at every phase where access is available or influence may be exerted.

The first front is the well-understood activity of nominations and elections. As the political parties decline in importance as centers for the origination of policy, the need to influence party policy positions becomes less. However, the many interest groups still put in an appearance before the Resolutions Committee of the major parties when they are drafting party platforms.

Both indirect and direct influence is exerted on legislatures and administrative agencies. Indirect influence is exerted when a group encourages members, affiliates, and other publics to engage in political activities themselves. Direct influence occurs when a group communicates with legislators and administrators through letters, by appearances before legislative committees and other fact-finding agencies, by personal visits to legislators and administrators, and the like.

In some cases, political interest groups are actually invited to participate in the processes of government. Administrative agencies may use advisory groups consisting of interest group representatives, popular referenda of interest-group opinions may be held, or representatives of interest groups may be incorporated into an agency. In certain instances, as in the case of professional licensing boards, the authority to make public policy may be delegated to private groups.

While it is true that the most important factor in the success of any interest group is achieving a situation in which individual legislators and administrators are in agreement with the group's proposals, these individuals are not mere chips on a sea of pressures, subject to shifting winds and the ebb and flow of tidal changes. They are individuals possessing attitudes, values, and frames of reference which render them more receptive to some proposals than to others. They are more likely to be receptive to proposals that stem from sources comparable to those from which their own attitudes and values have been derived.[6]

The fact that the judiciary is a political institution is sometimes overlooked. The pattern of judicial action is so well established and the form and procedures of the courts are so well known and accepted that pressure group activity is much less. Yet, the judiciary is a principal holder of public power favorably situated so that it can influence the balance among the shifting interests in society. Moreover, if the courts operate markedly contrary to the expectations of significant segments of the community or if its role is attacked, the political character of the judiciary becomes apparent.

The attacks on the Supreme Court after the decision concerning segregation in schools and cases involving loyalty-security matters illustrate this point. The role of the judiciary in economic regulation provides another example. Before 1937, business groups joined with the courts to defeat a number of acts of social legislation. The Supreme Court came under attack from liberal economic forces in the country which were allied with the President. The Court modified its position toward social legislation in a decision involving the Wagner Act which has been aptly referred to as "the switch in time that saved nine."

After 1937, a new alliance was formed between certain economic interests and powerful groups within Congress which could no longer rely on the Supreme Court for support. In fact, experiencing decisions that were adverse to their interests, they proceeded to overrule the Court by legislative action and were successful in a number of instances. The Congressional effort to overturn the Court's ruling in the natural gas controversy was balked by a Presidential veto, as was the attempt to amend the antitrust law to allow businesses to absorb shipping costs in order to quote uniform delivered prices throughout the country after the Supreme Court had declared the basing-point system illegal. Successful were the tidelands oil legislation reversing the position of the Court that offshore oil lands were subject to federal jurisdiction, the McCarran Act exempting insurance companies from federal antitrust regulation, and the McGuire Act exempting nonsigner-resale-price-maintenance agreements from the antitrust laws after the Court ruled that the original exempting legislation did not include nonsigner agreements.

The impression that the decisions of the Supreme Court are final and binding is no longer accurate. The Supreme Court is properly viewed as one more level, not necessarily the final one, of official compromise and decision in the never-ending interplay between interest groups, the legislature, the executive, administrative agencies, and political parties.

Interest Groups in Democratic Government

An understanding of the cultural factors which condition the role played by interest groups in our society might provide insight into a fundamental paradox. Interest groups are necessary and essential elements in our policy-making process, but at the same time they can impair the effective operation of representative democracy. Moreover, we expect interest groups to exert influence on government, and we condone such action. Yet, we do not expect our officials of government to submit to such influence, and we condemn the fact that they do.

The activity and influence of pressure groups can be expected to increase. Interest groups beget interest groups and pressure begets pressure. The success of one group stimulates the opposition to more vigorous activity. The locus of decision for many problems is moved from the private to the public arena. As an illustration, the Wagner Act used federal power to prevent long established practices which interfered with the efforts of workers to organize and encouraged the practice of collective bargaining. However, the Act did not attempt a detailed regulation of employer-employee relations. Instead, it left the details of this relationship to be worked out by the parties in the labor negotiations.

In time business and industrial groups succeeded in modifying this law which they saw as weighing the balance too heavily on the side of labor. Groups, like the NAM, which had been vigorous opponents of labor's rights to organize and bargain collectively and of the principle of government involvement in the economy reconstructed their basic philosophy. Under the Taft-Hartley Act government was brought into labor relations more than it had been before, this time on the side of management. What was once regarded as a matter for private negotiations between interested parties is now subject to government direction. Important areas of negotiation have shifted from the bargaining table to Washington. Political power is substituted for economic power, and private problems are made public problems. Modification of basic elements in employer-employee relations now appears to require another act of Congress instead of a new contract between union and management.

There has been frequent comment on the alleged danger from pressure groups. One of the most serious charges is that they threaten the public interest. Such a criticism presumes that the public interest can be identified. One is forced to agree with Frank Sorauf who, after a detailed analysis of the various definitions of the public interest, concludes that "the term 'public interest' has no genuinely valid intellectual definition, and that it suffers as well from a multiplicity of inadequate definitions." However, he adds, "Americans do embrace a public interest or value in another sense. They are agreed upon a governmental process that reconciles divergent interests according to established rules and processes."[7] We accept the method of democracy, even though we may share no common policy goals, and, in fact, regardless of the policies it may produce. The wisdom or reasonableness of the democratic process does not lie in any specific policy, but in the process by which decisions are reached.

By focusing on the processes of government in operation rather than on the substance of policies, the effect of political interest groups on the public interest can be more objectively evaluated. The question, then, is not whether a public policy is undesirable, piecemeal, less rational, a partial solution, or lacking in comprehensive planning. Rather, the question is whether the process of formulating policy has been perverted by pressure-group activity.

From this point of view, an evaluation of pressure groups must consider procedure rather than the policy which results. Are the media of communications available to all groups? Are there effective mechanisms for the articulation of political demands? Do unorganized interests have the opportunity to organize? Does money, power, or prestige give undue advantage to certain groups? Is the procedure employed indirect and obscure? Can responsibility be fixed? Do the groups actually represent the members for whom they claim to speak? Can the members of groups maintain accountability? On questions like these does the final appraisal of the role of pressure groups in a democracy turn.

NOTES

1. For a more complete description, see the author's article, "The Jurisdiction of the Federal Power Commission over the Field Prices of Natural Gas," *Land Economics,* Vol. 32 (February 1956), pp. 39–56.

2. For a fascinating account, see Joseph P. Harris, "The Senatorial Rejection of Leland Olds: A Case Study," *American Political Science Review,* Vol. 45 (September 1951), pp. 674–92.

3. See the author's article, "NAM: Influential Lobby or Kiss of Death?" *Journal of Politics,* Vol. 15 (May 1953), pp. 254–73.

4. David B. Truman, *The Governmental Process* (New York: Alfred A. Knopf, 1951), pp. 245–61.

5. The concept of "access" is developed at length in Truman, *ibid.,* pp. 321–51. The effectiveness of a group's efforts to gain and exploit access, as well as to identify itself with relevant publics, is related to certain internal factors which are primarily within the control of the interest group and depen-

dent upon its activities. These internal factors, which are beyond the scope of this paper, include: the size of the group; the alliances it can make with other groups; its structure, organization, and policy-making procedures; the quality of its leadership; its financing; and its cohesion.

6.   See Truman, *ibid.,* pp. 338–39.

7.   "The Public Interest Reconsidered," *Journal of Politics,* Vol. 19 (November 1957), pp. 630–31, 633.

THE INSTITUTIONAL CONTEXT
Harmon Zeigler

Democracy ... is not dependent upon any given set of governmental institutions. Although we are accustomed to equate our particular form of government with the basic necessities of stable democracy, there are many democratic countries with forms of government different from our own. Nevertheless there are formal patterns of authority which coexist with American democracy. Pressure groups not only must cope with the intellectual environment or cultural atmosphere of the nation but must also operate within the framework of governmental institutions. This section will consider the relation of pressure groups to the following American institutions: (1) federalism, (2) separation of powers. . . .

Federalism and the Separation of Powers

Federalism and the separation of powers are closely related and will be discussed as a single unit. Federalism may be defined legally as a system of government in which power is divided between a central government and regional governments, each of which is supreme in its own area of jurisdiction. This system is to be contrasted with the unitary system, in which the central government is supreme and all powers held by regional government are delegated. Of course, such delegated powers may be withdrawn. In the American federal system the states are formally recognized as existing independently of the national government.

The Constitution, as every schoolboy knows, does not contain a formal definition of federalism. However, the Constitution does specify the powers held by the national government and provides, in the Tenth Amendment, that "the powers not delegated to the United States by the Constitution, nor prohibited by it to the States, are reserved to the States respectively, or to the people." The Constitution

From Harmon Zeigler, *Interest Groups in American Society,* pp. 42–53. Copyright © 1964. Reprinted by permission of Prentice-Hall, Inc., Englewood Cliffs, New Jersey. Footnotes renumbered.

also includes a system of separation of powers or "checks and balances" among the three branches of the national government. The theoretical argument for these provisions is centered upon the assumption that political power is potentially dangerous. Therefore the best way to reduce the danger is to provide for a balancing of authority between the nation and the states and between the legislative, executive, and judicial branches of the national government. Although one should avoid being so presumptuous as to speak with authority about the *motives* of the framers of the Constitution, it is possible to ascertain from their writings that the system of diffusion of power was designed to provide a barrier to the dominance of "factions" (whether interest group or party). Presumably it would be possible for a faction to gain control of one branch of government only to be thwarted by another; or to control a state government but not *all* the states. As Professor Arthur W. Macmahon states: ". . . federalism lessens the risk of a monopoly of political power by providing a number of independent points where the party that is nationally in the minority at the time can maintain itself while it formulates and partly demonstrates its policies and capabilities and develops new leadership." [1]

To what extent has the diffusion of legal authority succeeded in developing a dispersal of actual or social power? We must be cautious in answering this question in order to avoid becoming overly legalistic. First, there is little doubt that actual power is diversified in American society. Still, there is no way in which we can assert that federalism and the separation of powers cause this diversification. [2] The best that can be done is to provide illustrations of the problems encountered by pressure groups in a system of legal dispersion of authority.

In our system of government we observe groups which, although unsuccessful in achieving their goals on a national level, have established positions of power among state governments. One reason for this occurrence is the variation between the responsibilities of state legislatures as opposed to the national Congress. The state legislature has a narrower set of interests within its area of jurisdiction, whereas the national legislature is responsible to the vast array of interests spread among the entire United States.

One of the best examples of an interest group operating from a position of strength at the state level is the perennial conflict between chain stores and independent retailers.[3] In the years following World War I, chain stores had increased their activities to such a point that the economic lives of thousands of independent merchants were threatened. The coming of the depression of the 1930's added to the menace of the chains and increased the fear on the part of the independent businessman that he would be driven from business. The problem was most intense among grocers because chain operations had been most successful in this field. However, other types of retailers and some wholesalers were also affected. Whatever the type of the business, the mass buying techniques of the chains and the subsequent lower prices charged to consumers were techniques against which there was no economic defense.

To meet this threat the retail and wholesale merchants tried unsuccessfully to prevent chain store growth by boycotting manufacturers who sold directly to chains. Next, independent merchants tried to "educate" the public via mass media to the "evils" of chain stores. However, chain sales continued to rise. Finally the problem was attacked by seeking governmental aid. However, in spite of the fact that chain operations directly injured millions of retailers, no national organization arose to ward off the "chain store menace." Instead, the problem was approached on a state-by-state basis with no connection between the activities of retailers from one state to the next. In most of the states the legislature was urged to enact tax legislation sharply restrictive on the activities of chains. As early as 1927 four states had adopted special taxes on chain stores and thirteen other bills had been introduced but failed to pass. In 1931 the Supreme Court upheld the constitutionality of the chain store tax, and the floodgate was opened. By 1935, two hundred and twenty-five chain tax bills had been introduced and thirteen had passed; by 1939, twenty-seven states had enacted such taxes. One commentator ruefully remarked that "wherever a little band of lawmakers are banded together . . . you may be sure that they are . . . thinking up things they can do to the chain stores."[4]

For our purposes, the significance of this episode is the fact that every success in retaliatory legislation occurred at the state level. Joseph C. Palamountain notes that "taxes vary so extremely from state to state as to show that no national group was able to coordinate the activities of its state and local units. . . ."[5] In fact, there is considerable evidence to suggest that, had the proponents of restrictive chain store taxation not worked through the states, the anti-chain campaign would have been much less successful. By the middle 1930's the chains had developed a counterattack program through the use of effective public relations. By skillful propaganda they converted potential supporters to active participants. Housewives, farm organizations, and food processors combined to ebb the tide of tax legislation. In 1936 California voters, in a popular referendum, voted down a chain tax. Thereafter few states considered chain-tax legislation.

The conclusion of the anti-chain drive occurred when an effort was made to have the national Congress adopt a nationwide restrictive tax in 1938. This would have seriously hampered the operations of chains doing business in several states. However in the arena of Congress, the chains were less at a disadvantage than they had been before the state legislatures. At the state level, home town sentiment against "foreign big business" went a long way toward balancing out the lack of money or organization on the part of the independent merchants. Nationally, the independents did not have the resources to compete with the vast potential of the chain stores. Only the National Association of Retail Druggists worked consistently for the legislation, although a few other retailers' groups testified at committee hearings. The chains, however, marshalled a formidable coalition in order to oppose the bill. The chains gained the support of the American Farm Bureau Federation, the National Association of Real Estate Boards, and many large food manufacturers. In addition, the support of labor unions figured prominently in the chain store coalition. Chain stores also had the backing of the Departments of Agriculture and Commerce.

The independent merchants were outmanned once they sought to expand their sphere of influence to the nation as a whole. The chain-tax bill, introduced by Representative Wright Patman of Texas, was lost in a maze of parliamentary delays. No hearings were held until 1940 and the bill never cleared the committee hearing stage. Thus the federal system of government played a part in the solution to a problem of public policy. Although the anti-chain interests were able to secure federal legislation in the form of the Miller-Tydings amendment to the Sherman Act in 1937, the existence of two levels of decision-making bodies enabled one interest to maintain a position of strength that might not have been possible under a unitary system.

The chain store episode is an example of a conflict within the business community in which each had access to a different decision-making area. In this particular case the larger business group, the chain stores, found a more satisfactory environment in the national legislature. Often, however, corporate interests find it more compatible with their goals to advocate the expansion of state jurisdiction at the expense of the national government. Some large corporations have financial resources greater than many state governments. With respect to the regulation of business, many states lack the necessary administrative machinery to provide thorough supervision. Under these circumstances, the cry of "states' rights" has become an important part of the struggle among pressure groups. As Donald C. Blaisdell has noted: "Federalism is particularly pleasing ... to the managers of industrial enterprise. While their charters to do business are obtained not from the federal but from state government, under federalism they get the benefits of a trade area of continental proportions, at the same time escaping effective federal regulation." [6]

The use of states rights as a symbol or propaganda device is important not only because it serves to clarify the relation of interest groups to the structure of government but also because it plays upon the myths of American society. Indeed the "specter of a centralized federal bureaucracy invading the reserved rights of the states" is invoked on the assumption that our values are biased toward a commitment to "grass roots" democracy.[7]

The use of the states' rights argument by interests seeking to avoid the intervention of the national government into certain economic and social matters began with the surge of industrial expansion after the Civil War, although some businesses still feared the erraticism of the state legislatures and preferred federal regulation. This was the period in which popular reform movements, such as the National Grange, advocated strict regulation of business activity in order to ameliorate the dangers of monopoly. In defense of their status, business interests argued that regulation by the federal government infringed upon the reserved rights of the states while simultaneously maintaining that state regulation was a violation of the right of Congress to regulate under the powers of the commerce clause. A large part of this activity serves to illustrate the use of the doctrine of separation of powers. The normal pattern was for business to challenge regulatory legislation through the courts. Such memorable decisions as *Hammer v. Dagenhart,* in which the Supreme Court invalidated the Child Labor Act as an invasion of the reserved rights of states, reflect this technique.[8] While legislative arenas mirrored the values of those supporting regulation, the courts became the citadel of business.

This technique of "divide and rule," in which federalism was used as a vehicle to produce inaction, made it possible for corporations to turn themselves into clusters of private power, sometimes to the extent of dominating the state governments. Many examples from contemporary economic life illustrate this technique. Oil companies interested in controlling the vast reservoirs of tidelands oil have relied extensively on the doctrine of states' rights. Robert J. Harris has written with perception that "the solicitude of the oil companies for states' rights is hardly based on convictions derived from political theory but rather on fears that federal ownership may result in the cancellation or modification of state leases favorable to their interests, their knowledge that they can successfully cope with state oil regulatory agencies, and uncertainty concerning their ability to control a Federal agency."[9]

The position of large dairy chains is comparable to that of the oil companies. Because the marketing of milk is usually perilous due to the highly perishable quality of the product, many states have created agencies to regulate the distribution of milk. These agencies have usually been ineffective in dealing with the huge interstate chains, such as Sealtest, Borden's, and Foremost, which dominate the market. On occasion, overtures have been made to the Federal Trade Commission by states to assist them in the task of regulation, only to face the determined opposition of the dairies.

These examples should serve to illustrate that federalism does not involve a struggle between the nation and the states, but rather a struggle among interests who have favorable access to one of the two levels of government. The recent controversy over integration fits into this assumption. After the Supreme Court had ruled against the continuation of the practice of segregation in public schools, the states' rights argument was well suited for groups of people in the South who sought to defend their regional customs against the dominant attitudes of the rest of the nation. Local and statewide organizations, known variously as White Citizens Councils and States' Rights Councils, demanded, in the name of the right of each sovereign state to exercise the authority of self-determination, that attempts to end segregation cease. Their efforts are given the official sanction of the state governments. State officials regularly attend meetings and pledge the support of the administration. Letters urging support of these movements are mailed from governors' offices. In Mississippi the state legislature established the State Sovereignty Commission in 1956 to combat integration efforts. The Governor, Ross Barnett, became chairman of this commission and also served as chairman of the Citizens Council, a private organization with the same aims as the official State Sovereignty Commission. The relations between the two bodies became so intimate that the private nature of the Citizens Council was blurred. The legislature actually allocated state funds for the propaganda efforts of the Citizens Council, thus making it a quasi-official body.

In contrast to the warm reception given segregationist groups by the southern state governments, the National Association for the Advancement of Colored People and related organizations have been subjected to constant harassment. Attempts to gain legal access to NAACP records, challenge of tax-exempt status, and other similar tactics continually frustrate the efforts of pro-integration groups. Under these circumstances it is only natural for these organizations to concentrate their efforts at the national government level. The argument between the opposing groups is not, whatever the verbalization, one of the rights of states against an ever-encroaching federal government. Rather the argument concerns more basic values. The states' right argument is an example of the manipulation of symbols for the purpose of creating a satisfactory attitudinal framework for the achievement of political goals. When one realizes that the southern states regularly pay into the federal treasury less than they get back in the form of grants-in-aid, the issue may be seen in a more complete perspective.

Turning to separation of powers, we are confronted with the same patterns of activity expected under any system of divided authority.

Access by a particular group to one branch of government does not necessarily mean access to another. Examples of congressional overturning of decisions by the Supreme Court come most readily to mind. The problem of differential access was brought into focus by two recent instances of judicial decisions which damaged the economic security of trade associations that were influential in Congress.

In 1948 the Supreme Court, in the case of *Federal Trade Commission* v. *Cement Institute,* held that the basing-point system of pricing was illegal. Under this system, prices were determined by formulas which eliminated the right of the consumer to choose between competitive producers. The basing-point system provided that the price of a commodity delivered anywhere in the United States included shipping charges estimated from a geographical basing point, irrespective of the actual point of departure of the merchandise. The Cement Institute, a trade association organized in 1929, had administered such a system rigorously. The assumption which guided the tenacity with which the Institute held to its pricing system was that "ours is an industry above all others that cannot stand free competition, that must systematically restrain competition or be ruined." [10]

The reaction to the Court's decision was swift and decisive. The steel industry, which also used the basing-point system, soon began to work for legislation that would legalize the system. Representatives from the state of Pennsylvania, national center of steel production, introduced resolutions calling for a moratorium suspending further action under the decision. United States Steel abandoned the basing-point system and raised the price of steel seven dollars per ton, although there is evidence suggesting that the change in pricing systems actually reduced the cost to the steel companies by one dollar per ton. The strategy was to raise a demand for legislation among the customers of the steel companies. The clamor finally resulted in the passage of S.1008. This bill provided that the Federal Trade Commission Act be amended so as not to regard the absorption of freight charges by sellers as an unfair trade practice. Thus the Congress had minimized the effects of the Supreme Court's decision.

However, the political process does not stop with the passage of a law. There was still another branch of government which had a role to play. President Truman's sympathies were not usually in accord with the desires of big business, which had guided the legislation through Congress. In addition, his political strength was believed to rest among the lower-income groups. Consequently, the opponents of the basing-point legislation, unable to bring their desires into reality in Congress, were in a more favorable position when they appealed to the President. The congressional delegation which urged Truman to veto was composed entirely of Democrats long conspicuous in their championing of vigorous enforcement of anti-trust legislation such as Senators Kefauver of Tennessee and Douglas of Illinois. In addition, organizations such as the United Automobile Workers of America, the National Association of Retail Druggists, and the United States Wholesale Grocers Association met with the Chairman of the Democratic National Committee. The net result of this activity was a Presidential veto in 1950.

The case of the basing-point legislation gives us a situation in which group interests fought for their goals through the entire national government. Those interests which failed in one area succeeded in another. A similar development can be seen in the Supreme Court decision in *Federal Maritime Board* v. *Isbrandtsen,* handed down in 1958.[11] In this case the Supreme Court struck down the legality of the "dual rate" or "exclusive patronage" contract employed by steamship conferences. Oceangoing carriers have for years been organized into voluntary conferences. These conferences consist only of those vessels furnishing regular service and not the independent lines and "tramps." The principal purpose of these conferences is to establish cargo rates and conditions of carriage. Under normal circumstances such agreements might violate the anti-trust legislation. However, the Shipping Act of 1916 exempted agreements between oceangoing carriers from anti-trust penalties, provided these agreements are approved by the Federal Maritime Board. By 1959 one hundred and ten conferences had negotiated agreements which had subsequently been approved.

One such type of contract was the "dual rate" agreement. This is an agreement binding shippers to transport all cargo loaded or discharged at ports served by the conference in vessels belonging to conference members. The rate charged to shippers who refuse to sign is higher, even for identical items. The "spread" between contract and noncontract rates sometimes was as high as 20 per cent.

However, there was always the question of whether such obviously discriminatory measures did not violate section fourteen of the Shipping Act, which forbids unfair or discriminatory agreements. Although the dual rate agreement had been before the Supreme Court on numerous occasions beginning in 1932, the *Isbrandtsen* case was the first time that the Court had faced the question of its legality. This decision literally was felt around the world since over sixty conferences were affected.

Since the decision of the Court threatened serious economic disruption to the shipping industry, an almost frantic appeal was made to Congress through the American Merchant Marine. On the same day that the decision was issued, a bill was introduced in the House legalizing all dual rate agreements. During a hurriedly arranged series of hearings, the only opposition came from a few scattered small traders who were hurt by dual rate agreements. As far as the reaction of congressmen can be ascertained, the shipping industry was believed to present a united front. In approximately one month Congress established a two-year period of immunity for all contracts operative at the date of the *Isbrandtsen* decision. The Shipping Act was amended, with only one opposing vote in either house, to read that "nothing in this section or elsewhere in this Act shall be construed or applied to forbid or make unlawful any dual rate contract arrangement in use by the members of a conference on May 19, 1958. . . ." The stated purpose of the law was to "defer the impact of the Court decision." [12]

These examples of interest groups and separation of powers are not intended to provide an exhaustive account. Indeed, instances such as those cited above could be described almost *ad nauseam*. However, one further point should be made. In the interplay between groups and formal institutions the Executive Office of the President may be checked by strong concentrations of power in the other branches. The famous struggle between President Franklin D. Roosevelt and the Army Corps of Engineers, perhaps the most widely discussed case of successful pressure group opposition to executive goals, will conclude the analysis. [13] The Army Corps of Engineers is legally responsible to the President as Commander in Chief. However, the Corps of Engineers has built a close relationship with Congress primarily through the mechanism of the National Rivers and Harbors Congress, an organization to which many members of Congress belong. The Corps has performed river development tasks since the beginning of the nation's history, when it was the only agency with engineers trained for such work. However, since the increasing expansion of government services, the Corps has been almost incessantly involved in struggle with other agencies doing the same thing. The Hoover Commission drew attention to these jurisdictional disputes and concluded that, irrespective of the legal position of the President, the executive branch could not marshal sufficient power to coordinate a water program against the wishes of the influential "rivers and harbors bloc."

The independence of the Corps of Engineers is strikingly borne out in the struggle over the Kings River Project in California. Both the Corps and the Bureau of Reclamation wanted to develop a program to provide more adequate water supply for the arid area surrounding the river. President Roosevelt decided that the project was primarily one of irrigation and consequently should be handled by the Bureau of Reclamation. However, at Congressional hearings on the project the Corps continued to urge that it be given authority. It was supported by its loyal following in Congress, and the final solution had both the Bureau and the Corps authorized to undertake the development of the river. Even though the President's 1945 budget contained an appropriation for the Bureau and none for the Corps, the appropriation acts passed by Congress reversed these positions. President Roosevelt, usually classified as a "strong" President, could not cope with the entrenched strength of the Corps of Engineers built upon Congressional loyalties and close relationships with the National Rivers and Harbors Congress.

NOTES

1. Arthur W. Macmahon, "Problems of Federalism: A Survey," in Arthur W. Macmahon, ed., *Federalism Mature and Emergent* (Garden City, N.Y.: Doubleday and Company, Inc., 1955), p. 11.

2. See Franz Neuman, *The Democratic and the Authoritarian State* (New York: The Free Press of Glencoe, Inc., 1957), pp. 216–232, for a discussion of the limitations of the concept of federalism as an independent causal factor.

3.   This description is drawn from Joseph C. Palamountain, *The Politics of Distribution* (Cambridge: Harvard University Press, 1955), pp. 155–187.

4.   Quoted in Merle Fainsod, Lincoln Gordon, and Joseph C. Palamountain, Jr., *Government and the American Economy* (New York: W. W. Norton and Co., Inc., 1959), p. 545.

5.   Palamountain, *op. cit.,* p. 163.

6.   Donald C. Blaisdell, *American Democracy Under Pressure* (New York: The Ronald Press Company, 1957), p. 50.

7.   Robert J. Harris, "States' Rights and Vested Interests," *Journal of Politics,* XV (Nov. 1953), 466.

8.   Hammer v. Dagenhart, 247 U.S. 251 (1918).

9.   Harris, *op. cit.,* 467.

10.   Quoted in Earl Latham, *The Group Basis of Politics* (Ithaca: Cornell University Press, 1952), p. 56.

11.   Federal Maritime Board v. Isbrandtsen, 356 U.S. 481 (1958). This account is taken from Jerrold L. Walden, "The Dual-Rate Moratorium—End of the Isbrandtsen Odyssey," *Journal of Public Law,* X (Spring, 1961), 78–99.

12.   House Report No. 2055, 85th Cong., 2d Sess., 1946, p. 2, Quoted in Walden, *op. cit.,* p. 78.

13.   *See* Robert de Roos and Arthur Maass, "The Lobby that Can't be Licked," *Harper's Magazine,* Aug. 1949, pp. 20–30, for a more complete description of this episode.

POLITICAL PARTIES AND ECONOMIC POLICY
William J. Keefe and Morris S. Ogul

Popular political thought seldom has taken account of the virtues of party or of the potential of party government. The vices of party, by contrast, are persistently deplored; it is not too much to say that American parties have grown up in an atmosphere of general hostility.[1] Independence from party, in the public mind, appears often to be the mark of a good man, the justifiable claim of a good legislator. Yet there is little evidence to suggest that the obloquy which hangs over the party system is the result of a careful assessment of the workings of political parties or of their contributions to representative government. One point of departure in assaying the importance of parties is to evaluate their role and potential in the legislative process.[2]

Party Voting in Congress.

In the ritual and practices of Congress, as of nearly all American legislatures, the party can perform a variety of functions. In varying degrees and with varying success, the parties organize the legislature, select the leadership, shape the ground rules for negotiation and decision-making, rationalize the conduct of legislative business, monitor the activities of the executive branch, and assist in familiarizing the public with the work of government. The parties' tasks in representative government are formidable and their functions indispensable.

One phase of the party role in the legislative process is especially vague: the direct contribution of the party to shaping legislation. The parliamentary machinery is, of course, controlled by majority party members. But to what extent does legislation bear the imprint of party *qua* party, to what extent is it simply the product of transient nonparty majorities or of persistent coalitions? Do the parties present genuine policy alternatives in Congress—i.e., do the parties differ? Can the

From William J. Keefe and Morris S. Ogul, *The American Legislative Process: Congress and the States,* pp. 270–274, 276–283. Copyright © 1964. Reprinted by permission of Prentice-Hall, Inc., Englewood Cliffs, New Jersey. Footnotes have been renumbered.

voting behavior of a Republican congressman be distinguished from that of a Democratic congressman, the voting behavior of a Republican senator from that of a Democratic senator? How much party responsibility for a legislative program do we want? How much do we now have? If party performance falls short, is it reasonable to expect otherwise—given the milieu in which parties function?

Satisfactory answers to these questions are hard to determine, even though an impressive number of studies of legislative parties have been made in the last half-century, particularly in the last two decades. At the risk of exacerbating the problem of understanding, let us have a good look at the relationship between party and public policy. Our analysis leans on a variety of studies.

There are two principal views of the *raison d'être* of political parties. The first argues that parties have ideological roots and that principle undergirds their organization. In the classic definition of Edmund Burke, "Party is a body of men united, for promulgating by their joint endeavors the national interest, upon some particular principle in which they are all agreed."[3] The other view finds party preoccupation with winning elections as the fundamental basis of organization. James Bryce put it this way:

[Legislation] is not one of the chief aims of party, and many important measures have no party character. [The] chief purpose [of political parties] is to capture, and hold when captured, the machinery, legislative and administrative, of the legal government established by the constitution.[4]

Conflicting claims such as those of Burke and Bryce have often been investigated.[5] The pioneering study traces to A. Lawrence Lowell, who, in 1901, published *The Influence of Party upon Legislation in England and America*.[6] Lowell assumed that the main test of party influence lay in the behavior of party members on roll-call votes. He defined a "party vote" as one in which 90 per cent of the voting membership of one party was opposed to 90 per cent of the voting membership of the other party. His analysis disclosed that party rivalry of this order was much less in evidence in Congress than in the British House of Commons in the nineteenth century. Legislative proposals before Congress were not frequently passed or lost in "party votes." The "influence" of party upon legislation in the state legislatures was even less than in Congress. Party affiliation, it was plain to Lowell, did not often affect the deliberations of American legislators, and party lines were not often drawn.

Party voting in Congress was re-examined by Julius Turner in 1951. Using Lowell's "90 per cent versus 90 per cent" test, he found that in various congressional sessions between 1921 and 1948 about 17 per cent of the roll-call votes in the House were "party votes. . . ."[7] Not only is party voting found much less frequently in the House of Representatives than in the [British] House of Commons, but it has declined markedly since the early days of the New Deal. There are few hints in this statistical picture which point to the development of cohesive and responsible congressional parties.

That the congressional parties function only sporadically as cohesive units has been documented sufficiently to put the matter to rest. More important in any case is the question of party differences over legislation. What policy matters are at stake when "party votes" (or approximations) do develop? Turner's analysis is especially useful here.

Conflict between the parties has cropped up consistently on legislation involving the tariff, agriculture, labor and social legislation, and on a variety of subjects where the issue is one of government versus private action. The parties' orientations have been plain for some time: (1) Democrats have persistently favored a low tariff, Republicans a high one. "When the tariff is considered, most Democrats unite against most Republicans as a matter of principle."[8] (2) Where agricultural problems have arisen, Democrats ordinarily have argued that the federal government should assume responsibility for the development of programs (such as parity payments) to assist the farmer, while Republicans ordinarily have offered an alternative of free enterprise in agriculture and, therefore, have opposed the development or extension of federal programs. (3) Democrats have been steadily more vigorous than Republicans in their support of government action to assist labor and low-income groups—through social security, relief, housing, and wage and hour regulation. (4) In general, Democrats have been more inclined to call for government action to remedy domestic problems or to launch new projects (farm relief, TVA, power development) than have Republicans. Where a choice is posed between government involvement or private action, a larger or a smaller federal role, party lines have tended to form rapidly, with the Republicans moving strongly to the defense of private means and a limited federal role.

On other issues Turner found members of both parties ranged at all points of the compass. Party lines were hazy and party positions inconsistent from one session to the next. Among the issues which failed to produce distinctive and continuing differences between the parties were veterans and claims, women's rights, District of Columbia business, civil service, public works, states' rights, armament, foreign affairs, and business claims. Democrats generally were more disposed to the extension of executive power than were Republicans, though this could be due in part to their control of the presidency during periods when the issue frequently arose. . . .

Voting on labor and social welfare legislation in Congress shows two distinct patterns. First, it is plain that this legislation produces significant cleavages within each party. Second, party disunity is not so serious that it blots out the major differences between the parties on "liberal-labor" legislation.

A fair test of party differences is available in the voting behavior of senators on legislative questions of concern to the AFL-CIO. Figure 1 shows the range of opinion in the Senate on issues covering a thirteen-year period, 1947–60. Each issue, in the view of the AFL-CIO, has a "right" and a "wrong" side. A senator voting "right" in the 86th Congress, for example, would have voted against a ban on secondary boycotts, in favor of extensive area redevelopment, in favor of a change in the rules to limit Senate debate, against an amendment to cut the number of public housing units to be constructed, in favor of federal aid to education in the form of grants for classrooms and teachers' salaries, in favor of an amendment to repeal a tax credit on dividend income, and in favor of a major extension of the Temporary Unemployment Compensation Act.[9]

Despite the absence of high cohesion within each party, real differences between the parties are unmistakable. Figure 1 shows that 70 per cent of the votes cast by Democratic senators were in support of the "liberal-labor" point of view, as contrasted with 27 per cent of the votes cast by Republican senators. The congressional parties plainly do not look at the country in the same way when it comes to legisla-

Figure 1. *Democratic and Republican support of key liberal-labor legislation, by section and individual members, 1947–1960, U.S. Senate.**

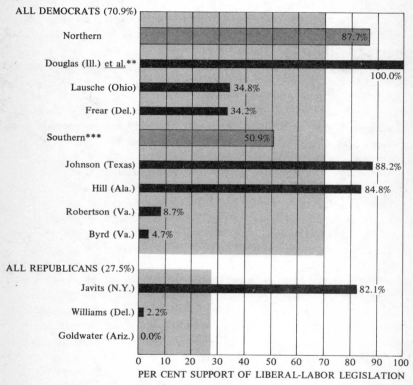

This graph is adapted from data presented by the AFL-CIO Committee on Political Education, How Your Senators and Representatives Voted, 1959–1960. *This publication contains a cumulative voting record for each senator between 1947 and 1960, totaling 46 major issues. The number of votes cast by each senator varies according to length of service.*

***Other Democrats with "perfect" records, as judged by the AFL-CIO, were Carroll (Colo.), Long (Hawaii)—only three votes, Muskie (Me.), McNamara (Mich.), Hart (Mich.), Humphrey (Minn.), McCarthy (Minn.), Hennings (Mo.), Symington (Mo.), Young (Ohio), Lusk (Ore.)—only two votes, Clark (Pa.), Jackson (Wash.), and Proxmire (Wis.).*

****Ala., Ark., Fla., Ga., La., Miss., N.C., Okla., S.C., Tenn., Tex., and Va. All non-Southern Democrats are classified as "Northern."*

Political Parties and Economic Policy

tion of this sort,[10] although the fact is obscured partially by the behavior of a conservative band within the Democratic party and a liberal band within the Republican party.

The most noticeable division appears in Democratic ranks, making it tempting to generalize that Northern (non-Southern) Democrats are the liberals of the party while Southern Democrats are the conservatives. But this masks as well as explains, as Figure 1, showing the behavior of individual senators lodged in the wings of their groups, should demonstrate. It will readily be seen that Senator Douglas of Illinois has had far more in common with Senator Hill of Alabama than with Senator Lausche of Ohio; the civil rights issue apart, Hill

Figure 2.   Democratic and Republican support of key liberal-labor legislation, total party and section, 1947–1960, U.S. House of Representatives.

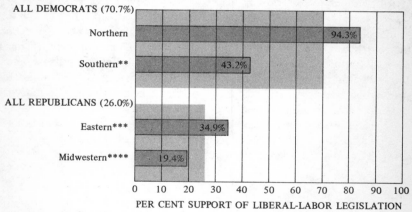

Adapted from same source as that of Figure 1. Calculations are based on a summary of 42 major liberal-labor votes between 1947 and 1960 in the House. The categories include those congressmen serving in 1960 and their voting histories in all sessions they served between 1947 and 1960. Ten of the 42 votes singled out by the AFL-CIO took place in the 86th Congress (1959–1960).

**Ala., Ark., Fla., Ga., Ky., La., Miss., N.C., Okla., S.C., Tenn., Tex., and Va.*

***Me., Mass., N.H., N.J., N.Y., and Pa.*

****Ill., Ind., Iowa, Kan., Mich., Minn., Mo., Neb., N.D., S.D., Ohio, and Wis.*

and Douglas share common ideological ground. Two Southern senators, Byrd of Virginia and Johnson of Texas, appear to have been in agreement on labor and social welfare legislation on but the rarest of occasions. Senators Byrd and Goldwater, though divided by party, have records virtually indistinguishable. The most that can be said is that the center of Democratic liberalism is located in the North, but not all Northern Democrats are liberals, while the center of Democratic conservatism is located in the South, but not all Southern Democrats are conservatives. Party life is about the same in the House (Figure 2).

People who like their party politics neat and logical will be offended by similar scattering within Republican ranks. Senators such as Javits of New York or Case of New Jersey are more frequently aligned with Northern Democrats on "liberal-labor" legislation than with members of their own party such as Goldwater of Arizona. And there are other cases. Nonetheless, when all the exceptions are listed, totaled, and explained, there are still important differences between the parties. Over the years a majority of the Democratic party has been determined to chart a liberal course for the federal government on labor and social legislation, while a majority of the Republican party has been equally insistent in posing a conservative alternative. The latter choice has varied with circumstances—a smaller expenditure for the same program, a project of more modest proportions, state rather than federal responsibility, defense of the rights of property as against those of labor unions and workers.

Party Fragmentation and Interparty Coalitions in Congress

The burden of the previous pages has been to mark the policy positions which differentiate the parties in Congress. It should be clear by now that the congressional parties are by no means "Tweedledum and Tweedledee"; that, despite the indifferent success which characterizes some party efforts, there are still important policy distinctions between the two groups. No claim has been made, of course, that party performance in Congress is either "disciplined" or "responsible," in the usual sense of these words; indeed, it is quite obvious that antithetical views are present within each party.

At this point, therefore, it is appropriate to examine the party fabric for snags and tears. Finding them is no problem; the difficulty comes with mending.

Table 1 provides strong evidence of the failure of party unity among congressional Democrats in six consecutive sessions. It is a bleak picture for those who believe that party loyalty should weigh heavily in the deliberations of members. In the second session of the 86th Congress, a majority of Southern Democrats opposed a majority of "Northern" (all other) Democrats on 40 per cent of the roll-call votes. For the most part, the issues which split the party in this session were those which have conspicuously troubled relations between the two wings. About one-quarter of the disputes involved civil rights legislation and another one-eighth concerned foreign aid authorizations and appropriations. In addition, Southern Democrats in large numbers left the fold (i.e., the Northern majority) to oppose depressed areas legislation, revision of the minimum wage, federal aid to education, extension of certain taxes, public housing, grants for urban renewal and slum clearance, federal supervision of campaign expenditures, and medical care for the aged financed through an increase in the Social Security payroll tax.[11] The percentage of "splits" declined after the party's capture of the presidency in 1960; nevertheless, they developed on one-third of the roll-call votes in 1961 and on one-fifth in 1962.

Table 1. Northern vs. Southern Democrats in Congress*

Year	Total roll-call votes, both chambers	North-South Democratic splits†	Percentage of splits
1957	207	64	31
1958	293	84	29
1959	302	83	27
1960	300	119	40
1961	320	107	33
1962	348	74	21

*This table is used with the permission of the Congressional Quarterly Service. See the *1962 CQ Almanac,* Vol. XX, 733–34.

†A majority of voting Southern Democrats opposed to a majority of voting Northern Democrats.

Not all Southern Democrats voted this way, to be sure, and some members were consistently opposed to the new Southern orthodoxy. Nonetheless, the general outlook of Southern legislators has become one of increasing conservatism—based on states' rights, resistance to federal spending programs (certain kinds), probusiness commitments, and fiscal "integrity." Among major interest groups, organized labor in particular has felt the cold hand of the Southern contingent in Congress.

The main paths along which Congress moves are not always staked out by the majority party or by a majority of the majority party. . . . Two facts in particular emerge. The first is that Republicans and Southern Democrats (at least a majority of each) have progressed from furtive courtship to virtual wedlock.[12] At the least, to continue the metaphor, amatory adventures across party lines have become increasingly common. In 1960, the coalition was brought to bear on more than one-fifth of the roll-call votes; in 1962, under a Democratic President, the percentage declined to one-seventh. And, second, not only do the groups get on well together, but their efforts have proved notably effective. This untidy combination, as the party-government school instinctively views it, won about six of every ten roll-call battles in 1962, seven of ten in 1959, and eight of ten in 1958. The coalition is fused on about the same issues that split Southern from Northern Democrats.[13]

Two or Four Parties?

The American party system provides a good illustration of the proposition that it is just about as difficult to abandon ideas concerning an institution as it is to abandon the institution itself. Conventional interpretation reassures us that our politics is of the common two-party variety, consisting of Republicans and Democrats. But there is a good deal of evidence that, at least at points in the political process, the two parties have been undermined by other persistent combinations. James Burns argues that we should accept the fact that, in practice and where it counts, we have a "four-party" system.[14] The main lines of his argument can be noted without going into a detailed analysis.[15]

The American "four-party" system consists of two presidential and two congressional parties: Presidential Democrats, Presidential

Republicans, Congressional Democrats, and Congressional Republicans. On a left-right, liberal-conservative continuum, they line up in the order listed, though some overlap is, of course, inevitable. Congressional Democrats like Hubert Humphrey of Minnesota and Joseph Clark of Pennsylvania, among others, are "members" in good standing of the Democratic Presidential party; and Congressional Republicans like Clifford Case of New Jersey and Jacob Javits of New York, among others, belong also to the Republican Presidential party. But the main divisions are intact.

The distinguishing mark of the "parties" is policy. *Both* presidential parties are more liberal and more internationalist than *both* congressional parties. "They are separate parties in that each has its own ideology, organization, and leadership. In political outlook, the Congressional Republican party slants sharply to the right, and the Congressional Democrats lean almost as far in that direction." Control of the national committees and national conventions has enabled both presidential parties to choose liberal candidates for the presidency; the congressional parties acquiesce because they cannot do otherwise and, moreover, a liberal presidential candidate helps them in the battle for a congressional majority. Elections, therefore, decide "what kind of liberals will run the White House and what kind of conservatives will run Congress." The result of this split, typically, is eventual stalemate, no matter which party wins the presidency.[16]

NOTES

1. See E. E. Schattschneider, *Party Government* (New York: Holt, Rinehart & Winston, Inc., 1942), especially Chapter 1.

2. Difficulties in generalizing about the role of party in the legislative process are troublesome, but the major problem is the formulation of a general theory of parties. See Frederick C. Englemann, "A Critique of Recent Writings on Political Parties," *Journal of Politics, XIX* (August, 1957), 423–40, and Aaron B. Wildavsky, "A Methodological Critique of Duverger's Political Parties," *Journal of Politics,* XXI (May, 1959), 303–18.

3. *The Works of Edmund Burke* (London: G. Bell and Sons, Ltd., 1897), I, 375.

4. *Modern Democracies* (New York: The Macmillan Company, 1927), II, 42–43.

5.   A summary and analysis of the studies dealing with party and legislation is available in Neil A. McDonald, *The Study of Political Parties* (New York: Doubleday & Company, Inc., 1955), pp. 69–75.

6.   *Annual Report of the American Historical Association for 1901* (Washington, 1902), I, 321–543. Another early study of party cohesion is Stuart Rice, *Quantitative Methods in Politics* (New York: Alfred A. Knopf, Inc., 1928). For critical reviews of studies of party cohesion modeled after Lowell's or Rice's, see Robert T. Golembiewski, "A Taxonomic Approach to State Political Strength," *Western Political Quarterly,* XI (September, 1958), 494–97, and Wilder Crane, Jr., "A Caveat on Roll-Call Studies of Party Voting," *Midwest Journal of Political Science,* IV (August, 1960), 237-49.

7.   Turner did not regard the "party vote" concept an adequate test of party pressure on legislation. His analysis of congressional parties at the roll-call stage was based on the *chi*-square test—a statistical method for determining whether the behavior of two objective groups is significantly different. Party differences would of course register more easily under a *chi*-square test than under Lowell's rigorous requirement of a "party vote"—90 per cent of one party voting against 90 per cent of the other. On the basis of the *chi*-square test, Turner concluded: "Party pressure seems to be more effective than any other pressure on Congressional voting, and is discernible on nearly nine-tenths of the roll calls examined." *Party and Constituency* (Baltimore: Johns Hopkins Press, 1951), p. 23. Smith and Field contend that Turner's determination that "two groups differed significantly by the *chi*-square test . . . amounts only to saying that the chances are less than 1 in 100 that two purely random groupings would differ to the extent evidenced. One would expect the behavior of even the loosest aggregations of politicians rather frequently to meet this test." *Southwestern Social Science Quarterly,* XXXIV, 34.

8.   Turner, *op. cit.,* p. 68. This study is based on the House sessions of 1921, 1930-31, 1937, and 1944. See especially Chapter 3. In addition to "principle" as a force in influencing voting on tariff legislation, cited by Turner, the realities of constituency interest plainly have a bearing. The economic factor in constituencies is an obvious explanation, but it is not the only one. In recent years the Democratic position on tariff legislation has undergone substantial change as a number of Southern Democrats have abandoned their traditional low-tariff stand. The developing opposition of Southern congressmen to reciprocal trade legislation is part of a new mood in the South, described by Charles O. Lerche, Jr., as the "new isolationism." This mood consists of much more than attitudes toward international questions. At bottom, it is a mass political protest, the momentum for which is furnished by the race issue. Among its advantages, the isolationist stance suits the South's

desire to be left alone. On a related matter, it is interesting to find that the states that are most opposed to foreign aid—Mississippi, South Carolina, Louisiana, North Carolina, and Georgia—are among the states with the largest Negro populations and all have explosive race problems. There are further dislocations in these states as a result of rapid urbanization. "Southern Congressmen and the New Isolationism," *Political Science Quarterly,* LXXV (September, 1960), 321–37. In the Senate, Southern support for reciprocal trade similarly has declined, but not nearly so sharply as in the case of foreign aid. Between 1953 and 1958, Southern Democrats supported reciprocal trade in about the same degree as Northern Democrats. See Malcolm E. Jewell, "Evaluating the Decline of Southern Internationalism Through Senatorial Roll Call Votes," *Journal of Politics,* XXI (November, 1959), 630–31.

9.   The issues on which the AFL-CIO kept score in the House in the 86th Congress were similar to those of the Senate: "anti-labor" provisions regarding boycotts and picketing, area redevelopment, civil rights, public housing, home mortgages, federal aid to education, federal funds to combat water pollution, increase in minimum wage, and a federal water project.

10.   Another analysis by the *Congressional Quarterly* confirms this difference between the parties. Using key roll-call votes on legislation that would *enlarge federal responsibilities* (e.g., area redevelopment, temporary unemployment compensation, aid to education, housing, public power, manpower retraining, standby public works, Social Security medicare, grants for educational television), the CQ studies show the Democrats generally voting in favor of a larger federal role and the Republicans generally voting for a smaller federal role. The data for the 86th and 87th Congresses looked as follows:

	86th Congress		87th Congress	
	Dem.	Rep.	Dem.	Rep.
Larger Federal Role				
Both chambers	74%	19%	75%	24%
Senate	74	27	65	26
House	74	17	78	24
Smaller Federal Role				
Both chambers	23	78	23	74
Senate	25	71	33	70
House	23	80	21	75

These data are used with the permission of the *Congressional Quarterly.* See the *Weekly Report,* XIX (Week ending October 20, 1961), 1751, and the *Congressional Quarterly 1962 Almanac,* p. 717.

11. See the *Congressional Quarterly Weekly Report* (Week ending December 2, 1960), p. 1929.

12. Northern Democrats are those mainly troubled by the alliance, but some Republicans also take a dim view of it. In a Republican caucus preceding the opening of the 87th Congress, Representative Thomas Curtis (R., Mo.) and six Republican colleagues offered a resolution to repudiate "any suggestions of a coalition with any group that would commit us to oppose civil rights legislation or, in general, other constructive legislation." The resolution was referred to the Republican policy committee with instructions that the committee report the matter back to a subsequent caucus. *The New York Times*, January 4, 1961.

13. Wilfred E. Binkley's view of the coalition, set down in the middle 1940's, is worth quoting: "Here is a congressional bloc not to be explained by any resort to the dogma of original sin. It is motivated as normally as any sectional group at any time in American history. The assumption that Republican congressmen combine with anti-administration Democrats merely to embarrass the administration constitutes a misconception of the nature of our representative system. These coalition congressmen, whether Democrats or Republicans, represent the dominant social forces, that is to say, the most influential interests in their predominantly rural districts. By and large theirs is an anti-metropolitan ideology induced by a phobia of our American Babylons with their slums and laboring masses organized in unions that exert pressures at the polls through political action committees." *President and Congress* (New York: Alfred A. Knopf, Inc., 1947), p. 276.

14. The "four-party" system appears to be more nearly "factional" than "party" in character. It might be said that on legislation having clearly defined "liberal" and "conservative" dimensions, there are two empirical parties in Congress: the conservative coalition (Southern Democrats and Northern Republicans) and the "liberal" coalition (mainly Northern Democrats plus a small group of Northern Republicans). But there are exceptions, since some Southern Democrats are usually in the liberal coalition and some Northern Democrats are usually in the conservative coalition.

15. The theme of an American "multi-party" system is found in several articles. See James M. Burns, "America's 'Four-Party' System," *New York Times Magazine*, August 5, 1956; "Two-Party Stalemate: The Crisis in Our Politics," *The Atlantic Monthly*, February, 1960, pp. 37–41; "White House vs. Congress," *The Atlantic Monthly*, March, 1960, pp. 65–69; "Memo to the Next President," *The Atlantic Monthly*, April, 1960, pp. 64–68. The most complete analysis of the four-party system, coalition politics, and the consequences of

these arrangements for the government and the people is James Burns, *The Deadlock of Democracy* (Englewood Cliffs, N.J.: Prentice-Hall, Inc., 1963). For a review of this book by Austin Ranney, followed by a rebuttal by Burns, see *The Reporter,* issues of March 14 and April 11, 1963. Ranney contends that the four parties do not have "as good a claim to be called parties as the aggregations that now bear the labels."

16. Burns, "White House vs. Congress," *op. cit.,* pp. 65–66.

THE SIGNIFICANCE OF BELIEF PATTERNS IN ECONOMIC REGULATION
Emmette S. Redford

Beliefs determine social action. It is true, of course, that if beliefs are the chicken, there are many eggs in its lineage, and that these have yolks of social force and whites of environment. Beliefs may be rationalizations of need, symbols for interests, links in a chain between the forging of interests and the institutionalization of behavior. It is true, nevertheless, that our concepts are guides for our action. It may be, as Justice Holmes remarked, that "the decision in a particular case will depend on a judgment or intuition more inarticulate than any major premise";[1] but behind a decision or a line of decisions there are some thought formations, vague or precise, about fairness, reasonableness, efficiency, duty to decide, and other matters.

Some beliefs are deeply rooted in the cultural heritage and are called traditions, some are interpretations of recent experience, others are responses to current need. Some are frozen, others are fluid before the face of circumstance. Some yielding to organic factors may normally be expected, and also some compromise with competing beliefs. Yet they are crystallizations and therefore clues to tendencies. They are consensus for the present and direction-setters for the future. They are one source of understanding about a series of decisions, a trend in policy, or the evolution of a social program.[2]

This paper reflects my search for belief patterns behind a system of economic regulation—that for domestic commercial air transport. The analysis is limited to this single area of regulation, but out of your own awareness you may see in the analysis explanations of a larger complex of social behavior—the whole system of public regulation of private economic activity.

The beliefs have all been stated repeatedly, though perhaps not in the same words used by the author. The author's contribution, if such there is, lies in isolation of the beliefs from total reality, in imputations of significance, and in elaborations on what is explicit and implicit in

From *Western Political Quarterly,* XIV, supplement (September, 1961), 13–24. Reprinted by permission of the University of Utah, copyright owners.

belief and circumstance. It may lie also in the ordering of these beliefs and in the resulting conclusions about relevant political science study. The beliefs, or patterns of belief, will be stated categorically under seven numbered headings and grouped in rather loose areas of correlation.

Basic Assumption

1. Public needs are dominant.   In our basic thinking economic purpose and political purpose are the same. The public is king. It is occupants of houses, not architects and builders, whose needs are to be satisfied. It is the common needs of people in the community, not the purposes of wielders of public power, which legitimize the efforts of the state. Not gain for capital and labor, not power, is the ultimate business of economics and politics, respectively. Not even economic and political freedom solely for their own ends. Abstract impressionism has its place in the arts, but the accounting is on the other side of the ledger in economics and politics. The basic belief for unregulated and regulated enterprise is that public needs are dominant.

Our public records—notably judicial opinions, congressional committee reports, and preambles of statutes—provide us abundantly with explicit statement of accepted public needs. In the case of civil aviation the needs were defined out of both experience and prospect. Mail—carried by air since 1918—was the first need met by civil aviation. In the twenties passenger service was required by the Postmaster General and the vision of a new transportation system expanded. The importance of civil aviation as an "adjunct of defense" was also recognized. Consequently, in the organic statute for civil aviation passed in 1938 the objectives were stated to be "the present and future needs of the foreign and domestic commerce of the United States, of the postal service, and of the national defense." [3]

In the committee hearings preceding the passage of the Act these needs were regarded as so important that frequent references were made to the need for law which, as the father of the organic law—Senator McCarran—put it, would "encourage and promote aviation." [4] In five of the six statements of purpose in the Act of 1938 the words "encouragement," "development," or "promotion" appear and they are implicit in the other statement.

A further need was inherent in the nature of the service. Safety was recognized as interrelated with the development of air transportation, and hence was both stated as a statutory objective and supported by an extensive system of regulation.

The belief that public needs are dominant led, under the conditions which existed, to the development of a public policy. The nature of the policy was dependent, however, on other beliefs. These were part of our economic and of our legal and political-administrative traditions.

Economic Assumptions

2. *Private enterprise is superior.*   From the classical tradition came the idea that private enterprise was more efficient than public enterprise. Smithian economics and utilitarian philosophy supplied the arguments and these have been parroted by politicians, journalists, and academicians. The issue was changed when it was recognized that choice, if choice there was, was between public management and regulated corporate management. John Stuart Mill saw defects in both systems though less in regulated corporate management,[5] and the socialists argued the advantages of public enterprise. But in this country where private capital was plentiful and government was amateurish, most commentators saw no reason to ponder the issue. Public enterprise would be accepted where private capital was not attracted or where gross abuses were revealed. Yet rarely, except for electric supply, would the issue between regulated corporate enterprise and public enterprise be presented as one of alternative choice. Private enterprise was ready and superior; regulation, its necessary complement, would be accepted, whatever its limits and defects.

For air transportation—which is public enterprise almost universally in the rest of the world—private enterprise was confirmed in this country in a series of events. Although the government initially flew the mails, the Kelly Act of 1925 inaugurated a system of private flying under government contract. When fraud was revealed, the government flew the mails.[6] This, however, was intended to be temporary and a series of tragic accidents brought an abrupt end to the venture. The government returned to the contract system and the first decisional position was irrevocably fixed in the development of civil air transport: it would be a private system.

This initial position set circumferences for further moves in public policy. Public service would be dependent upon attainment of business goals. There was new technology which could be used for a universal air mail system, a mass national transportation service, and greater national security. These objectives could be attained, however, only to the extent that profit could be anticipated by private investors. The rate and timing of use of technology for public ends was conditioned by the balance sheets of private companies. Private enterprise could take great risks in the reach for markets, but its reach would be limited by the chance for profit. All moves in public regulation would be conditioned by this ubiquitous business fact.

The effects of this conditioning of regulation can be overlooked or misinterpreted. By overlooking it, the defects in regulation may be attributed entirely to weakness in regulatory mechanism or in the men chosen as regulators. Through misinterpretation, the conditioning of regulation may be imputed entirely to the influence of the regulated upon the regulators. Though these factors may indeed be very significant, the conditioning of regulation is inherent in the basic institutional system of regulated private enterprise. When the institutional arrangement of private supply of a service with regulation as a supplement is chosen, then the regulators must give attention to the welfare of the companies supplying the service. This is certainly true when the public goal is expansion of service, when investment required is large and must be renewed recurrently because of rapid depletion and obsolescence, when continuity of service is desired, and when high maintenance standards are necessary for safety—all of which were conditions in civil air transport. The result is that planning turns inward to business facts. That this inward pull of regulation may obscure vision of public goals and call for compensations in regulatory approaches is part of reality to be faced, not reason for denying the existence of conditioning fact.

The public had, for air transport, certain tools through which it could reconcile public and business needs. It could grant subsidies, presumably to any extent necessary to supply the amount of service desired. Subsidy was an inevitable point of policy, just as deficit would have been in public ownership and operation. A second tool was the certificate system. This system was the logical replacement for the contract system for determining scope of service when passenger service became as important as mail service. It had, moreover, definite advantages for government and business. For government it was means of channeling and limiting subsidy. For business it was route to stability. This leads to the third belief.

3. Regulated competition is the means of promoting public service. The term "regulated competition" has had two meanings in American usage. Woodrow Wilson and Louis Brandeis used it to apply to restrictions necessary to maintain competition.[7] In this usage it would include laws against combination and unfair methods of competition. Those who discuss regulated industries use the term to refer to controls over such things as entry, mergers, and rate agreements. In this usage the term means control of the amount of competition.

There was apparently universal agreement among the legislative fathers of aviation regulation that competition was desirable.[8] A few favored or looked with sympathy on unlimited competition. During committee hearings extending through five legislative sessions Congressman Sadowski repeatedly questioned the desirability of limiting entry through certificates of public convenience and necessity.[9] Amelia Earhart thought limitation "now would be really a little premature. . . ."[10] Spokesman for the Post Office Department, straining to retain jurisdiction, feared monopoly for various reasons.[11] Nevertheless, the near-unanimous opinion was that limited competition, i.e., regulated competition, was the desirable objective for commercial aviation.

Belief in regulated competition was the result of several factors. One was interpretation of railroad experience. Mr. Joseph E. Eastman, long-time member of the Interstate Commerce Commission and venerated as a statesman of regulation, figured prominently in the events leading to the enactment of the Civil Aeronautics Act of 1938. He found in the facts of railroad history and the techniques of railroad regulation the pattern of regulated competition that should be adopted for air transportation.[12] Senator McCarran and Congressman Lea, leaders in the development of the legislation in the Houses of Congress, both regarded the existence of the certificate system in railroad regulation as sufficient reason for its use in air transport regulation.[13] In fact, we have here an outstanding example of how institutional history fixes an idea which in turn becomes determinative of future policy.[14] Another influence was the experience with air mail contracts. It was repeatedly argued that the award of contracts to the lowest bidder favored the strong, who could stand temporary losses and hence could bid at unremunerative prices. Senator McCarran called it a "vicious method of awarding new routes" which should be changed "to allow intelligent selection of the routes to be served and of those best qualified to operate them economically and safely."[15] Finally, the air transport industry favored regulated competition. Mr. Edgar S. Gorrell, President of the Air Transport Association, pointed out that only 60 of 125 million dollars invested in the industry remained; he strongly urged limited entry and protected investment as the foundations for stable advance of the industry.[16]

The hearings, reports, and debates on a regulatory measure are replete with condemnations of "unbridled," "cut-throat," "disastrous," "destructive," "wasteful," "unregulated" competition and of "chaotic conditions," "unsound ventures," "haphazard growth," "blind economic chaos," and industry sowing of "wild oats." What was favored was "orderly and sound growth," "orderly planning," "a measure of stability," "financial stability."[17]

This pattern of belief was accepted by the regulatory agency. The first *Annual Report* of the Civil Aeronautics Authority declared: "For the first time air carriers and the public are safeguarded against uneconomic, destructive competition and wasteful duplication of services by the statutory requirement that no person or company may engage in air transportation without first receiving a certificate of public convenience and necessity."[18]

The result is that management of the system of competition has been the chief task of regulation. The Board first moved into a period of restricted competition. It declared in the Delta case in 1941[19] that there were enough passenger trunk-lines already in the business, and it followed a restrictive policy with respect to the airlines offering irregular service. Then in 1955 it adopted a policy of expanded competition.[20] Now there are indications that the jet age will lead to a period of reduction of competition.

The mechanisms of regulation have been developed to meet this belief in regulated competition. With the exclusion of new companies from trunkline service the Board's task became the apportionment of opportunities among about a dozen companies. Balanced competition among those in the industry has been an objective. To meet this objective an elaborate set of rights and restrictions are couched in certificate terminology dealing with stopover, turnabout, through, and other forms of service. The time of the Board and its staff is devoted in large part to the refinements of balanced competition and stable growth. And the inwardness of the system of regulation has been increased as the refinements of balanced competition have become more complex.

4. Private responsibility should be preserved.   Years ago Justice Brewer in an opinion for the Supreme Court of the United States said: "It must be remembered that railroads are the private property of their owners; that while from the public character of their work in which they are engaged the public has the power to prescribe rules for securing faithful and efficient service and equality between shippers and communities, yet in no proper sense is the public a general manager." [21] It can be argued that government regulation has now been extended to the extent that it is in fact co-manager of regulated industries.[22] Yet the fact remains that there is a prevailing opinion that government action should be minimal and should not intrude too deeply into managerial and policy judgments.

The concept of private managerial responsibility was recognized by the fathers of air transport regulation. It was more assumed than expressed.[23] It is implicit in the division of public and private position embodied in the law and has been influential in its execution.

The law rings public power with restrictions, substantive as well as procedural. Foremost perhaps is the denial of any public administrative control over scheduling.[24] This is limitation of vast significance on public power to insure adequate service. It leaves to private judgment decisions as to hours of departure, even though such decisions affect community interests and even though they may, in competitive rendition of service, result in some duplication in schedules at the best hours while there is lack of service at others. In addition, the Act grants no authority to the Civil Aeronautics Board over security issues, the framers of the Act of 1938 having accepted only the protection given through the Securities Exchange Commission. It has been held also that the Board has no power to regulate depreciation allowances through uniform reporting requirements,[25] and argued in rate proceedings that management must be allowed a wide range of discretion in determining depreciation expenses.[26]

Private judgment is the foundation on which airline service has been developed. This is true because the initiative rests with the private companies. In addition to decisions on scheduling, private judgment determines the adoption of new types of service, such as coach service; the development of rate structure, through which choices are made between favoring high-price or low-price transportation; the addition of fringe, perhaps luxury, benefits; and most significant, the development of the route system. In all these cases, and many others, the initiative rests with the companies.

The powers granted to the Civil Aeronautics Board by the regulatory act are primarily enabling, rather than directive.[27] It normally acts on petition. This does not necessarily prevent advance planning by the agency. It could develop route patterns and service patterns to guide its judgment in decision on petitions from companies. It also does have a considerable power of action on its own initiative. Nevertheless, circumstances of various types have prevented public planning from being a dominant factor. One circumstance is that the inbasket of petitions is accepted in considerable measure as the determinant of work priority; another is that action on petition is an inevitable outgrowth of the use of private enterprise; but still another is the belief that public action should be minimal and corrective and private judgment broad. The result is that most of the planning of the airline system is done in company staffs and that the perspectives of planning are, in large measure, those set by company objectives.

Legal and Administrative Assumptions

5. *Business affected with a public interest should be subject to utility-type controls.* The term "affected with a public interest" has ceased to have significance as a criterion of constitutional law. The words, however, have had another significance. They have been a form of expression denoting that the American people think of some industries as being of such a nature that certain types of control are appropriate for them. The appropriate form of control is the utility type, and this type of control is both an institutional system and a pattern of beliefs.

This pattern of beliefs arose in the Granger period and has now been institutionalized through some ninety years of experience with regulatory technique. Through this experience the American people have been provided with a ready-made set of techniques in which they place much of their hope for implementing the basic belief that public needs should be dominant.

The National Association of Railroad and Public Utility Commissioners was represented on several occasions in the hearings on the aviation act. It was stated to be the view of the "association that any important public utility industry requires regulation in the public interest." [28] Congressman Lea said that regulation should have "two economic fundamentals"—issuance of certificates and control of rates.[29] These obviously are the core of utility regulation. To Mr. Gorrell a system based on certificates was "rooted in very early common-law conceptions." [30]

The details of the Civil Aeronautics Act followed closely those of the railroad and public utility acts. The same or similar types of provisions were included with respect to suspension of, hearings on, and setting of rates, to grant or denial of certificates, and to allowance of mergers.

As in some other regulated industries there were some special objectives different from those behind utility regulation. One was safety—called the "keystone of the entire situation." [31] Another was the promotional objective. This was strongly and repeatedly emphasized in the legislative history of the Civil Aeronautics Act: it has been stressed also by the Civil Aeronautics Board. Reporting to Congress in 1956 it said that in use of the certificate power "the Board must apply the specified standards so as to maintain an appropriate equilibrium between the two major policies of the Act—that of controlling the air transport industry along the traditional lines of public utility regulation and that of fostering and promoting air transportation."[32] Belief in utility-type controls is therefore one, but only one, of the background concepts.

6. *Regulation should be fair and this requires judicial process.* In American thinking about regulation fairness is probably a stronger concept than efficiency. In fact, fairness is essential for efficiency where private enterprise is chosen as the instrument of service—for without fairness to the regulated the springs of initiative and the streams of investment go dry. Yet fairness is sought for its own sake and is protected both by the power of the regulated and by judicial and popular conceptions of due process.

The thing that gives special significance to the belief in fairness is that it is married to another belief—that fairness is achieved only through judicial processes. Note the history of rate making as an example. It is called, in some of its manifestations at least, legislative; but it is believed to have some judicial attribute; it must, therefore, be done in a proceeding similar to that of a court. This is the pattern of beliefs in which fairness and judicial procedure lie bedded together.

The experience in air transport regulation is similar to that in other fields where utility-type controls are imposed. Provisions of the regulatory act and of the Administrative Procedure Act, judicial decisions or administrator's assumptions on what the judiciary would decide, and administrative practice follow the deeply set belief that judicial procedure is the only sure route to fairness.

In the development of regulatory process great emphasis was placed on the idea that proceedings of administrative agencies would be simpler than those of courts. Yet experience shows a tendency to round the circle and move toward the same point from which departure was sought.

The significance of the judicialization of processes is patently revealed in recent studies. James M. Landis has described the "inordinate delay" which "characterizes the disposition of adjudicatory proceedings before substantially all of our regulatory agencies," and the backlog of pending cases which confronts them.[33] Louis J. Hector, recent member of the Civil Aeronautics Board, has shown how decisions on determination of community route needs is merged with and submerged in the judicial consideration of which carrier will be awarded the route.[34] My study of the General Passenger Fare case in the Civil Aeronautics Board shows a similar merging of consideration of policy standards with that of application of standards, and the serious impairment, if not virtual destruction, of rate-making authority through procedural involvements.

Correctives for deficiencies in technique are essential for successful operation of a system based on the first two beliefs set out above—one in which public needs are dominant but private enterprise is used to supply them. The routes toward correction have been indicated in many discussions of regulatory technique: use of informal methods, simplification of formal procedure in judicial proceedings, use of other types of process whether called planning, policy making, or legislative proceedings. Innovations along these lines are inhibited, nevertheless, by the underlying belief that in regulatory matters there is only one certain route to fairness.

7. Regulation should be nonpolitical. The idea that regulation should be nonpolitical is a complex of many beliefs. Regulatory work is rationalized as judicial or legislative. It is easy to conclude, therefore, that it is not executive *in any sense* and should be independent from presidential direction and control. It seems obvious that judicial work should be performed with freedom from any external influence. It is *not* on its face self-evident that policy elaboration within the limits of statutory delegation should be nonpolitical or is nonexecutive, but the conclusions have been drawn nevertheless. The conclusions satisfy leaders in the congressional committees dealing with regulatory agencies because they support jurisdictional claims; they satisfy industry because it fears novelty in policy; they have not been strongly challenged from the executive branch; they were embalmed by the judicial hand in *Humphrey's Executor* v. *United States* three years before the charter for commercial aviation became law.[35]

In the development of aviation legislation the representative of the commercial industry asked for legislation which would "place aviation behind an insulated wall, where politics cannot get at it, where the quasi-legislative features will be handled by the Commission without interference from politics, and where also the quasi-judicial functions will likewise be so handled."[36] Senator McCarran summarized his view when the final bill was under debate: "I have stood for a policy throughout this contest ... whereby the air industry would be independent, and not under the subjugation and control of political agencies."[37] He referred specifically to merger controls as something which should be "in a nonpartisan, quasi-judicial body,"[38] and wished "to keep the element of safety [which had executive aspects] clear of any political influence, clear out of politics."[39] Congressman Lea in the final debates said the board being created had been limited "as far as possible" to "quasi-judicial and quasi-legislative functions," and summarized the prevailing view: "We desire that this commission, being a regulatory commission, shall be as independent as we can make it."[40]

The Administration's position on regulatory organization was clarified in January 1938. The President originally favored delegation of regulation to the Interstate Commerce Commission, but now supported the original McCarran view for separate regulation of air transport. The Administration had received the Brownlow Report in 1937 which recommended placing executive and policy determining functions under executive control, and had approved this recommendation in a message to Congress. But the belief pattern of the Brownlow Committee gained little acceptance. The Administration chose in 1938 to recommend that only "executive" functions in aviation regulation be under presidential direction. Mr. Clinton M. Hester, the Administration's spokesman, told a congressional committee: "In the exercise of its quasi-legislative, or so-called quasi-judicial functions ... the agency would sit as an administrative court entirely independent of the executive branch of the government."[41]

The draft of legislation supported by the Administration in 1938[42] contained no limitation on the President's power of removal and provided that the exercise of powers "which are not subject to review by the courts of law shall be subject to the general direction of the President."[43] Mr. Clinton M. Hester, who represented the Administration in the hearings, explained that this provision was designed to insure that "the executive work of this agency shall not be placed beyond the constitutional control of the President. . . ."[44] The bill also protected the President's control over international relations by providing for approval by him of foreign and overseas air permits. The latter provision remained in subsequent drafts and is in the act, but the provision for presidential direction on executive duties was removed. In both houses, moreover, a provision was added stating that the President could remove members of the agency for "inefficiency, neglect of duty, or malfeasance in office," which was construed as a limitation on his power of removal. In the Senate Senator Truman proposed an amendment to remove this provision, and it was argued in debate that the provision should come out because of the executive functions of the agency. Although the amendment was vigorously opposed by Senator McCarran, the Senate adopted it. Nevertheless the provision remained in the House Bill, and the House view for limitation of the power of removal prevailed in conference committee and in the two houses.

It is clear that the prevailing belief pattern was that quasi-legislative and quasi-judicial functions should be exercised independently. The so-called executive functions related by and large to safety regulation; and by executive order separating these functions, the Civil Aeronautics Board came to have functions regarded generally as quasi-legislative and quasi-judicial. Tradition has supported the notion of independence for these functions.

The significance of the tradition is to obscure the function of policy development. The notions that regulation should be nonpolitical and that the process should be judicial have tended to make regulation a pragmatic process of searching for the appropriate answer in each particular case with only vaguely defined policy guides. Independent boards are drawn away from policy by their absorption in day-to-day business and their isolation from the policy-making departments of the government. And the view that regulation should be nonpolitical results in inattention to the substantive problems of regulation in the office of the President and in the executive departments. The result is that the trend toward inwardness inherent in a system of regulation of private enterprise is enhanced—in my opinion greatly enhanced—by the organizational arrangements chosen for regulation.

Conclusions for Political Science

It is appropriate on this occasion to conclude this brief analysis with comments on its significance with respect to the task of political science. Of what relevance is description of this kind for our discipline?

First, it may remind us that any universe of political phenomena can be understood only if a variety of approaches to its study is used. Interest group analysis has served as one useful approach in study. The role and behavior of individuals has been another. Yet it seems clear that a full understanding of the system of regulation, or of any other system of political action, must extend beyond the immediacies of pressures and motivations of persons, to the wider canvas of technological dynamics, which this paper has only assumed, and of institutional framework and societal belief, which this paper has revealed as interacting in one system. And there is nothing, I submit, more behavioral than study of such interaction.

Second, it is clear that on the side of applied science both limitations and needs combine to shape the search for feasibilities. Proposals to be practical must either operate within the interstices of belief patterns or modify these patterns; the meeting of needs for effective public action is dependent upon the feasibility of developing favorable belief patterns.

Third, it is clear that regulatory administration has been more influenced by business and legal concepts than by management concepts. This may be due in part to the early limitations set for themselves by students of public administration. They concentrated on pure administration and yielded the quasis to the lawyers. They dealt with housekeeping and left the methods of making substantive decisions to lawyers and subject-matter specialists. There has only recently been any effort to develop a managerial science dealing with the process of decision. Our profession has met its obligation in the education of personnel, budget, and O & M specialists; but it has not even grasped a consciousness of its function in substantive areas.

I suggest that that function is definable. It may be defined on two levels. One is the level of administrative technology. The core of such technology must relate to substantive performance—to policy—to decision-making. It must deal with the ways facts may be gathered and verified and with the synthesis of facts and policy objectives in decision-making. It must deal with the role of planning, and with the place of legislative hearings and the methods by which they should be conducted. It must deal with efficiency and administrative due process in the making of decisions in substantive fields.

NOTES

1.   *Lochner* v. *New York,* 198 U.S. 45, 76 (1905).

2.   The outstanding analysis of the influence of opinion on law is A. V. Dicey, *Lectures on the Relation between Law and Opinion in England, During the Nineteenth Century* (New York: Macmillan, 1905).

3.   Civil Aeronautics Act of 1938, 52 Stat. 973, 980, Title 1, Section 2; the Act of 1938 was replaced by the Federal Aviation Act of 1958, in which the same words appear, 72 Stat. 731, 740, Section 102.

4.   *Hearings before a Subcommittee of the Committee on Interstate Commerce,* U.S. Senate, 75th Cong., 1st Sess. 38 (March 8, 1937).

5.   *Principles of Political Economy* (Ashley ed.; New York: Longmans, Green, 1909), pp. 960–63.

6.   See Paul D. Tillett, *The Army Flies the Mails* (University, Alabama: University of Alabama Press, 1954).

7.   For use of the term by Brandeis, see *The Curse of Bigness: Miscellaneous Papers of Louis D. Brandeis,* ed. Osmond K. Frankel (New York: Viking Press, 1935), p. 130; by Wilson, see John Wells Davidson (ed.), *The Crossroads of Freedom: The 1912 Campaign Speeches of Woodrow Wilson* (New Haven: Yale University Press, 1956), p. 183. The concept as used by them has been discussed in James E. Anderson, *The Emergence of the Modern Regulatory State: A Study of American Ideas on the Regulation of Economic Enterprise, 1885–1917* (Ph.D. dissertation, University of Texas, Austin, 1960).

8.   See the comments in Hardy K. Maclay and William C. Burt, "Entry of New Carriers into Domestic Trunkline Air Transportation," *Journal of Air Law and Commerce,* XXII (Spring 1955), 131–56.

9.   For examples see *Hearings before the Committee on Interstate and Foreign Commerce on H.R. 5234 and H.R. 4652,* 75th Cong., 1st Sess. 40 (March 30, 1937); 70 (March 31, 1937); 112–13 (April 1, 1937); *ibid., on H.R. 9738,* 188 (March 24, 1937).

10. *Hearings before a Subcommittee of the Committee on Interstate Commerce on S. 3027,* 74th Cong., 1st Sess. 103 (July 31, 1935).

11. See, for example, letter from James A. Farley, Postmaster General, and testimony of Karl A. Crowley, Solicitor, Post Office Department, *Hearings before the Committee on Interstate and Foreign Commerce on H.R. 5234 and H.R. 4652,* 74 Cong., 1st Sess. 119 ff and 149 (April 2, 1937).

12. *Hearings before a Subcommittee of the Committee on Commerce on H.R. 5234 and H.R. 4652,* 75th Cong., 1st Sess. 15–21 (March 30, 1937).

13. *Hearings before a Subcommittee of the Committee on Commerce on S. 3659,* 75 Cong., 3rd Sess. 156 (April 7, 1938) (McCarran); *Hearings before the Committee on Interstate and Foreign Commerce on H.R. 5234 and H.R. 4652,* 75 Cong. 3rd Sess. 159 (April 2, 1937) (Lea).

14. Senator McCarran: "I want to say that in the preparation of this bill I have followed the Interstate Commerce Act, and I have selected the best out of it that I thought applied to this science with a view to the future development of the science itself." *Hearings before the Committee on Commerce, U.S. Senate,* 73rd Cong., 2nd Sess. 5 (April 12, 1934).

15. In Senate Debates, 83 *Cong. Rec. 6635* (May 11, 1938).

16. *Hearings before the Committee on Interstate and Foreign Commerce on H.R. 5234 and H.R. 4652,* 75th Cong., 1st Sess. 51 ff (March 31–April 1, 1937).

17. For examples of use of these latter terms see House of Representatives, 83 *Cong. Rec.* 6507 (May 9, 1938) (Congressman Randolph of West Virginia); *Hearings before the Committee on Interstate and Foreign Commerce on H.R. 5234 and H.R. 4652,* 75th Cong., 1st Sess. 18 (March 30, 1937) (Eastman); *ibid.,* 66 (March 31, 1937) (Gorrell); 83 *Cong. Rec.* 6407 (May 7, 1938) (Lea.).

18. 1939, p. 2.

19. Delta Air Lines *et al.,* Service to Atlanta and Birmingham, 2 *CAB Reports* 447, 480. On competition generally, see *The Role of Competition in Commercial Air Transportation,* Report of the Civil Aeronautics Board submitted to the Subcommittee of Monopoly, Senate Select Committee on Small Business, Subcommittee Print No. 9, U.S. Senate, 82d Cong., 2nd Sess.

20. New York-Chicago Service Case, 22 *CAB Reports* 973 (September 1, 1955); Denver Service Case, 22 *CAB Reports* 1178 (November 14, 1955); Southwest-Northeast Case, 22 *CAB Reports* 52 (November 21, 1955). For decision at the same time on irregular carriers see Large Irregular Carrier Investigation, 22 *CAB Reports* 853 (Nov. 15, 1955).

21. *I.C.C.* v. *Chicago G. W. Ry. Co.,* 209 U.S. 108, 118–19 (1908); for an equally positive statement fifteen years later, see *State of Missouri ex rel. Southwestern Bell Telephone Co.* v. *Public Service Commission of Missouri,* 262 U.S. 276, 288.

22. For such an argument see F. F. Blachly and Miriam E. Oatman, *Federal Regulatory Action and Control* (Washington: Brookings, 1940), esp. pp. 19–25, and Emmette S. Redford, *Administration of National Economic Control* (New York: Macmillan, 1952), pp. 16 ff.

23. Though Eastman said concerning leaving in a bill under consideration a salary limitation for airline officers of $17,500 per year: ". . . what becomes of the theory of private management and why not have direct Government management?" Letter to Senator B. K. Wheeler, printed in *Hearings before a Subcommittee of the Committee on Interstate Commerce on S. 3027,* 74th Cong., 1st Sess. 69 (July 31, 1935).

24. Civil Aeronautics Act, Section 401 (f); Federal Aviation Act, Section 401 (e).

25. *Alaska Airlines* v. *Civil Aeronautics Board,* 257 F. 2d 229 (1939).

26. E.g., by the commercial airlines in *The General Passenger Fare Investigation.* See my monograph bearing this title in the Inter-University Case series (University, Alabama: University of Alabama Press, 1960), pp. 45–46, 48.

27. See Ernst Freund, *Administrative Powers Over Persons and Property* (Chicago: University of Chicago Press, 1928), particularly pages 10–18.

28. *Hearings before the Committee on Interstate and Foreign Commerce on H.R. 5234 and H.R. 4652,* 75th Cong., 1st Sess. 163 (April 6, 1937).

29. 83 *Cong. Rec.* 6407 (May 7, 1958).

30. *Hearings before a Subcommittee of the Committee on Interstate Commerce on S. 2,* 75th Cong., 1st Sess. 502 (April 12, 1938).

31. *Hearings before the Committee on Interstate and Foreign Commerce on H.R. 9738,* 75th Cong., 3rd Sess. 259 (March 24, 1938).

32. *Materials Relative to Competition in the Regulated Civil Aviation Industry,* 1956, transmitted by the Civil Aeronautics Board to the Select Committee on Small Business, U.S. Senate, 84th Cong., 2d Sess. 8 (April 18, 1956).

33. *Report on Regulatory Agencies to the President-Elect* (Committee Print, Subcommittee on Administrative Practice and Procedure, Committee on the Judiciary, U.S. Senate, December 1960, pp. 5–6.

34. *Problems of the CAB and the Independent Regulatory Commissions* (Memo-

randum to the President of the United States, September 10, 1959), pp. 4–9.

35. 294 U.S. 602 (1935).

36. *Hearings before a Subcommittee of the Committee on Interstate Commerce on S. 3659,* 75th Cong., 3rd Sess. 25 (April 6, 1938).

37. 83 *Cong. Rec.* 6726 (May 12, 1938).

38. *Hearings before a Subcommittee of the Committee on Interstate Commerce on S. 2 and S. 1760,* 75th Cong., 1st Sess. 115 (March 11, 1937).

39. *Ibid.,* p. 451 (April 12, 1937).

40. 83 *Cong. Rec.* 6407 (May 7, 1938).

41. *Hearings before the Committee on Interstate and Foreign Commerce on H.R. 9738,* 75th Cong., 3d Sess. 37 (March 10, 1938).

42. *Ibid.,* p. 36.

43. *Ibid.,* p. 25.

44. *Ibid.,* p. 39. The executive functions related primarily to safety. Hester thought they would be 90 per cent of the work of the agency (p. 49).

chapter two

Economic Stability Policy

A major development in American economic policy in the post World War II era has been the national government's assumption of responsibility for the maintenance of economic stability. While once it was thought that the economy was regulated by natural economic laws unamenable to government control, the Employment Act of 1946 now commits the national government to use its various policies and programs to maintain "maximum employment, production, and purchasing power." Although most persons, whether Democratic or Republican, liberal or conservative, seem agreed that this is a proper task for the government, there is no general agreement as to what kinds of stabilizing actions should be taken when to meet what conditions. Is inflation or unemployment the major problem? Should emphasis be on the use of monetary or fiscal techniques for stabilization? At what time is action required? Such are the questions which policy-makers must seek to resolve when fashioning stability policy.

The two major components of economic stability policy are fiscal and monetary policy. Fiscal policy involves the use of government taxation and expenditures to influence the total volume of purchasing power in the economy and thereby combat recession and inflation. Professor James Schlesinger indicates that compensatory fiscal policy, a matter of much controversy during the 1930's, has gained general acceptance and that with this has come the "death" of the annually balanced budget as an operational fact, if not as a potent political symbol. Many people still believe in the wisdom of an annually balanced budget, a fact which contributed to the difficulty encountered by the Kennedy and Johnson Administrations in winning congressional approval of the 1964 reduction in the income tax. The tax reduction was designed (successfully) to stimulate the economy. In application, the use of fiscal policy is affected by both political and economic considerations which make especially difficult the raising of taxes or the lowering of expenditures. In the latter part of his article Schlesinger sketches various choices open to the makers of stability policy, along with some of the political, ideological, and economic factors that help shape such choices. Clearly, the formation of fiscal policy is both political and technical in character.

Although taxation is a major tool of fiscal policy, it has many purposes in addition to economic stabilization: raising revenue to finance the operation of the government, promoting economic activity, influencing consumption patterns, regulating business activity. Moreover, taxes typically affect some persons and groups more than others, with most people preferring to shift the burden of taxation to someone else. Surrey's discussion of the enactment of special tax provisions by Congress provides meaningful insight into the federal taxing process and considerations affecting congressional tax decisions. This constitutes part of the context within which decisions on taxation for stabilization purposes are made and complicates the use of taxation to stabilize the economy. The use of both taxation and expenditures for economic stabilization would be much simplified if that were the only purpose for which they were used.

The second major part of stability policy is monetary policy, which can be briefly defined as governmental control of the volume of money and credit (and the interest rate) in the economy. To counteract inflation the money supply would be restricted and to offset recession it would be expanded. Monetary policy is primarily under the control of the Federal Reserve Board, one of the national independent regulatory commissions. Consequently, the formation of monetary policy takes place largely in the administrative process and thus differs substantially from fiscal policy-making. Professor Michael Reagan examines the structure of the Federal Reserve Board and Federal Reserve System and shows that their actual operation is much different than is indicated by their formal structure and allocation of activities. Reagan is primarily concerned with how the Board and System operate rather than with the substance of their decisions or their motivations for action. A significant finding concerns the domination of the Federal Reserve Board by the chairman, although legally the seven board members are equals. In all, Reagan nicely illustrates the divergence which often occurs between formal prescriptions and actual behavior in the policy-making process.

Broad fiscal and monetary policy have often been described as too blunt to deal adequately with some stability problems, such as cost-push inflation in which prices and wages rise because of the actions of large corporations and labor unions with substantial market power. The Kennedy Administration found itself confronted with a situation of this sort in 1962 when the steel industry decided on a general price increase, a situation complicated by the fact that this action was apparently contrary to an implicit agreement with the Administration not to raise prices. Theodore Sorensen, special counsel to President Kennedy, discusses the background of the steel price crisis and the efforts of the Administration to secure a reversal of the industry's price-increase decision. Some of the subtle and not-so-subtle aspects of presidential policy-making are reviewed. Those wishing other viewpoints on this significant episode should consult Grant McConnell, *Steel and the Presidency, 1962* (New York: Norton, 1963) or Wallace Carroll, "The Steel Price Crisis of 1962," *New York Times* (April 23, 1962). McConnell's treatment suggests that the situation confronting the Administration was not as unambiguous as Sorensen implies. While participant-observers can provide valuable insight and information on the policy-making process, their reporting may be skewed by their personal involvement.

EMERGING ATTITUDES TOWARD FISCAL POLICY
James R. Schlesinger

President Kennedy's [1961] proposals for tax reform have been indicative of the period of rapid transition through which fiscal policy is now passing. Aside from the recent request for executive authority temporarily to adjust income tax rates (a proposal which stands little chance of approval by Congress), the key feature of his program has been the tax credit which, as originally planned, would have permitted business firms to deduct directly from their tax bills a variable proportion of new investment. The plan has now been altered to provide a straight 8 percent credit for all investment activity. Nevertheless the possibility of varying the deductible percentage depending on economic conditions, makes the tax credit device potentially the most promising new weapon in the arsenal of stabilizing devices since World War II. It would permit regularization of investment outlays and thereby encourage stability of the economy-at-large. Yet the proposal runs directly counter to the tenets of political liberalism which perennially have favored stimulation of consumption spending and have tended to view tax relief for business as an inequitable sop to the interests. New lines have been formed over this issue. Paradoxically, the business community has been resisting what may well be regarded as a powerful stimulus for private initiative and the free enterprise system, while the liberal movement has been split, with the unions and many liberals opposing the tax credit for the traditional reasons. The detached observer can only be struck by the sharp contrast between the extraordinary changes in fiscal practice and instruments in recent years and the public discussion of fiscal policy which remains mired in the stale ideological issues of ten and even twenty years ago. A re-evaluation of fiscal policy, which eliminates the dross and winnows out the issues pertinent to contemporary realities, is now in order. It is hoped that this paper may make a small contribution in that direction.

Reprinted by permission from the *Political Science Quarterly*, LXXVII (March, 1962), 1–18. Some footnotes deleted.

1. The Old Debate

Some fifteen years have passed since the climax of the feverish academic debate over fiscal policy which occurred toward the close of the second World War, during the brief period of flowering plans and hopes when it appeared this evil old world might at long last be made over. Certain it was that the scourge of unemployment could be eliminated forever. Through the use of the government's tax and expenditure powers, aggregate demand or total money expenditures could be *precisely* equated to potential supply,[1] and, as a consequence, no factor of production needed to remain more than temporarily idle. This conviction, molded in academic circles especially by Professor Alvin Hansen and his supporters, had obtained widespread public acceptance. Although the Full Employment Act of 1946 did not satisfy the enthusiasts, since it failed to provide the desired *guarantee* of full employment, it did reflect the prevailing confidence in fiscal policy.

Elsewhere the hopes held out for fiscal policy had been even higher. In Great Britain such attitudes reached their culmination in the Beveridge Report[2] (1944), which may be taken to represent the high tide of enthusiasm for fiscal policy. Just prior to the Korean War a United Nations study, in reviewing the main ingredients of full employment policy, came to rather optimistic conclusions regarding the possibility of attaining both domestic and international stability. Yet by the time of the U. N. report, not only had the deepening antagonism between Russia and the West revealed that the world was not to be reformed and was still to be dominated by power politics, but several years of steady inflation had raised widespread doubts whether unemployment was likely to be the main postwar economic problem. For whatever reason, the ambitious proposal of the report attracted considerable attention in the academic world but was almost ignored by the governments represented in the U. N. Apparently the public's attention had been diverted to other matters.

The reaction of indifference by governments, many of which were already making use of fiscal policy for stabilization purposes, is symptomatic of the ebbing of interest in the debate over employment. So many wartime hopes for achieving a brave new world having died, it does not seem strange that the employment programs planned during the war now appear to be a form of castle-building, useful for arousing the public to greater efforts but somewhat removed from postwar economic realities.

Attitudes toward fiscal policy have reflected these changing conditions. If one were to ask what fiscal policy had achieved in the postwar period, the answer might well be: both everything and nothing. From the standpoint of its early opponents, compensatory fiscal policy has clearly conquered all obstacles and possesses the field. All administrations, all parties, and almost all politicians—some with seeming enthusiasm, some with seeming reluctance—have embraced compensatory fiscal policy. Yet the reluctance of some and the skepticism of all concerning fiscal policy would appear puzzling to the fiscal innovators of the middle forties, whose expectations had been pitched much higher. From the standpoint of the proponents, conditions have "improved" surprisingly little. In periods of recession and of inflationary pressure, the government appears strangely restrained in using the fiscal weapon. Serviceable in many respects, fiscal policy has failed to provide the utopia of employment security that was hoped for a scant fifteen years ago.

2. The Authentic Death and the Political Survival of the Annually Balanced Budget

The case for the annually balanced budget is at its strongest when the public sector accounts for a fairly small proportion of national income, for under such circumstances it may be argued that the nation's fiscal policy will have slight effect on economic conditions and that, for psychological reasons, balancing of the budget is the most appropriate policy. As the size of the public sector increases, the case for attempting to attain an annual balancing of the budget weakens while the case for compensatory finance grows correspondingly stronger. For, in periods of recession when aggregate demand is already declining, the attempt to balance the budget either through the reduction of government expenditures or through the increase of tax rates tends to bring a further diminution of aggregate demand. Adherence to the balanced budget concept is likely to intensify the recession. Cutting government spending would reinforce the decline in private spending—hardly a sensible procedure. It would seem more reasonable to cushion the fall in total expenditures by holding government expenditures constant or even by increasing them. On the revenue side, the attempt to increase tax *receipts* by increasing tax *rates* would be equally frustrating, for the increase in rates by reducing disposable personal income and/or by weakening incentives and business confidence is likely to accelerate the decline in private expenditures and further to reduce national income.

Thus the case against the balanced budget is a two-sided one. First, it would seem wise for the government to refrain from reinforcing the contractive tendencies by its own act and, therefore, it should fulfill its expenditure commitments while refusing to increase taxes. Such action, or refusal to take action, implies the incurring of a substantial budgetary deficit as revenues sag in unison with the decline of national income. Secondly, the *attempt* to balance the budget is in reality quite hopeless. Industrial nations have discovered that expenditure commitments rise in periods of depression. (Despite the best of intentions both Presidents Hoover and Roosevelt discovered this to be the case.) Moreover, it is hard to find additional sources of revenue in depression and the attempt, for the reasons given above, is likely to be self-defeating. Depressions breed budgetary deficits. The existence of a deficit, if not its size, is unlikely to be affected by whether the deficit is looked upon as an appropriate method of ameliorating the recession or as an evil blot on the fiscal escutcheon which is to be both fought and endured.

Despite its survival, as a political catchword, the annually balanced budget is now dead in practice. The effectiveness of a budgetary principle can never be discovered by listening to the professions of politicians but must be inferred from their actions. Despite the lip service, no actual effort is made to balance the budget during periods of recession. On the contrary, both parties vie with each other to increase rather than reduce the size of the deficit. In the 1958 recession, to take a recent example, the actions of *both* political parties tended to increase the deficit. The differences between the two concerned the degree of response that was necessary, whether reliance should be on tax reduction or expenditure increases and so on, rather than the appropriateness of a deficit in itself.

From their pronouncements at the time, however, one would have assumed that the balanced budget remains the lodestar of both parties. The balanced budget may be dead for practical purposes but, embalmed within a glass case, it is treated with a touching respect by most politicians. The reason for this is quite simple: by and large the public continues to regard the balanced budget as the criterion of sound finance. Since political parties are institutions designed to give, or at least to promise, the public what it wants, it should not be surprising that boundless devotion to the balanced budget will be expressed in political pronouncements. Thus the Republicans, in 1958, took pride in the speed with which the economic downturn was reversed, yet were deeply apologetic about the $12 billion deficit in fiscal 1959, which was certainly in large measure responsible for the mildness of the recession. The Democrats, on the other hand, whose plans for increasing the deficit had only been held in check by the President's veto, simultaneously castigated the administration for failure to take more aggressive action to deal with the recession and for incurring so enormous a deficit. It was clearly implied that under a different administration so monstrous a case of fiscal irresponsibility would never have occurred.

Both parties are aware that the bulk of the voters are primarily interested in ending a recession and only secondarily in avoiding a budgetary deficit. So long as the public fails to connect the stimulative powers of the federal budget in recession with the existence of a deficit, so long will the political parties pretend that they are separable. Simultaneously, a party will attempt to take credit for any stimulative effect of fiscal policy while decrying the inevitable financial accoutrements of that policy. Plainly the budgeting deficit, produced by the automatic fall in revenues and rise in expenditures, is the chief instrument for curing recessions. In practice, all parties make use of automatic stabilization.[3] If the public wishes to hear deficits denounced, political parties stand ready to perform the intellectual *tour de force* of disassociating the deficit from the operation of the automatic stabilizers.

It is clear that the proponents of fiscal policy have obtained the substance of their desires, while leaving to their rivals only empty forms and slogans. Consequently, it would seem that the former have won a great victory, and that they would be content to see their dreams fulfilled. Paradoxically, however, this is not the case. Although the use of fiscal policy in achieving stability is universally accepted today, the hopes of those who originally formulated it have gone unfulfilled. For various reasons our method of employing fiscal weapons, our attitudes toward fiscal policy, and our experience with employment programs, have all proved to be something of a disappointment to them. In several respects current practices and attitudes *are almost as far from those suggested in the wartime period as they are from the orthodox Treasury views of an earlier era.*

3. Economic Limitations

The goal of the formulators of full employment programs was not merely the *mitigation* but the virtual *elimination* of economic fluctuations. If, through the use of the fiscal weapon, aggregate demand could be more or less precisely matched to potential supply, then no (competent) man need be more than temporarily unemployed. And the original proponents did believe that fiscal policy might be employed so flexibly. By varying expenditures or the tax structure whenever deflationary or inflationary pressures became apparent, full employment without inflation could be permanently achieved. This attitude toward employment policy, which may be called the perfectionist view, was embodied in the Beveridge program and supplied the initial impulse for the Full Employment Act in this country. Since proponents of these policies would not be satisfied with mere palliatives, the automatic stabilizers, which could only mitigate but not eliminate fluctuations, were viewed as desirable but insufficient. To achieve a permanent state of full employment, the automatic stabilizers would have to be supplemented by discretionary fiscal policy, flexibly employed. In the view of their critics, this "attempt to drain the last dregs of employment out of the system" was likely to do more harm than good. They thought that discretionary fiscal policy too ambitiously employed was characterized by inherent defects which the formulators of the programs had to perceive. Time has proved the skeptics to have been very perceptive.

Part of the difficulty of the perfectionist view lay in the economic realm. The biggest error, perhaps, was the failure to appreciate the strong upward pressure on wages, costs, and prices which would exist under full employment conditions. American theorists underestimated the strong preference on the part of individual unions to preserve their autonomy rather than to observe a general wage-price formula. They overestimated the willingness of pressure groups in general to exercise self-restraint in the public interest. They overestimated both the effectiveness and public tolerability of the control of prices in "bottleneck sectors." Consequently, they failed to appreciate adequately the tendency of demand to leak off into higher wages and prices rather than into expanded output, once the sanction of unemployment was removed. One apparent effect of a full employment guarantee has been to make a steady rise in the price level inevitable.

Advocates of the employment programs failed to perceive another defect in the perfectionist view. Although it is a very powerful instrument, fiscal policy is also a *crude* one and may not be sufficiently subtle to achieve the *delicate* kinds of adjustment required in an economy which is dependent upon the *voluntary* action of individuals to achieve necessary adjustments. This type of difficulty is shown most clearly in the case of unemployment in export industries, which depend after all upon foreign buyers. An expansionary fiscal policy, by raising domestic costs and prices and making domestic goods less attractive to foreign purchasers, may actually magnify rather than diminish the problem of unemployment in the export industries—to say nothing of intensifying any balance of payments difficulties which may exist.

Even within the domestic economy, fiscal policy may be incapable of dealing with the problem of structural unemployment. When changes occur in consumer preferences or in the pattern of industrial production, the shift in the structure of output is likely to create a declining industry concentrated in a particular region. This is the problem of the depressed area about which fiscal policy can do little. Any increase in aggregate demand brought about by an expansionary fiscal policy is likely to result in continued unemployment in the depressed area, associated with a rise in the price level in other sectors of the economy. The problem in this case is that the simple Keynesian model upon which fiscal policy is based may be misleading. Aggregate supply may be equated to aggregate demand in the over-all sense, without the hoped for results, since demand may be concentrated upon industries in which capacity is insufficient, while unemployment continues in those industries against which consumer preferences have been shifting. In West Virginia, for example, the chief industry, coal, has suffered simultaneously from: a) a substantial fall-off in foreign demand since 1957; b) a gradual diminution of demand on the part of domestic consumers; and, c) improvements in the methods of coal-mining which have diminished the need for miners. Unemployment in West Virginia remains high, on account of the reluctance of the population to move away from their homes despite the shrinkage of employment opportunities. Irrespective of the statements of office seekers on the campaign trail, there is really very little that the federal government can do about this condition, short of *directing* industrial investment into the state. Due to the handicaps of location under which West Virginia labors, the effect of an expansionary fiscal policy on its unemployment problem will be modest at best.[4]

4. *Political Realities in a Democracy*

Failure to take account of its economic limitations has not, however, proved to be the chief drawback to fiscal policy in the postwar period. A far graver defect was the failure of its proponents to recognize the limits to its political workability, especially in the context of the American political system. Under *ideal* conditions, it could be expected that flexible use of fiscal policy could prevent unemployment, except for very short periods, outside of depressed areas. But such a result presupposes that the nation's fiscal machinery is controlled by rational and detached experts uninfluenced by pressures, interests, or impassioned controversies. Such is not the case, although at one time fiscal theorists naively assumed that it was. The nation's fiscal policy is decided by members of Congress subject to the strong and somewhat irrational demands of ordinary voters and of special interest groups. The practical results have consequently diverged considerably from the expectation of those who formulated the employment programs. As a result, since early in the postwar period, discretionary fiscal policy has been viewed with some skepticism by all except academic observers.

The most obvious of fiscal policy's political difficulties is its asymmetry or lopsidedness. According to the original conception, fiscal policy was intended to be a dual-purpose weapon, effective in dealing with excessive as well as insufficient demand. In times of inflation, budgetary surpluses would restrain total expenditures and ease inflationary pressures, just as in times of depression, demand was maintained by a budgetary deficit. In practice, nothing has been so hard to attain or to retain as a budgetary surplus. Paying taxes is burdensome and unpleasant to the voters, so that Congress is under constant pressure to reduce taxes. Moreover, expanded expenditures are quite satisfying to whatever groups are benefited, and Congress is under steady pressure to increase its outlays. Under these circumstances it is difficult even to balance the budget in times of prosperity, let alone obtain a surplus (which incidentally helps to explain the aura of fiscal rectitude which came to be built up around the balanced budget rule). Fiscal policy readily serves as a stimulant in periods of depression, but not as a restraint in periods of excessive demand. Whenever a surplus appears, there is a strong tendency either for expenditures to creep up or for tax cuts to be given—either action intensifying the pressure and throwing a larger burden on monetary policy.

There is a second facet to the lopsidedness of fiscal policy. If the onset of a recession brings about discretionary increase of expenditures on the part of the government, vested interests are created in such expenditures and, with the return of prosperity, it becomes difficult to reduce them. Associated with the reluctance to increase tax rates, the result could be perennially unbalanced budgets. Moreover, permanent increases in federal expenditures in recession, even if matched by an increase in taxes in prosperity, might mean that a rising proportion of national output is incorporated into the government sector—a condition which is not consistent with the political goals of a good many citizens. This tendency of government expenditures to creep up in recession without receding in prosperity is sometimes referred to as the "ratchet effect"—it has made political conservatives, at any rate, suspicious of the aggressive use of fiscal policy.

The assumption of fiscal theorists that the tax structure is far more flexible than conditions really warrant creates another difficulty. Theorists may view the tax structure as a technical instrument to be used for the manipulation of demand. The public, however, tends to regard the tax system as a matter of balanced rights and responsibilities, based upon justice and equity. Continued variation of tax rates may undermine the willingness to pay taxes upon which, in the final analysis, the effectiveness of fiscal policy depends. The willingness to pay taxes, particularly income taxes, is not a universal phenomenon. It could be that the attempt to overuse the fiscal instrument might destroy the delicate structure upon which it rests. At some point in the future the public may come to appreciate the desirability of viewing taxation simply as a device for influencing expenditures in the private sector. It clearly does not do so at the present time, thus making it hard to increase taxes or to reimpose them once they have been removed.

A barrier to the kind of flexibility envisaged by the theorists arises from the fact that any variation of the tax structure may mean a shift in the *distribution* of the tax burden among different classes of citizens and taxpayers. Any change in the tax structure which forces a reappraisal of the appropriateness of relative burdens almost inevitably breeds both intense political controversy and a degree of social friction which is disturbing. Each group's notion of equity in the tax structure is based upon the (tacit) belief that a larger share of the burden should be shifted to others—labor pleads for higher exemptions, while business pleads for a lower corporate income tax. It is for this reason that a wise rule-of-thumb in public finance is that "an old tax is a good tax." Avoiding changes in the tax structure means avoiding the reawakening of controversy and harmful passions. Fiscal theorists who urge continuous modification of the tax structure ignore the fact that fiscal policy is only in some respects a *general* control. Both tax and expenditure policies operate by directly affecting the interests of specific groups which are likely to feel resentful when those interests have been damaged. Continued modification of the tax structure may lead to social controversy, a feeling of ill usage, a decline in morale which weakens the social fabric, and, by weakening the willingness to pay taxes, may undermine the fiscal policy instrument itself.

With some notable exceptions most fiscal analysts have failed in their theorizing to appreciate the fragility of the fiscal system in a democracy, particularly under the Congressional system. Political confidence is delicate and quite easily disturbed. One way to achieve this result is to introduce continual friction over the tax and expenditure pattern. The tax system must be consistent with popular notions of equity; to be acceptable, temporary tax remissions would therefore have to be proportional or something close to it. Since under the American fiscal system frequent change is disturbing to political confidence, it would appear unwise to tamper with the system too frequently, even in the quest for continuous high employment.

Even more than the economic difficulties, the political clumsiness of discretionary fiscal policy has increased the reluctance to employ it aggressively in counteracting mild downturns, and has made it almost impossible to use fiscal policy effectively in dealing with inflationary pressures. To be sure, this defect refers only to discretionary fiscal policy rather than to the automatic stabilizers which do not require either precise forecasting or rapid and frictionless adjustments brought about through cumbersome political machinery. Only when a gross maladjustment exists between aggregate demand and supply, is it clear that discretionary fiscal policy can be employed. The tricky problems thus arise when one tries to decide what to do in in-between situations in which the automatic stabilizers have failed to prevent more unemployment developing than one would desire, yet the unemployment has not gone deep enough to warrant the risks of discretionary fiscal policy. Both the inflexibility of expenditures in the downward direction (the ratchet effect) and the political frictions generated by variation of the tax structure have made all postwar administrations loath to employ fiscal policy in as flexible a way as the academics of the 'forties hoped. The convenient theoretical assumption of *ceteris paribus,* which academicians employed in building their models of fiscal policy, has failed to provide an appropriate guide to the real world with its rapid changes of economic conditions and its combative behavior of political man.

Although in one respect fiscal policy has revolutionized budget policy, in another it has left conditions surprisingly unchanged. It has revolutionized budget policy in that as much has been accomplished from fiscal policy as could reasonably be expected. On the other hand, the early models have proved to be misleadingly simple and the gap between theory and reality has proved to be much greater than was anticipated in the bright glow of enthusiasm in the period of the war. Although the rule of the *annually* balanced budget has met its end, in fact if not in fiction, it has proved to be impossible to frame budget policy solely in terms of "functional finance" or "the economic requirements of particular conditions." Such concepts provide too elastic a criterion for budget policy, and it is for this reason that the balanced budget remains relevant as an aspiration, if not as a rule. Democracies appear to be reluctant to discipline themselves. The projected balancing of a target budget for conditions of full employment provides a disciplinary value in a society in which the public is inclined to overlook the fact that costs must be paid—a disciplinary value which the original proponents of fiscal policy may have treated too lightly.

5. Vistas of the Future

In two other respects attitudes toward fiscal policy have been changing rapidly. First, we have come to recognize that a given level of effective demand may be obtained through an incredible variety of fiscal devices which can be fitted together in an array of distinct patterns of tax and expenditure policies. Secondly, we have learned that fiscal policy does not exist in a vacuum; it must be effectively coordinated with monetary and debt management policies in order to achieve the nation's goals, whatever they may be. These two changes are closer together than one might think, for together they represent a departure from stale ideological controversy which has enormously broadened the range of the potential components of the nation's policy-mix.

The first point requires some amplification. In contrast to a widespread view of fifteen years ago that the "marginal propensity to save" was too "high" to permit reliance on the tax reduction route to stimulate total expenditures, tax reduction is today viewed as an effective instrument for stimulating not only consumption but investment as well. Peacetime levels of taxation much higher than were anticipated in the 'forties have meant that the leeway for stimulating expenditures through tax reduction is much greater than hitherto. These higher levels of taxation have meant that a large share of tax revenues has come from the lower and middle income groups; consequently a reduction in taxes may more easily stimulate mass consumption expenditures than was anticipated earlier. Moreover, upper income groups are more willing to consume out of increased aftertax incomes than was believed possible even ten years ago. The recognition of the expansibility of consumption is most vividly illustrated by the shift of the main focus of the critics of our economic system from "the mature economy" to the "affluent society"—that is, a shift from a view that the propensity to consume is too low to the view that it is too high. In addition, the abandonment of the notion that the volume of investment is "autonomously" determined has meant recognition that it is not at all difficult to stimulate additional *investment* expenditures via the tax reduction route. Particularly is this true when fiscal policies of a somewhat wider scope, including tax credits for investment expenditure or more generous treatment of depreciation allowances, are considered.

The widening range of activities which it is regarded as appropriate for the government to support has meant a similar broadening of opportunities on the expenditures side. In the depression the choice lay between traditional public works which provided tangible results and relief expenditures which did not. The inflexibility of public works and the inhibitions of Harold Ickes help to explain the insignificance of the PWA as a disburser of funds relative to the WPA which provided little or no direct value in return. Expenditures resulting in tangible benefits now include the housing program, slum clearance, and a greater expanded conception of resource development. With respect to expenditures for intangible benefits the government may now spend for education, for unemployment compensation and for a variety of welfare measures, without indulging in the leaf-raking fiction that there is a direct *quid pro quo*. In light of the broadened array of fiscal weapons, increasingly there are differences concerning the appropriate mixture of fiscal devices to achieve a given level of demand.

The second point reflects the recognition that monetary policy and the closely allied debt management policy can have a substantial influence on effective demand. Moreover, fiscal and monetary policies are closely associated in determining the availability of capital funds, and the allocation of resources as between consumption and investment. In the days when monetary policy was regarded as hopelessly ineffective, the problem of coordination could be blithely ignored. Now it is seen that a tighter fiscal policy permits a more lenient monetary policy, and vice versa. For effective monetary policy the problem of debt management must be under control, both with respect to its structure and its trend, and the trend of the debt reflects government surpluses and deficits, that is, fiscal policy. Thus there is a question of choice involved in the policy-mix. Accepting the goal of full employment, one can choose either to emphasize or deemphasize fiscal policy depending on whether one wishes to place a smaller or greater burden on monetary and debt management policy respectively.

Put together, both the centrifugal tendency for the scope of fiscal policy to widen and the centripetal tendency for it to become more closely intertwined with monetary and debt management policy in the over-all policy-mix have vastly increased the number of possible combinations of policy ingredients to achieve a given policy goal. Figure 1 illustrates this range of possibilities. On the highest level, a choice must be made between emphasizing fiscal policy and emphasizing monetary policy. Just below these two policy areas, not quite independent but not altogether dependent, is debt management, more subordinate to monetary than to fiscal policy but still reflecting immediate budgetary pressures. One may attempt to use debt management countercyclically or one may have the more modest and traditional Treasury objective of managing it "for its own sake."

Within the area of fiscal policy, one has a variety of choices. One may choose to rely exclusively on automatic stabilizers (accompanied by flexible monetary policy) or one may attempt to use discretionary fiscal policy. Under the latter heading there will be an opportunity to

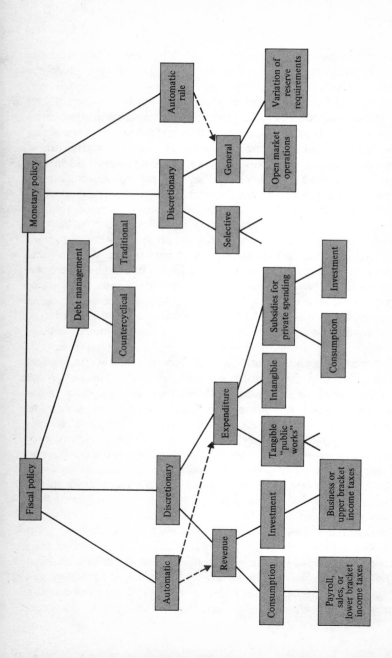

Figure 1

emphasize the revenue or the expenditure side (just as would be the case for automatic stabilizers, though not to the same degree). If the emphasis is placed on the revenue side, a choice will be made between influencing demand by affecting consumption, which implies variation of sales-type taxes, payroll taxes, or lower bracket income taxes, or by influencing investment, which implies changes in business taxes, upper bracket income taxes or depreciation policies. (Relying on investment changes must mean, of course, considerable reliance on monetary policy.) On the expenditure side, a choice may be made between changing expenditures for tangibles or for intangibles, or the decision might be made directly to subsidize private consumption or investment.

Monetary policy, though it remains wholly discretionary at the present time, may also be subdivided. One may rely on general controls, or one may make some use of selective controls. Under the heading of the traditional quantitative weapons, a choice will have to be made between emphasizing open market operations or utilizing changes in reserve requirements in determining monetary strategy.

In choosing the ultimate policy-mix, value judgments are unavoidable. As a general, if not universal, rule, the political right with its deep distrust of concentration of power, particularly in the government, has tended to favor monetary policy over fiscal policy. When fiscal policy is employed, the preference is for total reliance on the automatic stabilizers. If discretionary fiscal policy is employed, the preference is for reliance on changes on the revenue side, especially those that stimulate investment activity.[5] When expenditures must be adjusted, it is preferred that increases be for tangibles (such as roads) rather than intangibles (welfare benefits broadly construed). Curiously enough, in the case of subsidies the right has little aversion to subsidizing investment outlays, but a deep repugnance for subsidizing consumption outlays, although as a rule, subsidization of private expenditures is preferred to increased state activity.

The political left tends in the other direction. Fiscal policy, even discretionary fiscal policy, is *preferred* to monetary and debt management policies. Changes on the expenditure (that is, increases) are preferred to changes on the revenue side. If changes on the revenue side are accepted, the preference is normally toward stimulating mass consumption rather than investment (though, as President Kennedy's tax proposals indicate, this has changed in recent years as concern over the issue of growth has increased). There is no aversion to expenditures for intangibles. Subsidization of certain types of private consumption seems highly desirable, but direct subsidization of private investment is viewed with extreme suspicion. In employing monetary policy, the left, unlike the right, has some partiality for the selective controls, and has a preference for higher reserve requirements with open market purchases by the Federal Reserve, while the right prefers lowered reserve requirements.

At the present time, it should be emphasized, most of the disputes superficially concerning stabilization policy are really about value judgments on issues other than stabilization. When labor unions insist that recession should be fought by lowering sales or first bracket taxes, increased expenditures or subsidies, and looser money, but also insist that *reversal* of these policies is *not* the proper way to fight inflation (but rather business and upper bracket income taxes should be increased and selective controls on spending adopted), plainly the argument is not over stabilization *per se* but rather over increased consumption, decreased income inequality, and the appropriate role of the state. Similarly, when the political right recommends diminished progressivity of the income tax in *inflation* and in *deflation*, this clearly is not a question involving stabilization policy alone. Both sides are likely to insist that failure to adopt their particular remedies will be destabilizing, but that is the merest window dressing. Any detached observer will note a variety of ways of skinning the stabilization cat. Stability can be achieved through a vast number of combinations of policy measures, each one of which will reflect a different set of value judgments. The greater variety of fiscal devices and the increased flexibility of fiscal policy, in combining it with monetary or debt management policies, has increased the latitude for controversy over issues different from, but still unhappily confused with, the appropriateness of using fiscal policy for stabilization purposes.

NOTES

1.   If national income (Y) is divided into private expenditures (E) and government expenditures (G), which together comprise effective demand and

determine the level of national income, then to achieve full employment income, $E + G$ must be equal to total potential supply at full employment. Fiscal policy, it is hoped, will achieve this goal by directly increasing G or by inducing a rise in E (through tax reduction) when a deficiency of demand appears, or by reversing this process when excess demand appears. Thus it is hoped aggregate demand can be controlled with precision, permitting the maintenance of full employment without inflation.

2. William H. Beveridge, *Full Employment in a Free Society* (New York, 1945).

3. Any lingering hopes, doubts or fears that the Republican party might still be clinging to the annually balanced budget rule were eliminated by a final report to President Eisenhower by his Budget Director, Maurice H. Stans, generally regarded as a fiscal conservative (see *Federal Fiscal Behavior During the Recession of 1957–58,* Executive Office of the President, Bureau of the Budget, January 1961). While the report is quite critical of "deliberate (discretionary) countercyclical steps" in the recession of 1957–58, it attributes the rapid recovery to the action of the "built-in stabilizers," upon which, it argues, primary reliance should be placed in any future recession.

4. The debate in early 1961 between Walter Heller, Chairman of the Council of Economic Advisers, who argued that existing unemployment was primarily "cyclical" and could be eliminated by an increase in spending, and William McChesney Martin, Chairman of the Federal Reserve Board, who argued that it was "structural" and could not be, represented a revival of the controversy of the 'forties. Heller's position represented a reiteration of the faith of those who formulated the original employment programs: that unemployment was essentially a consequence of deficient demand. More recently there has been a change on the part of administration economists who are now ready to concede that in places like West Virginia or Michigan unemployment may well be structural and therefore intractable.

5. A characteristic example is provided by the tax program of Secretary Humphrey during the 1954 recession. Its underlying assumption was that prosperity depended upon investment activity; its chief features were more generous treatment of depreciation allowances and an income tax cut on an across-the-board basis. The Democratic minority in Congress favored greater relief for lower bracket income tax payers, including an increase in exemptions. Under the Kennedy administration the Democratic position has shifted dramatically, with the administration sponsoring the tax credit to encourage *investment* spending, and apparently favoring substantial reduction of income tax rates at the *upper* end of the structure.

THE CONGRESS AND THE TAX LOBBYIST—
HOW SPECIAL TAX PROVISIONS GET ENACTED
Stanley S. Surrey

The development of a proper tax structure for an economy as large and as complex as ours is a task of the first magnitude. Given the dimensions of the task and the political arena in which it must be undertaken, the Congress has performed the essential work successfully. It has shown remarkable collective wisdom in shaping our federal tax structure, and its accomplishment in this field may be measured favorably against the tax systems of other countries. Since we live in an era when both professional learning and public opinion regard a progressive income tax as the most appropriate method of raising governmental revenue, and since the progressive income tax is the mainstay of our tax structure, this accomplishment is remarkable. For a progressive income tax is also the most complicated and difficult of taxes to maintain. It places a premium on sensitivity to economic changes and to public attitudes. It demands high technical skills on the part of those who shape the legislative structure, who administer and interpret its provisions, who advise the public how to order its business and family affairs under the tax. It requires a literate citizenry with a respect for law and a willingness to shoulder fiscal burdens. Our over-all successful record in relying on the progressive income tax is thus a noteworthy achievement in public finance.

The continuation of this success with our federal-tax structure demands, however, constant alertness to the correction of faults as they appear. Recently there has been considerable criticism directed against the existence in our tax laws of provisions granting special treatment to certain groups or individuals. This criticism is aimed at both the increasing number of new provisions of this kind and the continuation of old provisions the significance of which has become far more important with passage of time. Some, it is true, have irresponsibly resorted to criticisms of this character as a justification for

Reprinted from the *Harvard Law Review*, LXX (May, 1957), 1145–1182, with the permission of the author and publisher, Copyright 1957, by the Harvard Law Review Association. This is a condensed version of the original article.

discarding the income tax. But nearly all who have voiced objections to special-treatment provisions have done so in the hope that a consideration of the problem would result in a strengthening of the income tax. . . .

Often these provisions are spoken of as "loopholes" or "special tax privileges." Of course, the use of the appellation "loophole" is a matter of viewpoint. What is a "tax loophole" to a CIO or an ADA meeting is merely "relief from special hardship or intolerable rates" to an American Bankers Association or NAM meeting—and vice versa. . . . But despite an absence of consensus on any particular list of provisions there seems to be considerable agreement that Congress in its tax legislation has adopted provisions favoring special groups or special individuals and that these provisions run counter to our notions of tax fairness. Moreover, the tendency of Congress to act this way seems to be increasing.

Against this background, the purpose of this article is to consider the question of why the Congress enacts these special tax provisions, to use a fairly neutral term. . . .

I. Some Major Factors

1. High rates of tax. The high rates of the individual income tax, and of the estate and gift taxes, are probably the major factor in producing special tax legislation. This is, in a sense, a truism, for without something to be relieved of, there would be no need to press for relief. The point is that the average congressman does not basically believe in the present rates of income tax in the upper brackets. When he sees them applied to individual cases, he thinks them too high and therefore unfair. Any argument for relief which starts off by stating that these high rates are working a "special hardship" in a particular case or are "penalizing" a particular taxpayer—to use some words from the tax lobbyist's approved list of effective phrases—has the initial advantage of having a sympathetic listener. Put the other way around, an advocate of the "Louis B. Mayer amendment" would simply make no headway with a congressman who firmly believed in a ninety-one-percent top tax rate.* But most congressmen apparently do not believe in such a rate—certainly not in the concrete and perhaps not even in the abstract. Since they are not, however, willing to reduce those rates directly, the natural outcome is indirect reduction through special provisions. . . .

2. *Tax polarity.* The existence of two rate structures in the income tax and of two types of taxes on the transfer of wealth permits a congressman to favor a special group by placing its situation under the lower rate structure or the less effective tax. Thus, the presence of the twenty-five-per-cent capital-gains rate enables Congress to shift an executive stock option from the high rates applying to executive compensation to the lower capital-gains rate. If there were no special capital-gains rate, or if we did not tax capital gains at all, this shift could not be made, since a congressman would not completely exempt the stock option. Similarly, the presence of a gift tax permits certain transfers of wealth, such as transferred life insurance, to be shifted from the higher estate tax to the lower gift tax. As a consequence, given this congressional tendency, we reach the paradox that having a gift tax as well as an estate tax may, given the present lack of proper co-ordination of the two taxes, result in less effective taxation of certain transfers of wealth than if we relied only on an estate tax.

3. *Technical complexity.* The high rates of tax, the complexities of modern business, the desires of the wealthy and middle-income groups for clear tax charts to guide their family planning, the Government's need for protection against tax avoidance, the claims of tax equity, and various other factors have combined to make the income, estate, and gift taxes exceedingly complex in technical detail. These technicalities involve the drawing of countless dividing lines. Consequently, a case on the high-tax side of a line may closely resemble the cases on the other side receiving more favorable tax treatment. The result is a

*[In 1964 the maximum rate was lowered to seventy percent. The "Louis B. Mayer amendment" is a special provision of the Internal Revenue Code, adopted in 1951, which saved Mayer about $2,000,000 in taxes. At the time it was assumed that the amendment covered only Mayer and one other person. Ed.]

fertile ground for assertions of inequity and hardship as particular taxpayers desire legislation to bend the dividing lines and thereby extend the favorable treatment to their situations. Also, faulty tax planning, ill-advised legal steps, or transactions concluded in ignorance of tax law can produce severe tax consequences. These "tax penalties" could have been averted under an informed tax guidance that would have taken the taxpayer safely through the technical tax maze. In these circumstances, the taxpayer facing severe monetary hurt because of a "mere technicality" (to use the phrase that will be pressed on the congressman) is quite likely to evoke considerable sympathy for his plight.

4. History and politics. The accidents of tax history also play a major role in the existence of special provisions. Tax-exempt securities in large part achieved their favored status through the vagaries of constitutional interpretation and not through any special desire to relieve the wealthy. Percentage depletion for oil and gas and the deduction of intangible drilling expenses have their roots in legislative compromises and administrative interpretation which for the most part do not appear to have been planned as special-interest relief. It is only later that the extent of the tax generosity inherent in such provisions is comprehended. But by then they are in the law, the problem of the group benefited is one of defense rather than attack, and the strategic advantages are all with that group. This is especially so when the area involved touches on major political matters, as in the case of percentage depletion and tax-exempt securities.

Political considerations naturally overhang this whole area, for taxation is a sensitive and volatile matter. Any major congressional action represents the compromises of the legislator as he weighs and balances the strong forces constantly focused on him by the pressure groups of the country. Many special provisions—capital gains, for one—are caught in these swirling pressures. The response of the legislator to issues raised by these provisions is, like his response to the general level of tax rates or to personal exemptions, a political response of considerable significance. It is an important part of the fabric of political responses which determines whether he will remain a congressman and whether his party will control Congress. In this group of provisions highly affected by political considerations are those "tax relief" provisions which have a broad public appeal and are thus likely to be regarded by the congressman as useful "vote-getters"—a "baby-sitter" deduction, the exclusion of "retirement income," or an extra exemption for the "aged." The political appeal of favorable action on these issues is quite likely to outweigh what a congressman would regard as "technical" tax arguments to the contrary.

5. Separation of executive and legislative branches of government. But many of the tax provisions we are considering do not lie at this political level. They are simply a part of the technical tax law. They are not of major importance in their revenue impact. But they are of major importance to the group or individual benefited and they are glaring in their departure from tax fairness. The inquiry, therefore, must here be directed toward some of the institutional features in the tax-legislation process which may be responsible for special provisions of this technical variety. Lacking direct knowledge, I must leave to others the task of describing the types of pressure from constituents or other groups which may be operative in a particular case. While these pressures may explain why the congressman who is directly subject to the pressures may act and vote for a special provision, they do not explain why other congressmen, not so subject, go along with the proposal. We must look for reasons beyond these pressures if we are to understand the adoption of these special tax provisions. A number of these reasons lie in the institutional aspects of the tax legislative process.

Basic to a consideration of these institutional aspects are the nature of our governmental system and the relationship between the Congress and the executive. A different governmental structure might give the legislator little or nothing to say about tax provisions. Under a parliamentary government, the revenue department retains tight control over the statutory development of tax law. It is responsive only to the broad political issues that require decisions of a party nature. Beyond these, the governmental tax technicians mold the structure, so that the tax lobbyist pressing for special legislative consideration or the legislator seeking to ease a constituent's problem by special tax relief is not a significant part of the tax scene. . . .

The United States picture is quite different, for here Congress occupies the role of mediator between the tax views of the executive and the demands of the pressure groups. This is so whether the tax issue involved is a major political matter or a minor technical point. The Congress is zealous in maintaining this position in the tax field. A factor of special importance here is article I, section 7, of the Constitution, which provides that "All Bills for raising Revenue shall originate in the House of Representatives." The House Committee on Ways and Means jealously guards this clause against possible inroads by the Senate. It also protects its jurisdiction over revenue legislation from encroachment by other House committees. When senators and other congressmen must toe the line, the executive is not likely to be permitted to occupy a superior position. Further, a legislator regards tax matters as politically very sensitive, and hence as having a significant bearing on elections. It is no accident that the tax committees are generally strong committees, whose membership is carefully controlled by the party leaders.

The Congress, consequently, regards the shaping of a revenue bill as very much its prerogative. It will seek the views of the executive, for there is a respect for the sustained labors of those in the executive departments and also a recognition, varying with the times, of the importance of presidential programs. But control over the legislation itself, both as to broad policies and as to details, rests with the Congress. Hence a congressman, and especially a member of the tax committees, is in a position to make the tax laws bend in favor of a particular individual or group despite strong objection from the executive branch. Under such a governmental system the importance to the tax structure of the institutional factors that influence a congressman's decision is obvious.

II. Some Institutional Factors

1. The congressman's desire to be helpful. A congressman's instincts are to be helpful and friendly. If it were otherwise, he would not be in Congress. When a constituent, or some other person who is in a position to claim attention, seeks legislative action, the congressman likes to respond within reason. If the proposal presented to him is at all rational he will, in all probability, at least introduce it in bill form so as not to offend the constituent. If the congressman is not a member of one of the tax committees, that may end the matter—but it may not, for the proposal has been launched and lies ready to be pushed ahead by whatever pressures may be generated in its behalf.

The desire—sometimes the need—of a congressman to be useful often places a congressman who sits on one of the tax committees, the House Committee on Ways and Means or the Senate Committee on Finance, in a difficult position. A fellow congressman who sits on the Public Works Committee, for example, can respond to constituent pressure by approving the project involved; a member of the Appropriations Committee can respond by a favorable vote on a specific appropriation. But a congressman on a tax committee can respond only by pushing through a special tax provision. His legislative stock in trade, so to speak, is special tax treatment. This difficulty is especially acute in the case of those congressmen who come to sit on a tax committee only after they have been members of other committees and have become so accustomed to using their committee powers in helpful ways that the habit persists. And after all, the congressman who sits on a tax committee is frequently regarded as a powerful personage at home, in part because the fact of membership is often used by the congressman as an argument to support continued reelection. The congressman must be able to live up to this stature and obtain successful action on a proposal—as a senator on the Senate Finance Committee once put it, "What's the good of being on this committee if you can't get through a little old amendment now and then?" Sometimes, however, a senior congressman on a tax committee has enough influence and personal friendships around the Congress so that he can, when necessary, take care of his constituents in legislative ways other than tax proposals; if so, he is more likely to be quite objective when it comes to tax problems. . . .

2. *Lack of congressional appreciation of departure from fairness.* In many cases the congressman considering a special tax provision may not realize that tax fairness is at all involved. He sees only the prob-

lem of the particular constituent or group concerned. The case in this focus may be very appealing, for human beings are involved with human problems. The income tax, always an impersonal, severe, monetary burden, becomes an oppressive force bearing down on men in difficulty. The congressman may therefore not even appreciate that arguments of over-all fairness and equity have any relation to the question, or may very well think them too intangible and remote. Provisions for the relief of the blind and the aged are perhaps illustrations. Or the congressmen, moved simply by a desire to help a constituent, may not understand the ramifications of the proposal. He is not a tax technician and he may view the proposal in isolation rather than perceive its relationship to the intricate technical structure of the revenue code. The proposal, so viewed, becomes merely a "little old amendment" which helps a constituent and does no harm. His brother congressmen are quite willing to be good fellows and go along, especially if the congressman urging the proposal is well-liked. After all, they too from time to time will have "little old amendments" to propose. Thus, in 1955 the Ways and Means Committee decided that in the initial consideration of members' bills dealing with technical matters it would allow each member one bill to be considered and then reported by the full committee if the bill met with unanimous agreement. . . .

3. *The Treasury Department's presentation.* The congressman's failure to recognize that tax fairness is at all involved may often be due to the inadequacy of the Treasury Department's presentation of the issues. This is not said critically, but by way of explanation. The problem facing the Treasury in these matters is formidable. The interested constituents or groups are generally skillful in presenting their cases in appealing form. Their energies are concentrated on one matter; they have time and money to devote to it; they may have the advantage of personal acquaintance, directly or through intermediaries, with the congressman; they can obtain skilled counsel informed on the ways of the Congress. The Treasury's tax staff must tackle all of these problems; its members are usually not chosen for skill in the presentation of issues or in handling congressmen; although on the

whole remarkably good, considering the compensation, they are rarely among the ablest in the tax field, nor do they usually have the needed experience.

Further, private groups concentrate on making the best case possible and in so doing gloss over or forget the unfavorable aspects. They present the proposal in its simplest form and often avoid the complications involved in embodying the proposal in statutory drafts. At times a congressman is misled by this simple but convincing presentation and commits himself before he is aware of the full implications of the proposal. The treasury staff, on the other hand, feels compelled to present the pros and cons and to point out the complications. It is both explaining and criticizing—not just attacking—and its presentation may seem confusing rather than informative to the congressman. When he compares the complex, technical, "on the one hand, but on the other hand" explanation of the treasury staff with the deceptively simple and certainly forceful description of the problem presented by the private group, the latter is bound to achieve a considerable advantage. Congressmen, and even most congressmen on the tax committees, are laymen in tax matters; they are not tax technicians. Again this is not said critically. A congressman has a great many tasks to perform and decisions to make, so that he cannot—and really should not—be immersed in the technicalities of everything. After all, how skillful in tax law is the average lawyer? . . .

Also, the treasury staff is usually not well known to the congressman. Its members, not being political, ordinarily do not mix with him at the same level, nor do they meet him socially. Hence the congressman is generally not in a position to act on the assumption that, although he doesn't fully understand all of what they say, he knows them to be good fellows and they are probably right. Nor do they spend with an individual congressman the amount of time needed to develop the problem fully. Thus in a committee meeting, the congressman must often decide an issue after only a minimum amount of discussion and before his biases and preconceptions have been replaced by a real understanding of the issues. The interested groups and the tax lobbyists, on the other hand, have the time to brief the various congressmen on their proposals. They are pushing one proposal and can concentrate on it. The treasury staff is faced with considering all of the proposals, and the time and personnel needed for an adequate informal discussion on each proposal with the necessary congressmen are not available. . . .

4. Lack of omniscience on the part of the Treasury. The treasury tax staff is not omniscient. Yet understanding approaching omniscience is needed to do its job. A lack of knowledge on any particular matter, a failure of skill at any moment, can be fatal. The approach of the average congressman is to hear the private group, find out in general what it wants, react sympathetically for a variety of reasons, and then ask the Treasury whether there is any objection to the proposal. If the Treasury is off its guard and acquiesces, the proposal becomes law. If the Treasury is unprepared and presents a weak case, the proposal becomes law. Equally serious is the in-between situation in which the Treasury acknowledges that some hardship is present in the particular situation, but points out that the difficulty is but a phase of a general problem and that it has not yet been able fully to analyze the general area. It therefore urges that the particular proposal be postponed until further study is given to the whole matter. But recognition of some hardship and of some merit in his particular proposal is all that the congressman needs. His constituent wants relief from that admitted hardship now, and not years later when the whole matter has been thought through and his case fitted into a solution appropriate for many cases. Hence the congressman will seek approval of the proposal in the limited form necessary to solve the particular problem presented to him—and a special tax provision is thereby born.

It is obvious, given the vast number of proposals to which it must react, that the Treasury must sometimes fail. The failure rate will vary with the competence of the treasury staff at any particular time, and there is a considerable variation in that competence. It will vary, moreover, with the degree of importance which the treasury policy-makers attach to research on tax matters, and here also differences in attitude are marked. But even when competence is at a high general level and there is a proper appreciation of the need for extended staff research, errors in judgment or gaps in knowledge are inevitable. The whole matter of capital gains for pension-trust terminations, for example, started with an error in judgment on the Treasury's part in

1942 when it acquiesced in capital-gain treatment as a solution for the bunched-income problem present in this area. It so happened that the problem was presented in the context of a pension trust in which only the lower-bracket taxpayers received lump-sums distributions, and as an *ad hoc* solution the result was not too objectionable. But there was a failure to think through the problem, a failure caused by lack of time and lack of knowledge about the provisions respecting termination of pension trusts. Thus the provision got its start—and the rule of the camel's nose is cardinal in the field of tax privileges . . . .

5. Lack of opposition apart from the Treasury Department to proponents of special tax provisions. The critical importance that attaches to the level of treasury competence and the fatal consequences of any slip on its part derive from its unique position in tax legislation. The question, "Who speaks for tax equity and tax fairness?," is answered today largely in terms of only the Treasury Department. If that department fails to respond, then tax fairness has no champion before the Congress. Moreover, it must respond with vigor and determination, and after a full explanation of the matter it must take a forthright stand on the issues. A Treasury Department that contents itself with explaining the issues and then solemnly declaring the matter to be one for the policy determination of Congress abdicates its responsibility. The congressman understands aggressiveness and a firm position. He is often in the position of the small boy inwardly seeking parental bounds for his conduct while outwardly declaiming against them. He may not accept policy guidance from the treasury policy spokesman, but he wants it presented. He will invariably interpret a treasury statement that the matter is one for his own policy decision as a victory for the seeker of the special provision.

Thus, in the tax bouts that a congressman witnesses the Treasury is invariably in one corner of the ring. Assuming the Treasury decides to do battle, which is hardly a safe assumption at all times, it is the Treasury versus percentage depletion, the Treasury versus capital gains, the Treasury versus this constituent, the Treasury versus that private group. The effect on the congressman as referee is inevitable. He simply cannot let every battle be won by the Treasury, and hence every so often he gives the victory to the sponsors of a special provision. Moreover, the Treasury is not an impersonal antagonist—it is represented before the Congress by individuals. These individuals are constantly forced to say that enactment of this proposal will be unfair, and the same of the next, and the next. The congressman, being only human, is bound from time to time to look upon these individuals as the Cassandras of the tax world. To avoid this dilemma, the Treasury in a close case will sometimes concede the issue if the proposal can be narrowly confined. It feels compelled to say "yes" once in a while simply to demonstrate that it maintains a balanced judgment and possesses a sense of fairness. A special provision is thus enacted simply because it happens to have somewhat more merit than the numerous other special proposals before the committees and because an affirmative answer here by the Treasury will protect negative responses to the other proposals.

At another level, what should the Treasury reply to a congressman who says, "I have fought hard in this committee for your position on all of the major issues. Yet when I introduce a minor amendment to take care of a problem of one of my constituents, you take a self-righteous stand and tell me and the committee that the amendment is inequitable and discriminatory. Is that any way to treat your real friends on the committee?" Faced with such a protest, a treasury policy official with a major program hanging in the balance before the committee may well look the other way when a special provision comes up for discussion. Once again a dilemma is raised by the fact that to the congressman the Treasury appears as one protagonist before the committee rather than as a representative of taxpayers in general. . . .

6. *The congressional tax staff.*   The description of the Treasury as the principal and often the sole defender of tax fairness calls for a consideration of the role of the congressional tax staff. Most of the congressional tax technicians are members of the staff of the Joint Committee on Internal Revenue Taxation and as such serve both the House Ways and Means Committee and the Senate Finance Committee. There are a few technicians attached to the separate committees, and the clerks

of the committees can play a very important role if they are personally so inclined. But institutionally the chief guidance given to Congress by its own employees comes from this joint committee staff.

The members of this staff work closely with the treasury tax technicians. Their work on the details of proposals and drafts is highly important, but the task of policy formulation and policy guidance to the congressmen appears to be reserved exclusively to the chief of that staff. His role is a difficult and unenviable one. Many congressmen pass along to him the tax proposals that they are constantly receiving from their constituents. Undoubtedly, the Chief of Staff discreetly but effectively blocks many of these proposals from proceeding further. But he also, whatever his inclinations may be, cannot in his situation always say "no." Perhaps inevitably on the crucial issues his role tends to be that of the advocate of the congressman advancing a particular proposal on behalf of a special group. The special-interest groups cannot appear in the executive sessions of the committees, and the congressman sympathetic to their point of view is not technically equipped to present their case; he tends to look to the Chief of Staff to assume that task. Further, he looks to the Chief of Staff to formulate the technical compromises which will resolve the dispute between the special-interest group and the Treasury. The Chief of Staff must therefore work closely with the congressmen and be "brilliantly sensitive to their views."* He must necessarily be able to gauge the degree of interest that a congressman may have in a proposal and weigh that in the consideration of the guidance he will give.

Because of these institutional pressures the Chief of Staff is very often the opponent of the Treasury Department before the tax committees. As a result, the difficulties for the average congressman on the tax committees become even greater. The issues get more and more complex as the "experts" disagree, and the congressman can hardly follow the technical exchanges. He is quite often content to fall back on the comfortable thought that, since the congressional expert appears to disagree with the treasury experts, there is adequate technical justification for voting either way. Hence the congressman is free

*Darrell, "Internal Revenue Code of 1954—A Striking Example of the Legislative Process in Action," in *U. of So. Calif. School of Law, 1955 Tax Inst.* I, 6.

to be guided by his own sympathies and instincts. Since generally these sympathies are in favor of the private groups, their proposals obtain his vote.

Unfortunately agreement between the congressional Chief of Staff and the Treasury can sometimes present just as difficult a problem. When the two disagree, at least the congressman who is seeking to discover the real issues may find them exposed at some time through this disagreement of experts. But if the experts agree, the effect is often to foreclose any real committee consideration of the issues. The congressman may be lulled into thinking that no significant issues are involved, and the proposal therefore becomes law. But if the government experts have erred, or if they have incorrectly gauged the congressional sentiment, special benefits may well result which the congressman would not have sanctioned had he understood what was involved. . . .

7. Lack of effective aid from the tax bar. The lack of any pressure-group allies for the Treasury in its representation of the tax-paying public could have been remedied in part by effective aid from the tax bar. Yet for a good many years the vocal tax bar not only withheld any aid but very often conducted itself as an ally of the special pressure groups. Many a lawyer representing a client seeking a special provision could without much difficulty obtain American Bar Association or local-bar-association endorsement for his proposal. He could then appear before Congress and solemnly exhibit the blessing of the legal profession. In fact, the activity of the Bar Association in this respect became so obvious that it seemingly boomeranged—many a congressman began instinctively to smell mischief when presented with a Bar Association tax proposal or endorsement. . . .

8. Lack of public knowledge of special tax provisions. Perhaps the most significant aspect of the consideration of special tax provisions by the Congress is that it usually takes place without any awareness of these events by the general public. Almost entirely, these matters lie outside of the public's gaze, outside of the voter's knowledge. The special provisions which are enacted lie protected in the mysterious complex statutory jargon of the tax law. This technical curtain is impenetrable to the newspapers and other information media. The public hears of debate over tax reduction or tax increase and it may learn something about the general rate structure. But it seldom learns that the high rates have no applicability to much of the income of certain wealthy groups. Nor does it understand how this special taxpayer or that special group is relieved of a good part of its tax burden. All of these matters are largely fought out behind this technical curtain. Hence the congressman favoring these special provisions has for the most part no accounting to make to the voters for his action. He is thereby much freer to lend a helping hand here and there to a group which has won his sympathy or which is pressing him for results.

It is true that under our governmental system we have given to the Congress, subject to presidential veto, the responsibility of deciding what is "fair" in the federal sphere from our collective standpoint. Its decision is our democratic answer. But all this presupposes that the congressman's decision will be known to the voters and that he will have to account to them for his view. In the tax field this accounting does not exist, so that the presuppositions that on most matters stamp final congressional action as "fair" in a democratic sense are here lacking. . . .

9. The relationship of special tax provisions to private-relief bills. Some of these special provisions represent simply private-relief claims for the particular individual benefited. While phrased as amendments to the tax law, they are only money claims against the Government based on the equities asserted to exist. Thus, it is said of a senator skilled in congressional ways that he would ask the legislative draftsman preparing the draft of a particular tax provision to make the amendment as general in language and as specific in application as was possible. The tax committees and the Treasury have not solved the problem of how to handle these special bills. Curiously enough, some tax situations do come through the judiciary committees as private-relief bills along with other private-relief bills involving claims against the Government. These bills may involve, for example, a removal of the barrier of the statute of limitations in cases thought equitable, or the recovery of funds spent for revenue stamps lost in some fashion. Here they are subject to the criteria developed over the decades by those committees in the handling of private-claims bills. These criteria are reasonably strict, and few of the bills pass the Congress. Of those that do succeed, a number are vetoed, and a veto is customarily regarded as a final disposition of the bill.

Many situations come before the tax committees that are quite comparable, in that the tax proposal is equivalent to a money claim against the Government, equal to the tax to be saved, sought for a specific taxpayer on equitable grounds. This is especially true in the case of proposals of a retroactive character. In the tax committees these special proposals tend to take on the coloration of an amendment to the tax code of the same character as all the various substantive tax matters before these committees. In essence, all amendments to the tax laws that private groups push on their own behalf are designed to lower taxes for the proponents and thereby relieve them from a tax burden to which they are subject. The special proposals thus become simply one more amendment in the long list of changes to be considered. The proponents of these special proposals are thereby able to cloak the fact that they are presenting private-relief claims against the Government. This is especially so when the proposal is considered as merely one more item in a general revenue bill. Here it is also protected from the threat—and fate—of a presidential veto. Even when the proposal is considered as a separate bill, the fact that it is merely one of the bills before a tax committee that is considering a great many substantive bills involving amendments to the tax code generally produces the same result. The committee will tend to focus on the proposal as curing a substantive defect in the law and lose sight of the fact that the special proposal is essentially a private-relief bill. . . .

THE POLITICAL STRUCTURE OF
THE FEDERAL RESERVE SYSTEM
Michael D. Reagan

Public policy is not self-generating; it emerges from institutions. Foremost among the institutions charged with monetary and credit policy formation—an area, like fiscal policy, that has not received from political scientists the attention accorded to micro-economic regulation of particular firms or industries—is the Federal Reserve System. The purpose of this paper is to examine the "fit" of the System's formal structure to (1) the policy functions and the informal policy-forming mechanisms of the "Fed," and (2) the pattern of interests and values affected by monetary policy. Its thesis is that a substantial gap has developed between these elements.

A brief sketch of the formal structure of authority and the historical development of System functions is needed to begin with; this is followed by analysis of the formal and the effective roles of each component of the System along with the internalized interest representation at each level. Then the linkage between the Federal Reserve System and general economic policy is explored. Finally, the conclusion summarizes the findings and suggests briefly how formal structure and policy functions might be brought into closer, more effective alignment.

1. Structure and Functional Development

The pyramid. The Federal Reserve System[1] can be described as a pyramid having a private base, a mixed middle level and a public apex. At the apex stands the Board of Governors (frequently referred to as the Federal Reserve Board or FRB). Its seven members are appointed by the President, with the consent of the Senate, for fourteen-year, over-lapping terms, one term expiring at the end of January in each even-numbered year. Members are removable for cause, but the removal power has not been exercised. In making appointments,

From *The American Political Science Review,* LV (March, 1961), 64–76. Reprinted with the permission of author and publisher.

the President must give due regard to "fair representation of financial, agricultural, industrial, and commercial interests, and geographical divisions of the country," and not more than one member can be appointed from a single Federal Reserve District. The Chairman is selected by the President for a renewable four-year term. The Board is independent of the appropriations process, for its operating funds come from semi-annual assessments upon the twelve Reserve Banks.

At a level of equivalent authority to the Board itself, but in the "middle" of the public-private pyramid, stands the statutory Federal Open Market Committee. It is composed of all FRB Members plus five of the twelve Reserve Bank Presidents, with the President of the New York Reserve Bank always one of the five and the others serving in rotation. The Chairman of the Board of Governors is, by custom, the Chairman of the Committee.

The Reserve Banks are quasi-public institutions: their capital stock is subscribed by the member banks—all national banks and about one-third of the state-chartered banks, at the statutory rate of six per cent (one-half paid in) of their capital and surplus—but their role is public as a part of the central banking system. While a six per cent cumulative dividend is paid to the member-bank stockholders, and a surplus equal to twice the paid-in capital has been accumulated, the remainder of the Reserve Banks' now sizeable earnings is surrendered to the national Treasury. The growth of the Banks as money-makers, especially in the past decade, is indicated in Table 1;[2] their annual contribution to the Treasury currently amounts to about a tenth of the annual interest cost of carrying the public debt. In contrast with their paid-in capital of $387 million (as of December 31, 1959) their assets included some $27 billion in Treasury securities, and their earnings derived chiefly from the interest paid on these holdings.

The Reserve Bank Presidents are not government appointees: they are elected by the boards of directors of their respective Banks, subject to FRB veto; and their compensation—far above civil service levels—is fixed in the same way. Thus their selection is initially private, but with public supervision. The Board of Directors of each Reserve Bank consists of nine persons, six of whom are elected by the member commercial banks of that District (these banks, the "owners" of the Reserve Banks, constituting the private base of the pyramid),

Table 1. Combined reserve bank net earnings, dividends to stock-holder banks, and transfers to U.S. Treasury and to surplus, selected years, 1914–1960 (thousands of dollars)

Year	Net earnings	Dividends paid	Paid to U.S. Treasury	Transferred to surplus	% Dividends to earnings
1916	2,751	1,743	—	—	63.4
1920	149,295	5,654	60,725	82,916	37.9
1922	16,498	6,307	10,851	−660	38.2
1925	9,449	6,916	59	2,474	73.2
1932	22,314	9,282	2,011	11,021	41.6
1935	9,438	8,505	298	635	90.1
1945	92,662	10,183	248	82,232	11.0
1950	231,561	13,083	196,629	21,849	5.6
1957	624,393	20,081	542,708	61,604	3.2
1959	839,771	22,722	910,650	−93,601	2.7
1960	949,000	24,500	897,000	42,000	2.6
Total 1914–1960	6,885,077	477,706	5,476,395	945,476	6.9

Source: *Annual Report of the Board of Governors, 1959,* pp. 116–117. Figures for 1960 approximate, from *New York Times,* Jan. 6, 1961, p. 35.

while three (including the Chairman and Deputy Chairman) are appointed by the FRB in Washington.

Off to the side stands the final element of statutory organization, the Federal Advisory Council (FAC). This group of twelve men is composed of one commercial-banker representative from each District, annually elected by the respective regional Boards. The FAC meets quarterly with the FRB to discuss general business conditions and may make recommendations to the Board on matters of policy. The twelve Reserve Bank Presidents constitute a non-statutory Conference of Presidents that meets three times a year; a Conference of Reserve Bank Chairmen meets annually with the FRB.

The location of policy powers. The three major tools of monetary policy are the rediscount rate charged by Reserve Banks to member bank borrowers on their loans from the System; the setting of reserve requirement levels for the member banks; and—most important to-day—open market operations in securities of the federal government. Decisions regarding each of these instruments is formally located in a different organ of the System, although (as will be developed below) channels for advice and influence cause a mingling of the decisional powers in fact. The levels of reserve requirements are set by the FRB; open market policy is a function of the Open Market Committee (OMC), thus providing the regional and quasi-private elements of the System with formal access to the heart of monetary policy formation; and the Reserve Bank Boards of Directors share with the FRB formal authority over the discount rate. The rate is "established" every fourteen days by each regional Bank, but "subject to the review and determination" of the Board of Governors. In addition the FRB shares with the Comptroller of the Currency, the FDIC and state authorities a very considerable list of regulatory and supervisory powers over member banks and their officers.

Functional change since 1913.   When established, the Federal Reserve System was thought of as exercising only the technical function of quasi-automatic adjustment of an elastic currency supply to the fluctuating needs of commerce and industry. The System was pictured as a "cooperative enterprise" among bankers for the purpose of increasing the security of banks and providing them with a reservoir of emergency resources.[3] To this day the Federal Reserve Act mandate reflects this view: it instructs that the discount rate and open market policy shall be operated with "a view of accommodating commerce and business," and that reserve requirements shall be handled so as to prevent "excessive use of credit for the purchase or carrying of securities." Nothing in the Act relates the monetary authority to the function of national economic stabilization; yet this is its prime task today.

In 1913, it was not foreseen that the techniques of monetary policy would become instruments of economic stabilization with their consequences for employment, growth and price stability overtaking their specific banking objectives in importance. Yet this is what has happened, beginning in the Twenties but more strongly and with more explicit recognition in the policy process since the Great Crash.[4] With this shift, the operation of the Federal Reserve System necessarily moved into the political mainstream, for the goal of stabilization requires making choices among alternatives that have important and visible consequences for substantial interests and community values. Once macro-economic policy had become the primary *raison d'être* of the System, the breadth of interests involved became coterminous with the nation, not just with the bankers; and monetary policy, as well as depositors' safety, became a public concern rather than a private convenience.

A corollary of the rise of stabilization to stage center is that the scope of FRB action has become essentially national, belying the assumption of relative regional independence that underlay the original legislation. Divergent policies for each region become undesirable—even impossible—if national stabilization is to be achieved in an increasingly interdependent national economy.

II. Roles and Interests of the Components

We turn now to a comparison of formal roles and interest composition with the informal roles and interest-impact of each level of the System's structure.

The commercial bank base.   The formal role of the member banks is that of an electoral constituency in the selection of six of the nine directors for each Reserve Bank. While the member banks have no direct policy voice, this electoral role originally gave them an indirect one, on the assumption that the regional boards would be policy-making bodies through their authority over the discount rate. That authority is negligible today. Furthermore, the "ownership" of the Reserve Banks by the commercial banks is symbolic; they do not exercise the proprietary control associated with the concept of ownership nor share, beyond the statutory dividend, in Reserve Bank "profits." As in the large, publicly held corporation, ownership and control have been divorced. No doubt the FRB, for example in the adjustment of reserve requirements, has been solicitous for the maintenance and improvement of commercial bank earnings. But if the record of the other "independent" regulatory commissions is any guide, this would have been true regardless of their stockholdings in the Reserve Banks.

Bank ownership and election at the base are therefore devoid of substantive significance, despite the superficial appearance of private bank control that the formal arrangement creates.

Reserve Bank Boards of Directors. The Reserve Bank Boards' authority to set rediscount rates, subject to "review and determination" by the FRB, is considerably diminished by the ultimate formal authority of the latter, for "determination" includes final decision and even initiation of rate changes. It is further reduced by informal practice: to avoid the embarrassments of public disputes, discount rate policy is discussed at OMC meetings and the determinations settled upon therein are usually followed through uniformly at the next meetings of the respective regional Boards of Directors.[5] The special formalities are "of little significance; rediscount policy is made in much the same way and on essentially the same considerations as is reserve and open-market policy."[6] The nationalization of function has thus removed the basis for the assumption of regional autonomy that underlay the original grant of authority to the Reserve Banks. The major tasks of the Directors now are to provide information on regional conditions for OMC and the FRB to take into account, and to serve as a communications and public relations link between the System and local communities—both the general community and the specific "communities" of commercial banking, industry, merchants and other financial institutions. They do not exercise important substantive authority.

This may be fortunate in view of the structure of interests that prevails at this level. For the range of interests, reflecting the banker-business orientation of 1913, is narrow by legal specification and narrower still in fact. By statute, each regional Board has three classes of membership: Class A consists of three commercial bankers; Class B of three men active in commerce, agriculture or "some other industrial pursuit"; and Class C, without occupational restriction. Class C members are appointed by the FRB; the others are elected by the member banks of each region.

Class A directors are elected by a method that groups the member-bank stockholders into size categories for voting purposes and assures the selection of one director from a large bank, one from a middle-sized bank and one from a small bank within the District. Informally, Classes B and C tend to be quite similar. Both are dominated by executives of manufacturing firms, utilities, oil and chemical firms, and large distributors—although Class C also includes an occasional academic economist or publisher. Very large firms predominate; very small firms, "family farmers," and labor are not represented. The list of Directors reads like a *Who's Who* of American industry.[7]

The propriety of excluding other segments of the economy from these Boards is not a substantively important question at present because of the decline in the Boards' authority, though the appearances could themselves become a political issue. But it is worth asking what functional value this elaborate structure possesses and whether the Boards would be missed if they were simply abandoned. The informational role of the Directors could be as well—perhaps better—performed by the Reserve Bank Presidents, who are full-time officials in close daily contact with their districts.

The Reserve Bank Presidents. The Presidents, by virtue of the membership of five of their number on the OMC (and the participation of all twelve in OMC discussions) are more significantly related to the policy process than are their nominal superiors, the regional Boards.

Selection of the Presidents is by the respective Boards, but subject to FRB veto: initially private but finally public. Increasingly, they are men with substantial Reserve System experience. Two-thirds of the incumbents have had such experience; one-third have come to their posts from careers in commercial banking. Their daily contacts are with private bankers and one observer suggests that they have been "inclined to favor more cautious, mild policies that would be less disturbing to the normal courses of banking and the money markets" than has the FRB.[8] Yet another writer, granting a "commercial banker mentality" in the early days of the System, argues that a public, central banking view is coming to prevail as a majority come up through the System.[9] In one respect the Presidents have clearly differed from the FRB: in their support of a change urged by commercial bankers that would place authority for all monetary actions in the OMC—a change the FRB has opposed.

As a statutory minority on the OMC, the views of the Presidents cannot be controlling in themselves. In the apparently unlikely event of a split within the FRB segment of the Committee, however, a solid front by the five President-members would enable them to determine public policy. Since they are not appointed by the President, nor removable for policy differences with either the President or the FRB within their five-year terms, the present structure allows the possibility that policy with a highly-charged political potential may be made by men who lack even indirect accountability to the national public affected. Former FRB Chairman Marriner Eccles has pointed out the uniqueness of the arrangement in these words: "there is no other major governmental power entrusted to a Federal agency composed in part of representatives of the organizations which are the subject of regulation by that agency." [10]

The situation of the Reserve Presidents reverses that of the regional Boards: while the latter's structurally important place has been downgraded by loss of function, the former's structurally inferior position has been upgraded by increased authority.

The Board of Governors and the Board Chairman. The gap between formal and informal roles in the Federal Reserve is readily apparent at the FRB level. By statute, it controls by itself only one of the major monetary instruments, the setting of reserve requirements. In fact, it is in a position to, and does, exercise authority in varying degree over all three instruments of policy—and is popularly recognized as *the* monetary policy authority. Further, the effective voice within the Board is that of the Chairman, despite the formal equality of all seven Members—and this too is popularly recognized. William McChesney Martin's name may not be a household word, but it is far better known than those of his colleagues. Over the years, the Board has seldom contained, besides the Chairman, more than one or two members at a time whose stature commanded independent respect.

The Board has final authority over discount rates through its power to "review and determine" the decisions of the Reserve Directors. The Members of the FRB constitute a seven-to-five majority in the OMC and thus—barring defections—control the most important of monetary tools. In fact, decisions on all three instruments of policy are taken on the basis of discussion within OMC. Since 1955 the Committee has been used as a "forum, a clearinghouse for all of the aspects of policy determination in the System." [11] Thus the formal distribution of authority is belied in practice by unified consideration.

Unified control seems inevitable, since the types of decision are logically related and it would be unthinkable to have them operating in contradictory directions. Because of the political importance of monetary policy, however, and the desirability of fiscal-monetary coordination, it is questionable whether a twelve-man, quasi-private body provides an adequate or appropriate locus for policy determination; of this, more presently.

The size, length of term and interest composition of the FRB have been the subject of considerable Congressional attention and have undergone some change over the years. The Board began with five appointed Members with staggered ten-year terms and two *ex officio*—the secretary of the Treasury and the Comptroller of the Currency. Both the latter were removed in the 1935 revision of the Banking Act, at the insistence of Senator Carter Glass, then chairman of the Banking and Currency Committee. Now there are seven Presidential appointees, and the term is fourteen years. No Member, incidentally, has yet served a full fourteen-year term, but a few have served *more than* fourteen years through successive appointments to unexpired terms.

The Chairman is selected by the President for a four-year, renewable term. This definite term was adopted in 1935, apparently with the intent that an incoming President should have a free hand. Resignations and new appointments have not coincided with presidential inaugurations, however, with the result that the incumbent's appointment, for example, expires in 1963.

The Federal Reserve Act has from the beginning stipulated group-interest qualifications for FRB Members. Originally, two had to be experienced in banking or finance, and the total membership had to provide "fair representation" of industrial, commercial and financial interests—as well as a regional balance designed to avoid eastern "domination." In 1922 the requirement of financial experience was dropped and agriculture was added to the list of represented interests. The actual composition for the 1914–50 period was as follows: thirteen from banking, five each from business and agriculture, and four from law.[12] Those appointed since 1950 have included one from private banking, two from business, two from agriculture and one each from the deanship of a business school and from a government career. Two of the post-1950 group also had experience of several years each on a Reserve Bank Board and one appointee's major experience had been as a Reserve Bank officer. "Promotion from within" is the trend. Among the major organized interests, labor is conspicuous by its absence. Business has been represented, but by substantial independents (ranchers, lumbermen, realtors) rather than by executives of large industrial corporations.

The size, length of term, interest composition and geographic distribution are all of questionable value to the System's policy functions and administrative effectiveness. It has been argued that fourteen-year terms provide an opportunity for Members to develop a knowledge of monetary economics and that they insulate the Board from partisan considerations. But many posts of equal technical complexity in other agencies are adequately staffed on a much shorter basis and, more importantly, insulation from politics is as impossible as it is democratically undesirable for an agency functioning so near the center of national economic policy. I shall return to this point later.

Although replacement of the Board by a single executive has been suggested only rarely, many observers, including Chairman Martin, are on record as favoring a smaller group than seven, on the ground that more capable men might then be attracted to the Board.[13] Clearly a seven-man board cannot collectively negotiate effectively with the President, the Secretary of the Treasury, the Chairman of the Council of Economic Advisers, or the lending agencies whose programs impinge on economic stability; yet coherent policy requires negotiation, consultation and program coordination constantly. Nor would a five-man board be notably better in this respect.

As it is now, the Chairman *is* the Federal Reserve Board for purposes of negotiation. In recent years he has lunched with the Secretary of the Treasury weekly,[14] and has sat in with the President's informal inner council on economic policy.[15] Congressional committees rely upon the Chairman to speak for the Board and rarely bother to interrogate other Board members. These arrangements apparently work because none of the other members is strong enough, personally or politically, to challenge the Chairman; and also, it seems reasonable to suggest, because there is no alternative save chaos. It is supported too by the tradition of secrecy that attends the actions of central banks, and that is defended as necessary to prevent the exploitation of leaks to private advantage: the fewer the negotiators, the less the likelihood of leaks. The gap between formal structure and the necessities of action reflected in the informal but decisive accretion of power to the Chairman (not only to the incumbent, but to McCabe and Eccles before him) is too great to be bridged by a minor adjustment in the size of the group.

Because of the importance of the Chairmanship, and the necessity for cordial relations between the head of the FRB and the President, Martin and McCabe have both suggested that the four-year term of the Chairman should end on March 31 of the year in which a President begins his term of office. Simpler still is the suggestion that the Chairman's term should be at the President's pleasure, as with most other national regulatory commissions. Whichever way the matter is handled, the need is for a relationship of mutual trust between President and Chairman, both for the sake of consistent economic policy and for democratic accountability through the President as chief elected representative of the public.[16] The present system of a fixed four-year term that (accidentally) does not coincide with Presidential inaugurations is unfortunate on both counts. Moreover, since the staggered 14-year terms of members expire in January of even-numbered years, a new President—even if the Chairman stepped aside—would be confined to the membership he inherits, in choosing a new Chairman, unless some member resigned to create a vacancy.

The policy suitability of geographic and interest qualifications for membership on the Board is a question that would become moot if the Board were replaced by a single head. If not, the answer must be that such qualifications are unsuitable because they are irrelevant and, in their present form, inequitable as well. They are irrelevant because the function of the Board is no longer simply to accommodate business, but to stabilize the national economy. The Board is not engaged in mediating group conflicts where the direct representation of parties-in-interest may be an irresistible political demand, but in a task of economic analysis and political judgment affecting the interests and values of *all* groups and individuals. Given the agency's function, independence of mind and familiarity with government finance and money markets, and with macro-economic analysis, are far more desirable qualifications than group representation.[17] Sensitivity to basic political currents—a quite different kind of "expertise"—is also pertinent, but not sensitivity only to the needs of a few special segments of the economy. The geographic qualification is equally irrelevant because of the nationalization of economic forces; five of the twelve districts must go unrepresented at any given time, as it is. And some geographic spread would be secured in any event, although without the severely restrictive effects of the current requirement upon the availability of capable men, simply because Presidential politics would work in this direction in the FRB as it does in cabinet and Supreme Court appointments.

The inequity of existing group representation requirements lies in the exclusion of interests as much affected by monetary policy as those that are included by statute. The present range reflects the original, restricted concept of the System. Today if groups are to be represented as such labor has as strong a claim as the farmers or industrialists, because employment levels are dependent on monetary policy to a significant extent; fixed-income receivers, whether corporate bond-clippers or Social Security pensioners, are directly and adversely affected if the tools of the FRB are not used with sufficient vigor to combat inflationary tendencies. Chairman Martin has even defined the objectives of monetary policy as providing job opportunities for wage earners and protection of those who depend upon savings or fixed incomes.[18]

One political consequence of the existing interest exclusions is to lessen the acceptability of monetary policies in the eyes of organized labor—or, at least, in the eyes of its leadership. The AFL-CIO Executive Council launched an attack in February, 1959, on banker and corporate-executive "domination" of the Fed, drawing a direct connection between the pattern of representation at both national and regional levels and what it called "misguided anti-inflation measures" that stifle growth while increasing bank profits.[19] As we have seen, the regional Boards lack the power to determine policy independently and the labor complaint is misdirected to that extent. Yet the *appearance* of the System may be as important as the substance in determining reactions to policy, and the appearance leaves the System open to this type of charge. As regards the national Board, the charge *could* have relevance: a labor representative might be more hesitant than other members in espousing "hard" policies that could dampen employment; but it is equally possible that he would in time adopt the coloration of his surroundings, which in the case of the Federal Reserve would apparently mean an institutional bias for "sound money" and a priority for anti-inflation goals.

Even if labor and pensioner representation were added, however, the list of affected interests would be far from exhausted. As Emmette Redford has written of interest representation in regulatory agencies generally, "It is difficult, if not impossible, to include representation of all the interests which might legitimately make a claim for some representation."[20] A non-interest or "general interest" criterion for appointments would be the simplest way to avoid the problem entirely if a multi-member Board is retained. A statement expressing the views of the House Committee on Banking and Currency in 1935 sums up the matter nicely:

It is important to emphasize in the law that Board action should reflect, not the opinion of a majority of special interests, but rather the well considered judgment of a body that takes into consideration all phases of the national economic life.[21]

The Open Market Committee and policy unification. In origin and development, the OMC represents the leading structural response of the Federal Reserve System to its change in function. But the response has not been entirely adequate and further modifications in the structure and scope of authority of the Committee have been advanced from a number of quarters.

When the System began operations, the discount rate and the levels of reserves were thought to be the major tools of policy. As the public debt grew, and as the macro-economic function of stabilization developed, open market operations by the Reserve Banks increased in importance. The initial structural response came in 1922 when an Open Market Committee was established informally, more under the leadership of President Benjamin Strong of the New York Reserve Bank than of the FRB. The Banking Act of 1933 gave the OMC statutory recognition as a twelve-man group, selected by the Reserve Banks, to carry on open market operations under rules laid down by the FRB, thus substantially increasing the power of the national, public component. The Banking Act of 1935, largely written by then-Chairman Eccles as an effort to enhance the centralized, public character of the monetary authority, reorganized the Committee into its present form: the seven FRB members and five Reserve Presidents.[22] (The House version—not enacted—of the 1935 Act would have gone further with the centralizing process by transferring authority for open market operations to the Board alone, with a requirement of consultation with an advisory committee of the regional Banks.) In short, change in economic circumstance, *i.e.,* the growth of a large federal debt as an inescapable component of the nation's financial structure, and the development of a new function led to an institutional addition to the System. Informally, the change has gone one step further: as mentioned earlier, the OMC is used as a forum for discussion of the entire range of monetary actions, not just for decisions regarding the tool that lies formally within its jurisdiction.

There is widespread agreement among participants and observers that unified handling of the three major techniques is essential for coherence; but there is sharp disagreement over the appropriate composition of the OMC and over the division of labor between OMC and FRB. The disagreements involve in a politically sensitive way the central-regional and public-private balances in the policy process. The range of specific proposals is as follows:

1. Consolidate all instruments in a publicly appointed Board, either the present FRB or a smaller one, abolishing the OMC but requiring consultation with the Reserve Bank Presidents. Variants of this have been suggested by the Hoover Commission Task Force, Eccles, and Bach, who see this approach as the proper way to secure the advantages of both public responsibility and "grass roots" information.[23]

2. Consolidate by merging the OMC and FRB into a single Board constituted of three Members appointed by the President and two Reserve Bank Presidents, each of the latter group serving full time for a year on a rotating basis. This was proposed by former Chairman McCabe in 1949 as the proper change if any were to be made at all;[24] it would have the effect of displacing the New York Bank President from his present permanent seat on the OMC.

3. Consolidate in the OMC as presently constituted. This is the position once favored by the regional Presidents.[25]

4. Consolidate reserve requirements and open market policy in a reconstituted OMC consisting of the present five Reserve Bank representatives and a smaller FRB of five Members—thus creating an even balance between central and regional, publicly and semi-privately appointed elements. This proposal was advanced by the New York Clearing House Association, which also urged that in case of a disagreement between a Reserve Bank and the FRB over the rediscount rate, either party should be allowed to refer the question to the OMC for final decision.[26] The Association apparently felt that commercial bank influence was greater with the Presidents than with the national Board.

Those preferring no change at all include Martin, who has defended the existing arrangement as consistent with the "basic concept of a regional" System and as a way of promoting close relations between the Presidents and the Board.[27] The Patman subcommittee saw no reason, as of 1952, to disturb the *status quo*, but Representative Patman has more recently proposed consolidation in an enlarged FRB of twelve Presidential appointees.[28]

The rationale underlying the all-powers-to-the-Board approach can be summarized in the principle that public functions should be lodged in public bodies, and the assertion that open market operations are in no sense regional in character. Eccles has pointed out that the Reserve Presidents are not appointed by or accountable to either the President or Congress, and for this reason argues that their participation in national, public policy formation is inappropriate.[29] Bach has emphasized the national character of open market policy,[30] and he is joined in this view by Jacob Viner, who has said that:

The regional emphasis in central banking is an obsolete relic of the past. No country, not even Canada, which is much more a collection of distinct economic regions than is the United States, has thought it expedient to follow our initial example of introducing regionalism into central banking.[31]

The argument for OMC as the top body derives from the importance attributed to regionalism and (inferentially at least) from a belief in the financial community that the Committee is more sympathetic than the FRB to the felt needs of bankers. The regional case has been most strongly stated by President Delos C. Johns of the St. Louis Reserve Bank:

Each Reserve bank president is in a position to judge possible alternatives of national monetary policy with due regard to the particular characteristics of his region. This makes for adoption of national monetary policy that squares realistically with actual conditions in the regions. . . .[32]

Macro-stabilization as the major function of the System clearly forecloses regional devolution in the making of policy, yet regional circumstances should be considered. The valid claims of regionalism, however, require only a consultative voice, not a decisional one. And public policy, I would agree with Eccles, should not be made by a body containing men who are not accountable to the national public whose welfare is affected by the decisions made.

In *operations,* as distinct from policy determination, regionalism may well possess continued utility; and centralization of policy is entirely compatible with a considerable degree of regional diversification in operations. The point of greatest overlap between national policy and Reserve Bank operations appears to be in the handling of the "discount window," that is, the ease or difficulty with which a member bank may avail itself of the rediscount privilege. A uniform national policy could, for example, suggest "easier" loan conditions in any District whose area rate of unemployment was "x" percentage points above the national average, and thus provide for regional differentiation while maintaining central policy control.

Federal Advisory Council. The Federal Advisory Council began as a compensation to the commercial bankers for their failure to obtain direct representation on the FRB.[33] Its function today has been described as providing "firsthand advice and counsel from people who are closely in touch with the banking activities of their particular districts,"[34] although available information does not explain how these bank representatives are able to contribute something that the Reserve Bank Presidents, with their extensive staff aids, could not supply as well or better. Assuming that their advice is not redundant, however, it is questionable whether the FRB should accord *statutory* advisory status to commercial bankers only, now that the System's policy may affect many other social groups just as significantly as the bankers; *e.g.*, non-bank financial institutions, home builders, state and local governments, Golden Age Clubs, wage-earners, and so on. The Board has at times used formal consultants from outside the commercial banking sphere, as when consumer credit regulations were being formulated;[35] but this is apparently infrequent. Once again, we see that the System's structure has become outmoded by the change in scope of function.

III. The Federal Reserve and National Economic Policy

The analysis to this point has focused upon internal factors. We come now to the questions: What is the source of the Federal Reserve's policy goals? Does existing structure adequately relate the monetary authority to the President and to the monetary management operations of the Treasury, to lending agency decisions, and to the Council of Economic Advisers? Does an adequate mechanism exist for resolving disputes that threaten the coherence of an Administration's over-all economic policy? These can only be answered by going beyond the internal organization of the Fed to a consideration of its external relationships.

The first place to look for the mandate of an agency is in its organic statute; but the Federal Reserve Act deals sparsely with the matter of goals, and has in any case, as already noted, been outpaced by events. Since the law does not provide a mandate fitted to the modern concerns of the System,[36] it is to the Employment Act of 1946 that one must look for goals written in macro-economic language: "it is the continuing policy and responsibility of the Federal Government to use all practicable means ... to promote maximum employment, production, and purchasing power." This declaration applies to the Federal Reserve as to all other agencies of the national government, and is often mentioned in FRB descriptions of the System's role. But as a policy guide it is less than complete. For one thing, it does not mention price stability, although it has been widely interpreted as including this goal by logical extrapolation from those explicitly speci-

fied. For another, it leaves open such questions as, should employment be maximized today by measures that may bring on unemployment tomorrow by over-stimulating a "boom," or conversely, contribute to unemployment today lest inflation come tomorrow?

Thus the Employment Act mandate shares the imprecision of
most such statements. While it could perhaps be sharpened, a need for
interpretive subsidiary definition probably cannot be eliminated because any language tight enough to do this would inevitably place too
inflexible a straight-jacket on agency operation.[37] Elaboration of goals
at later stages of the policy process may be expected to continue. The
President, who enters office with a vague mandate that is partly personal, partly party doctrine, commonly sets at least the tone for the
specific interpretation of statutory directives, by the nature of his
appointees. But the President's authority over the Federal Reserve is
restricted, unless vacancies occur, to one appointment of a member
(for fourteen years) every other year starting a year after his own term
begins; and to appointment of the Chairman for a fixed four-year
term. The independence of the agency conflicts with the President's
responsibilities for overall economic policy.

In support of the position that independence should prevail—*i.e.,*
that the FRB should not take its mandate from the President—the
argument is advanced that anti-inflationary measures are unpopular
though necessary; that "hard" decisions are more acceptable "if they
are decided by public officials who, like the members of the judiciary,
are removed from immediate pressures,"[38] and that the accountability
of the System to the electorate is adequately achieved through its
responsibility to Congress.[39] On the other side, the President is required by the Employment Act to submit a program for achieving the
Act's goals; such a program must include recommendations on monetary policy to be meaningful; and thus the President must be "the
coordinating agent for the whole national economic program."[40] Men
on both sides agree on one point: there should be a strong advocate
within the government for the monetary stability viewpoint, and the
central bank is the logical home for such advocacy. The major disagreements are whether a substantial degree of insulation from other
agencies engaged in economic policy determination helps or hinders

the expression of that viewpoint, and whether a clear locus of authority is required for settlement of disputes between the institutions variously responsible for monetary and fiscal policies.

The issue of FRB accountability to Congress is a false one and should be exposed as such. Contrary to a myth strongly held by System spokesmen—and many Congressmen—the FRB, even more than the other regulatory commissions, is *less* accountable to Congress than are the line departments in the Presidential hierarchy. The Federal Reserve does not depend on appropriations and thus is freed from the most frequently used tool of Congressional administrative supervision. And Congress has exercised an unusual degree of restraint in even suggesting its policy views to the Board. All executive agencies that have statutory bases may be said to be "creatures of Congress," and those with single heads are more easily held accountable than those with boards that diffuse responsibility.[41] For agencies with substantive powers, the price of accountability to Congress is accountability to the President.

On the need for a coordinating authority, Martin's position has been to grant the need for coordination but to argue that it can be achieved adequately through informal consultation.[42] The Advisory Board on Economic Growth and Stability established by President Eisenhower in 1953 would appear to be in line with his thinking: ABEGS (under leadership of the then CEA Chairman Arthur Burns) could bring about full exchange of information and full discussion, but could not *commit* the participating agencies to a unified course, even before it fell into desuetude after Burns' departure. The same was true of the Treasury Secretary-FRB Chairman luncheons and the President's informal economic policy discussions with agency heads during the Eisenhower Administration. Thus the problem of a possible stalemate or contradiction between Presidential and FRB policy is not resolved by these consultative arrangements.[43] A stronger incentive toward reaching consensus would be provided by the Clark-Reuss bill.[44] This would make it the "sense of Congress" that the President's Economic Reports under the Employment Act should include "monetary and credit policies to the same extent as all other policies affecting employment, production and purchasing power," with provision for inclusion of an FRB dissent, if necessary, in the Reports.[45] But again, unity would not be assured and accountability would remain obscure. Only if the FRB Chairman served at the will of the President, and a centralized authority directed the use of all credit instruments, would a formal basis for cohesion and accountability be laid.

Would a proposal of this kind mean the subordination of monetary stability to a frequently assumed low-interest, easy money predilection in the Treasury Department and the White House? While an unambiguous "No" cannot be given in reply, the weight of argument is in the negative direction. Independence may mean isolation rather than strength, for independent agencies lack the power of Presidential protection and Presidential involvement. Paradoxically, the real ability of the Fed to influence national economic policy might very well be increased if its formal independence were diminished. Have not the informal steps taken in the past seven or eight years toward closer liaison between the FRB and Presidential policy makers already made the Board (*i.e.,* the Chairman) somewhat stronger than was the case during the Truman Administration?

In addition to Presidential elaboration of Congressional policy statements, further interpretation is invariably made at the agency level. When the FRB or OMC decides to change, or not to change, the degree of restraint or ease in credit policy it is deciding—*necessarily*—whether to place emphasis for the short-run on the price stability or the maximum-employment-and-growth side of its imprecise mandate. The question of internal interpretation, therefore, is whether the policy preferences of the monetary authority are likely to coincide with those of the politically accountable originators and interpreters of the mandate. The probability is that the central banking agency will be to some extent more conscious of the monetary than of the employment-and-growth aspects of stabilization, the major reasons being (1) the role of the institution, (2) the inevitably close relationships of the policy makers to their commercial banking "clientele" as the focal point of immediate policy impact, and (3) the social backgrounds of the policy makers. The Administration (of whichever party) and Congress, however, are likely to give greater weight to employment than are the central bankers, simply because the political consequences of unemployment are likely to be—and are even more likely to be perceived as—more unfortunate for elected office holders than those of price inflation. This difference may be pronounced or slight, depending on the personal emphasis and understandings of the men involved; but that they will continue to exist even when the general orientation of both sides is similar was shown by the occasional disputes between the President's economic advisers and the FRB during the Eisenhower Administrations.[46]

The internal structure of authority affects FRB policy in one other respect pertinent to the mandate question. This is the absence of an instrument for dealing with what has come to be known as "administered price" or "market power" inflation; *i.e.*, inflation caused, not by excessive demand, but by the ability of unions and companies in situations of diminished competition to raise wages and prices even in periods of unutilized manpower or productive capacity. Such inflation can only be dealt with effectively by monetary or fiscal techniques if employment and growth are depressed beyond the political limits of public acceptability. A policy dilemma results. The Fed does not have (and probably does not want to have) authority to take direct action against this type of inflation. Nor, since the tools for such action would be non-monetary in nature,[47] is it appropriate that the central banking agency take on such a task. Yet in the absence of any but the traditional instruments the FRB is faced with a cruel choice: its own rationale calls for it to fight inflation, but doing so would create rising unemployment. If it refrains from acting, in order to preserve high employment, it may fail to stop inflation. Does it have a mandate to make such a choice? One could be extrapolated from the general stabilization directive, but not with any clear political sanction. As economist Gardiner C. Means has said, "there is a good deal of question whether such a momentous decision should rest with the Federal Reserve Board."[48]

IV. Conclusion

The basic finding of the analysis presented above is that the formal structure of the Federal Reserve System is inappropriate to its functions and out of line with informal arrangements that have the logic of necessity behind them. These gaps flow from changes in the monetary authority's function and in the structure of the economy. Devised as a service agency for banking and commerce—to achieve a semi-automatic adjustment of the money supply—the Federal Reserve has become as well a policy-making institution with major responsibility for national economic stabilization. Ancillary arrangements for interest representation based on an assumption that monetary actions were of important concern only to bankers and businessmen now have the appearance of unjustified special access because the range of affected interests and values is seen to be as broad as the nation itself.

Informal developments—most notably the unified handling of major monetary techniques and the preeminence of the Chairman's position—and the formal changes of 1935 that in a degree public-ized and nationalized the Open Market Committee did something to improve the fit of form to function. But these alterations have not been sufficient to ensure adequate accountability for what is today an authority of first rank political importance; they have not brought the quasi-private "face" of the System into line with its public responsibilities; and they do not provide a sufficient organizational base for coherent integration of the fiscal and monetary components of national economic policy. A more complete face-lifting is in order.

The Chairmanship is the key both to accountability and to effective performance. The four-year fixed term, having produced a result contradictory to the one intended, should be repealed in favor of service at the pleasure of the President. The informal preeminence of the Chairman should be recognized formally by abolishing the Board and the OMC and centralizing authority over the discount rate, reserve requirements and open market operations in the hands of the Chairman, who might be re-titled the Governor of the Federal Reserve System. The need for information from below could be handled through regularized reporting from the Reserve Bank Presidents on regional conditions, and by strengthened staff analysis in the Office of the Governor. By these alterations, the public, *i.e.,* political, quality of monetary policy would be accorded appropriate recognition; responsibility would be clearly located; a means of settling possible disputes between fiscal policy under the President and monetary under the Fed would be created; and the process of consultation and negotiation by the Fed with the Treasury, the CEA and the lending agencies would be made more effective. In short, a single head, enjoying the confidence of the President, would be able to speak with vigor for the central banking viewpoint in the formation of economic policy; yet once the deliberations had been completed an assurance would exist that the Fed would be at one with the rest of the government in executing the policy determined upon.

A second, lesser category of structural change would have the object of revising the Fed's appearance to fit the public nature of its responsibilities. Election of two-thirds of the Reserve Bank Directors by commercial banks, and "ownership" of the Reserve Banks by commercial banks, are admittedly matters of no great substantive importance today. But since they are functionless elements, and their appearance of special interest access is harmful to the legitimacy of monetary actions, the Reserve Boards should be eliminated (or, at least, all of their members should be publicly appointed) and the commercial banks' shares in the Reserve Banks should be bought out by the government—thus making the Reserve Banks in form what they largely are in fact: field offices of the national, public monetary authority.

Adoption of this series of proposals—or others, perhaps milder in form but having the same essential consequences—would significantly improve the economic policy machinery of the national government. These changes represent a logical extension of the premises of the Employment Act:

In no major country of the world today, except in the United States, is there a central bank that can legally, if it wishes, tell the head of its own Government to go fly a kite. It seems to me that if we are to hold Government responsible for carrying out the new doctrine of economic stabilization, there must be a chain of responsibility reaching through the Presidency to all the instrumentalities that do the stabilizing.[49]

NOTES

1. For more detailed description of the formal organization, see Board of Governors, *The Federal Reserve System* (Washington, D. C., 1961) and G. L. Bach, *Federal Reserve Policy-Making* (New York, 1950).

2. The original Federal Reserve Act imposed a 90 per cent "franchise tax" on Reserve Bank earnings after expenses, dividends and an allowance for

surplus. In the mid-1920s earnings were still a major concern, and the principal reason for the Banks' holding government securities, against the opposition of Secretary Mellon. In 1933 half the Banks' accumulated surplus was appropriated to furnish the initial capital of the new Federal Deposit Insurance Corporation; to allow the replenishment of surplus the franchise tax was dropped. By 1946 the surplus reached proportions that led the Board to decide as a matter of policy to pay 90 per cent of earnings to the Treasury, under the label of "interest" on outstanding Federal Reserve notes; this policy continued from 1947 through 1958. In 1959 the surplus was cut back to an amount equal to the subscribed (*i.e.,* twice the paid-in) capital, and the balance, together with all earnings after dividends, was paid over to the Treasury. *Annual Report of the Board of Governors,* 1959, pp. 96–99.

3. E. A. Goldenweiser, *American Monetary Policy* (New York, 1951), p. 295.

4. In the mid-1920s it dawned on the Reserve Banks—sooner than on the Treasury or the FRB—that open market purchases, first undertaken to improve Reserve Bank earnings, could be managed to offset declines in member banks' outstanding loans; see L. V. Chandler, *Benjamin Strong, Central Banker* (Washington, Brookings, 1958). The Banking Act of 1935, reorganizing the FRB and the System, ratified emergency improvisations in 1932–33 to restore bank liquidity by enabling advances to be made to member banks on the security of any of their assets deemed acceptable, and not just on "eligible" commercial paper as before. Federal deposit insurance was introduced in 1934, in recognition of the fact that more public policy objectives than the rescue of depositors in failing banks were at stake in the maintenance of confidence in the safety of bank deposits. The architects of the 1913 act supposed they had, by and large, provided for the safety of deposits by establishing the rediscount privilege and strengthening bank examination powers.

5. Joint (Patman) Committee on the Economic Report, *Monetary Policy and the Management of the Public Debt, Replies to Questions,* Sen. Doc. 123, 82d Cong. 2d sess., 1952, pp. 278–79. Cited hereafter as Sen. Doc. 123.

6. Bach, pp. 81–82.

7. See, for example, the *Forty-Sixth Annual Report of the Board of Governors of the Federal Reserve System* (Washington, 1960), pp. 134–48, for the list of names and affiliations as of December 31, 1959.

8. Bach, pp. 57–58.

9. Goldenweiser, p. 296.

10. Joint (Douglas) Committee on the Economic Report, *Hearings, Monetary, Credit and Fiscal Policies,* 81st Cong., 1st sess., 1949, p. 221.

11. Chairman Martin in Senate Committee on Finance, *Hearings, Investigation of the Financial Condition of the United States,* 85th Cong., 1st sess., 1957, p. 1260. Cited hereafter as Senate Finance Committee *Hearings.*

12. Bach, p. 119.

13. Sen. Doc. 123, p. 30.

14. Senate Finance Committee *Hearings,* 1959, p. 2180.

15. Conversation with staff members, Council of Economic Advisers.

16. Bach, pp. 227–28.

17. See Chairman Martin's remarks, Sen. Doc. 123, p. 300, and Bach, p. 121.

18. Senate Finance Committee *Hearings,* p. 1262.

19. Statement (mimeograph) of the AFL-CIO Executive Council on *Monetary Policy,* San Juan, Puerto Rico, February 24, 1959. See also, *New York Times,* February 26, 1959, p. 30, and March 6, 1959, p. 24.

20. *Administration of National Economic Control* (New York, 1952), p. 270; and see ch. 9 generally.

21. House Report No. 742, 74th Cong., 1st sess. (April 19, 1935), p. 6.

22. Marriner S. Eccles, *Beckoning Frontiers* (New York, 1951), pp. 167–71. These pages contain an excellent capsule summary of OMC development.

23. Commission on Organization of the Executive Branch of the Government, *Task Force Report on Regulatory Commissions,* Appendix N, January, 1949, pp. 113–14; Eccles, pp. 224–26; Bach, pp. 234–35.

24. Joint Committee on the Economic Report, *Monetary, Credit and Fiscal Policies, A Collection of Statements,* 81st Cong., 1st sess., 1949, pp. 68–69.

25. *Ibid.,* p. 162. By 1952, the Presidents were less enthusiastic for change (see Sen. Doc. 123, p. 673). They perhaps feared that the unified control might go to the FRB rather than to the OMC if the subject were opened up at all.

26. New York Clearing House Association, *The Federal Reserve Reexamined* (New York, 1953), pp. 138–39.

27. Sen. Doc. 123, p. 294.

28. Subcommittee on General Credit Control and Debt Management, Joint Committee on the Economic Report, *Monetary Policy and the Management of the Public Debt,* Sen. Doc. 163, 82d Cong., 2d sess. (1952), p. 54; H. R. 2790, 86th Cong., 1st sess. (1959).

29. Joint Committee on the Economic Report, *Hearings, Monetary, Credit and Fiscal Policies,* 81st Cong., 1st sess. (1949), p. 221.

30. Bach, p. 234.

31. Subcommittee on General Credit Control and Debt Management, Joint Committee on the Economic Report, *Hearings, Monetary Policy and the Management of the Public Debt,* 82d Cong., 2d sess. (1952), p. 756, cited hereafter as General Credit Control Subcommittee *Hearings,* 1952. Regionalism in the Federal Reserve—or at least its modern defense—perhaps owes more to an unexamined bias in favor of "federalism" as a matter of political ideology than to an empirical examination of the national economic structure.

32. Sen. Doc. 123, pp. 677–79.

33. Robert E. Cushman, *The Independent Regulatory Commissions* (New York, 1941), p. 160.

34. Martin, in Senate Finance Committee *Hearings,* 1957, p. 1261.

35. Letter, Kenneth A. Kenyon, Assistant Secretary, Board of Governors, to the author, August 17, 1960.

36. Had Eccles been successful in writing his ideas into the 1935 amendments to the Federal Reserve Act, the Act would have anticipated by eleven years the declaration of national economic policy adopted in the Employment Act. The Eccles mandate would have directed the FRB "to exercise such powers as it possesses in such manner as to promote conditions conducive to business stability and to mitigate by its influence unstabilizing fluctuations in the general level of production, trade, prices, and employment so far as may be possible within the scope of monetary and credit administration." H. Rept. No. 742, 74th Cong., 1st sess. (1935), p. 9.

37. An attempt to clarify the Federal Reserve's role by means of a clearer mandate has been urged by Senator Paul Douglas and by Jacob Viner, see Sen. Doc. 163, p. 74; General Credit Control Subcommittee *Hearings,* 1952, pp. 771–72. It has been opposed by Goldenweiser and the Reserve Bank Presidents: *ibid.,* p. 765; Joint Committee on the Economic Report, *Monetary, Credit, and Fiscal Policies, A Collection of Statements,* 81st Cong., 1st sess. (1949), p. 101. The absence of any mandate legislation since the Employment Act suggests insufficient Congressional consensus upon its substantive content. Organized labor has opposed amendments to add price stability to the goals of that Act, as intended to water down its emphasis on "maximum employment."

38. Martin, in Sen. Doc. 123, p. 242.

39. See, for example, FRB Research Director Ralph A. Young's remarks, Antitrust Subcommittee, Senate Committee on the Judiciary, *Hearings, Administered Prices,* 86th Cong., 1st sess. (1959), Part 10, pp. 4887–91.

40. See H. Christian Sonne's comments, from which the quotation is taken, in General Credit Control Subcommittee *Hearings,* 1952, pp. 848–50.

41. For discussion of this and other pertinent administrative myths, see Harold Stein's remarks in General Credit Control Subcommittee *Hearings,* 1952, pp. 758–59.

42. Sen. Doc. 123, pp. 263–73.

43. See the remarks of Leon H. Keyserling and Roy Blough in Sen. Doc. 123, pp. 848–51.

44. Its most recent form, at the time of writing, was embodied in S. 2382, 86th Cong., 1st sess.

45. For extended discussion of the Clark-Reuss proposal, see: Executive and Legislative Reorganization Subcommittee, House Government Operations Committee, *Hearings, Amending the Employment Act of 1946,* 86th Cong., 1st sess., 1959, and Subcommittee on Production and Stabilization, Senate Committee on Banking and Currency, *Hearings, Employment Act Amendments,* 86th Cong., 2d sess., 1960.

46. *E.g.,* in the spring of 1956; see discussion in Senate Finance Committee *Hearings,* 1957, pp. 1361–63.

47. See Emmette S. Redford, *Potential Public Policies to Deal with Inflation Caused by Market Power,* Joint Economic Committee, Study Paper No. 10 for Study of Employment, Growth and Price Levels, 1959.

48. Antitrust Subcommittee, Senate Committee on the Judiciary, *Hearings, Administered Prices,* 86th Cong., 1st sess. (1959), Part 10, p. 4917.

49. Elliott V. Bell, "Who Should Manage Our Managed Money?" An address before the American Bankers Association Convention, Los Angeles, California, October 22, 1956.

THE STEEL CRISIS OF 1962
Theodore Sorensen

The most direct and dangerous challenge by a powerful private interest group to the President's anti-inflation efforts—and to the President's office and trust—came from the steel industry in 1962.

While the dramatic confrontation between John Kennedy and United States Steel reached its climax in April of that year, the President's own concern went back more than a year earlier. In one of his first post-inaugural conversations with Secretary Goldberg, a former counsel to the Steelworkers Union, he expressed concern over the effects any steel price rise would have on his balance of payments and anti-inflation efforts.

The President's concern was well founded. Not only was steel one of our largest industries; its prices were also a direct or indirect cost in almost every other commodity. It played so large a part in the American economy, and its products were an essential part of so many other capital and consumer products, that its price actions had long been a bellwether for all industry. "As goes steel, so goes inflation" had long been the epigram which accurately summarized this nation's price movements.

Senator Robert Taft of Ohio, in Senate hearings of 1948, scolded the industry for raising its prices, predicting that such an increase would force up other prices and encourage further wage demands by labor. His scolding was in vain, but his forecast was unfortunately accurate. Between 1947 and 1958 steel prices more than doubled, increasing more than three times as fast as other industrial prices. Economists estimated that the largest single cause of the rise in the Wholesale Price Index prior to 1958 was inflation in steel.

Labor was partly to blame. Because of the dominant influence of a comparative handful of companies, both sides in steel labor negotiations privately assumed that management would be able to adjust its prices to pay for whatever wage bargain was reached. As a result, steel

Pages 443–459 of *Kennedy* by Theodore Sorensen. Copyright © 1965 by Theodore C. Sorensen. Reprinted by permission of Harper and Row, Publishers, and the author.

wages had been rising between 1947 and 1958 faster than productivity, and steel prices had been rising even faster than labor costs.

Since 1958 steel prices had been stable, and so had wholesale prices as a whole. But, as earlier noted, our balance of payments and gold supply were far from stable. American steel prices having risen in earlier years far more rapidly than those of our competitors overseas, this country's share of world steel export markets had steadily declined, while foreign imports into this country more than tripled, accounting for nearly one-fourth of the rise in our payments deficit between 1957 and 1961. American machinery, machine tools, equipment and vehicles, which comprised the bulk of our durable goods exports, also depended on steel products and prices—as did our exports of most other important commodities—and it was clear to President Kennedy in 1961 that another major price rise in steel could potentially spark not only a new inflationary spiral but a disastrous payments deficit and gold outflow.

His immediate concern that year was an automatic increase in steel wages scheduled to take place on October 1 and the growing talk in the steel industry, as reported in the press, of a price increase at that time. The October 1 wage rise was the third and final increase promised under a 1960 settlement which had ended the longest steel strike in history. That settlement, under the auspices of Vice President Nixon, was accompanied by solid rumors that the companies had agreed not to increase prices until after the election. Kennedy asked Goldberg, who had helped negotiate the contract, whether the Steelworkers Union should be asked to forego the October 1 wage increase in the national interest. But this would have been a dubious precedent for the stability of collective bargaining contracts, and analysis by the Council of Economic Advisers showed that the October 1 step was within the range of rising productivity and could be absorbed without a price increase. Labor costs per ton of steel, said the CEA, in figures the industry would later dispute, were no higher than they were in 1958. The real problem, warned Secretary Goldberg, would be the 1962 negotiations for a new contract.

On September 6 the President wrote an open letter to the presidents of the twelve largest steel companies, urging that prices not be increased on October 1 or thereafter, detailing the damage higher steel prices would do to the nation's balance of payments and price stability in general and to steel exports in particular, pointing out the excellent profit and income position of their stockholders, and reminding them that the restrictive monetary and fiscal measures required to halt any inflationary spiral they started would retard our nation's recovery from recession and steel's hopes for greater capacity utilization. He then made this key point:

I do not wish to minimize the urgency of preventing inflationary movements in steel wages ... the steel industry has demonstrated a will to halt the price-wage spiral in steel. If the industry were now to forego a price increase, it would enter collective bargaining negotiations next spring with a record of three and a half years of price stability. It would clearly then be the turn of the labor representatives to limit wage demands to a level consistent with continued price stability. The moral position of the steel industry next spring—and its claim to the support of public opinion—will be strengthened by the exercise of price restraint now.

Some of the replies were thoughtful, some were rude, none made any promises—but prices were not raised. A week later the President wrote an old friend, President David McDonald of the Steelworkers, emphasizing the need in 1962 for a steel-labor settlement "within the limits of advances in productivity and price stability ... in the interests of all of the American people." Republicans protested that Presidents should concern themselves with "inflation," not with price rises in particular industries. But no one misunderstood the President's desire that the 1962 settlement neither necessitate nor lead to a price increase.

To lessen disruptive stockpiling of steel by customers who thought either a strike or a large price increase was inevitable, the President requested both parties, through Secretary Goldberg and in a press conference, to accelerate their negotiations. With his approval, the Secretary talked first with the industry's chief negotiator, R. Conrad Cooper, then with Steelworkers President McDonald, and subsequently with others on both sides, including a telephone conversation with U.S. Steel Chairman Roger Blough. On January 23, 1962, Kennedy met privately with Goldberg, Blough and McDonald at the White House, having also met with Blough the previous September.

In all these talks both the President and Goldberg emphasized their interest not only in an early settlement, which by itself was not of great importance, but in a settlement which would make a price rise unnecessary. More specifically, President Kennedy's considerable influence with the union and the good offices of the Secretary of Labor were offered as a means of helping achieve such a settlement if both sides were agreeable. No formal pledge from the industry to hold prices steady, if the President succeeded, was requested, and none was forthcoming. For the government to have asked for such a commitment, the President said, would have been "passing over the line of propriety." But, while Blough and other industry spokesmen grumbled on each occasion about rising costs and the profit squeeze in what was assumed to be the usual "poor-mouthing" that opens labor negotiations, the industry accepted the administration's help without any illusion as to the President's only purpose and without any indication that it intended to raise prices no matter what settlement was reached.

While Roger Blough would later claim that all kinds of public hints about a pending price rise had been made—hints which no one else in either industry or the press seemed to have grasped—he and other industry officials in direct contact with the administration made no use of those opportunities to inform the President of such an action. On the contrary, the industry voluntarily made itself party to what was in effect a tripartite transaction clearly based on the President's premise that steel price increases were undesirable and, unless necessitated by a wage increase exceeding productivity increases, not to be attempted.

Nor was it a passive acceptance of minimal help. Goldberg did not even talk to McDonald until Cooper had advised him, after talking with his colleagues in the industry, that they were agreeable. A series of wires, calls and visits from the Secretary on behalf of the President helped to get the negotiations started several months early in February, helped get them resumed when they had broken up in March and, most importantly, helped persuade McDonald to accept the industry's most modest settlement in postwar history. "They did it in part," concluded the President later, "because I said that we could not afford another inflationary spiral, that it would affect our competitive position abroad—so they signed up." The agreement provided for no general increase in wage rates at all, and fringe benefit improvements costing about 10 cents an hour, or 2.5 percent.

This over-all figure—well under the 17 cents originally sought by the union, well under the 1960 settlement, less than one-third the cost of the average steel settlement for twenty years, and based on an earlier Council of Economic Advisers analysis—had been presented by Goldberg to Blough in a private conversation on March 6 as a figure well within the capacity of the industry to absorb without a price increase, a conclusion which neither Blough nor other industry leaders disagreed with. Goldberg then urged the same figure upon McDonald in a private conversation on March 12 as appropriate to price stability. Negotiations were resumed on March 14 and concluded on March 31.

The 1962 steel settlement, the first without a strike since 1954 and the first clearly and completely within the bounds of productivity increases in memory, was hailed throughout the nation. The President, in identical telephoned statements to management representatives and union headquarters, praised the agreement as "responsible . . . high industrial statesmanship . . . obviously noninflationary . . . a solid base for continued price stability. I . . . extend to you the thanks of the American people." The union members, he remarked to me as he put down the phone after the second call, had cheered and applauded their own sacrifice, while the management representatives had been "ice-cold."

But neither side expressed any disagreement with his conclusions on price stability. Newspapers and magazines representing every shade of opinion breathed a sigh of relief that steel price increases were no longer a danger. The following week, as the individual companies executed their formal contracts with the union, the President telephoned Goldberg that Charlie Bartlett had a tip from steel sources that a price rise was imminent. The Secretary scoffed at the report. Nothing had happened to alter the cost picture of the industry in the preceding months. On the contrary, the competition from low-cost foreign producers, competing metals and other materials, and the higher profits which could be realized from greater sales and capacity utilization, would cause any normally competitive industry at such a time to be considering price decreases.

The price of scrap, iron ore and coal, the three major materials used by the steel industry, were below their 1958 levels. Under the new labor contract, which did not even go into effect until July 1, employment costs per ton of steel would continue to decline. In the years of general economic slack since 1958, the profit position of several companies had improved and others had worsened, making it impossible to justify a uniform price decision by all. "We should be trying to reduce the price of steel, if at all possible," President Edmund Martin of Bethlehem Steel was quoted as telling his annual meeting on April 10, "because we have more competition, particularly from foreign sources."

On Tuesday, April 10, the last major contract having been signed, the President was surprised to note that his appointment calendar included a 5:45 p.m. appointment for Roger Blough. O'Donnell said Blough had requested it that afternoon. Goldberg said he had no idea what Blough might have in mind but agreed to stand by in his office.

What Blough had in mind was soon clear. Seated on the sofa next to the President's rocking chair, he handed him U.S. Steel's mimeographed press release announcing a $6-a-ton price increase, four times the cost of the new labor settlement. The President was stunned. He felt that his whole fight against inflation, his whole effort to protect our gold, was being reduced to tatters. If the industry in which he had made his greatest effort for stability, an industry plagued by foreign competition and underutilization, could make a mockery of his plea for self-restraint in the national interest, then every industry and every union in the country would thereafter feel free to defy him.

Above all, he felt duped. The man sitting across from him had personally, knowingly accepted his help in securing from the workers a contract that would not lead to an increase in prices. The prestige and powers of the Presidency had been used to help persuade the Steelworkers to accept less from the companies in the interest of price stability, and now the contract had no sooner been signed than the industry was announcing a large, across-the-board price increase for all products. "The question of good faith was involved," as the President said later. "The unions could have rightfully felt that they had been misled"—and no other union would ever listen to his plea for self-discipline again. "I think you're making a mistake," he coldly told Blough, who would not learn until later the enormity of his mistake.

Angry but contained, the President sent for Arthur Goldberg, who was less contained. The Secretary, learning that Blough's press statement had already been distributed to the wire services and networks for 7 p.m. release, harshly rejected the U.S. Steel Chairman's explanation that as an act of "courtesy" the President of the United States had been handed a mimeographed press release about an accomplished fact. Goldberg called it a "double cross," an act of bad faith, contrary to what was obviously understood by all concerned in the negotiations, contrary to the best interests of both the nation and the industry, and contrary to the assurance Goldberg had given the President that both Blough and McDonald could be relied on. Blough expressed his regrets, attempted to justify his action as necessary for his stockholders and departed. "They were not willing to accept my explanation," he said later with some degree of understatement.

The President's next scheduled appointment was a review of questions for the next day's press conference—an extra session, before the usual breakfast, which Assistant Press Secretary Andrew Hatcher had scheduled in Salinger's absence. Hatcher, Walter Heller, McGeorge Bundy and I were waiting for this meeting in Ken O'Donnell's office outside the President's door. When Blough left, the President asked us to come in and told us the news. His own anger was rising. His trust had been abused, his office had been used. He had intervened only with the industry's consent, with the unmistakable intention of holding the price line, and that intervention was now being made to appear at best weak and at worst stupid to the workers and to the American people. "My father always told me," he said, recalling the Ambassador's brief service in the steel industry and his fight with its leaders while on the Maritime Board, "that steel men were sons-of-bitches, but I never realized till now how right he was."

Little time was spent on recriminations. A price rise at that time and in that context was not only an economic setback—it was an affront to the office of the Presidency and to the man who held it. "If I had failed to get a rescission," he said later, "that would have been an awful setback to the office of the Presidency." No President should have accepted it without a fight; no one could have thought that John

Kennedy would. "U.S. Steel," one of those present would remark later, "picked the wrong President to double-cross."

The steel industry had successfully defied Presidents, however, for more than half a century. Its challenge to Kennedy was in an arena where he had few weapons and no precedents. Had it not been for the fact that the industry, in addition to its economic defiance, also accepted his good offices and then failed to honor his trust, history might well have been different. But the first question the President asked us after breaking the news was: "What can we do about it?"

Our primary *hope* was to create a climate that would discourage other companies from joining in the increase and encourage U.S. Steel to rescind. We recognized that market pressures would force the price leaders to back down if only one or two important companies refused to go along with the increase. Our primary *obligation* was to ascertain whether the ability of a powerful company to announce an unjustifiable price increase, with confidence that it could be sustained despite all the obvious economic pressures against it, reflected a violation of the laws against monopoly. With these two courses in mind, the President promptly telephoned for press statements from the Attorney General and the chairmen of the Senate and House Anti-Trust Subcommittees, similarly discussed what the government was doing for or with U.S. Steel with his Secretaries of Treasury and Defense, and directed Goldberg, Heller and me to prepare a statement for his Wednesday afternoon press conference. He could not meet with us later that night, he complained, because of the annual White House reception for all members of Congress. Recalling that the previous year's reception had been similarly marred by the Bay of Pigs fiasco, he said with a rueful smile, "I'll never have another Congressional reception."

Moving to my office, Goldberg, Heller and the latter's colleague from the Council of Economic Advisers, Kermit Gordon, discussed with me the information needed for the next day's statements. Through the long night that followed, the Council and the Bureau of Labor Statistics worked to produce the necessary data on why the industry needed no increase and how it would harm the whole nation. At the Congressional reception the President, in between smiles and handshakes, talked action with the Vice President, with Senator Gore and with Goldberg and me when we arrived. Earlier, by telephone, he had talked almost apologetically to David McDonald, who assured him that the Steel Union members would not feel the President had intentionally misled them.

The press conference breakfast the next morning, Wednesday, was devoted almost entirely to steel. Arthur Goldberg, who attended, told the President that he intended to submit his resignation, that he could no longer preach wage restraint to any union, and that he wished to acknowledge publicly his failure in exposing the Presidential office to such abuse. The President deferred this request, and he also agreed finally to defer his own suggestion for an immediate message to Congress seeking legislation, and to concentrate instead on mobilizing public opinion in his press conference opening statement.

Presidential anger, Arthur Krock has written, "must be reserved for those rare occasions when the office and the nation as well as the man are basically offended." This was one of those rare occasions. With the economic data before me, with continuous news announcements of other steel companies raising their prices by identical amounts, and with considerable alterations by both the President and the Attorney General, the opening statement for that press conference was written and rewritten. Each new version reflected more strongly the President's by then wholly unemotional determination to impress upon the industry and the public the seriousness of the situation. It was completed only as we rode over to the State Department Auditorium in his limousine.

His voice was ice-cold but calm as he read, sounding more like Roosevelt indicting the Japanese for Pearl Harbor than a man displaying "unbridled fury" as some of those not present would later claim:

The simultaneous and identical actions of United States Steel and other leading steel corporations, increasing steel prices by some six dollars a ton, constitute a wholly unjustifiable and irresponsible defiance of the public interest.

In this serious hour in our nation's history, when we are confronted with grave crises in Berlin and Southeast Asia, when we are devoting our energies to economic recovery and stability, when we are asking reservists to leave their homes and families for months on end, and servicemen to risk their lives—*and four were killed in the last two days in Vietnam*—and asking union members to hold down their wage requests, at a time when restraint and sacrifice are being asked of every citizen, the American people will find it hard, as I do, to accept a situation in which *a tiny handful of steel executives whose pursuit of private power and profit exceeds their sense of public responsibility* can show such utter contempt for the interests of 185 million Americans.

Seated in the audience, I heard a gasp from the reporters around me as the President continued:

If this rise in the cost of steel is imitated by the rest of the industry, instead of rescinded, it would increase the cost of . . . most . . . items for every American family . . . businessman and farmer. It would seriously handicap our efforts to prevent an inflationary spiral . . . make it more difficult for American goods to compete in foreign markets, more difficult to withstand competition from foreign imports, and thus more difficult to improve our balance of payments position, and stem the flow of gold. . . .

Price and wage decisions in this country, except for very limited restrictions in the case of monopolies and national emergency strikes, are and ought to be freely and privately made, but the American people have a right to expect, in return for that freedom, a higher sense of business responsibility for the welfare of their country than has been shown in the last two days. *Some time ago I asked each American to consider what he would do for his country and I asked the steel companies. In the last twenty-four hours we had their answer.*

The words italicized above were among those added to the statement by the President just prior to the conference or inserted spontaneously as he delivered it. Less pointed remarks, he was convinced, would have been noted, answered and then forgotten.

The statement also cited convincing and detailed facts on the industry's strong economic position without an increase, on the widespread damage the increase would cause and on the various branches of the government already looking into the matter; and it was followed by equally harsh comments in answer to all questions. Example:

. . . the suddenness by which every company in the last few hours . . . came in with . . . almost identical price increases . . . isn't really the way we expect the competitive private enterprise system to always work.

Even answers to unrelated questions on service wives and Vietnam were related by the President to the actions of the steel companies. From the moment of that press conference on, he had the initiative in the fight.

But as we discussed the situation back in his office, the steady parade of companies rushing to imitate precisely U.S. Steel's increase cast gloom over his hopes for a rescission. Nevertheless he was determined to fight on, and he asked me to call a meeting for him in the Cabinet Room early the next morning to coordinate the various efforts needed or already under way, some of them initiated the previous evening.

Days later, when it was all over, several Republicans—who had remained discreetly silent during the fight, refusing to approve either the price hike or the President's opposition to it—would term these various administration efforts an example of "overreacting," "tyranny" and "executive usurpation." Roger Blough spoke of "retaliatory attacks," and said that "never before in the nation's history had so many forces of the Federal Government been marshaled against a single industry." Clearly there was at the time an atmosphere of mobilization and crisis, much of it more apparent than real, based on words rather than actions, and deliberately designed to encourage rescission. But once the smoke of battle had blown away, it should have been clear to all—as it had been clear to the group which met Thursday morning in the Cabinet Room—that the only concrete governmental actions available were two rather modest steps, neither representing "illicit coercion" or "intemperate retaliation":

First, the Defense Department sought to meet its obligation to the taxpayers to purchase steel at the lowest available price. Secretary McNamara reported to the President that the steel industry's action could increase the cost of national defense by one billion dollars, not, as widely reported, merely because of increased steel costs, which were but a fraction of that total, but because of increased costs in all other sectors of the economy which followed steel. "To minimize the effect of the price increase on Defense costs," McNamara directed, the use of alternative materials would be studied, and "where possible, procurement of steel for Defense production shall be shifted to those companies which have not increased prices."

Any prudent steel customer would have done the same. McNamara, whom the President had called regarding this approach after

Blough's visit, underscored his intentions by announcing the award of a small Polaris armor-plate contract to the tiny Lukens Steel Company, which had not raised prices. He noted publicly that U.S. Steel and Lukens were the only producers of this kind of high-strength steel. Similar announcements were planned for the General Services Administration, the Agency for International Development and others. But this was not a massive weapon. It was insufficient by itself to persuade the few holdout companies not to join the price increase parade and wholly useless once they did. The Lukens award, in fact, was announced after the fight was almost over.

Second, the Justice Department sought to meet its obligation to law enforcement by initiating an inquiry as to whether a series of simultaneous and identical price increases, justified neither by cost nor by demand, and undertaken by companies in totally different financial positions, reflected normal free market behavior, coincidence, collusion or monopoly. Whatever the answer, I doubt that any self-respecting Antitrust Division under any administration could have sat back and idly watched this occur, given the long history of price conspiracies in steel. In no fully competitive industry could one company raise its prices in confidence that virtually all others would follow. The Federal Trade Commission, which had ordered the industry in 1951 to halt certain monopolistic practices, also announced a reopening of its inquiry. "Steel," said an eminent scholar commending the President's action, "is not really a competitive market. It's one big company." And a leading professor of antitrust law wrote us:

Price leadership without overt collusion is inevitable in tightly organized oligopolies, schooled to habits of cooperation, afraid to discriminate, without possible new entrants. . . . Using the latent powers of the Sherman Act . . . the Courts have plenty of power . . . to reorganize industry leaders.

No such reorganization was attempted. Those who assailed the Kennedys for immediately summoning a Grand Jury investigation, however, had less to say when seven major antitrust indictments for secret price-fixing conspiracies were returned against the steel industry in the two years that followed. The largest indictment was returned in April, 1964, by a Grand Jury receiving information from its predecessor organized by the Kennedys.

One of the items that particularly interested the trust-busters in April, 1962, was the statement by Bethlehem President Martin, made shortly before the Blough announcement, that this was no time to raise prices. Bethlehem was the first to join U.S. Steel in the increase. Was this evidence of conspiracy, monopoly power, deliberate deceit or, as claimed, a misquotation? The Antitrust Division had an obligation to find out. Federal Bureau of Investigation agents, in their normal role as investigators and fact-finders for all divisions of the department, interviewed not only all company officials (U.S. Steel's General Counsel told them that he and his associates were "too busy" to talk to them then) but also the three reporters who had covered the Bethlehem meeting (all of whom stood by their stories).

Unfortunately, two overzealous agents, misunderstanding either their role or their instructions, called and visited one of the reporters in the middle of the night to check his story, and telephoned another who put them off. The latter, as well as the third reporter, were interviewed at their offices, although subsequent reports talked of "state security police" swooping down unannounced to grill all three in their beds. Some members of the newspaper fraternity—who never, as the President pointed out, showed the slightest hesitation in waking anyone else up at night—encouraged violent Republican talk about "Gestapo tactics," "press suppression" and accusations that the Kennedy brothers had personally ordered a 3 a.m. "third degree." As always, neither of the Kennedys would publicly blame the career men responsible, but the Attorney General's deputy had in fact specified to the FBI that all those to be interviewed should be telephoned at their place of business, not their homes, for an appointment in the usual hours. No orders were ever given to awaken anyone or to obtain the information by 7 a.m., and neither Kennedy knew about the calls until the next day.

The antitrust and Defense procurement actions were the only two tangible items on the list I drew up for Thursday's meeting in the Cabinet Room, and, although both contributed to the general atmosphere of concern, neither provided a means of rescission. Among those present at 8:50 that morning, in addition to the President and myself, were Messrs. Robert Kennedy, Goldberg, McNamara, Hodges, Under Secretary of the Treasury Fowler, FTC Chairman

Dixon, Walter Heller, Larry O'Brien and several sub-Cabinet members and assistants. Roughly the same strategy group met the following day as well.

The only other concrete action available, it appeared, would be new legislation. The President regarded this as a difficult route, despite early Democratic support for his stand on the Hill. Remembering Truman's ill-fated move to draft railroad strikers, and having reconsidered his position of the previous morning, he did not want to act in haste. The Steelworkers having fulfilled their obligations, he did not want to take action against the industry—on its tariffs or tax proposals, for example—that would diminish its employment. Secretary Dillon, on vacation in Florida, argued against any change for the time being in the proposed investment tax credit and depreciation reform. But if rescission could not be obtained soon, said the President, he would go to Congress. His press conference statement had not been an act.

But the legislative alternatives, canvassed in a meeting in my office Friday morning, were not too promising. They ranged all the way from a simple resolution condemning the price rise to permanent legislation placing steel and similar price and wage decisions under various degrees of governmental supervision. A proposed ninety-day "Steel Price Emergency Act of 1962" would have temporarily rolled back prices to their April 9 level until a Presidential board of inquiry could report on what increase, if any, was proper and in the national interest; and the industry, though not bound to accept the Board's recommendations, would be on notice that further legislation was the alternative. A proposed amendment to the existing Defense Production Act would have revived Presidential authority to stabilize, with a March, 1962, base, prices and wages either in all industries or in those producing basic commodities. Other suggestions called for a variety of Executive Orders, Presidential panels, court reviews or temporary rollbacks and controls. Most suggestions were too little, too late or too much. They either failed to assure correction of the immediate problem or went so far as to be undesirable.

The President was left chiefly with his effort to obtain a voluntary rescission without legislation through both public and private appeals. At our Thursday morning meeting Secretary of Commerce Hodges was designated to hold a press conference in reply to one scheduled by Roger Blough that afternoon. Arrangements were made to supply Hodges with rebuttal material, and to supply a few friendly reporters at the Blough conference with pertinent questions. Other Cabinet members and agency heads were asked to hold press conferences on the impact of a steel price increase on their various concerns—defense, balance of payments, farmers, small businessmen.

All the economists in government were to pull together a "Fact Book" or "White Paper" on steel to be widely distributed. Democratic governors were asked through the National Committee to deplore the increase and request local steel men not to join in it. Administration spokesmen were to be supplied to the various TV interview shows.

On Capitol Hill Senator Kefauver had already welcomed the President's call to arms and scheduled an investigation by his Anti-Trust Subcommittee. The House Anti-Trust Subcommittee, the Small Business Committees in both houses and other committees and individual members threw their weight behind the President. The Republican candidates for Senator and Governor of Pennsylvania, Congressmen Van Zandt and Scranton, wired Roger Blough that the increase was "wrong for Pennsylvania, wrong for America and wrong for the free world." With a handful of expected exceptions, the nation's editorial writers and columnists refused to support the price rise and most supported the President.

Blough's press conference statements that afternoon were defensive but mild. Hodges in his reply struck back hard against a "handful of men who said in effect that United States Steel comes first, the United States of America second." He ridiculed Blough's contention that price *increases* were justified by foreign competition, and refuted the corporation's plea that increasing the cost of everyone else's machinery was the only way U.S. Steel could obtain enough funds to modernize its own.

But while the public barrage continued, the President was exploring private avenues of persuasion as well. He had early in the fight asked all those in his administration with business ties—including Hodges, Gudeman, Heller, McNamara, Gilpatric, Fowler, Dillon, Goldberg, Roosa and others—to place calls to any contacts they had among steel companies still holding the price line, among steel companies who might consider rescinding, among steel bankers and steel buyers and steel lawyers. No threats were made, no inducements were offered, but the nation's interest in price stability and a better balance of payments was made clear, and reliable channels of communication between the government and the steel companies were established.

There was little time, very little time. When steel prices had last been increased in 1958, all the major companies had been in line two days after the first company's announcement. The rush of other companies to join U.S. Steel on Wednesday, both before and after the Kennedy press conference, cast gloom over the possibility we had discussed the previous night of bringing U.S. Steel back by persuading the others to hold fast. "I am hopeful," the President said at his press conference, "that there will be those who will not participate in this parade.... But we have to wait and see on that, because they are coming in very fast."

Many of the hopes for this divide-and-conquer strategy focused on the Inland Steel Company of Chicago. Inland's President, Joseph Block, was regarded as an "industry statesman" and served on the President's Labor-Management Advisory Committee. Block was in Japan, but a series of administration calls reached other Inland officials. Recognizing the national interest in preventing a worsening in balance of payments and inflation, and recognizing the administration's role in helping obtain a noninflationary labor settlement, Inland agreed that April, 1964, was no time to be raising prices, and announced Friday morning that it would not. Promptly the President called another friend, Edgar Kaiser of Kaiser Steel, and that much smaller company made a similar announcement. Still another company, Colorado Fuel and Iron, announced that it would consider at most only selective price increases on some items in the future.

A note of optimism entered our Friday meeting in the Cabinet Room. The companies announcing no price raise, along with an as yet uncertain holdout, Armco, probably had no more than 15 percent of the industry's capacity and could, by holding out, increase it to no more than 25 percent. "But," said Robert McNamara, on the basis of his days with Ford, "none of the others will be willing to give up any part of that additional 10 percent, and they'll all have to come down." We agreed that a primary effort should be made to reach Armco.

Absent from this Friday conference was Arthur Goldberg, on his way to New York for the last of three secret meetings with U.S. Steel officials. The President, after the first blush of anger, had no animosity toward either the company or the industry which had challenged him. He sought not revenge but rescission. Those with a more over-simplified class warfare view of big business argued that the steel industry had deliberately abused him and should be the object of punishment, not negotiations. But my own belief is that the industry's misdeeds—which resulted in the President of the United States being misled as to its intentions, informed too late of its action and made to look bad by its timing—were the product of thoughtlessness rather than malicious intent; and, while most steel executives, having held the line in 1960 after a far more expensive settlement, might have been a little less thoughtless had the occupant of the White House been Richard Nixon, I believe their motivations were based primarily on narrow and shortsighted economic grounds rather than political ones.

U.S. Steel, unlike most of those imitating its action, had in fact suffered a decline in profits, although it had maintained its usual dividends; and Roger Blough, the man whom it paid each year several times the amount the United States people paid their Chief Executive, impressed Kennedy as a sincere, if somewhat dull, individual. Some of Blough's colleagues in the industry may well have had a "let's show that man in the White House who's boss" attitude, but Blough and others seemed genuinely surprised and concerned by the President's response.

The President, therefore, upon learning late Wednesday night through the Charlie Bartlett channel that a meeting of the minds might be possible, directed his Secretary of Labor to meet with U.S. Steel Finance Chairman Robert Tyson; and later, when Goldberg's history as an adversary seemed to prevent the company from bending, Kennedy asked Clark Clifford, as a corporation lawyer with no job in the government, to represent him also. Earlier, two bankers friendly to Blough had been asked to point out to him the error of his ways. Wilbur Mills, whose Ways and Means chairmanship commanded respect in the industry, had wired Blough to revoke the increase. And Walter Heller had been removed by the President from a televised debate with Tyson when the latter suggested through intermediaries that it might only harden the lines.

Tyson met separately with Goldberg and Clifford on Thursday afternoon, meeting the latter on board U.S. Steel's private plane at the Washington airport. Neither meeting made any progress. But word reached the President that Blough wanted talks to continue, and a luncheon meeting of Goldberg, Clifford, Tyson, Blough and U.S. Steel President Worthington was scheduled for Friday.

Goldberg—who had not, contrary to Blough's later report, initiated the negotiations—pressed hard on both days for a rescission of the increase and for the appointment of a high-level Presidential review committee. Both Goldberg and Clifford stressed that the timing of the increase, after Blough had failed to use many opportunities to warn the President of his intention, looked like a double cross, whether it was or not. Under instruction from the President, they warned of the darkening climate between steel and government, expressed doubt that Kennedy could restrain the more fiery members of Congress intent on harsh legislation, and insisted that there was one, and only one, action acceptable to the President: a complete rescission.

But by the time lunch was served on Friday, their arguments were largely unnecessary. The holdouts in the industry had prevailed. During the luncheon both Blough and Goldberg received telephone calls with the same message: Bethlehem Steel, the nation's second largest producer, a rival of Inland's in Midwest markets and of Kaiser's on the West Coast, and a major Defense Department contractor, had rescinded its increase.

Back in the White House the Bethlehem announcement caused jubilation. Already on his way to a review of the Atlantic Fleet off the Carolina coast, the President asked me, first, to prepare a brief statement thanking, on behalf of all consumers and businessmen, those companies who had held the line, and, second, to check with the others with whom we had worked as to whether any Presidential statement was desirable. Late that Friday afternoon, as I reported on this by telephone through Andy Hatcher at a Norfolk, Virginia, naval base, a secretary from the Press Office placed a scrap torn from the wire service ticker in front of me:

Bulletin—New York, A.P.—United States Steel Corporation rescinded today the steel price increase it initiated Tuesday.

Roughly seventy-two hours had passed since Roger Blough's visit to the White House—seventy-two hours in which nearly every waking moment of the President, regardless of whether he was toasting the visiting Shah and Empress of Iran, preparing for his press conference and trip, hosting the Congressional reception or fulfilling a dozen other duties, had been spent in either meditation or action on how best to preserve his purpose and policies in this struggle. Even the Chicago *Tribune* could not avoid admiring such "decisiveness in the executive." Foreign newspapers were almost unanimous in their praise of his victory, although the Communist press was hard put to explain how a government controlled by capitalist monopolists had cracked down on one of its masters. "Oh," cried Robert Frost, "didn't he do a good one! Didn't he show the Irish all right?" But what he had shown primarily was not his Irish temper, not "naked power" as the *Wall Street Journal* called it, but the ability to mobilize and concentrate every talent and tool he possessed and could borrow to prevent a serious blow to his program, his prestige and his office. While steel 1962 was the key battle in John Kennedy's war on inflation, his victory was less a victory against Big Steel than a victory for the American Presidency.

chapter three
Antipoverty Activity

Although both poverty and public policies concerned with poverty have long existed in the United States, the elimination of poverty became a major focus of public policy, and a major political issue, in the 1960's. The planning of a major antipoverty program began in 1963 under the Kennedy Administration and was continued by the Johnson Administration, being designated by President Johnson as "my kind of program." Early in 1964 he announced that his Administration had declared an all-out "war on poverty." A legislative proposal to implement this declaration was formulated in the executive branch, and was enacted into law with few changes in August, 1964, as the Economic Opportunity Act.

The initial selection in this chapter, a reprint of one of my own articles, surveys national antipoverty activity during the 1961–1966 period. After discussing the nature of the "poverty problems," antipoverty policy strategies, and major antipoverty legislation, I seek to account for the development of concern about poverty and the initiation of a war on poverty in an affluent society in which the poor lack really effective political power. One of my major conclusions is that, within the context created by growing concern about poverty in the early 1960's, strong presidential support was a crucial element in the enactment of antipoverty legislation. Whereas this first article is concerned with what can be called the macro-politics of poverty, the next two selections focus on particular decisions and controversies in the war on poverty.

As passed by Congress, the Economic Opportunity Act authorized a total of nine different antipoverty programs, to be administered either directly by the Office of Economic Opportunity or by delegate agencies under its supervision. Many of the provisions of the original Act received little consideration in their way through Congress and were unclear in their meaning or intent. Perhaps the most controversial of the poverty programs has been the Community Action program, which was designed to initiate and coordinate antipoverty activities at the community level. Especially productive of turmoil here was Section 202 (a) (3) of the Economic Opportunity Act, which provided for "maximum feasible participation" of the poor in local community action programs. How much participation should there be by the poor? What form should participation take? How should representatives of the poor be selected? Such questions, arising when the Office of Economic Opportunity began to implement the community action program, were left unanswered by the statute and its legislative history. John Donovan discusses the OEO's early efforts to administer the "maximum feasible participation" provision and the ensuing political controversy. His treatment illustrates both the blending of politics and administration which is so often characteristic of the governmental process and the development of policy by administrative activity. In 1966 Congress adopted an amendment to the Act which required that the poor constitute at least one-third of the boards of local community action agencies.

Because of the many conflicts and controversies created by Economic Opportunity Act programs, and the waning of presidential support for the war on poverty, there was substantial doubt early in 1967 as to whether Congress would extend the life of the legislation. (Up to 1967, the poverty program was authorized on a yearly basis.) Opposition to the Act was especially strong in the House of Representatives, which has customarily been more conservative than the Senate on social welfare legislation. Still a major issue was the maximum feasible participation of the poor in the community action program. Joseph Loftus, then a *New York Times* reporter, provides one version of the maneuvering engaged in by some of the Act's supporters to secure adoption of the "Green Amendment" and to build a favorable majority coalition. The Green Amendment provided that local governments could take direct control of community action programs and that up to one-third of the members of community action agency boards of directors could be local public officials. So amended, the life of EOA was extended for a two-year period.

Interestingly enough, in the fall of 1968 OEO reported that only three percent of the local governments involved had indicated an intention to take control of community action agencies as permitted by the Green Amendment. However, whether symbolic or substantive, the issue of "local control" often significantly influences the actions of national policy-makers.

The Appalachian Regional Development Act, discussed in the last selection in this chapter, stands in sharp contrast to the Economic Opportunity Act in its approach to poverty. Originating in the actions of the governors of the Appalachian states, it seeks to combat poverty by bringing about the economic development of an entire region through fairly conventional public-works-style programs, especially highway construction. Presenting no strong challenges to local interests, public or private, it has become a generally accepted (and little heard-about) program.

POVERTY, UNEMPLOYMENT, AND ECONOMIC DEVELOPMENT: THE SEARCH FOR A NATIONAL ANTIPOVERTY POLICY
James E. Anderson

The focus of this paper is on the antipoverty campaign of the 1960's. After an examination of the nature of the poverty problem, consideration will be given to antipoverty strategies, the use of the curative strategy, and some of the political aspects of the war on poverty. In all, the discussion is intended to provide a broad perspective on the national government's war on poverty and the development of antipoverty policy in the United States.

I

It is quite apparent that many people have not shared in the general economic growth and prosperity which have characterized the United States since World War II. If one third of the nation is no longer "ill-housed, ill-clad, and ill-nourished," as Franklin Roosevelt stated in 1937, it is nonetheless true that many millions of people are still afflicted by poverty. Much debate has occurred in the past few years over what constitutes poverty and how many people are poverty stricken.[1] Among the questions in this "debate" are: Is poverty definable as a family income of less than $2,000 annually, or $3,000 or $4,000, or what? Should the poverty-line be higher for urban dwellers than for rural residents, for those under 65 years of age than for those over 65? Do the poor number 30 million, or 35 million, or 40 to 50 million, or how many? Is poverty only a "state of mind," a situation in which some think they are poor because they have less income or material possessions than others? Or is poverty merely a statistical phenomenon with, say, the lowest fifth of the income pyramid being considered poverty-stricken?

There is much room for controversy and statistical manipulation in answering such questions. In some studies the conclusions reached

Reprinted from *The Journal of Politics,* XXIX (February, 1967), 70–93, with the permission of the publisher.

appear to be skewed by ideological considerations, with the conservative defining poverty more narrowly and consequently finding both less poverty and less need for governmental action than the liberal. To wit: A study prepared for the conservative American Enterprise Institute used an income standard ranging from $1,259 to $3,155 for non-farm households whose size ran from 2 to 7 or more.[2] On this basis, one tenth of the nation's household units (around 17 million people) were in the poverty category. In contrast, Leon Keyserling and the liberal Conference on Economic Progress,[3] using an annual income of less than $4,000 before taxes as the poverty standard for a household, held that in 1960 almost 10.5 million families were living in poverty (or 23 percent of all families). Some 4 million unattached individuals with annual incomes below $2,000 were also designated as poverty-stricken.

A third study, which seems soundly conceived and ideologically "neutral" and which yields data similar to that used by many public officials, was prepared by the Department of Health, Education, and Welfare using the Census Bureau's sample statistics for 1963.[4] Annual incomes necessary to maintain nutritional adequacy were calculated for different types of families classified by farm and nonfarm residence, age and sex of head, and number of children. Using these criteria, a flexible poverty standard was developed, which ranged from $880 annually for a single female aged 65 or over living on a farm to $5,100 for an urban family of 7 or more headed by a male under 65 years of age. On the basis of the flexible standard it was calculated that, in 1963, 34.5 million persons (or 18 percent of the population) were in families with incomes insufficient to purchase a minimally nutritional budget. This supports the frequently heard statement that one-fifth of the nation still lives in poverty. It might be noted that the much criticized Council of Economic Advisers study, which used a fixed $3,000 standard, yielded similar results: 35 million people living in poverty [5]

To end this phase of the discussion, the disagreement over the nature and precise amount of poverty should not be permitted to obscure the "problem of poverty." As one close student of poverty has stated:

it would be a mistake to conclude from this [lack of agreement] that there is no evidence to demonstrate that tens of millions of people have incomes that are insufficient to provide minimum levels of living for this society. Most Americans would agree that a family is poor if its income is below the amount needed to qualify for public assistance. Many would also count as poor some families with incomes well above this level. The 1960 Census data show that *at least 23.5 million people—one person out of eight in the United States—live in a family with an annual income that is less than the amount needed to qualify for aid under the public assistance laws of each state.*[6]

In addition to aggregate statistics, an understanding of the poverty problem also requires discussion of the causes of poverty and the various groups included among the poor. This will focus attention on the problems facing policy-makers. In his *The Affluent Society,* Galbraith makes a useful distinction between case poverty and insular poverty.[7] Case poverty relates to the personal qualities or characteristics of the affected persons. Given our present socioeconomic system, some persons and families have been unable to participate satisfactorily in the nation's general prosperity because of such limiting factors as old age, inadequate education or illiteracy, lack of needed job skills, poor health, inadequate motivation, and racial discrimination, regardless of where they live—rural and small town areas, urban areas, or metropolitan areas.

Insular poverty appears in what are called "pockets of poverty" or depressed areas, as in West Virginia, much of the rest of Appalachia, and many parts of rural America.[8] Such areas are characterized by higher and more persistent rates of unemployment and underemployment and larger proportions of low income persons than in the country as a whole. The *proximate* cause of this condition is the lack of adequate employment opportunities for the current population. Some of the people in these areas will also suffer from lack of education, poor health, inadequate job skills, etc., because the two types of poverty are not mutually exclusive. The lack of job opportunities, in turn, may be the product of a number of factors, including technological change, depletion of national resources, shifts in consumer demand, and the movement of industries to other areas.[9]

Both insular and case poverty are usually viewed as "structural" in nature, resulting from individual shortcomings and from temporary or limited imperfections in the economic system. They differ from the "mass poverty" of the 1930's, which was a product of general economic decline and which was markedly reduced by the revival of the economy in the early 1940's. Poverty of the structural sort does not automatically disappear as the economy expands and general affluence increases.

A close relationship exists between unemployment, low wages, and poverty. Many of the poor are unemployed or are completely outside of the labor force. But poverty is also the result of underemployment and employment at low wages, as in the cases of migratory workers and unskilled domestic workers. Thus a Department of Labor study on the employment status of families with incomes below $3,000 in 1963 reported that 30 percent of the poor families were headed by persons who held jobs throughout the year. Another 14 percent were headed by persons who worked at fulltime jobs for part of the year but who were never counted as unemployed because they moved into or out of the labor force. The heads of 16 percent of the families experienced unemployment. Finally, 39 percent of the families were headed by persons who were completely outside the labor force in 1963. Included in this last category are many aged or retired workers, the disabled, the dispirited, and women with child-rearing responsibilities. While most of the persons in the first three categories listed would benefit from economic growth and increased job opportunities, most of those in the last category would not because they are largely outside of the productive economy.

Although poverty exists in all regions of the country, in both rural and urban areas, and among all elements of the population, its incidence is heaviest among the following: nonwhites (Negroes, Puerto Ricans, and Mexican-Americans); the aged; families headed by females; families without a breadwinner; the unemployed; families headed by farmers and unskilled laborers; families headed by very young persons or persons with less than an eighth-grade education; very large families; and unrelated individuals living alone.[10] As this listing and the previous discussion should indicate, the problems of poverty and unemployment are multiple rather than monolithic in nature. Consequently there must be a variety of policy responses, geared to particular forms of causation and need, if these problems are to be dealt with effectively.

II

There are a number of general strategies which the government may use in dealing with the problems of poverty and unemployment. The major ones are discussed in this section.

Aggregationist strategy. Involving the use of broad fiscal and monetary policies to maintain a high level of economic growth and employment, this strategy is based on the assumption that much unemployment and poverty are the product of inadequate demand for labor and insufficient employment opportunities. According to the Council of Economic Advisers:

The maintenance of high employment—a labor market in which the demand for workers is strong relative to the supply—is a powerful force for the reduction of poverty. In a strong labor market there are new and better opportunities for the unemployed, the partially employed, and the low paid. Employers have greater incentive to seek and to train workers when their own markets are large and growing. . . To fight poverty in a slack economy with excess employment is to tie one hand behind our backs.[11]

The national government is generally committed to the aggregationist strategy by the Employment Act of 1946, which pledges the government to use its various programs and policies to maintain "maximum employment, production, and purchasing power." The 1964 cut in the income tax rates and the 1965 excise tax reduction both were in line with the aggregationist strategy.

Alleviative strategy. This is the oldest strategy for aiding the poor and the unemployed. Emphasis here is on relieving or easing the hardships and misery associated with poverty and unemployment by providing financial or material aid to the distressed on either a short-term or long-term basis. Alleviative programs have become more numerous and more generous in recent decades as the views that poverty and unemployment are often neither individually caused nor controllable and that public aid is necessary to protect the dignity of the individual have gained increased acceptance. Programs which are primarily alleviative include unemployment compensation, public assistance, medicare, general relief, and work relief. All involve some sort of "transfer payment."

Curative strategy. In contrast to the alleviative strategy, the curative strategy stresses efforts to help the poor and unemployed become self-supporting and more capable of earning adequate incomes by bringing about changes in either the individuals themselves or in their environment. This strategy is expressed in the slogan "Rehabilitation not relief" and to use President Johnson's somewhat inelegant terminology, the desire "to make taxpayers out of taxeaters." Programs in accord with the curative approach include area and regional development, work training, vocational education, job experience and literacy training, and much of the community action program under the Economic Opportunity Act. Curative programs are largely a development of the past decade.

Equal opportunity strategy. The focus here is on eliminating discrimination against Negroes, Indians, Mexican-Americans, and Puerto Ricans and providing them with equal educational and employment opportunities. Almost half of all nonwhite Americans are poor, and discrimination—in employment, wages, education, housing—is an important cause of poverty here.[12] Negroes, for example, are often hired last, paid less, and fired first. Illustrative of this strategy is the Civil Rights Act of 1964, which bans discrimination on the basis of race, color, religion, national origin or sex by many employers and labor unions. The Act also prohibits discrimination under any program or activity—in education, welfare, manpower training, etc.—receiving federal financial assistance. The civil rights movement, by broadening its concern to economic as well as political discrimination, has stimulated increased use of this strategy.

It is now generally agreed that the aggregationist strategy alone is inadequate to eliminate poverty and unemployment. It is, however, a necessary condition for their elimination; and the other antipoverty strategies, to be most effective, presuppose a high level of employment. But even if increased job opportunities are available many will not be able to take advantage of them because of inadequate job skills, low education, old age, discrimination, geographical location, and the like. Curative and equal opportunity programs should help many of these to become self-supporting or to enlarge their incomes. But others will still be unable to provide for themselves—such as many of the aged and females with large families—and here alleviative programs come in. In short, the various strategies set forth are interdependent; and the national government is currently utilizing all of them in the war on poverty.

The strategies under consideration here can obviously be implemented by a variety of means or tactics, which can usefully be divided into economic and welfare categories.[13] Economic programs are tied into the regular economic system and either make previous employment a requirement for eligibility for benefits or they relate benefits to the economic value of the work done by the recipients. Illustrative of economic programs are unemployment compensation, public works, area and regional development, and most job training programs. Welfare programs provide benefits not directly related to previous employment or value of work done. When a means test is used to determine eligibility for benefits they are often designated as relief programs. The Job Corps is somewhere in between welfare and relief—no means test is used (in a strict sense) but the cost of providing jobs considerably exceeds the value of the work done. Examples of welfare programs include old age assistance, aid to families with dependent children, literacy training and work experience programs, and general relief.

The selection and use of antipoverty instruments are affected by existing policy objectives and traditional national values and beliefs. Our society has customarily preferred the use of economic programs over welfare programs as the former are generally in accord with beliefs and values relating to individualism, self-reliance, and personal dignity. Conversely, welfare-type programs, especially those of the relief sort, are often stigmatized as "doles," "handouts," and, less harshly, charity. Programs of cash subsidies to the poor, such as the negative income tax[14] and the Guaranteed Annual Income,[15] run counter to our ideas about the relation of work and income and thus far have had little support. Only recently has there been a great deal of pressure for major increases in benefits under such programs as old age assistance and Old Age, Survivors and Disability Insurance, which would do much to eliminate poverty.

To the extent that antipoverty programs appear to strengthen or expand the economy, the likelihood of favorable attitudes toward them is increased. Education and training programs gain considerable support as "investments in human capital" designed to increase opportunity for the poor and help assimilate them into the "mainstream" of American economic life. Programs which appear to encourage economic growth are also apt to gain favor while those that seem to reduce the incentive to work can be expected to encounter substantial resistance.

III

In this section some of the curative legislation enacted in the war on poverty will be surveyed in roughly chronological order to convey a notion of its evolution. The discussion will illustrate the multifaceted nature of the war on poverty and the essentially pragmatic approach followed in waging the war. Some particular political problems and controversies will be noted, although discussion of the "macro-politics" of poverty is reserved for the next section.[16]

Aid to Depressed Areas

Efforts to provide national aid to localities affected by chronic and heavy unemployment began in 1955 at the instigation of Senator Paul Douglas (Dem., Ill.).[17] Bills providing aid programs for such areas were passed by the Democratic-controlled Congress in 1958 and 1960 but both were vetoed by President Eisenhower, partly because he believed they involved too much national participation in local affairs and authorized larger expenditures than were necessary. Aid to depressed areas became a major issue in the 1960 Presidential campaign and President Kennedy took office pledged to assist such areas.

As adopted, the Area Redevelopment Act of 1961 established a four-year program of assistance for depressed areas—those in which the unemployment rate was above average and persistent—under the supervision of an Area Redevelopment Administration located in the

Department of Commerce. The broad objective of the Act was to reduce unemployment by encouraging the formation of new businesses or the expansion of existing businesses in depressed areas, thereby increasing the available number of jobs (i.e., by bringing jobs to the workers). To this end, the Area Redevelopment Administration was empowered to provide: long-term loans at low interest to attract or expand businesses in depressed areas; loans and grants to local governments for public facilities needed to attract businesses; technical assistance to help communities formulate economic development programs; and worker retraining programs. A total expenditure of $394 million over a four year period was authorized. The Act essentially followed a "trickle-down" approach to poverty and unemployment, with most of the direct benefits going to businesses and not to unemployed workers.

From its inception the ARA led a rather hectic life and was a continual center of controversy. Contributing to its difficulties were administrative problems, e.g., many of its activities required cooperation from other government agencies; Congressional impatience for results; dissatisfaction with some of the ARA projects, such as a $1.8 million loan to help construct a motor hotel in Detroit; Republican charges that the program was used in 1962 as a "pork barrel" to help re-elect Democrats; and continued opposition by business groups, such as the Chamber of Commerce, who believed the program was unneeded.[18] A Presidential request for continuation and expansion of the ARA program was rejected by the House in 1963 after favorable Senate action. The extension bill was not brought to a vote in 1964 because the Administration feared unfavorable House action and, consequently, the Area Redevelopment Act expired in July, 1965.

In the spring of 1965 President Johnson requested the Congress to replace the ARA with an expanded and broadened federal depressed areas program. According to the President individual counties and communities often were not capable of economic growth. Therefore, a broader areal approach to economic development than the locality-oriented aid policy of the ARA was necessary.

The Economic Development Act, passed by Congress in August, 1965, provides for a five-year, $3.25 billion program of grants and loans for public works, development facilities, technical assistance, and other activities intended to help economically depressed areas and to stimulate planning by them for economic development. Most of these funds are slated for public works projects, such as water systems, waste treatment plants, industrial streets and roads, airports, and other facilities which would directly or indirectly improve employment opportunities in depressed areas or, in the words of the Act, "primarily benefit the long-term unemployed and members of low-income families or otherwise substantially further the objectives of the Economic Opportunity Act of 1964. . . ." The Economic Development Act also provides for the creation of multi-county and multi-state development areas and districts designed to broaden the scope and the effectiveness of developmental activity. Another part of the law authorizes the establishment of multi-state regional planning commissions, similar to the Appalachian Regional Commission, to plan for the economic development of other regions of the country.

The Economic Development Act is really an amalgamation of features of three previous pieces of legislation: The Area Redevelopment Act, the Accelerated Public Works Act of 1962, and the Appalachian Regional Development Act of 1965. Since it is not mentioned elsewhere, a comment on the 1962 Act is in order here. This Act, which was extremely popular with Congressmen and local public officials (one Washington official termed it an "instantaneous success"), authorized a one-year appropriation of $900 million for public works projects to stimulate employment in depressed areas. Most of this money ($850 million) was actually appropriated, with the federal government paying up to 75 percent of the cost of many local public works projects.

Whether the Economic Development program will be more effective than the Area Redevelopment Act is a matter for future determination. However, it does have a new name and a new administrative agency (the Economic Development Administration), greater funds, and a broader policy orientation.

Manpower Development

Another curative approach to the problem of poverty and unemployment is illustrated by the Manpower Training and Development Act of 1962. This legislation attempts to attack poverty and unemployment wherever they may exist, in depressed areas or elsewhere, by helping workers who are unemployed or under-employed to acquire new job skills or to improve and update their existing skills. The 1962 statute, as amended, authorizes a program of loans and grants for worker training programs operated by state agencies and private institutions and for on-the-job training programs conducted by employers, state agencies, labor unions, and other groups. Subsistence payments are made to many workers while they are undergoing training. Basic literacy training may be provided for workers who need it in order to benefit from vocational training.

Although the MTDA program originally was scheduled to expire in 1965, it has proven to be quite popular with both parties in Congress. Legislation expanding and extending the programs was enacted in 1963 and again in 1965, with the 1965 legislation passing by votes of 76–9 in the Senate and 392–0 in the House.[19] The manpower training program has enjoyed general support from both business and labor groups although the Chamber of Commerce has suggested, but less than vigorously, that the matter should be left to the states. Liberals and conservatives alike prefer for people to support themselves and not be dependent on public funds. Both have shown considerable interest in retraining programs.

Two facets of the manpower training program merit mention here because of their political interest. Under the terms of the original Manpower Development and Training Act, after two years most of the training programs were to be financed by the national and state governments on a fifty-fifty basis. The states, however, showed a considerable lack of enthusiasm for this eventuality. During the first year of the program all of the states except Louisiana undertook training activities but only four states authorized the matching of funds. A survey of state directors of vocational education by the U. S. Office of Education revealed that directors in eighteen states felt that their states would not participate unless the 100 percent federal financing was continued after June, 1964. Another thirteen directors expressed "serious doubts" about participation on a matching basis by their states while only eight directors said there was "reasonable certainty" that their state would participate on a matching basis.[20] The subsequent amendments to the Act continued full federal financing through June, 1966. After that time the *local* governments involved in training programs will be required to pay 10 percent of in-school training costs. (This can be in kind, as in making buildings and equipment available.) The new matching requirement would not appear to be a serious impediment to state-local participation. The whole chain of events lends support to the contention that effective antipoverty activity requires national action.

Second, although manpower training has received general support, there has been opposition to particular aspects of the program, including the relocation of retrained workers. Provisions permitting partial payment of the costs of worker relocation were deleted from the 1962 legislation and the earlier Area Redevelopment Act, while the 1963 MTDA amendments permitted only some experimental relocation projects. The opposition in Congress to subsidized relocation of workers has been bipartisan and has come from both liberals and conservatives. Spokesmen from depressed areas have feared loss of population (and voters) and wastage of community resources. Sentiment and the belief people should have a right to live wherever they want have also been factors. Thus Senator Dirksen contended, in opposing aid for relocation, that just "as the Indians were reluctant to leave the graves of their ancestors . . . and rather than leave [their ancestral lands] were willing to fight it out," so later Americans were reluctant to move from their homes.[21]

The Economic Opportunity Act of 1964

This is an omnibus piece of legislation which seeks to deal directly with poverty, with both the causes and symptoms of poverty. Its various sections provide for programs geared to the needs and situations of different groups in the population. Much stress is placed on local initiative and leadership and voluntary participation, on giving "new opportunities to those who want to help themselves or their communities."[22]

A primary focus of the Economic Opportunity Act is on youth and breaking the "cycle of poverty," whereby poverty in one generation of a family often begets poverty in the next generation and so on. To realize this goal a number of programs are created, especially for youth between the ages of 16 and 21. First, the Job Corps is designed to provide education, vocational training, and work experience in rural conservation camps and residential training centers to increase the employability of youth and prepare them for "responsible citizenship." Second, under the Neighborhood Youth Corps program vocational training and work experience (and income) are provided for youth while living at home. Third, the work-study program helps students from low-income families remain in college by giving them financial assistance in the form of part-time employment. Only the first of these programs is handled solely by the national government. The latter two involve state or local initiative with the Office of Economic Opportunity, which administers the statute, paying up to 90 percent of the cost.

Another major section of the Economic Opportunity Act authorizes federal financial assistance for "grass roots" community action programs carried on by public or private nonprofit agencies. This program is intended to encourage the development of comprehensive and coordinated community efforts to help the poor become self-sufficient. Projects in these local antipoverty programs may include literacy training, health services, homemaker services, legal aid for the poor, or early childhood development activities. In the last category is Project Head Start, designed to provide "cultural enrichment" for preschool poor children. (It is now a permanent feature of the war on poverty because, President Johnson has stated, it has been "battle-tested" and "proven worthy.") Up to 90 percent of the cost of community action programs is paid by the national government.

Other antipoverty activities authorized by the 1964 law include: grants and loans to low income rural families to help them enlarge their income-earning capacity; loans to small businessmen, especially as these may contribute to work-training and job opportunities for low income persons; financial assistance to the states for special adult literacy programs; grants, loans, and loan guarantees to assist state and local governments in aiding migratory farm workers, grants to encourage the states to set up programs to help unemployed fathers and other members of needy families with children gain work experience and job training. The statute also established a domestic service corps—Volunteers in Service to America, or VISTA—to recruit and train workers for service in state and local antipoverty projects, slum areas, Indian reservations, hospitals, and the like.

The Economic Opportunity Act thus provides a quite varied, and highly experimental, set of techniques for combating poverty. Whether they represent the best set of means, or even an adequate set, for eliminating poverty is an open question. The Act, however, does represent a distinct departure from previous legislation, which can be regarded as both more conservative and less direct in its thrust (*e.g.,* ARA and the "trickle-down" approach, MTDA and the focus on training and unemployment). This, plus the vigor with which it has been implemented, explains why the 1964 law has generated considerably more political controversy than its predecessors. Conflict has developed over such matters as the location of Job Corps camps; the rate of pay for Neighborhood Youth Corps workers; the role of the poor in community action programs; the question of who should control local antipoverty programs; and the use of the governors' power to veto community action and Job Corps projects in their states.[23] A program as comprehensive as that of EOA is bound to challenge a variety of particular interests.

The Regional Approach: Appalachia and Beyond

The Appalachian Regional Development Act of 1965 manifests yet another curative approach to the poverty problem—the use of federal funds to promote the social and economic uplift of an entire geographical region and its inhabitants. The name Appalachia denotes an eleven state region centered around the Appalachian Mountains, extending from northern Pennsylvania to mid-Alabama, and including all of West Virginia and part of Pennsylvania, Ohio, Maryland, Kentucky, Tennessee, North Carolina, South Carolina, Georgia, and Alabama. The region has been described as a "victim of both geography and automation, [lagging] . . . behind the nation as a whole in employment, education, health facilities, housing, and virtually every other yardstick used to measure a healthy economy."[24] It is generally conceded to be the largest economically depressed area in the nation, although it does contain such "pockets of prosperity" as Charleston, West Virginia.

The Appalachian Act authorizes the expenditure of $1.1 billion in federal funds to encourage the economic development of the region. Around four-fifths of these funds will be used over a five year period for the construction of major regional development highways and local access roads. The national government will pay up to 70 percent of a project's cost with the remainder coming from the states involved. The emphasis on roadbuilding resulted from the facts that adequate highways are lacking in many parts of the region and that the governors, senators, and congressmen in the Appalachian states wanted roads to be given priority. Better road systems were believed necessary to open up the region and to stimulate new traffic.

The remainder of the funds provided by the Act are, it should be noted, for a two year period. They will go for such purposes as health facilities, vocational schools, land improvement programs, reclamation of mining areas, and the development of timber and water resources. A program for pastureland improvement was dropped from the Act because of the opposition of western cattle interests.

The various programs under the Appalachian Act will be carried out by the appropriate national and state agencies, such as the Bureau of Public Roads and the state highway departments. The entire program, however, is supervised and coordinated by the Appalachian Regional Commission, which is comprised of the governor from each state in the region (or a representative selected by him) and a federal representative chosen by the President. Subject to a veto by the federal representative, specific projects are initiated by the states and undertaken with the approval of a majority of the state members on the Commission. This arrangement, it is hoped, will result in greater local participation and in better adaptation of the program to local conditions.[25]

The Appalachia program is geared to the economic needs of the region, not to particular localities, and is intended to increase economic growth and employment opportunities in the region as a whole. The funds expended will not go directly to needy people nor, necessarily, to the most depressed towns and counties. There is no "means test," such as a level of unemployment, to determine eligibility for aid as in the Area Redevelopment Act and the Economic Development Act. The focus is on those areas and communities within the region which have the most potential for economic growth, thus substituting a region-wide approach for the "scattershot" approach manifested in other programs, such as the ARA. As John L. Sweeney, federal co-chairman of the Appalachian Regional Commission, has stated: "Most programs of economic help in the past have been based on the theory that a man has a right to a job where he lives and that government should bring him that job. The Appalachia approach is that a man has a right to a job, but it is reasonable to expect him to be willing to commute to it or move to it if necessary." [26] This new theory is made manifest by the emphasis on road-building and assistance to "economic growth centers."

The Appalachia program, in short, stresses economic development and is a long range program whose impact on poverty will be largely indirect. It is not "people centered," as one ARC official put it, in contrast to the Office of Economic Opportunity which "concentrates on helping people, through training education, and the like, to live a middle-class existence." [27] It will probably be a decade or more before the "real results" of the Appalachia program are apparent.

One immediate "by-product" should be remarked here, however. The Appalachia program stirred the interest of congressmen from other areas in regional programs. To get them to support the Appalachia plan the administration agreed to consider regional development programs for other parts of the country. Consequently, Title V of the Economic Development Act authorizes the establishment of "regional action planning commissions." More specifically, the Secretary of Commerce, with the approval of the states involved, can create economic development regions in areas which have "lagged behind the whole nation in economic development." Each such region will have a federal-state commission which will develop recommendations for new programs of economic development. A number of new regions have been proposed, including the Ozarks, the New England States, the Upper Great Lakes area, and the Great Plains. [28]

Although the new regional approach to economic development is still in the experimental and planning stage, it has proved to have considerable political appeal. What impact it will have on the impoverished is uncertain at this point. It should be borne in mind, however, that while economic growth and prosperity are necessary conditions for an effective war on poverty, by themselves they may have little direct impact in reducing poverty.

IV

This section will deal with two aspects of the macropolitics of poverty. First, why is there now so much concern about poverty? Poverty has been around for a long time without arousing such involvement as we now witness. For example, little attention apparently was paid to Henry George when he wrote about *Progress and Poverty* in the late nineteenth century. Why, then, in an era of general prosperity and a time when poverty is considerably down from past levels, has the world's wealthiest nation chosen to launch a "war on poverty?" Why has poverty become a political issue of major national concern?

Second, beyond the concern about poverty, how can one explain the enactment of this substantial body of antipoverty legislation? What are some of the operative factors? Here we are confronted with an apparent paradox. The poor themselves, as Michael Harrington has contended, lack political power:

the poor are politically invisible. It is one of the cruelest ironies of social life in advanced countries that the dispossessed at the bottom of society are unable to speak for themselves. The people of the other America do not, by far and large, belong to unions, to fraternal organizations, or to political parties. They are without lobbies of their own; they put forward no legislative program. As a group, they are atomized. They have no face; they have no voice.[29]

In a political system in which action is often a response to strong organized demands by those affected, how does one account for the antipoverty legislation enacted?

Why has poverty become a major political issue? Several factors can be mentioned. First, both Presidents Kennedy and Johnson have used the presidency to inform the population of the existence of poverty in prosperity, the evils of poverty, and the need for governmental action to eliminate it. Motivated at least partly by the desire to be recognized as great presidents, which requires important accomplishments, they identified poverty as a major subject for national action. Second, the writings of various scholars and publicists have helped focus attention on poverty and inform people about its causes and consequences. The books by Galbraith, Harrington, Caudill, and Myrdal come readily to mind.[30] Third, the "race problem" and the civil rights movement have also been contributory. The incidence of poverty is much higher among nonwhite than white groups and, in many large cities, a majority of those seeking public assistance are Negro. The Negro leadership is focusing attention on the poor and the civil rights movement is demonstrating much concern for jobs as well as legal rights. Herman P. Miller makes the point:

The rural poor, the aged poor, and even the poor hillbillies in Appalachia and the Ozarks could not arouse the nation to their urgent needs. They continued to suffer indignities of body, mind, and spirit year after year in quiet desperation while they lived in hovels and their children were poorly educated. Action came only recently. It followed a prolonged period of marches, sit-ins, and other forms of protest by the Negro community. There is no reason to believe that the war on poverty and these protest activities are unrelated.[31]

Fourth, the belief that poverty is a significant cause of crime and delinquency and growing concern about mounting welfare expenditures are also worth mention. In his opening statement on the Economic Opportunity Act, Representative Landrum (Dem., Ga.), who served as its floor manager in the House, advocated its enactment partly as a means of lowering welfare costs and of reducing crime and delinquency.[32] Fifth, the paradox of poverty in the midst of affluence is both ugly and disturbing to many who are not poor, while many of the poor are less than quiescent in their poorness. An attitudinal change has occurred. As one commentator states:

A revolution of expectations has taken place in this country as well as abroad. There is now a conviction that everyone has the right to share in the good things of life. . . .The legacy of poverty awaiting many of our children is the same as that handed down to their parents, but in a time when the boon of prosperity is more general then the taste of poverty is more bitter.[33]

Finally, many people have become convinced that the problem of poverty requires political action for its solution, the play of automatic economic processes being viewed as insufficient. Moreover, success in the war on poverty is perceived as quite probable by many persons.

Success, or the good prospect thereof, in dealing with a problem is often highly productive of both concern and action on the part of reformers. Also contributory may be the apparent fact that many Americans are presently more "cause-minded" than they were a decade ago.

To turn now to our second question, in contrast to most important economic legislation, the various antipoverty acts discussed in the preceding section did not originate in the demands of strong, organized interest groups. Rather, these programs have been developed largely within the executive branch and Congress. (The principal exception is the Appalachia Act, which grew out of efforts by the region's governors to solve common problems.) Thus, the Area Redevelopment Act, was started on its way by Senator Paul Douglas and was a product of the interest in depressed areas which he developed while campaigning for re-election in Southern Illinois. Again, it is said that the idea for the Economic Opportunity Act originated with Robert Lampman, then associated with the Council of Economic Advisers. The idea was taken up and promoted by Walter Heller, Chairman of the CEA, partly as a way of doing something directly for the poor and partly as a way of stimulating the economy through spending. Given tentative approval by President Kennedy just prior to his assassination, the proposal was quickly and strongly accepted by President Johnson within a few days after his accession to the presidency.[34]

Organized group support and opposition to proposals for antipoverty legislation have formed after their development. A wide variety of labor, liberal, welfare, civil rights, civic, and professional organizations have supported the various antipoverty laws. Among the groups supporting the Economic Opportunity Act were the AFL-CIO, National Grange, National Farmers Union, National Urban League, National Council of Churches, National Education Association, General Federation of Women's Clubs, American Friends Service Committee, and the National Association of Counties. The group support for antipoverty legislation is somewhat generalized in nature, lacking the intensity which characterizes, say, the AFL-CIO's support of legislation to repeal the right-to-work laws and the National Right To Work Committee's opposition to repeal. Although the broad group support would seem to make legislative and executive support of such legislation "good politics," it does not appear to be a really compelling force.

Opposition to the antipoverty programs has come primarily from the Chamber of Commerce, the National Association of Manufacturers, and the American Farm Bureau Federation. (Some right-wing ideological groups are also in opposition.) These three groups have not been vigorously opposed to such legislation as it does not significantly impinge on their interests. It does run counter to the conservative ideology they espouse and they oppose it as unnecessary, or as improperly and hastily prepared, or as not really a proper activity for the national government. Then, too, the position of the opponents has been weakened by the fact that one appears to be in favor of poverty when he opposes legislation put forward as necessary to eliminate it.

The contention here is that, given a climate of opinion favorable to antipoverty action and generalized favorable group support, a political situation emerged in which Presidential action has been a (if not *the*) crucial factor in securing antipoverty legislation. Presidents Kennedy and Johnson have been strong supporters of antipoverty legislation and this, within the context of a "permissive" political environment, appears to have been the determining factor. It seems quite doubtful, for example, that either the Economic Opportunity Act or the Appalachian Regional Development Act would have been passed without President Johnson's strong endorsement and support. Conversely, area redevelopment legislation was not enacted during President Eisenhower's administration because of his opposition in the form of vetoes.

Most of the major antipoverty legislation has come during the Johnson administration. While Johnson has been a vigorous and skillful legislative leader, he appears to have benefited initially from the favorable climate of opinion and congressional cooperation resulting from the Kennedy assassination. Following his sweeping victory in the 1964 presidential selection, he regarded himself as having a clear mandate to implement his proposals for the "Great Society," which include the elimination of poverty. Moreover, the 1964 Goldwater debacle served to emasculate the opposition to Johnson's program within Congress and apparently to demoralize it elsewhere. These broad developments have obviously favored the antipoverty campaign.

Within Congress the various antipoverty bills have been passed by substantial majorities, especially in the Senate. The one exception is the House defeat for the ARA in 1963. This appears to have been caused by such factors as poor leadership and the loss of some southern votes because of the reaction to President Kennedy's 1963 civil rights proposals. Northern Democrats have been almost unanimous in their support of the various statutes, with somewhere between half and two-thirds of the Southern Democrats also in favor. A scattering of Republicans from Eastern and urban states have been among the supporters. In opposition have been two-thirds or more of the Republicans, a third to a half of the Southern Democrats, and an occasional Northern Democrat. However, large majorities of both parties have supported manpower training and vocational education legislation. The vote on the Vocational Education Act was 378 to 21 in the House and 80 to 4 in the Senate.

What has caused the broad pressure group and Congressional support for antipoverty legislation? Material or economic interests are certainly one factor affecting group and Congressional action here, but they are clearly not the only factor. Most of the members of Congress voting for the Appalachia Act did not come from states and districts directly benefiting from it and, it can be added, some who came from such states and districts voted against the Act. While some were perhaps swayed into support by the promise of regional programs of their own, these were few in number.[35]

Party affiliation and ideological orientation have undoubtedly been vital in shaping the positions of many persons. The large proportion of Congressional Democrats voting for the legislation is what one would expect because of the party's general orientation in favor of liberal-labor legislation. Further the supporters of antipoverty legislation articulate, and presumably are influenced by, a liberal ideology of action which combines humanitarianism and practical economic considerations with a belief in the need for national action. Antipoverty legislation is generally advocated as necessary to alleviate and prevent misery and to improve the economic opportunities and quality of life of the poor. At the same time, it is frequently advanced as a way of aiding economic growth and reducing welfare costs. This thought-pattern is illustrated by the following statement: "We pay twice for poverty; once in the production lost in wasted human potential, and again in the resources devoted to coping with poverty's social by-products. Humanity compels our action, but it is sound economics as well."[36]

The opposition to antipoverty legislation also can be explained in a variety of ways: material interests; southern concern about segregation; partisan politics; and ideology. Much of the opposition has been within the framework of a conservative political-economic philosophy which includes hostility toward big government and national action (which are often treated as synonyms), a preference for localized solutions to economic problems, and considerable faith in the operation of the market place.

In short, the argument here is that the enactment of antipoverty legislation can not be satisfactorily explained in terms of pressure group politics and material interests. These have had greater impact on the details of legislation than on its broad outline and final adoption. A favorable climate of opinion, strong executive support, party affiliation, and ideology are more useful variables in accounting for the war on poverty programs.

V

Whether the various antipoverty programs established to date will eliminate poverty is problematical. So indeed is the question whether poverty can ever be entirely eliminated. Taken together, however, the various measures are a decisive rejection of economic Darwinism and indifference regarding poverty and a strong commitment to positive action. This seems likely to continue for the next few years because there appears to be no room for poverty in President Johnson's vision of the Great Society, although financial pressures generated by the war in Vietnam could lead to some reduction in effort.

The various antipoverty measures also represent a practical and experimental approach to the problem of poverty. A variety of strategies and tactics are currently being employed. Whether one considers the total effort too great or too small, it certainly can not be characterized as doctrinaire. While the search for a national antipoverty policy is still underway, some of its general features are beginning to emerge: continuing encouragement of general economic growth and prosperity; greater attention on curative approaches, with alleviative activity reserved for such groups as the aged and the unemployable; and the maintenance of the equal employment opportunities.

In contrast to the welfare programs established by the Social Security Act of 1935, which seek to provide the individual with a floor of security in the form of minimal maintenance, the main thrust of the current antipoverty campaign is to increase the economic opportunities open to the poor and their abilities to maintain themselves. To this end efforts are being made both to increase the number of available jobs in the economy and to equip the poor through education, job training, work experience, and the like, to secure jobs or better paying jobs.

But if the antipoverty programs represent a departure in strategy and technique from the New Deal approach to welfare and poverty, they are nonetheless essentially based on the "traditional" view of poverty—that is, poverty is individual and peripheral in nature and is not, therefore, the consequence of major structural weaknesses in the American socio-economic system. Consequently, the antipoverty programs do not generally involve major institutional change (at least in the short run) and no vested interests have been sharply threatened or disturbed by them. Groups whose interest are divergent in other areas—labor policy, taxation—have found it relatively easy to unite in general support of antipoverty programs. Viewed from the perspective of institutional change, the antipoverty legislation has been essentially conservative in orientation, which has undoubtedly eased its enactment.

NOTES

1.   Important statistical examinations of poverty include: Robert J. Lampman, *The Low Income Population and Economic Growth,* Study Paper No. 12, prepared for the Joint Economic Committee, 86th Cong., 1st Sess., 1959; Conference on Economic Progress, *Poverty and Deprivation in the U. S.* (Washington: Conference on Economic Progress, 1962); Michael Harrington, *The Other America* (New York: The Macmillan Company, 1963), pp. 187–203; Herman P. Miller, *Rich Man, Poor Man* (New York: Thomas Y. Crowell Company, 1964); Council of Economic Advisers, *Annual Report, 1964* (Washington: Government Printing Office, 1964), pp. 55–84; Mollie Orshan-

sky, "Counting the Poor: Another Look at the Poverty Profile," *Social Security Bulletin,* XXVIII (January, 1965), pp. 3–29; and James N. Morgan, *et al., Income and Welfare in the United States* (New York: McGraw-Hill Book Company, 1962).

2.   Rose D. Friedman, *Poverty: Definition and Perspective* (Washington: American Enterprise Institute, 1965).

3.   Conference on Economic Progress, *op. cit.,* pp. 19–23.

4.   Orshansky, *op. cit.* See also the discussion by Herman P. Miller, "Changes in the Number and Composition of the Poor," in Margaret S. Gordon, ed., *Poverty in America* (San Francisco: Chandler Publishing Company, 1965), pp. 81–101.

5.   *Annual Report, 1964, op. cit.*

6.   Herman P. Miller, "Statistics and Reality," *The New Leader,* XLVII (March 30, 1964), p. 18. (His emphasis).

7.   John Kenneth Galbraith, *The Affluent Society* (Boston: Houghton Mifflin Company, 1958), ch. 23.

8.   For examples of the latter, see *Incomes of Rural Families in Northeast Texas,* Bulletin 940 (College Station, Texas: Texas Agricultural Experiment Station, 1959); and *Incomes, Resources, and Adjustment Potential of Rural Families in the Clay-Hills Area of Mississippi,* AEc. M. R. No. 29 (State College, Mississippi: Mississippi Agricultural Experiment Station, 1960).

9.   Sidney C. Sufrin and Marion A. Buck, *What Price Progress?: A Study in Chronic Unemployment* (Chicago: Rand McNally and Co., 1965), esp. chs. 1, 2.

10. See Oscar Ornati, *Poverty Amid Affluence* (New York: The Twentieth Century Fund, 1966), *passim.*

11. *Annual Report, 1964, op. cit.,* pp. 73–74. Cf. Hyman P. Minsky, "The Role of Employment Policy," in Gordon, *op. cit.,* pp. 175–200.

12. See *e.g.,* Alan Batchelder, "Poverty: The Special Case of the Negro," *American Economic Review,* LV (May, 1965), pp. 530–540.

13. Joseph M. Becker, William Haber, and Sar A. Levitan, *Programs to Aid the Unemployed in the 1960's* (Kalamazoo, Mich.: The W. E. Upjohn Institute for Employment Research, 1965), pp. 4–8.

14. Under the negative income tax proposal, grants would be paid to poor families whose incomes were too low to permit them to take full advantage of the exemptions and deductions to which they are entitled under existing tax

laws. See Robert J. Lampman, "Approaches To the Reduction of Poverty," *American Economic Review,* LV (May, 1965), pp. 526–527.

15. Michael D. Reagan, "For a Guaranteed Income," *The New York Times Magazine,* June 7, 1964, pp. 20 ff. A group of publicists, economists, and educators, calling itself the Ad Hoc Committee on the Triple Revolution, has proposed that every family be guaranteed an income of $3,000 a year.

16. On the concept of macropolitics, see Emmette S. Redford, *American Government and the Economy* (New York: The Macmillan Company, 1965), pp. 58–60.

17. Roger H. Davidson, *The Depressed Areas Controversy: A Study in the Politics of American Business* (New York: Columbia University, unpublished doctoral dissertation, 1963), provides an excellent account of the enactment of the Area Redevelopment Act.

18. Julius Duscha, "The Depressed Areas," *The Progressive,* XXVII (September, 1963), pp. 29–32; and Conley H. Dillon, *The Area Redevelopment Administration: New Patterns in Developmental Administration* (College Park: University of Maryland, Bureau of Governmental Research, 1964).

19. *Congressional Quarterly Almanac,* XXI (1965), pp. 810–815.

20. *Congressional Quarterly Almanac,* XIX (1963), p. 525.

21. Senate Committee on Banking and Currency, *Hearings on Area Redevelopment Act,* 86th Cong., 1st Sess., 1959, p. 63.

22. House Committee on Education and Labor, *Hearings on the Economic Opportunity Act of 1964,* 88th Cong., 2nd Sess., 1964, Vol. I, pp. 20–22.

23. "Shriver and the War on Poverty," *Newsweek,* LXVI (September 13, 1965), pp. 22–30; and William F. Haddad, "Mr. Shriver and the Savage Politics of Poverty," *Harper's,* CCXXXI (December, 1965), pp. 43–50, are especially useful. A running account of the political conflicts generated by the Economic Opportunity Act programs can be found in *The New York Times.*

24. Marjorie Hunter in *The New York Times,* February 7, 1965, p. E5.

25. Jerald ter Horst, "No More Pork Barrel: The Appalachia Approach," *The Reporter,* XXXII (March 11, 1965), pp. 27–29.

26. Quoted in *ibid.,* pp. 28–29.

27. Interview with the writer, September, 1965.

28. Cf. Don Oberdorfer, "The Proliferating Appalachias," *The Reporter,* XXXIII (September 9, 1965), pp. 22–27.

29. Michael Harrington, *The Other America: Poverty in the United States* (New York: The Macmillan Company, 1963), p. 14.

30. Galbraith, *The Affluent Society, op. cit.;* Harrington, *The Other America, op. cit.;* Harry Caudill, *Night Comes to the Cumberlands* (Boston: Little, Brown and Company, 1963); and Gunnar Myrdal, *Challenge to Affluence* (New York: Pantheon Books, Inc., 1963).

31. "Poverty and the Negro," in Leo Fishman, ed., *Poverty Amid Affluence* (New Haven: Yale University Press, 1966), p. 104. Cf. Nathan Glazer, "A Sociologist's View of Poverty," in Gordon, *op. cit.,* p. 20. Many of the Washington officials interviewed by me spontaneously mentioned the civil rights movement as a major cause of antipoverty action.

32. *Congressional Record,* CX, pp. 18208–18209 (August 5, 1964).

33. Orshansky, *op. cit.,* p. 3.

34. The comments on the Economic Opportunity Act are based on a report in *Newsweek, op. cit.,* and an interview with Sar A. Levitan.

35. Oberdorfer, *op. cit.,* p. 26.

36. Council of Economic Advisers, *Annual Report, 1964, p. 56.*

COMMUNITY ACTION:
POOR PEOPLE
AGAINST CITY HALL
John C. Donovan

With the exception of the youth programs in Title I, which borrow heavily from the Kennedy administration version of the Youth Employment Opportunities Act, it must be said that community action, as it appears in Title II of the Economic Opportunity Act, provides not only the largest single program in the Johnson antipoverty attack but also represents an innovation of surpassing importance. Title II also has a direct impact upon urban politics in this country and at its most sensitive points.

Perhaps it is not completely remarkable that community action moved so effortlessly through the first congressional round without stimulating either congressional curiosity or anxiety. Title II, when read casually, sounds pedestrian enough:

Section 202 (a)

The term "community action program" means a program—

(1) which mobilizes and utilizes resources, public or private, of any urban or rural, or combined urban and rural geographical area (referred to in this part as a "community"), including but not limited to a State, metropolitan area, county, city, town, multi-city unit, or multi-county unit in an attack on poverty;

(2) which provides services, assistance, and other activities of sufficient scope and size to give promise of progress toward elimination of poverty or a cause or causes of poverty through developing employment opportunities, improving human performance, motivation, and productivity, or bettering the conditions under which people live, learn and work;

(3) which is developed, conducted, and administered with the maximum feasible participation of residents of the areas and members of the groups served;

(4) which is conducted, administered, or coordinated by a public or private nonprofit agency (other than a political party), or a combination thereof. . . .

Reprinted by permission of the publisher from John C. Donovan, *The Politics of Poverty* (New York: Pegasus, 1967). pp. 39–40, 50–59. Footnotes have been deleted.

One develops a certain amount of sympathy for the men in Congress when he realizes that he has just read language which is loaded with political dynamite; Section 202 (a) (3) is the famous section which stipulates "maximum feasible participation" of the poor (although it does not read "the poor") and thereby stimulates a process of major social change. It all sounds innocuous enough when phrased by the legal draftsman. . . .

The fact that community action rapidly came to have some meaning in hundreds of communities is significant in itself. One point of view which emerged in the discussions during the formulation of the Economic Opportunity Act asserted that community action ought to be applied in a limited number of large cities. There was the experience of the Ford Foundation "gray areas" program to build upon and there were some sixteen communities in which the President's Committee on Juvenile Delinquency had already placed "seed money." This school of thought inclined to the view that it would be well to make a maximum effort in perhaps ten communities having the toughest problems.

Mr. Shriver, director of the new Office of Economic Opportunity, personally came to favor a broader attack through a national program which would begin just as rapidly as possible in hundreds of communities. The director was evidently supported in this by the White House; thus, community action as an administrative and political reality almost immediately became a national phenomenon. This high-level decision *not* to limit community action to a selected and limited list of communities profoundly affected the nature of the organization Mr. Shriver's Office of Economic Opportunity was to be. It also led to a certain amount of confusion concerning OEO's role in the poverty war.

OEO: Fish or Fowl?

In one sense, by placing the Office of Economic Opportunity in the Executive Office of the President and by appointing a man of national prominence as director, the Johnson administration appeared to be creating a White House-level coordinating agency with a mandate to pull together the efforts of all relevant agencies and departments in a combined federal attack on poverty. In another sense, since it was decided early in the game that OEO should be directly responsible for administering the community action program which was to affect hundreds of communities, urban and rural, large and small, across the country, Mr. Shriver actually was assuming responsibility for a major operating program. Thus, from the very beginning of the program, Mr. Shriver's new organization has been torn between the role of overall coordinator, which would seem to call for a relatively small, elite planning group (somewhat analagous to the Bureau of the Budget with its highly competent five hundred specialists), and that of an operating agency requiring a bureaucratic staff numbering in the several thousands.

In addition to the enormous responsibilities which community action (Title II) imposes, Mr. Shriver also made it clear from the very beginning that the Job Corps was to be administered directly out of his office. This again was a key decision with the greatest possible implications for the kind of administrative structure which the Office of Economic Opportunity was to become. The Job Corps was a major operating program—in some ways as complex and as difficult as community action—and yet it was to be administered from the level of the Executive Office of the President. OEO also immediately took responsibility for VISTA, a kind of domestic peace corps.

The fish or fowl dilemma has plagued OEO from that day forward. A White House agency may try coordinating the overlapping programs of executive departments and agencies. As soon as it undertakes operating programs of its own and comes into conflict with other operating programs, it will have to be coordinated by someone else, quite possibly the Bureau of the Budget.

Actually, Mr. Shriver's official life has been even more complicated than this brief summary suggests. The President, for reasons that have always been obscure, kept Mr. Shriver for many months as director of the Peace Corps as well as director of the inherently bifurcated OEO. In addition to this, various parts of the Economic Opportunity Act were negotiated away to the various operating departments—most notably the Department of Labor and the Department of Health, Education, and Welfare—for purposes of administration. Thus Title IB, which makes possible a national program of work-training for young people, was delegated immediately to the Secretary of Labor who established a Neighborhood Youth Corps as part of that department's new Manpower Administration. In terms of the number of youths served, the Neighborhood Youth Corps soon became the largest single youth program in the antipoverty program. Likewise Title IC, which provides for a work-study program for college students, was delegated a year later to the Office of Education for administrative purposes. Title V, which provides for a program of training for heads of households who have been on relief, was delegated immediately to the Department of Health, Education, and Welfare.

Two years after the program was launched, Mr. Shriver had to defend himself against charges that the antipoverty program was an "administrative shambles." His defense was that if it were an administrative shambles, he was proud to be in charge. A better defense would have been that if it were *not* an administrative shambles he and his associates in OEO had performed a modern miracle. To conceive a new multimillion-dollar national program which is to be administered in part by a White House-level coordinating agency and in part by operating departments, and which at the same time is to be coordinated by some new White House office which itself becomes part of the administrative overlap, is to postulate administrative chaos. Only a nation as gifted as we are in organizational talent would risk launching a promising new program in such a highly disadvantageous administrative setting.

Mr. Shriver also faced the problem which any new agency head faces of finding a competent staff, including high-powered associates, gifted enough to want to take on the administrative and political headaches of complex operating programs such as community action and the Job Corps. In this connection, the loss of Adam Yarmolinsky in August was a serious blow. Indeed, it might have been critical but for Shriver's good fortune in having acquired previously the services of Jack Conway, long-time assistant to Walter Reuther. Mr. Conway who was on leave from his position as executive director of the Industrial Union Department of the AFL-CIO had been working with the Shriver task force since March and was responsible for developing the community action program. Although Conway had expressed his personal desire to return to his trade-union position at an early date, he was willing to accept the position of deputy administrator during the initial phase in order to help get the program into operation. Conway was another key man in the Johnson poverty war who had strong Kennedy ties—having served as deputy administrator of the Housing and Home Finance Agency during the early Kennedy years. Conway's previous experience indicated that he would bring to the OEO deputy position a combination of administrative ability, political sophistication, and, not least important, a sense of how to move within the confines of the bureaucratic maze which pervades official Washington. Conway's principal assignment was one that he liked, to get Title II (community action) into operation *in as many communities as possible, as soon as possible.* Conway's right-hand man in this undertaking was Richard Boone, a young professional from the staff of the President's Committee on Juvenile Delinquency who had previously worked for the Ford Foundation.

Time was of the essence. Although the appropriation for the war on poverty was through Congress by October 3, 1964, a high-level decision held up the funding of any specific projects until after the presidential election (a rather handsomely non-political gesture from the Johnson White House). The first projects were announced by Mr. Shriver on November 25. Hence, the largest single problem Mr. Shriver and Mr. Conway faced was to find worthy projects for $800 million between November 25 and June 30, 1965, the end of the fiscal year. The first year of the war on poverty, in fact, was telescoped into about six and a half months of administrative action.

Shriver Faces Congress: Round One

The second most immediate problem facing OEO in mid-November, 1964, was having something to say to the Congress shortly after the first of the year. Only experienced Washington hands and a few specialists in the federal budgetary process will realize that the executive budget for the next fiscal year (in this case, beginning on July 1, 1965), starts taking final form by mid-November of the previous year. Mr. Shriver did not have anything more than a skeleton organization in

November, 1964. He had the problem of disbursing $800 million in hundreds of local communities in a period of about six months. Yet, in half that time, Shriver would be facing congressional committees, asking for more money for another year and answering questions about how his new program was going. And during the period from mid-November to mid-December, 1964, the embryonic Shriver office had to make basic budget decisions about the shape and scope of their massive program which was yet to be seen in operation.

One does not exaggerate the problem in stating it in this fashion. Actually, Mr. Shriver testified before a House subcommittee on April 2, 1965, about the new program. Was Congress likely to be curious about the results of the new program before there could possibly be any results? Or was Congress willing to defer a close examination until the following year—1966—by which time presumably there would be enough administrative experience to offer a basis for judgment?

If he took time to glance back, Mr. Shriver must have remembered that the program moved through the Congress with relative ease in 1964; only in the appropriations committees was there anything resembling a hard look, and in that case the billion-dollar program was trimmed to eight hundred million by a rule of thumb, because OEO would have less than twelve months in which to put the program into effect. Looking ahead to 1965, Shriver found himself in a situation in which his new program would be under review in Congress before there could be any administrative results worth examining. Hence, there was the distinct possibility that the Johnson antipoverty program would be given virtually a free ride through another session of Congress.

This is approximately what happened in 1965. The Republicans who felt they had been bluntly turned aside in 1964 might be ignored with impunity now that President Johnson had been to the polls in November and had won a landslide victory in his own right. In the process, the LBJ coattails carried into Congress the largest Democratic majorities since the days of FDR. The Johnson landslide added forty-two new Democratic seats in the House. Once again we encounter basic legislative arithmetic. Since each vote counts double (add one Democrat, subtract one Republican), the strongest president since

Roosevelt had acquired a plus eighty-four advantage in the House of Representatives in the Eighty-ninth Congress.

What this meant for the poverty program was that any effective critique would have to come from administration Democrats in the Congress, and it was fairly predictable that administration loyalists would not go out of their way to give the war on poverty a hard time during its first year of operation. It was after all only a six-month-old infant. Any significant congressional review of the antipoverty program would have to wait at least until 1966.

In the meantime, OEO experienced no shortage of administrative problems; a good many of them soon revealed themselves to be political problems as well.

The Mayors React

Community action was hardly underway before the first signs of resistance were felt. They came with increasing intensity from San Francisco all the way to New York City. John F. Shelley, Democratic mayor of San Francisco, charged that OEO was "undermining the integrity of local government" by organizing the poor into militant, politically active groups. Mayor Shelley was candid in his insistence that the "elected city official must retain control." By June of the first year, Shelley and Mayor Samuel Yorty of Los Angeles (another Democrat) sponsored a resolution at the U.S. Conference of Mayors accusing Sargent Shriver of "fostering class struggle." Democratic Mayor Wagner of New York told a House subcommittee, "I feel very strongly that the sovereign part of each locality . . . should have the power of approval over the makeup of the planning group, over the structure of the planning group, over the plan."

What seemed to be causing the greatest difficulty was Section 202 (a) (3) of the act which defines a community action program as one which " . . . is developed, conducted, and administered with the maximum feasible participation of residents of the areas and members of the groups served." We recall that this section was the creature of the staff of the President's Committee on Juvenile Delinquency and that it received very little attention from the committees of Congress in 1964.

Section 202 (a) (3) was not being overlooked or neglected in the development of OEO's national program. As early as February, 1965, OEO issued a community action program guide to be used by local communities which stated: "A vital feature of every community action program is the involvement of the poor themselves—the residents of the areas and members of the groups to be served—in planning, policy-making, and operation of the program."

The same program guide clarified the meaning of "maximum feasible participation": the poor were to participate "either on the governing body or on a policy advisory committee," or to have "at least one representative selected from each of the neighborhoods" involved in the program.

The guide went one step further and recommended elections among the poor to fill these positions "whenever feasible." The guide did not state, but it was widely understood, that OEO was using a rule-of-thumb standard requiring that one-third of the local poverty board members were to be drawn from the poor.

No matter how seriously the Office of Economic Opportunity intended its administrative policy to be taken at the local level, one can imagine that the national director of the program, Mr. Shriver, would prefer having some flexibility of action on the troublesome issue of representation of the poor. It is one thing to insist on the one-third ratio in Portland, Maine, where there is no mayor, weak or strong, and no boiling dark ghetto; but it is quite another thing in Mayor Richard Daley's Chicago with its powerful Democratic political machine and the nation's largest Negro ghetto. The student of American public administration realizes that this was not the first time that an unsettling (and unsettled) new policy had to be adjusted a little bit this way, a little bit that way as the pressures shifted and mounted.

The pressures mounted and the policy adjusted and shifted. Atlanta, Georgia, developed a community action program which soon became Mr. Shriver's pride and joy; yet the poor were conspicuously absent from its board. Newark, New Jersey, at the other extreme, established a board from which city hall was virtually excluded. OEO was reluctant to take on Mayor Daley in Chicago; it courageously struggled with Mayor Shelley in San Francisco. All through the months of 1965, Sargent Shriver resembled nothing so much as a skilled tightrope walker as he moved with a certain nimbleness of tread.

In Miami Beach on August 11, Mr. Shriver denied that his agency had set arbitrary quotas for representation of the poor; he also explained that representatives of the poor did not have to be poor themselves. A week later, Mayor Yorty of Los Angeles publicly blasted Shriver, accusing him of cutting off federal funds as a means of forcing Los Angeles to increase the number of poor people in the planning process. A month later, at a ceremony celebrating an additional grant of funds to Atlanta, Mr. Shriver praised the local antipoverty program as a "shining example." On this occasion, under questioning from a newsman, Mr. Shriver was careful to explain that the involvement of the poor in policy-making was an evolutionary process.

Pressure from the mayors mounted steadily. At the annual meeting of the U.S. Conference of Mayors in June, the mayors' executive committee approved a resolution urging that OEO recognize existing or city hall–endorsed local agencies as the proper channel for community action projects. The mayors formed a new antipoverty committee with Mayor Daley of Chicago as chairman.

The selection of Mayor Daley would have special meaning in Washington where it already seemed to be well understood that *no* antipoverty programs were to be set up in Chicago except through city hall. Mayor Daley and his committee lost no time meeting with Vice-President Humphrey *(not* with Mr. Shriver) and Theodore Berry, who was the man directly responsible for community action in the rapidly expanding OEO headquarters staff. The mayors expressed concern over OEO's tendency to support community action projects which were independent of city hall. According to John Gunther, executive director of the Conference of Mayors, the Vice-President told the mayors' antipoverty committee the Johnson administration intended to work closely with the mayors. In August Vice-President Humphrey addressed the National League of Cities: "I can tell you now that your important role is assured in this program. I'm your built-in Special Agent to make sure that you are represented in this program twenty four hours a day, 365 days a year. I've been hired for you."

These words coming from a former mayor must have been especially reassuring to the current crop of mayors.

Citizens' Crusade: The Voice of Conscience

In September, 1965, Jack Conway left his position as deputy to Sargent Shriver and returned to his position as executive director of the Industrial Union Department of the AFL-CIO. At almost the same point of time, it was announced that a new group, the Citizens' Crusade Against Poverty, was to be formed, and that Mr. Conway would be prominently involved in its activities. Mr. Conway took with him from OEO to serve as director of the Citizens' Crusade Richard Boone, the former JD committee staff man who had helped write the concept "maximum feasible participation" of the poor into the Act and into OEO administrative practice. The Citizens' Crusade Against Poverty, a private organization, was chaired by Walter Reuther; its members included individuals prominent in civic, civil rights, church, and liberal organizations; finances were supplied by the United Auto Workers and by the Ford Foundation. Those close to the new organization hoped it might become the "conscience" of the antipoverty program. The position of deputy to Mr. Shriver was now taken by Bernard L. Boutin, a Democrat from New Hampshire who had served throughout the Kennedy years as administrator of the General Services Administration. Mr. Boutin was appointed deputy director of OEO on October 21, 1965, reasonably close to the first anniversary of the antipoverty program. Mr. Boutin, who had once served as Mayor of Laconia, New Hampshire, arrived on the OEO scene amidst growing rumors and newspaper reports that the Johnson administration was disenchanted with the political repercussions of community action programs in big cities.

On November 5, 1965, Joseph Loftus reported in the *New York Times* that the Bureau of the Budget had told the Office of Economic Opportunity that it would prefer less emphasis on policy-making by the poor in planning community action projects. The story continued:

Maximum feasible participation by the antipoverty program is called for by the law. In the Bureau's view this means primarily using the poor to carry out the program but not to design it. This viewpoint was acknowledged today by a high government source who refused to be identified.

Someone was talking out of school—or was he?

It requires little imagination to realize how rapidly this story spread to every city hall and to a great many poor neighborhoods in America. Mr. Shriver, who was delivering an address in Scottsdale, Arizona, when the story broke, issued an immediate denial which Mr. Loftus carefully reported in the *Times* the next morning. "Unfortunately," said Mr. Shriver, "the article gives the impression that the Bureau of the Budget's 'alleged' position is official government policy that is about to be implemented by OEO." "Moreover," he continued, "it seems to imply that such a policy has been enunciated by the White House. Frankly, no such change in OEO's policy has been directed or ordered by anyone in the Administration. Our policy is today and will remain exactly what it has been from the very beginning."

Perhaps this strong statement from Mr. Shriver helped clear the air, assuming that all concerned understood what OEO's policy had been from the beginning. On the other hand, if Mr. Shriver had wished to keep some degree of administrative flexibility, he was now more firmly committed than ever to "maximum feasible participation" of the poor—or so at least it seemed late in 1965.

In the present case, the policy was made, in a sense, when the original task force put the concept "maximum feasible participation" in Title II of the proposed bill. Congress helped to harden the policy decision when it endorsed (albeit uncritically) the concept which remained in Title II of the Economic Opportunity Act of 1964. But Congress did not read substance into the words, and so it was left to Mr. Shriver, whose office assumed responsibility for administering Title II, to determine what "maximum feasible participation" was to mean in Chicago, in New Haven, in Portland, in San Francisco, in Atlanta, and in hundreds of other American communities.

HOW POVERTY BILL WAS SAVED IN HOUSE
Joseph A. Loftus

Washington, Dec. 24, 1967. "A few months ago," said a House member even before the final roll-call began, "nobody would have bet a nickel we would approve a poverty program in this Congress."

His exaggeration, if any, was slight. Yet the bill signed by President Johnson yesterday authorizes not a one-year but a two-year program. And awaiting his signature is another bill to appropriate $100-million more for the Office of Economic Opportunity this year than Congress gave the poverty agency a year ago.

The legislation would continue a wide variety of programs, first enacted in 1964, to help the poor.

These include remedial education, vocational training for teenagers and adults, preschool training, health care, legal services and community action programs, which are designed to involve the poor in community life and help them to take advantage of other local and Federal programs.

Congress passed the bill even while surfing on an economy wave that engulfed other agencies. This turnabout in the fortunes of the antipoverty agency can be explained largely, if not totally, by a strategy built around what has been variously called the Green amendment, the "bosses and boll weevil" amendment and the "city hall" amendment.

In short, an amendment sponsored by Representative Edith Green, Democrat of Oregon, was written to the specifications of Southern Democrats and some big city Northern Democrats who insisted on changes in the law as the price of their support.

The amendment permits Mayors or other locally elected officials to take control of community action agencies, which govern locally initiated poverty programs and account for about half the spending of Federal poverty funds. Most of these agencies now are private, nonprofit corporations.

House Problem Outlined

The poverty bill of 1967 was never in serious trouble in the Senate. The House problem was this:

By coincidence, the poverty bill of 1966 was signed on Election Day. On that day, 45 Democrats who had voted for the bill were defeated by Republicans. The poverty program could not afford to lose so many friends. Mathematically it looked as though it had lost its lease.

In the following months, criticism of the poverty program mounted. The agency was accused of inept administration, of vesting power in persons who were responsible to nobody, of funding black power advocates and "hate whitey" schools, of organizing the poor for demonstrations against City Hall.

To the Republicans, the poverty agency had the deepest partisan tinge. It became the most visible Great Society symbol, and the Republicans set out to dismantle it. They proposed distributing its functions among old-line agencies, and few in Washington were betting against them.

Last spring, after nose counts, informed Democrats on the House Education and Labor Committee said that they had no doubt that the Republicans and Southern Democrats could write their own ticket on poverty legislation.

The summer riots seemed to confirm the doom of the program. Foes of the antipoverty agency concluded that the disorders demonstrated the failure of the program, and some went so far as to blame beneficiaries of the program for fomenting the trouble.

Two of the worst riots occurred in Detroit and Newark. Detroit had been credited with operating one of the most successful antipoverty programs in the country. In Newark, the militant poor had snatched the program from the Mayor and other elected politicians.

Opinions Are Sought

In June and July, Representative Carl D. Perkins, Kentucky Democrat and House manager of the poverty bill, wrote to 80 selected mayors and chiefs of police for opinions.

The replies were so critical that Mr. Perkins decided that changes in community action controls were imperative if the program was to be saved. He decided that delay was important, too. Delay could not worsen the prospects for the bill and might dim the memory of the riots while giving friends of the program time to organize public support.

Nonaction rarely makes news, and many of these persons throughout the country were not aware of the antipoverty agency's legislative hazards. The agency sent out the alarm. It gave particular attention to Mayors, including Republicans, who began lobbying for poverty funds. Even Mayors who were unhappy with certain aspects of the community action program knew that the program represented badly needed cash.

Mr. Shriver, his general counsel, Donald M. Baker, and his legislative representatives, George D. McCarthy and Charles H. Holm, met daily at 9 a.m. and spent scores of hours lobbying on Capitol Hill. They and other departmental lobbyists met often at the White House with Joseph A. Califano and Harold Barefoot Sanders, Jr., special assistants to the President.

When Mr. Perkins could wait no longer, he summoned his committee to mark up the Administration bill. Mrs. Green began offering amendments, most of them viewed by the antipoverty agency as undesirable.

Safeguards Agreed To

Her major amendment, giving community action agencies to state and locally elected officials, was unacceptable to key Democrats on the committee, but they began to see the virtue of working with her instead of fighting her and possibly driving her to seek conservative coalition support.

Mrs. Green consented to meetings with Representatives James O'Hara of Michigan, Sam M. Gibbons of Florida, Hugh L. Carey of Brooklyn, John H. Dent of Pennsylvania and Mr. Perkins, all Democrats.

They persuaded her that the amendment as introduced would give Southern politicians a weapon to use against poor Negroes and might abolish church-sponsored poverty projects funded by the anti-poverty agency.

She agreed to safeguards and bypass provisions so that the agency director could fund alternative agencies if local politicians did not conform to certain criteria and regulations.

When these private meetings began to look fruitful, some of the committee group went to Mr. Shriver and worked out the rest of the strategy.

"This is your chance to get a bill you can live with," one member told him. "But you have got to pretend you are against it."

Mr. Shriver philosophically was uncomfortable with Mrs. Green's amendment. He preferred the total involvement of the community that he was striving for under the old law. But he was persuaded by the political realities.

It was important, he was told, that Mrs. Green play out her role as his antagonist, a credible role in view of her criticism of practices of the antipoverty agency in the last three years. Any semblance of a deal between Mrs. Green and Mr. Shriver might destroy important support among southern Democrats and a few Republicans.

The members of the committee group did not tell Mrs. Green what they were up to, and if she knows now she apparently has not given away the secret. She has acknowledged that the amendment that she sponsored was not entirely of her own authorship.

Coalition Vote Averted

When *The New York Times* reported in early November that Mrs. Green's amendment had the support of the White House and Mr. Shriver, the latter called to say that he was not supporting the amendment and if the White House favored such a change it had not told him.

Mr. Shriver's associates say now that he and they conceived of the amendment last spring. Other Administration sources credit Barefoot Sanders as the silent genius of the whole strategy. Key House committee members, however, say that White House assistance was minimal so far as they know.

It is possible, of course, that no one person knows the whole story. The support attracted to Mrs. Green's amendment cut the ground from under the Republicans and destroyed the possibility of a conservative coalition vote. The Republicans recognized as much on the first day of House debate when Representative Charles E. Goodell, Republican of upstate New York, flung the phrase "bosses and boll weevil amendment."

Meantime, Republicans and other conservatives had unwittingly created sympathy for the antipoverty agency by excluding its employes from the government pay rise bill, by letting its stopgap spending authority lapse and then voting to limit its authorization to $1.2 billion, a cut of $800-million below the budget proposal.

As antipoverty projects around the country started to close down or set closing dates, House members started to hear from home. Newspapers unexpectedly made community action their cause. The antipoverty agency reported that it had counted 450 favorable editorials in 296 newspapers in October and November. A number of friendly businessmen bombarded the House Republican Policy Committee, which avoided taking a position on the poverty bill.

The House authorized a $1.6-billion poverty bill, then increased it to $1.98-billion in a "compromise" with the Senate. George H. Mahon, Texas Democrat, said that he did not like that but was going to vote for it because, as far as he was concerned as chairman of Appropriations, the poverty program would get no more than $1.6-billion cash.

Those words from a conservative spender on the House floor gave some other conservatives a politically defensible rationale for supporting the bill, even though it was known that the House would have to raise the $1.6-billion part way toward the Senate's $1.98-billion later. It did, and the final figure was $1.773-billion.

Not all the Southern Democrats felt they could, with political safety, vote on the record for the poverty bill, but they helped out on the nonrecord head counts in crucial spots. By the time the House reached the final roll-call on adoption of the compromise authorization bill, 63 Republicans had decided to pitch in with "aye" votes.

One of them was cast by Albert H. Quie of Minnesota, who for three years had been the teammate of Mr. Goodell in attacking Administration poverty bills and offering their own substitutes. Neither had ever before voted for a Democratic poverty bill.

NO MORE PORK BARREL:
THE APPALACHIA APPROACH
Jerald ter Horst

If imitation is the sincerest form of flattery, then the Appalachia redevelopment program may indeed be the forerunner of a new era in Federal public-works spending. Similar programs are already being proposed for the Ozarks, the New England States, and the Upper Great Lakes area, each fashioned in the belief that the gateway to the Great Society is through regional concentration of Federal money instead of scattershot spending in the fifty states.

In its purest form, the 1965 Appalachia proposal would mean that the states and counties actually could tell Washington where and how to spend Federal tax dollars to achieve the economic and social uplift of a particular region. Ordinarily this alone would engender stiff opposition in Congress. But the eleven-state Appalachia concept dares to go several steps further. Federal money would go primarily to a region, not directly to impoverished people. It would not necessarily go to the neediest towns and counties, either, but to those with the greatest potential for economic growth. And the benefits, assuming that the program is successful, would not be immediately translatable into votes.

The Governors' Idea

This tradition-shattering concept did not originate in Washington. It was the collective idea of a group of governors who began meeting periodically in the late 1950's in an effort to seek solutions to the common economic blight affecting many areas of their states. By May 20, 1960, the consultations had reached the point where the group, meeting in Annapolis, Maryland, formally created the Conference of Appalachian Governors. The following October, meeting in Lexington, Kentucky, the conference gave birth to "a special regional program of development" that envisaged a combined attack on their problems through the resources of the local, state, and Federal governments, and the assistance of private industry, civic groups, and philanthropic foundations. At the meeting were the governors of Alabama, Georgia, Kentucky, Maryland, North Carolina, Pennsylvania, Tennessee, Virginia, and West Virginia. Joined later by Ohio and South Carolina, the group represents that portion of the Appalachian Mountains ranging from northern Pennsylvania into southern Alabama, an area largely bypassed by the tremendous economic changes at work in the rest of the country since the Second World War.

In 1963, the Appalachia governors prevailed on President Kennedy to create the Appalachian Regional Commission to analyze the needs of the region and develop a co-ordinated plan for attempting some permanent cures of their chronic problems. Represented on the commission were the states and all the Federal agencies involved in such aid programs as highways, hospitals, public health, education, timber, crops, livestock, manpower retraining, mining, flood control and stream pollution, wildlife, and recreation. Under its chairman, Under Secretary of Commerce Franklin D. Roosevelt, Jr., the commission toured Appalachia twice and discussed the region's needs with public and private experts in the various states. Its report last spring to President Johnson set the stage for an unusual concerted program of economic-resource development by the cities, counties, and states and the Federal government.

The various subregions of Appalachia, the commission said, share this unhappy distinction: "Rural Appalachia lags behind rural America, urban Appalachia lags behind urban America, and metropolitan Appalachia lags behind metropolitan America." It found, for example, that one-third of Appalachia's families earn less than $3,000 annually; two-thirds of its people do not finish school; unemployment is half again the national average, and out-migration is at the high rate of 200,000 persons a year. "The most serious problems which beset Appalachia are low income, high unemployment, lack of urbanization, low educational achievement, and a comparatively low standard of living."

Breaking New Ground

At first glance, the 1965 Appalachia program appears to be the usual grab bag of projects—new roads, soil improvement and erosion control, timber development, hospitals and treatment centers, vocational-education, sewage-treatment works, strip-mine reclamation, fish and wildlife projects—all intended to help Appalachia catch up with the rest of the nation.

But closer examination discloses that the Appalachia planners have broken new ground in the formulation and management of public-works spending. For the first time, the Federal government would delegate a major share of the decision-making to the participating states. The master plan for economic rehabilitation would be devised by the states or groups of counties in a multistate area with contiguous land and common problems.

While the actual operation of aid projects would be under the appropriate Federal agencies, the supervision and co-ordination of the whole Appalachia program would be vested in the Appalachian Regional Commission, to consist of the governor of each participating state, or his designee, and one Federal representative named by the President. Decisions would be made by a majority vote of the state members, plus the affirmative vote of the Federal representative, who would, in effect, have a veto over proposals by the state members of the commission. But the veto could be substantially limited, since a majority of state members could counter any move toward Federal "dictation" by withholding their votes.

This check-and-balance formula represents a major shift in bureaucratic thinking in Washington. It has inspired heated debate inside the administration and in Congress. Veteran agency heads still question the wisdom of letting states have such a large share of the decision-making process when most of the money comes from Federal revenue.

Congress has also been historically reluctant to appropriate money without a certain supervision over the decision-makers. This it can do most easily when funds are expended by Federal agencies—even to the extent of cranking into a program a few pet projects of a committee chairman and influential lawmakers. It is a precept of pork-barrel doctrine that a congressman and his constituents have a right to expect certain Federal benefits for their district to flow from his membership on key committees. Thus it comes as a minor miracle to find that both Federal bureaucrats and members of Congress seem willing to relinquish some of their authority in order to give the Appalachia program a trial.

One of the surprise converts is the Bureau of the Budget, known best as the "No" agency of government. "To be honest, this is a new venture," conceded Charles L. Schultze, until recently an assistant Budget Bureau director. "We are doing something different. While not saying it is experimental, we think it is an exceedingly interesting approach. We are going to have to work our way through this."

In his testimony before the House Public Works Committee, Schultze described the proposed Appalachia concept of multistate planning under Federal supervision as "a nice balance" of authority. Still to be tested, however, is just how the states will exercise their new license to tell Washington where to send Federal dollars. What's likely to happen, according to Senator Jennings Randolph, the West Virginia Democrat who steered the bill through the Senate, is that most of the hard bargaining will be done outside the commission's chambers. An Appalachia planner agreed. "We'll work it out informally before we take something in for a vote—just like they do in Congress."

The basis for this hope lies in the considerable give-and-take among the Appalachia governors and the Federal representatives in working out the terms of the legislation. For example, Georgia, North Carolina, and Maryland, because their needs are not so great, have consented to a smaller allocation of primary highway corridor mileage than is intended for West Virginia and Pennsylvania. Similarly, the governors of South Carolina and Alabama have agreed to take a smaller share of development highway money because their Appalachia counties will be adequately served by the Federal interstate highway program.

The spirit of compromise was equally apparent in Congress. The administration and Capitol Hill Democrats consented to a proposal by Senator Jacob K. Javits (R., New York) that no program for Appalachia should be implemented until the Appalachia commission had consulted with appropriate state officials and received their recommendations. The acid test, however, will come when individual lawmakers make their customary demands on Federal agencies for inclusion of projects dear to their constituents.

Leading from Strength

Another radical departure from tradition is the Appalachia concept of skipping the customary "means test" to determine which areas will be helped. The Area Redevelopment program, for example, uses specific criteria for establishing eligibility for Federal aid. A county must have a certain rate of unemployment in order to qualify for job-creating projects. But the Appalachia approach relies on "regional growth potential," a theory that economic uplift should be concentrated on certain cities or counties that have prospered in spite of Appalachia's general distress.

There is a hint of economic predestination here; the belief that many economically weak towns and counties do not have the potential to become thriving, prosperous centers of population. Instead, Appalachia planners believe that the economically strong places should be strengthened to support the weaker surrounding areas. One example is Huntsville, Alabama, with its space-industry complex and college environment in the midst of a depressed area. "Instead of trying to build up the area to compete with Huntsville, we should try to find ways of helping the rest of the region become auxiliary to Huntsville," one planner explained. "This could be done by improving the road networks, providing sewer and water facilities for residential expansion, perhaps improving farm production and recreational opportunities in some sectors of the region."

Wilkes-Barre, Pennsylvania, is considered another center for regional growth potential that could attract more industries and commerce and provide new job opportunities through co-ordinated planning designed to increase the "social overhead capital" needed for area self-sufficiency. In all, there are probably fifty such core cities or counties in the 360 counties included in the Appalachia region.

One of the continuing controversies in the Appalachia program is its heavy emphasis on roadbuilding. About one thousand miles will be "local access" roads, intended primarily to link Appalachia's almost inaccessible valleys with nearby cities and towns. Another 2,350 miles would be designated as "development highways," linking core cities with each other and with areas outside Appalachia.

"There's been a sort of liberal versus pragmatist debate on this thing," said John L. Sweeney, the able young administrator the President chose as chairman of the Federal Development Planning Committee for Appalachia. "Most programs of economic help in the past have been based on the theory that a man has a right to a job where he lives and that government should help bring him that job. The Appalachia approach is that a man has a right to a job, but it is reasonable to expect him to be willing to commute to it or move to it if necessary."

Using a mile-a-minute yardstick, Appalachia planners think it logical to expect people to travel forty minutes to reach their places of employment, a vocational school, or even a hospital. Thus a core-city plan will encompass an area extending as far as forty miles from the center, crossing county and state boundaries when necessary.

Roads or Education?

Not all economic and social planners agree, however, with the priority on roads. Doubts about its importance were heard at the American Institute of Planners conference in Newark, New Jersey, last year. One said he wished he could be "czar" of the Appalachia program just long enough to scrap the highway priority. Others said education should get first priority. An earlier Ford Foundation study concluded that the unemployed and unskilled coal and steel workers in Appalachia "must be written off as far as any major economic contribution is concerned." It advocated massive Federal aid to education, increased out-migration, and birth control.

The Appalachia rebuttal is both intriguing and indignant. "If we are going to be politically realistic about the Appalachia program, it is necessary to design a program that mirrors the political realities of the states involved," said Stuart F. Feldman, top staff aide for the Appalachia Development Committee. And the political realities are that the governors, senators, and representatives of the Appalachia states wanted a priority on roads—and so did the planning experts for the committee.

"From the point of view of public policy," Feldman told the planners' conference, "it is evident that Appalachia is an ongoing region whose 167,000 square miles, numerous metropolitan areas, and population of over sixteen million people represent a resource and an investment this nation cannot abandon through policies that encourage an outmigration of the able."

There is both historic and contemporary justification for the road priority. Appalachia once had been opened by the railroads, which came to fetch the coal for the steel mills and electric-power generation. But automation has hit each of the region's big three—coal, steel, and the railroads—throwing thousands upon thousands of men and their sons out of manual-labor jobs. Oil and natural gas became victorious competitors of coal for the fuel market; even the coal-burning locomotives gave way to diesels. In the old days, rail spurs ran back into almost every Appalachia hollow to reach the mines; because they were not built for private gain, roads seldom followed. There are still hamlets whose only connection with the outside world is over the abandoned rail roadbeds.

The Federal interstate highway system has helped to open Appalachia. But states and communities with a low tax base haven't been able to raise extra funds for the auxiliary highways and local access roads. In mountainous areas of West Virginia, for example, Appalachia planners note that it costs $2 million a mile to construct a two-lane paved highway. Moreover, Appalachia needs road money not so much to accommodate existing traffic as to stimulate new traffic.

Surprisingly, the press has been rather uncritical in reporting that seventy-six per cent, or $840 million, of the Appalachia program's $1.1-billion price tag is for roadbuilding. The road money actually is a five-year authorization; the rest of the money for other Appalachian needs covers the first two years only. Seen in perspective, then, the road ratio is not so lopsided as it appears.

The debate will be more intense over another aspect of the Appalachia program—namely, its assumption that there should be preferential treatment for an eleven-state area, as well as internal discrimination inherent in selecting one town as a growth center while bypassing another. One of Appalachia's problems is the inability of counties and cities to raise the usual local share necessary to obtain Federal matching funds for such things as airports, hospitals, vocational education facilities, libraries, and flood control. The Appalachia bill will make it possible for the Federal government to pay up to eighty percent of the total cost in such instances, even if other regions of the country would get only fifty percent Federal aid. Additionally, there are special supplemental funds to cover actual operating costs of hospitals for up to two years, plus a $36.5-million fund to alleviate land damage wrought by collapsed coal mines, underground fires, and acid seepage into streams. And Republicans charge gross discrimination in that the road program "is almost as large as the annual program for construction of Federal-aid primary and secondary highways" for the entire country.

There has been, inevitably, some compromise. The bill's current dollar total is about one-third of the $3 billion in Federal money originally sought. A proposed public development corporation, to be financed by bond sales and Federal funds, had to be scrapped when it appeared to be just another back-door raid on the Treasury. Western cattle interests knocked out a $17-million program for pastureland improvement. And administration lobbyists have had to tell envious lawmakers from other areas that if they will go along with the Appalachia plan, the White House will entertain similar regional development programs for other parts of the country.

Behind it all lies a growing conviction in Congress and in the councils of a Democratic administration that pork-barreling, accelerated public-works spending, and such things as the Area Redevelopment program—generally classed as economic pump priming—have missed the mark. The past, however, has not been a complete loss, at least not in the view of the President's Council of Economic Advisers. The council has analyzed the weaknesses of these earlier programs, and all of its conclusions point toward more Appalachia-type solutions. Add a pinch of Johnsonian consensus, and the rationale is simply that states and local communities cannot do the job alone— and that the Federal government should not.

chapter four

Business Regulation

A substantial volume and variety of regulatory legislation and activity in the United States is directed toward the business community. The focus of this chapter will be on two principal varieties of regulation: the maintenance of competition under the antitrust laws and the detailed control of particular industries by independent regulatory commissions. The maintenance of competition has long been a central goal of American economic policy, being expressed by the Sherman Antitrust Act (1890), Clayton Act (1914), and Federal Trade Commission Act (1914), and subsequent amendments to those statutes. For some industries, however, this pattern of regulation has been considered inadequate to protect the interests of the public, and consequently a more detailed and thorough form of regulation has been provided. This industry regulation, usually implemented by independent regulatory commissions, involves government in the management of business and, among other things, has typically resulted in at least some restriction of competition. The policy-making process, responding to different interests in different forms at different times, has yielded inconsistent results.

The Sherman Act was one of the first major regulatory statutes passed by Congress. While the trust issue reached such proportions in the 1880's that both major political parties felt obliged to respond to it, William Letwin's discussion of the Act's passage indicates that it was shaped by a variety of political, personal, and economic factors. He rejects some of the simplistic explanations for its adoption. He concludes that the Sherman Act was about as good a law as Congress could pass at the time, given its lack of knowledge and experience with the monopoly problem.

The wording of the various antitrust statutes is often general, ambiguous, or both. Letwin's discussion illustrates why this is so for the Sherman Act. Consequently, the operational meaning and impact of antitrust policy depends substantially on how the statutes are interpreted by the courts and implemented by the agencies having jurisdiction under them, particularly the Antitrust Division and the Federal Trade Commission. In my own article which follows Letwin's, I argue that antitrust administration is essentially a political process. I describe and comment upon a variety of political factors which play upon the antitrust agencies and help determine how they use their enforcement discretion. The agencies in turn, I contend, consciously gear their actions to "political realities."

Most of the independent regulatory commissions have been established to regulate particular industries (the FTC and NLRB are exceptions). Grant McConnell summarizes some of the issues and controversies relating to commission regulation (which is a policy issue itself). Of particular interest here is the charge that the commissions have failed to make law (or policy), though they have been delegated substantial policy-making, or rule-making, power by Congress. Have the commissions really failed to make policy? Or is it that they have not systematically and openly laid down general policies? Or does the charge really mean that the commissions have made the "wrong" kind of policy, that is, policy with which those making the charge do not agree? These questions should be kept in mind while the selections by Huntington and Bendiner are read.

Huntington has written a classic study of the relationships between a regulatory agency and its clientele (those whom it directly serves or regulates). Since the 1920's the railroads have been the primary source of political support for the Interstate Commerce Commission, and the ICC, in turn, has become highly responsive to railroad interests in its policy-making. Some have described the ICC as the "captive" of the railroads. Huntington's discussion indicates that the ICC has shown a marked preference for the railroad viewpoint in its policy decisions in the area of rail–motor carrier competition.

The economic conflict between the operators of nonscheduled airlines and the major airlines after World War II is chronicled by Robert Bendiner. The Civil Aeronautics Board, set up in 1938 both to protect the interests of the traveling public and to promote the development of air transportation, could not avoid being drawn into the dispute. It possessed discretionary power which could be exercised to the advantage of either party to the conflict. Bendiner's account illustrates the multitude of factors which, over time, produce a policy position. Whether one agrees or disagrees with the CAB, it did, in its own fashion, develop policy. The question becomes a normative one: Did it act correctly? Bendiner's study nicely demonstrates how an agency can become the focal point of political struggle over policy.

CONGRESS PASSES THE SHERMAN ACT
William Letwin

The deceptive simplicity of the Sherman Act has led many historians to believe that the intention of Congress was equally simple. Although they have not agreed on what the intention was, these historians have shared the view that the motives of Congress were elementary and unmixed and have differed chiefly over whether Congress was sincere. Some suppose that the congressmen of 1890 were committed to a policy of *laissez faire,* interpret that policy as a dogmatic faith in competition, and regard the Sherman Act as an effort to enforce that orthodoxy.[1] Others, less trustful, maintain that the Act was a fraud, contrived to soothe the public without injuring the trusts, and they insist that no other result was possible because the Republican Party, in control of the 51st Congress, was "itself dominated at the time by many of the very industrial magnates most vulnerable to real antitrust legislation."[2] Both these schools can draw support from distinguished men who lived while the Act was being passed.[3]

But the process by which laws are made in the American democracy is not so direct and obvious. Congress does not merely enact its private dogmas, nor does it simply supply whatever the people order. Public opinion is not so precise. Far from demanding a particular law, the public desires at most a certain kind of law, and more often only wants to be rid of a general evil. Sometimes, indeed, public opinion is practically silent and yet effective, for Congress often refuses to pass laws because it expects that the public would object, or adopts them in anticipation that the public will approve. Congress is not a factory that mechanically converts opinion into statutes. The congressman is a representative, who must recognize at least some tendencies of public opinion if he is to be re-elected. He is also a professional lawmaker, more likely than not a lawyer by training, who is not indifferent to his craft. He talks with lawyers, follows the decisions of judges, and reads law journals. He is willing to draw on the skill of other experts when

Reprinted from William Letwin, *Law and Economic Policy in America,* pp. 53–54, 85–99, by permission of Random House, Inc. Copyright 1954, © 1956 by the University of Chicago. Footnotes have been renumbered.

the need arises, and will take advice from businessmen, reformers, or economists. He is a member of a political party and may feel loyal to its traditional policies and obliged to support at least part of its current platform. Finally, he is an individual with beliefs, interests, ambitions, and idiosyncrasies quite his own.

It should not be surprising then that although the Sherman Act was passed by a virtually unanimous vote, and although its language is disarmingly clear, the administrations and courts charged with enforcing it have experienced so much difficulty in settling its meaning. The Sherman Act reflects not only the uncertainty present in every general law because its authors cannot foresee the particular cases that will arise, but also the ambiguity that colors many democratic laws because the authors cannot completely resolve the divergent opinions and cross purposes that call it forth. . . .

Legislative History of the Sherman Act

The political parties officially recognized the trust problem soon after it arose. The "third parties" needed no urging; they were eager to extend the campaign that the Greenback and Anti-Monopoly parties had carried on since 1880 against "land, railroad, money and other gigantic monopolies."[4] It was a matter of course that the Union Labor Party, formed by a coalition of Greenbackers, Knights of Labor, and farmer organizations, should make much of this new opportunity, and indeed they made it one of their great causes. The platform they adopted in the spring of 1888 concluded with the declaration: "The paramount issues to be solved in the interests of humanity are the abolition of usury, monopoly, and trusts, and we denounce the Democratic and Republican parties for creating and perpetuating these monstrous evils."[5]

The major parties were anything but anxious to appear as champions of the trusts. The Democrats had made the appropriate general statements against monopoly in 1880 and 1884,[6] but they had especially good reasons for carrying these further in 1888. For one thing, they could cite the new offense as additional evidence against their old enemy, protection. President Cleveland, in his annual message to Congress at the end of 1887, said it was "notorious" that the "combinations quite prevalent at this time, and frequently called trusts," strangled competition; he urged that action be taken against them, and suggested that Congress reduce the customs duties protecting them against foreign competitors.[7] Moreover, the trust issue was especially useful for appealing to farmers and laborers who might otherwise shift their vote to the third party. Cleveland, during his term of office, opposed the easy-money and silver-coinage schemes, supposedly popular in the South and West, that were advocated by the Union Labor Party[8] and supported by a wing of his own party. As a candidate for re-election he was no more pliable, and the Democratic national convention of 1888 was the only one between 1880 and 1896 that did not advocate silver coinage; it did not even mention the word "silver" in its platform. The party apparently felt obliged to make up for this somehow, and amidst sympathetic references to "the industrious freemen of our land," "every tiller of the soil," and "the cry of American labor for a better share in the rewards of industry," it asserted that, "Judged by Democratic principles, the interests of the people are betrayed when, by unnecessary taxation, trusts and combinations are permitted to exist, which, while unduly enriching the few that combine, rob the body of our citizens. . . ."[9]

The Republican Party had even more compelling need to condemn the trusts. They had since 1880 achieved the reputation of being the party of the rich, and in 1884 Ben Butler began calling them the "Party of Monopolists."[10] This label became especially current after their presidential candidate was given a banquet by a group of businessmen, among them Gould, Vanderbilt, and Astor, which the New York *World* titled "The Royal Feast of Belshazzar Blaine and the Money Kings," and during which, it said, the "Millionaires and Monopolists" sealed their allegiance to the party.[11] A party whose policies were subject to so crudely cynical an interpretation and which was undoubtedly supported—as were the others—by some millionaires, must have condemned the trusts in self defense even if it had not objected to them in principle. In their convention of 1888 the Republicans accordingly condemned "all combinations of capital, organized in trusts or otherwise, to control arbitrarily the conditions of trade among our citizens," and recommended "such legislation as will prevent the executions of all schemes to oppress the people by undue charges on their supplies, or by unjust rates for the transportation of their products to market." [12] Because they elected President Harrison and won decisive control of Congress in the following election, responsibility for carrying out the recommendation became theirs.

Congress began to concern itself with the trust problem in January of 1888. An antitrust bill was brought to the floor of Congress by Senator John Sherman, by now an aging man at times impatient and confused, but still the most prominent and esteemed Republican in Congress. He had served as representative for eight years, senator for over twenty-five, and had been Secretary of the Treasury under Hayes. He had been a candidate for the presidential nomination since 1880, and seemed finally to be winning it at the convention of 1888 until Harrison took the lead during the seventh ballot. Soon after this defeat he began to take serious interest in the trust question. His seniority and experience gave him great authority on financial questions and his recent disappointment gave him the urge to do something memorable. He began by establishing personal jurisdiction over the antitrust problem. The antitrust bills introduced earlier in the year[13] had been referred to committees, but none had yet been debated when, on July 10, Sherman successfully introduced a resolution directing the Senate Committee on Finance, of which he was a ranking member, to investigate all antitrust bills.[14] He maintained that the Committee would investigate antitrust bills "in connection with" tariff bills, which were undoubtedly its proper province; but this argument had its danger as well, for by stressing the connection between trusts and tariffs he was playing into the hands of the Democrats. He had already made this blunder when, in replying to Cleveland's annual message, he agreed that the trusts might be fought by reducing duties that protected them—though he then added that he knew of no trusts which had such protection.[15] Now he was a little more on guard, and argued that the trusts not only prevented "freedom of trade and production" but also subverted the tariff system; they undermined "the policy of the Government to protect and encourage American industries by levying duties on imported goods." [16]

The effect of Sherman's maneuver became evident a month later, when Senator John Reagan, a Democrat from Texas, introduced an antitrust bill which was read and about to be referred to committee.[17]

At this point Sherman rose to insist that according to the resolution the bill should be sent to the Finance Committee. He maintained that this was appropriate because the only constitutional provision enabling Congress to legislate against trusts was the power to levy taxes: though the Federal Government might not be able to attack trusts like Standard Oil, it could certainly use the taxing power to control monopolies like the Sugar Trust, which were aided by tariffs. But this doctrine was far from congenial to him, and when Senator Ransom replied that Congress derived its jurisdiction over trusts from its constitutional power to regulate commerce, Sherman was ready to shift ground. He answered: "I always take the revenue laws as commercial laws. They always go together, interchangeably." [18] Though this may have been an accurate interpretation of the Constitution,[19] it was less than an adequate reason for referring trust bills to the Finance Committee rather than the Commerce Committee, but the Senate was impressed by Sherman's determination and agreed to send Reagan's bill to his committee. Sherman immediately capped the day's work by introducing an antitrust bill of his own.[20]

His bill, unlike Reagan's, was returned in short order to the Senate floor, where it was briefly debated and considerably amended in January 1889.[21] By now it had begun to look like a serious effort, and was honored with a long attack by Senator James George of Mississippi, formerly a Confederate general and Chief Justice of the state supreme court, a Democrat and fervent upholder of states' rights.[22] George questioned both its effectiveness and its constitutionality. He declared that although he firmly opposed the trusts and was eager to destroy them, he saw no hope that the bill could do so. It declared illegal "all arrangements, contracts, agreements, trusts, or combinations between persons or corporations made with a view, or which tend, to prevent full and free competition" in certain goods, or "to advance the cost to the consumer"; yet these words, George said, would condemn not only the trusts and combinations but also arrangements made "for moral and defensive purposes." It would penalize not only the Southern farmers who had organized a boycott against the Jute-Bag Trust, but also combinations of farmers to raise the prices of their products and of laborers to raise their wages, and even temperance societies whose members compacted not to use spirits.

However serious this defect—and Sherman immediately assured the Senate that it was unintentional—the great objection to the bill was its utter futility. The bill, as it now stood, supposed that Congress derived its power over trusts from the commerce clause of the Constitution; it therefore outlawed combinations dealing in goods that had been imported from abroad or that might "in the due course of trade" be transported from one state to another. But according to the established interpretation of the Constitution, George insisted, Congress could control commerce only while goods were in the actual process of being transported into the country or from one state to another. It was apparent that a law punishing combinations because they dealt in goods that might once have been imported or that might some day be sent from one state to another was either unconstitutional, or if constitutional, then so limited in application as to be worthless. Having ended his critique, he took a little time to point out, with some relish, that Sherman had admitted that an antitrust law could not be based on the commerce power and had recognized, as he himself would, that trusts could be controlled in a constitutional manner only by reducing protective tariffs. Sherman did not answer, and before there was another opportunity for debate, the 50th Congress disbanded.

These preliminary skirmishes were continued during the early months of the 51st Congress. The moment the session began Sherman introduced a bill that, except for changes in detail, contained the words and principles of his previous drafts. It declared unlawful and void all combinations preventing competition in foreign and interstate commerce; it authorized any person injured by such combinations to recover damages; and it subjected all members and agents of such combinations to fine and imprisonment.[23] The bill, introduced on December 4, 1889, and very slightly amended by the Finance Committee, was brought to the floor of the Senate in February 1890, whereupon Senator George once again made a full-scale attack on it. He repeated his previous objections, and as before concluded that the bill was "utterly unconstitutional, and even if constitutional, utterly worthless."[24] The matter was left there, and it began to look as though antitrust legislation was a dim prospect. More than two years had passed since the first bills had been put before Congress, and as yet only one had been briefly considered. The machinery seemed to have come to a standstill. Two other bills in the Senate, introduced by George and Reagan, were still being held up by committees, as were seventeen bills that had been introduced by Representatives.[25] It was rumored that the reason for the delay since December was that McKinley, chairman of the House Ways and Means Committee, was thinking of attaching an antitrust section to his tariff bill,[26] which had already been passed by the House and was quite certain to become law. For the moment, however, nothing seemed to be happening.

Suddenly the situation changed, and in the last weeks of March 1890 the serious work of preparing an antitrust law was begun. The burst of energy may have come because the Republican congressmen gave up the idea, assuming they had ever had it, of treating the trust problem in the McKinley Tariff Bill. To have done so would have given the impression that they agreed with the Democrats about the causes of trusts and the constitutional powers available to destroy them. They may have felt that the public was becoming impatient, for congressmen were receiving an increasing number of petitions advocating antitrust legislation.[27] Or the new activity may have come at Sherman's insistence. He announced a few days before it began that he had revised his bill to meet George's objections, having deleted the provisions George had criticized because they would make the law a criminal one and thus oblige the courts to interpret it narrowly.[28] In any case, by the time Sherman submitted his new bill on March 21, the Senate was prepared to concentrate on it and spent the next five days doing little else.

The great debate opened with a long, formal address in which Sherman praised his bill.[29] He began by explaining its political and legal theory. It was intended, he said, to destroy combinations—not all combinations, but all those which the common law had always condemned as unlawful. It was not intended to outlaw all partnerships and corporations, though they were by nature combinations. The corporations had demonstrated their usefulness by the vast development of railroads and industry, and Sherman added—bearing in mind the lingering prejudice against them—that as long as every man had the right under general laws to form corporations, they were "not in any sense a monopoly." But any combination which sought to restrain trade, any combination of the leading corporations in an industry, organized in a trust to stifle competition, dictate terms to railroads, command the price of labor, and raise prices to consumers, was a "substantial monopoly." It smacked of tyranny, "of kingly prerogative," and a nation that "would not submit to an emperor ... should not submit to an autocrat of trade." Sherman went on to say that all such combinations in restraint of trade were prohibited by the common law, wherever it was in force; it had always applied in the states, and the "courts in different States have declared this thing, when it exists in a State, to be unlawful and void." Senator Cullom interrupted to ask, "Everywhere?" "In every case, everywhere," Sherman replied, and went on to list the recent decisions supporting his view. He first read the full opinion of the Michigan Supreme Court in the case of *Richardson v. Buhl*,[30] which had a double attraction for him. It struck at the Diamond Match Company's monopoly, and it branded as a monopolist General Russel Alger, one of his chief rivals in 1888 for the Republican presidential nomination, whom Sherman blamed for his unexpected defeat and publicly accused of having bribed delegates.[31] Sherman then cited other cases, which if they did not hold the same personal interest for him, all supported the view that monopolies and combinations in restraint of trade were unlawful and void in courts of common law.[32] But, he continued, the trusts were threatened by no similar law in the Federal courts and a statute was needed to enforce the common law that already applied in state courts. Once again, he insisted that Congress was authorized alike by the commerce and revenue clauses of the Constitution to regulate combinations affecting interstate and foreign commerce; and he concluded that his bill, based on this constitutional power and declaring the common-law rule, would effectively destroy the power of the trusts.[33]

The debate which occupied much of the following week was untidy but not without pattern. Many senators delivered great orations, but few were heard to say that the trusts were desirable or an antitrust law unnecessary. George repeatedly questioned the bill's constitutionality; certain of his Democratic colleagues took occasion to avow their opposition to tariffs. A number of senators tried to substitute their own bills for Sherman's; failing this, they attached them to his bill as amendments. By the end of the third day, the bill before the Senate consisted of sixteen sections.[34] Sherman's bill now had tailing after it:

Reagan's bill, which, instead of relying on common-law formulas, gave a long explicit definition of the term "trust", [35] Ingall's bill, which was a more or less independent effort to prohibit speculation in farm products; and George's clause, which exempted labor unions and farmers' organizations from the general prohibitions. Moreover, the constitutional issue was still confused, and George suggested that the bill be referred to the Judiciary Committee, whose members, chosen for their legal wisdom, might be able to restore order to the law. Sherman, piqued and impatient, objected that it was most unusual to transfer a bill from one committee to another; Reagan, whose original bill had never been reported to the floor by the Judiciary Committee, was equally adamant; and Vance called the Judiciary Committee a "grand mausoleum of Senatorial literature" in which this bill would be buried. But after two more days in which further amendments were added and further profound doubts expressed, the matter had become so tangled that little alternative remained, and the bill was referred to the Judiciary Committee with instructions to report within twenty days.[36]

The Judiciary Committee took the matter out of Sherman's hands, much to his regret and anger. But within a week, surprising everyone, the Committee produced a bill of its own. The work was done largely by its chairman, George Edmunds of Vermont. He disposed of the constitutional question very quickly: when the Committee first met to consider the bill, he proposed to his colleagues "that it is competent for Congress to pass laws preventing and punishing contracts etc, in restraint of commerce between the states." And they, including George, who had raised objections to this theory all along, unanimously agreed.[37] Edmunds then presented drafts of the critical sections of the Act, that made it a misdemeanor to engage in any combination in restraint of trade or to "monopolize" trade, and these were agreed to by all the committeemen present. Two of the remaining sections were written by others: George prepared the section authorizing the Attorney General to sue for injunctions against violators, and Hoar wrote the section authorizing private persons to sue violators for triple damages.[38] The Committee's draft was in broad outline the same as Sherman's original bill, yet Sherman was not pleased. He immediately denounced it as "totally ineffective in dealing with combinations and trusts. All corporations can ride through it or over it without fear of punishment or detection." [39] His reaction was particularly ungenerous, since aside from the fact that the new bill was simpler than his, it differed mainly in providing a greater number of more severe penalties. But when the time came, he voted for it, and as a matter of courtesy it bears his name. The Senate as a whole seemed well satisfied, and after hearing Edmunds' plea that they "pass a bill that is clear in its terms, is definite in its definitions, and is broad in its comprehension, without winding it up into infinite details," [40] they passed it by fifty-two votes to one.

The action of the House was less systematic. Representative Culberson, who was in charge of the debate, tried to limit it to one hour. His colleagues, who had not until now considered any antitrust bill, complained that they could not get printed copies of the one before them. A strong group insisted that a section should be added to the bill specifically aimed at outlawing railroad and meat-packing pools. After a rather desultory debate, the House passed the bill with one amendment, on May 1. During the next two months, conferences were held between the two chambers, and the House was eventually prevailed on to withdraw its amendment.[41] President Harrison signed the bill, and it became law on July 2, 1890.

Law and Policy in the Sherman Act

The Sherman Act was as good an antitrust law as the Congress of 1890 could have devised. Congressmen had been called on to give the Federal Government novel powers to control, directly and generally, the organization of economic life. They had little experience to teach them how such a law should be written or to inform them how the courts might interpret it. They realized from the beginning that whatever law they composed would be imperfect. Its strongest advocates frankly admitted that it would be "experimental," [42] and in the end the whole of Congress was reconciled to the limitation Sherman recognized when he said, "All that we, as lawmakers, can do is to declare general principles." [43] Yet if the Sherman Act was an experiment, it was the safest one Congress could make, and if it only declared general principles, they were at least the familiar ones of the common law. Sherman had repeatedly said that his bill was based on a tried formula: "It does not announce a new principle of law, but applies old and well-recognized principles of the common law to the complicated jurisdiction of our State and Federal Government." [44] Edmunds, principal author of the Judiciary Committee bill, and Hoar, who guided it through debate on the floor, said the same. [45] Of the eighty-two senators, sixty-eight were lawyers, and as one of them said, "I suppose no lawyer needs to have argument made to him that these combinations and trusts are illegal without statute." [46] They could not tell how the courts would construe a statute that gave the government power to indict and sue the offenders, but they believed that the courts would experience little difficulty in recognizing the offense.

Congress had reason to think, further, that the Act aimed at the proper goals. On the one hand, it satisfied the public demand for an antitrust law. It prohibited trusts in so many words: it declared illegal "every contract, combination in the form of a trust or otherwise, or conspiracy, in restraint of trade or commerce among the several States or with foreign nations." This specific mention of "trusts" had almost been omitted, for Edmunds so strongly desired to define the offense in "terms that were well known to the law already" [47] that his draft of the section used only the common-law words, "contract," "combination," and "conspiracy." But a majority of his colleagues on the Judiciary Committee had seen the political value of adding a term that was well known to the public and had agreed to insert Evart's phrase, "in the form of a trust or otherwise." [48]

On the other hand, the Act did not go farther than Congress thought it should. Congressmen were no more in favor of unlimited competition than the economists were. Sherman, in his great address, had emphasized that many combinations were desirable. He was sure that they had been an important cause of America's wealth, and he had no intention of prohibiting them. It was only "the unlawful combination, tested by the rules of common law and human experience, that is aimed at by this bill, and not the lawful and useful combination." [49] Edmunds and Hoar later said they had the same intention. [50] A majority of the representatives who conferred with senators about the House amendment opposed it for similar reasons. They said that the bill's "only object was the control of trusts, so called," but that the scope of the amendment was broader, and indeed too broad: "It declares illegal any agreement for relief from the effects of competition in the two industries of transportation and merchandising, however excessive or destructive such competition may be."[51] Senator Teller meant the same, although he used impolitic language, when he said that "a trust may not always be an evil. A trust for certain purposes, which may mean simply a combination of capital, may be a favorable thing to the community and the country."[52] Perhaps the clearest statement of this view, held by many congressmen as well as by many economists of the period, was that of Representative Stewart of Vermont:

[T]here are two great forces working in human society in this country to-day, and they have been contending for the mastery on one side or the other for the last two generations. Those two great forces are competition and combination. They are correctives of each other, and both ought to exist. Both ought to be under restraint. Either of them, if allowed to be unrestrained, is destructive of the material interests of this country.[53]

The common law was a perfect instrument for realizing the policy supported by Congress. It prohibited some monopolies but not all combinations, and congressmen felt that a statute based on it would have equally qualified effects.

Though the pattern of the law was sound, there were nevertheless defects in detail. Various ambiguities had crept in because so many men had taken part in drafting it, because they wanted it to be simple and general, and because they wanted to use common-law terms to define the offenses. In order to keep the law broad, Congress did not specifically exclude labor unions from its scope or include railroad pools. So far as their sentiments were expressed in debates and bills, they had favored unions or wanted to leave them immune from this law. Sherman said they should be specifically exempted and many agreed with him.[54] Edmunds almost alone spoke against a specific exemption, because he thought that labor unions should be treated like any other combination.[55] But when he came to write the bill he was mainly concerned with keeping it unqualified. His colleagues seem to have been convinced by his arguments in favor of simplicity. Although during the debates four of the eight members of the Judiciary Committee spoke for exempting labor unions,[56] they all voted for Edmunds' draft, probably because they agreed that the law should not be cluttered with details and felt that, in any case, it would not be construed against unions. Reasoning of the same sort explains why railroad pools were not specifically named as offenders, for Senator Vest, a member of the Judiciary Committee, in commenting on the House amendment said that he too had wanted to add an explicit prohibition, until the other committeemen convinced him it would be redundant.[57] In order to make the Act more inclusive, Congress introduced another note that added to its ambiguity. "Restraints of trade," as the common law understood them, could only come about through agreement between persons; but the Judiciary Committee felt that the Act should also condemn any individual who restrained trade by himself, and they therefore drafted a section making it illegal for any individual to "monopolize." Hoar and Edmunds assured the Senate that the word had a well-known meaning at common law,[58] and their advice was followed, although the word meant little more at common law than the engrossing of a local food supply. These were only a few of the blemishes that marred the Act; the courts in time found many more. But to have drawn up a more satisfactory solution for a new and difficult problem, congressmen would have had to be much more adept, much more remote from public opinion, and much more unanimous in their own views than the lawmakers of a democracy ever can be.

NOTES

1. See the authoritative text, Seager and Gulick, *Trust and Corporation Problems* 373 (1929) and Mund, *Government and Business* 145, 146, 150 (1950).

2. Fainsod and Gordon, *Government and the American Economy* 450 (1941). Cochran and Miller, *The Age of Enterprise* 171–2 (1942). See also, Papandreou and Wheeler, *Competition and Its Regulation* 213 (1954), in which the Sherman Act is described as a measure of "appeasement."

3. Senator Platt said that his colleagues were interested in only one thing, "to get some bill headed: 'A Bill to Punish Trusts' with which to go to the country." Coolidge, *An Old-Fashioned Senator: Orville H. Platt* 444 (1910). Justice Holmes thought that the Act was "a humbug based on economic ignorance and incompetence." *Holmes-Pollock Letters,* I, 163 (Howe ed.)

4.   Greenback platform of 1884; a virtually identical expression appeared in their platform of 1880, and a more expanded version in the Anti-Monopoly platform of 1884. McKee, *National Conventions and Platforms* 215, 192, 224 *et seq.* (1901).

5.   *Ibid.,* 251. Anti-monopoly planks appeared also in the 1888 platforms of the Prohibition Party and of the United Labor Party. *Ibid.,* 247, 252 *et seq.*

6.   *Ibid.,* 184, 206.

7.   Richardson, *Messages and Papers of the Presidents,* VIII, 588 (1900) (Message of Dec. 6, 1887).

8.   McKee, *National Conventions and Platforms* 250.

9.   *Ibid.,* 235.

10.   Butler, *Address to His Constituents* 8 (Pamphlet of Aug. 12, 1884).

11.   N.Y. *World* p. I (Oct. 30. 1884).

12.   McKee, *National Conventions and Platforms* 241.

13.   50th Cong. 1st Sess. Sen. 2906; H.R. 6113, 6117, 8036, 8054, 9449, 10049 (1888). The bills, as well as debates directly concerned with them, are conveniently gathered in 57th Cong. 2d Sess., Sen. Doc. No. 147, *Bills and Debates in Congress Relating to Trusts* (1903), from which, however, some relevant matter is omitted, e.g., H.R. 4406.

14.   19 *Cong. Rec.* 6041 (1888).

15.   19 *Cong. Rec.* 190.

16.   19 *Cong. Rec.* 6041.

17.   19 *Cong. Rec.* 7512.

18.   19 *Cong. Rec.* 7512.

19.   Crosskey, *Politics and the Constitution* parts 1–2 (1953).

20.   19 *Cong. Rec.* 7512.

21.   20 *Cong. Rec.* 1167–69 (1889).

22.   20 *Cong. Rec.* 1459–61.

23.   51st Cong. 1st Sess., Sen. 1 (1889).

24.   21 *Cong. Rec.* 1765–72 (1890).

25.   Sherman's Resolution (see p. 87 above) having expired with the end of the 50th Congress, Reagan's bill (51st Cong. 1st Sess., Sen. 62, [1889]) was referred to the Judiciary Committee, but George's bill (51st Cong. 1st Sess., Sen. 6, [1889]) was sent to the Finance Committee. Of the bills in the House

(H.R. 91, 179, 202, 270, 286, 313, 402, 509, 811, 826, 839, 846, 3294, 3353, 3819, 3844, 3925 [1889]) nine were referred to the Ways and Means Committee, six to the Judiciary, and two to Manufactures. 51st Cong. 1st Sess., H.R. 30 (1889), a proposal for a constitutional amendment prohibiting trusts, was also before the Judiciary Committee.

26. 7 *Ry. & Corp. L.J.* 201 (1890).

27. A few public petitions and resolutions for state legislatures were read into the record during the second session of the 50th Congress (Dec. 3, 1888 to March 3, 1889), 20 *Cong. Rec.* 514, 1234, 1253, 1273, 1500, 1589, 2135 (1888–89). But between Dec. 2, 1889 and March 21, 1890, forty-nine were entered. 21 *Cong. Rec.* (listed in Index, sub. "Trusts, Petitions").

28. N.Y. *Times* p. 6, col. 1 (March 19, 1890).

29. 21 *Cong. Rec.* 2456 (1890).

30. 77 Mich. 632 (1889).

31. The rumor that Alger, or his managers, bought votes of Southern delegates, reputedly at $50.00 each, was reported at the time and has been repeated since by disinterested witnesses: N.Y. *Trib.* (June 10, 1888); Stephenson, *Nelson W. Aldrich* 71, 434 n. 7 (1930); Gresham, *Life of Walter Quintin Gresham,* II, 574, 632 (1919). Sherman was convinced of its truth and was openly antagonistic to Alger. When President Harrison signed the Antitrust Bill, he is said to have remarked, "John Sherman has fixed General Alger," though this story may well be apocryphal. Gresham, II, 632. Though revenge cannot have been Sherman's chief motive in pressing for the Act, there is no doubt that he was bitter about the incident; he still referred to it angrily in his autobiography. Sherman, *Recollections of Forty Years,* II, 1029 (1895). And he did not forego the opportunity to indulge the passion; contemporary observers remarked the relish with which he read the opinion in Richardson v. Buhl. N.Y. *Times* p. 4, col. 3 (March 25, 1890).

32. Craft v. McConoughy, 79 Ill. 346 (1875); Chicago Gas Co. v. People's Gas Co., 121 Ill. 530 (1887); People v. Chicago Gas Trust Co., 130 Ill. 268 (1889); People v. North River Sugar Refining Co., 22 Abb. N.C. (N.Y.) 164 (1889), aff'd, 121 N.Y. 582 (1890).

33. 21 *Cong. Rec.* 2458 *et seq.* (1890).

34. *Bills and Debates* 217–22 (1890).

35. Reagan defined a trust as a "combination of capital, skill, or acts" by two or more persons or associations for any of the following purposes: to restrict trade, to limit production, to increase or reduce price, to prevent competition,

to fix prices, to "create a monopoly," to make any agreement to set minimum prices, to agree to "pool, combine, or unite" so as to affect prices. 51st Cong. 1st Sess., Sen. 62 (1889).

36. 21 *Cong. Rec.* 2600 *et seq.,* 2604, 2610, 2731 (1890).

37. Senate Committee on the Judiciary, Minute Book 226 (March 31, 1890) (Ms. in U.S. Archives).

38. The Committee Minute Book 227–33, shows that sections 1, 2, 5, and 6 were drafted by Edmunds, section 4 by George, section 7 by Hoar, and the phrase "in the form of a trust or otherwise" by Evarts. It does not indicate who drafted sections 3 and 8. There is a strong presumption, but no proof, to support Walker's assertion that Edmunds did; Walker, "Who Wrote the Sherman Law?," 73 *Cen. L.J.* 257, 258 (1911).

39. N.Y. *Times* p. 4, col. 4 (April 8, 1890).

40. 21 *Cong. Rec.* 3148 (April 8, 1890).

41. *Bills and Debates 327–402 (1890).*

42. E.g., Senators Sherman, Edmunds, Turpie, and Representatives Culberson and Heard; 21 *Cong. Rec.* 2460, 2557–58, 3148, 4089, 4101 (1890).

43. 21 *Cong. Rec.* 2460 (1890).

44. 21 *Cong. Rec.* 2456.

45. 21 *Cong. Rec.* 3146, 3148, 3152.

46. Sen. Teller, 21 *Cong. Rec.* 2458.

47. 21 *Cong. Rec.* 3148.

48. See note 38, above.

49. 21 *Cong. Rec.* 2457, and also 2460.

50. Washburn, *The History of a Statute* 9 (1927); United States v. Joint Traffic Ass'n, 171 U.S. 505, 544 *et seq.* (1898); *Hearings before Senate Committee on Interstate Commerce, pursuant to Sen. Res. 98,* 62d Cong. 1st Sess., Vol. II, pp. 1550, 2430 (1912).

51. 21 *Cong. Rec.* 5950.

52. 21 *Cong. Rec.* 2471.

53. 21 *Cong. Rec.* 5956.

54. Sherman, 21 *Cong. Rec.* 2562, 2611–12; Hiscock, at 2468; Teller, at 2561–62; Reagan, at 2562; Gray, at 2657. Consult also note 56 below. The exemptions were included in 51st Cong. 1st Sess., Sen. 1, 6, and H.R. 91, 402, 509, 826, 3819, 3844 (1890).

55. 21 *Cong. Rec.* 2726–29.

56. Hoar, 21 *Cong. Rec.* 2728; Wilson, at 2658; Coke, at 2613–15. George was the author of the proviso in the first place. It appeared in his 51st Cong. 1st Sess., Sen. 6 (1890), from which Sherman borrowed it, 21 *Cong. Rec.* 2611.

57. 21 *Cong. Rec.* 6116. See also the remark by Hoar, at 4560.

58. 21 *Cong. Rec.* 3151–52.

THE POLITICS OF ANTITRUST ADMINISTRATION
James E. Anderson

The antitrust laws are a cardinal feature of public economic policy in the United States and there appears to be strong generalized public support for them. The Sherman Act, the Clayton Act, the Federal Trade Commission Act, and the other statutes collectively designated as antitrust legislation manifest an intent to prevent monopoly and maintain competition in the economy. It has been remarked that antitrust in the United States "is best understood when it is treated as a form of national religion,"[1] and that it is "an expression of a social philosophy, an educative force, and a political symbol of extraordinary potency."[2] Any effort to repeal or drastically change any of the antitrust laws seems predestined to failure and indeed is unlikely to be attempted. Criticism of antitrust is most likely to be directed at the manner in which the laws are enforced by the antitrust agencies or are interpreted by the courts.[3]

It is common knowledge that a substantial difference often exists between policy as manifested in legislative enactments and policy as an "operational reality" applicable to the everyday behavior of persons. In the latter sense the substance of public policy depends greatly on the actions and decisions of administrative and judicial bodies in interpreting and implementing legislation. This is clearly the case with antitrust policy. Because of the generality and vagueness of the provisions, meaningful understanding of antitrust policy requires more than a reading of the antitrust statutes. It also requires consideration of a large number of court cases interpreting the statutes and the administration of the laws by the antitrust agencies. Since the agencies possess and exercise discretion in administering the laws, the actual meaning of antitrust policy will partly depend on how this discretion is exercised.

The focus here is on the antitrust administrative process. Very little will be said about such matters as the legal doctrines developed in antitrust cases, the impact of antitrust on the economy, or arguments as to the form antitrust policy should properly take. Nor will much be said about the administrative procedures and legal techniques used by the antitrust agencies. Taking the antitrust laws and their judicial interpretations as given, my purpose is to identify some of the factors which shape the efforts of the agencies in applying the laws. Thus, the concern of this paper is with the "politics of enforcement," by which is meant those arrangements, traditions, pressures, and conditions which influence the course of administration and consequently the substance of policy. Major attention is given to the Antitrust Division and the Sherman Act.

The Politics of Enforcement

Although the initiative in antitrust enforcement rests with the administrative agencies, it should be noted that the legal meaning of the antitrust laws ultimately depends on the interpretation of them by the courts, particularly the Supreme Court. In some instances, especially prior to 1937, the Court has made rulings which have had a restrictive impact on the agencies. The Knight Case, the U. S. Steel Case, and the decisions in the 1920's holding that mergers through asset acquisition were not prohibited by the Clayton Act are well-known illustrations.[4] Since 1937 the Supreme Court has generally been favorably disposed toward antitrust and has upheld the antitrust agencies in most of the cases reaching it, while at the same time substantially broadening the meaning and scope of the antitrust laws. During the 1956–1964 period the Antitrust Division won 36 of 41 antitrust cases decided by the Supreme Court.[5]

Generally speaking, at the present time it seems that the Supreme Court, in its interpretation of the antitrust laws, has provided the Antitrust Division and the Justice Department with all the authority, and perhaps a little more, than they want to exercise.[6] In 1965 *Business Week* reported that then Attorney General Katzenbach was "concerned about how to manage the overkill capacity that the courts have given him" and that he believed the laws as interpreted by the courts reached further than it was practical to go in enforcement.[7] Donald Turner, the head of the Antitrust Division from 1965 to 1968, expressed the belief that antitrust suits should not be brought simply because they could be won under the laws as interpreted, and he acted accordingly.[8] The Supreme Court has thus provided the legal basis for vigorous antitrust enforcement, but this is only one factor, albeit an important one, shaping the course of antitrust activity.

Presidential administrations and political conditions. With respect to the impact of presidential administrations on antitrust activity, an examination of the historical record reveals that laxity or vigor in enforcement has depended less on whether an administration was Republican or Democratic than on whether it had a conservative or liberal orientation and on the nature of the prevailing political environment.[9] During the first decade of the Sherman Act neither the Republican Harrison and McKinley Administrations nor the Democratic Cleveland Administration did much to enforce the law; together they initiated a total of 11 cases. In the next decade and a half both the Republican Roosevelt and Taft Administrations and the Democratic Wilson Administration are usually counted as strong enforcers of the antitrust laws. Moreover, Taft, who was considered the most conservative of the three, had the most active enforcement program in terms of number of cases started. In recent years the Eisenhower Administration was no less active in the antitrust area than the Truman, Kennedy, and Johnson Administrations, again using quantitative measures such as cases started.

The political conditions extant during an administration's tenure in office seem to have a much greater impact on its antitrust program than does its partisan character. These political conditions may be of either a long- or short-term nature. Examples of the long-term variety include the generally conservative, business-oriented eras of the 1890's and the 1920's, the Progressive Era, and the period since 1937 (which has been characterized by conditions broadly favorable to antitrust—favorable court interpretations, increased acceptance of government intervention in the economy, etc.). The first two periods are associated with lax antitrust enforcement, the latter two with more general tendencies. More immediate, particular political conditions may have a short-range influence on what a given administration does. Thus the Taft Administration instituted 18 antitrust suits in the winter of 1912–1913, just prior to leaving office. This seems at least partly explainable as Taft's response to the criticism of his antitrust program by Wilson and Roosevelt during the 1912 presidential campaign.[10] The Kennedy Administration, which lacked a venturesome antitrust policy, was partly motivated by a desire to overcome the anti-business image with which it had been tagged, especially after the 1962 steel price crisis. In point, in June, 1962, Assistant Attorney General Loevinger, then in charge of the Antitrust Division, stated that "it just doesn't seem like the time to file any breathtaking, world-shaking cases—even if we were ready to." Another antitrust official was quoted at the same time as saying: "It is probably true that we are affected by business uncertainties to the point where we are holding up cases with a novel or uncertain character or approach."[11] The higher priority given to antitrust by the Eisenhower Administration has been explained as an effort to counteract the pro-business label given it by the press.[12]

The record of Franklin Roosevelt's Administration during the 1930's offers an especially instructive example of the impact of political conditions on antitrust policy. The New Deal was the product of an alignment of political forces which would lead one to expect a vigorous antitrust program. However, the economic dislocation created by the Great Depression and the immediate concern for recovery led initially to continuation of the antitrust quiescence of the 1920's. The National Industrial Recovery Act of 1933 largely suspended the antitrust laws in favor of industrial self-regulation under codes of "fair competition." In the New Deal's second term the economic downturn of 1937, public discontent with economic conditions, and pressures from Congress for greater attention to antitrust matters, caused Roosevelt to sense that a shift in policy was in order. The result was the appointment in 1938 of Thurman Arnold to head the Antitrust Division and the beginning of a new era of more vigorous enforcement of the antitrust laws.[13]

President Johnson was considered by many as an "economic conservative on antitrust" and apparently discouraged enforcement of the antitrust laws which would have harassed business. The Antitrust Division and the Federal Trade Commission were criticized by liberals during the Johnson Administration for relative inaction in filing antitrust suits and in expanding the reach of the antitrust laws.[14] Tables 1 and 2 indicate that there was a marked decline in antitrust activity after 1963. Another indication of the Administration's impact is contained in a statement made by Donald Turner to a Senate committee:

> ... I still subscribe to the views Professor Kaysen and I set forth, now some eight years ago, in which we urged additional legislation which would make it easier to deal with monopoly and oligopoly problems. However, I suppose it is highly likely that if I sent such a proposal forward to the administration, it would not be rushed over to the Hill the following morning.[15]

Presidential administrations are thus clearly an important component of the antitrust environment and do much to affect the general patterns of enforcement.

Administrative agencies. The primary administrative agencies in the antitrust area are the Antitrust Division of the Department of Justice and the Federal Trade Commission. They have overlapping jurisdictions. The Antitrust Division has responsibility for the Sherman Act and the FTC for the Federal Trade Commission Act. However, many practices which violate the Sherman Act can be attacked as unfair methods of competition under the Federal Trade Commission Act. The two agencies are thus potential competitors for jurisdiction, but they have apparently developed a satisfactory division of authority and working relationship for themselves. Their relationship does not seem characterized by any real tendency toward "administrative imperialism" on the part of either.[16] However, there have been some conflicts between them on particular policy issues, such as basing-point legislation during the Truman Administration.[17]

Their generally peaceful coexistence is facilitated by their differing policy orientations. The Antitrust Division acts as the "defender of competition" against monopolistic activity. Its enforcement efforts have been concentrated on Section 1 of the Sherman Act, which bans restraints of trade, and the amended Section 7 of the Clayton Act, which prohibits mergers that may substantially lessen competition (see Table 1). The Federal Trade Commission is essentially a protector of consumers against deceptive practices and of small businessmen against the "predations" of their larger competitors.[18] Its enforcement program has heavily emphasized the prevention of unfair or deceptive practices (e.g., false advertising) and, under the Clayton Act, price discrimination.[19]

The Federal Trade Commission has completed several hundred cases relating to price discrimination since the Clayton Act was amended and strengthened by the Robinson–Patman Act in 1936.[20] The Antitrust Division has instituted a total of 11 such cases during the same time. One explanation for this is an Antitrust Division official's statement that "Budgetary limitations cause the Department to refer almost all complaints of violations of Section 2 of the Clayton Act to the Commission. . . ."[21] A better explanation is probably that the Division, given its procompetitive orientation, finds the price discrimination clause rather distasteful. In fact, the Division opposed the adoption of the Robinson–Patman Act when it was before Congress.

To avoid overlapping, duplication, and conflict in areas in which both have jurisdiction, the Division and Commission have developed a notification arrangement.[22] When one agency starts to investigate a matter which might be within the scope of the other, the other is immediately notified. If it happens that a related or overlapping proceeding is already underway, the matter is ordinarily left to the agency which acted first. This arrangement is a matter of comity rather than law. Within the areas where both are likely to act, the determination of which, if either, does act in a particular instance seems more a matter of chance than design. There appears to be little *active* cooperation between the two agencies. A former Justice Department official who was closely concerned with the liaison arrangement has stated: "We tried to take all that was good and give the Commission all that we didn't want."[23] The human element cannot be ignored in such matters.

Some of the implications of having two major antitrust agencies have been set forth by Massel:*

It is mainly by chance that an alleged violation is treated by one or the other of these agencies. On several occasions, the Antitrust Division has instituted antitrust suits taking little or no account of previous action by the Federal

---

*From Mark S. Massel, *Competition and Monopoly* (New York: Doubleday, Anchor Books, 1964), pp. 84–85. Quoted by permission of the publisher.

Trade Commission for the same practices. Lawyers for potential defendants try to have their problems handled by one agency or the other, depending on their feelings about which will give their clients easier treatment. In the same way, lawyers who seek informal clearance of prospective mergers or other business ventures select the agency that pleases them most.[24]

Antitrust administration is further complicated by the fact that some 18 other federal agencies also have a share of antitrust jurisdiction.[25] Some of these agencies have direct enforcement duties, some can exempt certain practices from prosecution, a few are authorized to suspend statutory exemptions, some provide information, and so on. The Federal Trade Commission usually does not get involved in imperialistic or competitive struggles with other agencies and has developed informal cooperative relationships with some. For instance, it has an agreement with the Small Business Administration whereby small businessmen can file complaints of unfair practices that come within the Commission's jurisdiction with any of the SBA's field offices, which will forward them to the FTC for action.

In contrast, conflict often attends interaction between the Antitrust Division and some of the other agencies. In recent years, the Division has been involved in some sharp conflicts with some of the independent regulatory commissions and federal banking agencies, especially the Comptroller of the Currency, over corporate mergers. The regulatory agencies usually act as both promoters and regulators of the industries under their jurisdiction and often are quite sympathetic and responsive to industry interests. In deciding whether to approve proposed mergers, the regulatory agencies are likely to hold that the "public interest" is not limited to competition and that such factors as business solvency, efficiency, or ability to meet the needs of the community served outweigh any adverse effects which a merger might have on competition. Such approval does not bar action by the Antitrust Division, which focuses on the anticompetitive aspects of mergers, and in recent years it has successfully challenged a merger of two natural-gas pipeline companies approved by the Federal Power Commission and several bank mergers approved by the Comptroller of the Currency.[26] One effect of conflicts of this sort is to leave public policy unsettled.

Agency personnel. Although antitrust administration is an institutional process, the persons appointed to head the agencies can have an impact on both the direction and the intensity of enforcement. Discretion in the process permits the official to give some expression to his political philosophy, notions of proper public policy, partisan inclinations, or whatever personally motivates him. If the impact of personnel is difficult to separate from political conditions, presidential support, and other factors, it is nonetheless operative. During the second Cleveland Administration (1893–1897), the first Attorney General, Richard T. Olney, had little liking for the Sherman Act and did little to enforce it. After the government lost the Knight Case (1895), he wrote: "The government has been defeated in the Supreme Court on the trust question. I always supposed it would be and have taken the responsibility of not prosecuting under a law I supposed to be no good . . . ." [27] Olney's successor, Judson Harmon, showed more initiative and was responsible for the actions culminating successfully in the Trans-Missouri and Joint Traffic Association cases. [28] Under the Eisenhower Administration, Robert Bicks, a firm believer in antitrust, displayed more enthusiasm for the antitrust laws as head of the Antitrust Division than did his predecessor, Victor Hansen. [29] Another head of the Division, Donald Turner, indicated that he would give less attention than formerly to winning price-fixing cases and to criminal antitrust prosecutions, and that one area of increased concern would be restrictive patent licensing. [30]

With regard to the Federal Trade Commission, the story of how William Humphrey dominated it in the 1920's and converted it from an agency to regulate business into one primarily concerned with helping business is familiar history. [31] The current chairman of the FTC, Paul Rand Dixon, was something of an old-style antitrust before his appointment in 1961. Under his guidance the Commission was initially more concerned with antimonopoly work than it had been during the 1950's, [32] although its momentum has tailed off recently. Dixon has also striven to make the Commission more responsive to the interests of small business.

Personality conflicts between officials involved in antitrust administration may also affect what is done. Anthony Lewis states that one cause of the Kennedy Administration's lack of a "venturesome antitrust policy" was that Lee Loevinger, the head of the Antitrust Division, did not get along well with Attorney General Robert Kennedy. Kennedy's lack of confidence in Loevinger, contends Lewis, dampened the activity of the Antitrust Division. This situation apparently ended with the appointment of William Orrick to succeed Loevinger.[33]

Appropriations. A frequently encountered statement in antitrust literature is that the volume of enforcement activity depends on the funds available to the enforcement agencies. A common complaint by the proponents of a strong antitrust program is that the agencies are hampered by inadequate appropriations. Other things being equal, the amount of funds available to the agencies does help determine whether antitrust enforcement tends to be lax or vigorous, as measured by case activity, and whether it is innovative or not. Until the mid-1930's the appropriation for the Antitrust Division was under $300,000 annually. As a consequence, in the view of Professor Edwards, antitrust enforcement was "merely symbolic in character." He continues:*

In any one year, from half a dozen to a dozen instances of law violation were arbitrarily selected for investigation and trial because of the importance of the defendants, the political ripeness of the issue involved, or the significance of the question of law upon which the decision would turn. With all available resources committed to these few cases, the enforcement agencies were helpless to undertake new work, and in consequence the prosecution of a few lawbreakers became in effect a guarantee of immunity to the rest. It was inevitable that the meager resources should be used primarily in attempting to prevent relatively obvious types of restriction, and for this reason many significant and controversial issues were ignored.[34]

In recent years the appropriations for the Antitrust Division and the Federal Trade Commission have increased substantially. Whereas the Division received three million dollars annually in the mid-1950's, its budget has ranged upward from five to seven million dollars per year in the 1960's. A larger increase has been registered by the FTC. Its budget was around four million dollars annually in the mid-1950's.

---

*From Corwin D. Edwards, *Maintaining Competition* (New York: McGraw-Hill, 1949), pp. 293–294. Quoted by permission of the publisher.

During the 1960's its annual appropriation has grown from six to fifteen million dollars. With this increase in funds has come a substantial increase in agency proceedings. More than twice as many antitrust cases have been started since 1940 than during the preceding 50 years. New cases averaged 60 per year during the 1957–1966 period. Obviously, however, there is not necessarily a direct, one-to-one relationship between amount of funds and volume of case activity. In 1965 and 1966 the Antitrust Division started only 43 and 44 cases, respectively, despite larger appropriations, perhaps because of reduced concern with winning easy cases which involve less agency expense.

Appropriations, of course, are not an independent variable affecting enforcement. Their volume depends on the support, or lack thereof, for antitrust in Congress, the administration, and society. Their growth can be viewed as a manifestation of increased support for antitrust, although within both government and society there is still considerable ambivalence, indifference, and opposition to antitrust. Consequently, less money still is provided for antitrust than many consider necessary for a really vigorous, full-scale enforcement program.

Appropriations are also significant for antitrust because the process by which they are provided represents a point of continuing contact between Congress and the agencies. It affords Congress or, more accurately, the appropriations subcommittees an opportunity to influence or control agency activity by both formal and informal means.[35] The ensuing discussion will focus on House action, since the Senate, acting in its usual appellate role in the budgetary process, has dealt only occasionally and briefly with the antitrust agency budgets. The time period involved is 1960–1967.

In the House Appropriations Committee the budget for the Antitrust Division is handled by the Subcommittee for the Departments of State, Justice, and Commerce, the Judiciary, and Related Agencies. Since 1955 the chairman of the Subcommittee has been Representative John Rooney (D., N.Y.), who has a reputation as an "economizer." Nonetheless, and despite the committee's budget-cutting orientation, in the last decade the Subcommittee has always approved the entire budget request for the Antitrust Division.[36] Mr. Rooney has dominated the Subcommittee's hearings on the antitrust appropriation, which have usually taken only part of a day. He has shown much concern for "concrete" data in evaluating the Division's requests—numbers of cases litigated or terminated, amount of fines collected, and the like. The hearings devote little attention to such matters as antitrust doctrine, the scope or impact of enforcement, or the relationship of antitrust to competition. Items such as these cannot be assessed or measured in any precise manner, and a focus on them would probably add more hyperbole than facts to the Subcommittee's information.

The Subcommittee's concern with hard facts is well illustrated by an incident which occurred during the 1965 antitrust hearings. Mr. Rooney remarked that "we have a situation where we only collected $1,200,000 in fines and no jail sentences. We wonder if that is a sensible expenditure of almost $7,000,000 of the taxpayers' money." This observation led into the following exchange with William Orrick of the Antitrust Division.

Mr. Rooney. What are they [the 294 lawyers in the Division] doing?

Mr. Orrick. They are preparing cases, going to the libraries, conducting grand juries, conducting investigations, and doing research, and I think the taxpayers' money is very well spent, indeed, on this activity. I might say with the continuing high-level investigations this is important.

Mr. Rooney. You have been in Government three years?

Mr. Orrick. Yes sir.

Mr. Rooney. And this is your third time up here?

Mr. Orrick. Yes sir.

Mr. Rooney. You should know that these gratuitous statements do not convince us at all. We would like to have some meat to digest. If you were to sit across there and tell us you had produced a case like the Philadelphia electric cases, then you would have something. [Rooney was apparently much impressed by these.]

Mr. Orrick. We are looking for those all the time, Mr. Chairman.

Mr. Rooney. And you have not found any?

Mr. Orrick. I have not found any since I have been there; no, but we are looking.

Mr. Rooney. It is pretty hard to understand that with the appropriation . . . of approximately five million dollars in 1961 there were 35 criminal cases won compared with 12 in 1962, and 18 in 1963.[37]

It appears that concern of this sort by the appropriations Subcommittee quite probably has helped cause the Antitrust Division in the past to stress statistical results and to focus on winning cases, whatever their significance. A comment by Paul Rand Dixon is in point here. "It is of course a valid observation that, so long as the performance of the antitrust agencies is measured by the number of proceedings brought or completed, the smaller cases and the consent order procedure 'could encourage a type of numbers game.' " He went on to say that the FTC did not believe that numbers were "the *sole* criterion." [38]

An illustration of the "numbers game" in operation can be drawn from the Antitrust Division's experience during 1962–1963. In its report on the appropriation for fiscal year 1963, the Subcommittee stated:

In allowing the full amount ($5,988,000) which is $113,000 over the appropriation for fiscal year 1962 the Committee expects an effective program of enforcement of the Antitrust laws. The Committee is much more interested in the successful conclusion of cases than in statistical work load charts.[39]

In its 1963 annual report the Division asserted that its "record during the fiscal year just closed shows that the committee's directions have been fully implemented." Sixty-two antitrust cases were filed and 88 were terminated during the year. "This is an all-time record," the report continued, "and almost three times the number of antitrust cases closed during the entire preceding year, when only 30 were terminated." The government won 80, lost 6, and requested dismissal of 2.[40] The Division also emphasized its compliance with the Subcommittee's directive during the hearings on its 1964 budget request. "I think we are doing what this committee suggested to do," remarked Assistant Attorney General Loevinger.[41] The Subcommittee recommended the Division's full request.

The Federal Trade Commission has also fared rather well in the appropriations process in recent years. The Subcommittee on Independent Offices of the House Appropriations Committee, which deals with the FTC, has typically followed the standard appropriations-committee practice of recommending less than the Commission requested but more than it received during the previous fiscal year. Some of the cuts in its requests have been appealed by the Commission to the Senate and partially restored. The Subcommittee has probed much more deeply and thoroughly into FTC activity—extent of activity, particular matters handled, use of personnel, nature of enforcement program—than has been the case for the Antitrust Division. Generally, the Subcommittee has been favorably disposed toward the Commission's program. The present Subcommittee chairman, Representative Joe Evins (D., Tenn.), and Chairman Dixon are long-term friends and both were once staff members on the FTC. That this situation bodes well for the FTC seems apparent from Representative Evins' opening remarks at the 1967 fiscal year hearings:

Mr. Evins.   The Committee will come to order.

We are pleased and delighted to see our friends from the Federal Trade Commission with us today, one of our favorite agencies. This is a very fine and distinguished group.

I did not think twenty or more years ago when I was attorney at the Commission that I would be sitting in on your budget. I did not visualize that, I did envision, [sic] that Paul Rand Dixon, a great football player and a driving man, would someday be driving against the forces of monopoly while heading this Commission.[42]

One complaint the Subcommittee has frequently voiced about the Commission's work has concerned its focus on minor matters rather than more important antimonopoly work. Representative Albert Thomas (D., Tex.), who preceded Evins as chairman of the Subcommittee, often chided the Commission about this. In 1964, after a reference to the electrical price-fixing case, he remarked: "In that case it was brought to light that it [the price-fixing conspiracy] cost more money than all the salts, pills, oils, and Serutan put together, and multiplied by a hundred. Why chase rabbits when you have these lions?"[43] The belief that the Commission should act on more significant matters has also been expressed by Representative Evins and stated in committee reports. In recent years, perhaps at least partly because of such pressures, the Commission has given more attention to antimonopoly work, roughly 60 per cent of its enforcement budget now going for this purpose. Dixon argues that the decline in formal activity is the result of an emphasis on informal enforcement techniques.

The appropriations process may also be utilized by congressmen to prevent or discourage agency actions which do not meet their approval. For fiscal year 1964 the Federal Trade Commission requested funds for a reporting program utilizing a questionnaire to collect detailed financial and product information and data on mergers and acquisitions from the thousand largest manufacturing and merchandising corporations. In the budget hearings the members of the Independent Offices Subcommittee expressed considerable concern about this proposal, although it had already been softened in order to get Budget Bureau approval. Objections were that it might involve self-incrimination, the information might be available elsewhere, it involved too much intervention in private affairs, and businessmen complained about having to spend too much time filling out government questionnaires.[44] The committee report on the Commission's appropriation indicated that this item had been rejected. "The $100,000 included in the 1964 budget program for a general questionnaire and economic study of intercorporate relations has been denied and a limitation has been included in the bill prohibiting the use of funds for that purpose."[45]

Another important participant in the budgetary process is the Bureau of the Budget with its authority "to assemble, correlate, revise, reduce, or increase" agency budget requests before they are transmitted to Congress. Budget Bureau action may relate both to the amount of agency funds and to the purposes for which funds may be used. Agency budget requests are sometimes reduced by the Bureau of the Budget before they reach Congress. In the appropriations hearings for 1965, the Chairman of the FTC reported that the Bureau had reduced the Commission's budget request from $15,178,000 to $13,270,000, as part of the President's economy drive.[46]

The Bureau of the Budget may also act to eliminate or modify particular purposes for which funds are requested.[47] In 1961 the FTC's original budget request included funds to conduct studies of credit terms and shopping center leases, since these involved problems for small businesses. Both items were deleted by the Bureau of the Budget before transmittal to Congress. Another set of 1961 requests was altered by the Bureau. The Commission originally sought funds for studies of collusive pricing policies of food chain stores (at the suggestion of the Senate Small Business Committee) and the decline of sources of supply because of the adverse implications for independent distributors. As altered by the Bureau, the final request provided for a grower-to-consumer study "to ascertain and analyze distribution trends, discounts, allowances, and the operation of different classes of buyers, sellers, and special organizations for marketing." If these examples are at all representative, they indicate that the Budget Bureau is less sympathetic to small business interests than the FTC and that the latter does not escape executive budgetary controls because of its independent status.

Other congressional activities.   In addition to the appropriations process, there are many other ways by which Congress, particular committees, or individual congressmen may seek to influence antitrust enforcement. Congress may enact legislation for the purpose of either facilitating or limiting antitrust enforcement. In the years since World War II a number of statutes in each of these two categories have been enacted. Legislation strengthening antitrust includes the Celler Antimerger Act; an act increasing maximum fines in criminal cases from $5000 to $50,000 per violation; an act permitting the government to recover damages from antitrust violators; a statute giving the FTC some jurisdiction over meat-packing companies; a law making FTC orders issued under the Clayton Act final unless appealed in 60 days; and the Antitrust Civil Process Act of 1962, which significantly strengthened the ability of the Antitrust Division to secure evidence in civil antitrust cases. Legislation restricting antitrust enforcement has usually involved the exemption of particular industries or activities from antitrust prosecution. Included here are fair trade agreements, railroad rate agreements, insurance companies, some national defense activities, bank mergers (partially), and most recently, the professional football merger.[48] Congress has thus made some efforts to strengthen the enforcement process while at the same time responding to the demands of particular interests for special treatment under the antitrust laws.

The House and Senate Judiciary Committees (particularly their antitrust subcommittees), the Select Committees on Small Business, and the Joint Economic Committee are important components of the constituencies of the Antitrust Division and Federal Trade Commission. The Committees, through their hearings and investigations, staff studies, personal contact, and other actions, variously act to encourage, admonish, persuade, or defend the antitrust agencies, customarily in support of the goal of vigorous antitrust enforcement. In 1958 the Antitrust Subcommittee of the House Judiciary Committee conducted a lengthy investigation of the use of consent decrees by the Antitrust Division during the Eisenhower Administration. It issued a report in which it expressed strong criticism of their use in some cases and cautioned against their misuse.[49] In 1965 a subcommittee of the House Select Committee on Small Business held hearings on the "Activities of Regulatory and Enforcement Agencies Relating to Small Business." The hearings took on the appearance of a campaign to persuade such agencies, including the Antitrust Division and the Federal Trade Commission, to be favorably disposed to the interests of small business. Dixon of the FTC was quite agreeable to this but Donald Turner of the Antitrust Division, while expressing concern for small businessmen, resisted committing himself to becoming their particular champion.[50]

In the performance of "case work" for their constituents, congressmen engage in much communication with administrative agencies, including the antitrust agencies. The Antitrust Division, for example, reported that it received and answered 617 letters of inquiry from congressmen in 1963. Agency officials frequently mention congressmen as comprising a major source of complaints concerning antitrust violations. Senator Sparkman has provided an account of a successful intervention:

Just recently I had a friend in my state call me on the telephone. He was the operator of a small bakery operating just in one town. He told me that a chain bakery, a big one, had reduced the price of bread by 3 cents a loaf in his town. In another town 6 miles away, there had been no change.

All of the circumstances he gave indicated that it was a move to freeze him out. And he told me he could be frozen out very quickly. . . . May I say that I took this matter up with your office [he was speaking to Lee Loevinger, head of the Antitrust Division], and also with the Federal Trade Commission, and both of you moved in quite promptly, and the matter was cured quickly.[51]

This is undoubtedly not an isolated story of success, at least so far as alacrity of response by the agencies is concerned.

Pressure groups. In the literature pressure groups are frequently cited as a major cause of inadequate enforcement of the antitrust laws.[52] If by this contention it is meant that overt "pressure" activities of organized groups, acting directly on the antitrust agencies, have forestalled or dulled agency enforcement activity, it seems at best a matter of conjecture. There is little solid evidence in the record to support such a theory. Indeed, Joseph Palamountain contends that the Federal Trade Commission is unique among the independent regulatory commissions "in that organized groups seldom apply strong and continuing pressure to it." Of course, trade associations and other groups may call alleged illegalities to the attention of the Commission. However, the jurisdiction of the Commission covers so much of the economy that few organized groups become its permanent clients and "none looms large in its environment." This condition would seem to be characteristic also of the Antitrust Division, with its similarly broad jurisdiction. In further explanation of the scarcity of organized pressures on the FTC, Palamountain notes that it is one of the most legalistic commissions and has preferred deciding individual cases to the exercise of rule-making power. Consequently, he concludes, "its policies and their political implications are spelled out so slowly as to minimize political reactions."[53]

There is, of course, much opposition and critical comment voiced with respect to both particular agency decisions and general patterns of action. In press statements, business magazines, law reviews and economic journals, the proceedings of the Antitrust Section of the American Bar Association, and elsewhere, one encounters much adverse comment. But there is also much support or approval expressed as well. Both categories of commentators offer many suggestions concerning the "proper" course of antitrust policy. How much impact all this commentary has on agency enforcement activity is problematical,[54] but it clearly indicates that there is no general agreement on the meaning or purposes of antitrust.

Strong, organized support is also lacking for antitrust enforcement. There is no "antitrust lobby," no set of active groups, no clientele upon which the agencies can depend for strong, continuing support. Consumers, who most clearly benefit from competition, are notoriously unorganized in our society. Among producer groups there is a substantial element of truth in the comment that everyone wants competition for everyone, except himself. This is attested to by the many efforts, frequently successful, of groups to gain exemption from the antitrust laws because "their situation is different."

The antitrust agencies, in sum, seem to exist in a sort of "no-party constituency," in which organized support or opposition tends to be shaped by particular agency decisions, and to rise and fall as the issues so created gain and then lose saliency. They stand in contrast to such regulatory commissions as the Federal Power Commission, the Interstate Commerce Commission, and the Civil Aeronautics Board, each of which has a well-organized clientele continuously concerned with its actions and to which it is markedly responsive.

An Agency Perspective

Thus far the politics of antitrust administration have been considered primarily in terms of the political forces impinging on the agencies. This section will briefly examine the Antitrust Division's enforcement activity and attempt to relate it to the agency's need for political support. Antitrust agencies, like others, "are in a continuous process of adjustment to the political environment that surrounds them—an adjustment that seeks to keep a favorable balance of political support over political opposition." [55] Let us see how this may influence agency action.

Roughly two-thirds of the antitrust cases filed under the Sherman Act have dealt with collusive practices in violation of Section 1, with price-fixing agreements being the activity most often singled out for legal action.[56] Only a small portion of the antitrust cases since 1890 have involved monopolization under Section 2, and most of these have not involved monopoly in a primary sense. From 1957 to 1967 monopolization cases averaged eight per year (see Table 1). It has been many years since a major monopolization case of the old fashioned trust-bearing variety was brought in an established industry.

In recent years, it is true, the Antitrust Division has given increased attention to antimerger cases under the Clayton Act, but this is a different matter.

Not only has antitrust enforcement emphasized Sherman Act Section 1 cases, it has also been concentrated on three industrial groupings: food processing and distribution, production and distribution of building materials, and the service trades. Around half of the antitrust cases have involved these industry groupings, even though they are far less concentrated than such industries as basic metals, chemicals, industrial machinery, and farm machinery, which have been rather infrequently considered under the antitrust laws.

Why have these patterns developed? For one thing, most antitrust cases arise out of private complaints, made either personally by the complainants or by their congressmen. By being somewhat passive and acting mostly on the basis of complaints received, the enforcement agency can appear as something of an impartial arbiter, a role which may reduce opposition and criticism. Much of the recent criticism of the Antitrust Division has involved antimerger activity, an area in which the Division acts largely on its own initiative. Also, the Division does not have funds sufficient to conduct extensive investigations in quest of violations.

About two-thirds of the complaints received by the Antitrust Division emanate from businessmen seeking protection against competitors, groups of competitors, or suppliers.[57] Such complaints are more likely to arise in industries, such as the three designated above, where there are many companies operating. There are also more customers and competitors available to complain, and apparently complain they do.

The industrial groupings most involved in antitrust proceedings either deal with the "necessities" of life, such as food, or come into contact with large numbers of customers and competitors, as in the case of building materials. It is probably politically expedient for the Division, in terms of public and congressional support, to bring cases in these industries. Protection of the consumer against illegal price-fixing has a certain appeal.

No matter what the industry, it is easier for the Division to win collusive practices cases under Section 1 than monopolization cases. The former do not entail the use of complex, economic concepts and data; indeed, many collusive practices, such as price-fixing, are *per se* violations. All that needs to be proved is their mere existence. Monopolization cases are more difficult to win and are more costly in resources required—time, personnel, and money. By concentrating on Section 1 cases, many of which involve obvious violations and are settled by consent decrees or pleas, the Division is able to bring more cases and win a very high percentage of them. Given the emphasis on statistical results, e.g., by Congressman Rooney's House appropriations subcommittee, this appears as a logical way for the agency to gain needed political support. Also, while price-fixing cases are in the oldest antitrust tradition, monopolization cases directed against large corporations and oligopolistic market structures would run counter to the present acceptance of substantial concentration in the economy. An effort to bring more such cases would undoubtedly be dubbed "anti-business." And, as Galbraith has remarked, "to declare the big corporation illegal is, in effect, to declare the modern economy illegal." [58]

The Sherman Act is thus applied with notable discrimination. The result is an enforcement pattern which appears to be beneficial to the Antitrust Division if not always significant economically.

Concluding Comments

Antitrust enforcement as here depicted exemplifies the blending of politics and administration so frequently remarked on in the modern literature of public administration. Antitrust administration is a political process carried on in an environment populated by a variety of political forces—such as presidential administrations, congressional committees, group pressures, administrative agencies, and public opinion—which influence the direction and volume of enforcement activity. The combination of forces which plays upon the antitrust agencies changes from one situation to another and from one time to another. This paper has been concerned with identifying some of the important political forces and qualitatively commenting on their activity and impact. Further research to permit generalizations as to what forces tend to operate in particular types of situations or cases would be desirable. While legal and economic considerations are also important

Table 1. Antitrust Division: Case Activity, 1957–1967

	1957	1958	1959	1960	1961	1962	1963	1964	1965	1966	1967
Cases Filed											
Civil	37	32	21	59	40	41	39	41	33	32	36
Criminal	18	22	42	27	22	32	23	23	10	12	17
Total	55	54	63	86	62	73	62	64	43	44	53
Price-Fixing Cases											
Civil	15	18	9	36	11	27	13	16	13	14	26
Criminal	13	17	40	23	18	31	20	11	7	12	16
Total	28	35	49	59	29	58	33	27	20	26	42
Merger Cases	5	4	6	13	15	10	14	10	17	14	7
Monopolization Cases											
Civil	10	6	3	7	4	9	4	5	6	5	6
Criminal	2	4	4	2	2	10	1	1	1	0	0
Total	12	10	7	9	6	19	5	6	7	5	6

Source: Antitrust Division, Department of Justice

Table 2. Federal Trade Commission: Formal Activity, 1957–1967

	1957	1958	1959	1960	1961	1962	1963	1964	1965	1966	1967
Complaints Issued											
Antimonopoly	55	86	79	157	120	234	230	96	26	94	24
Deceptive practices	187	268	271	346	290	240	129	129	66	48	108
Cease-and-Desist Orders											
Antimonopoly	31	45	64	57	103	92	261	136	39	94	30
Deceptive practices	148	228	267	289	265	319	161	121	67	51	95

Source: Federal Trade Commission

in antitrust enforcement, to neglect the political dimension is to neglect a vital part of the process, perhaps the most vital.

NOTES

1. Andrew Shonfield, *Modern Capitalism* (New York: Oxford University Press, 1965), p. 329.

2.   Robert H. Bork and Ward S. Bowman, Jr., "The Crisis in Antitrust," *Fortune, 68* (December, 1963), p. 138.

3.   Cf. Kenneth Elzinga, "Oligopoly and the New Industrial State," *Social Science Quarterly, 44* (June, 1968), pp. 49–57; and Bork and Bowman, *op. cit.*

4.   *U. S.* v. *E. C. Knight Co.,* 156 U. S. 1 (1895); *U. S.* v. *U. S. Steel Corp.,* 251 U. S. 417 (1920); *FTC* v. *Western Meat Co.,* 272 U. S. 554 (1926); and *Arrow-Hart & Hegeman Electric Co.* v. *FTC,* 291 U.S. 587 (1934).

5.   "Workload Statement—Antitrust Division" (Washington: Department of Justice, mimeo, 1965).

6.   See the excellent discussion of the Warren Court's antitrust decisions in Martin Shapiro, *Law and Politics in the Supreme Court* (New York: The Free Press, 1964), Ch. 6.

7.   "Antitrust Policy Gets a Long, Hard Look," *Business Week* (May 8, 1965), pp. 45–66.

8.   *New York Times,* (June 29, 1966), p. 65.

9.   Cf. Victor H. Kramer, "The Antitrust Division and the Supreme Court," *Virginia Law Review, 40* (April, 1954), pp. 433–463; and Walter Adams, "The Sherman Act and Its Enforcement," *University of Pittsburgh Law Review, 14* (Spring, 1953), pp. 319–343.

10. Kramer, *op. cit.,* pp. 437–438.

11. Quoted in the statement of Richard J. Barber, Joint Economic Committee, *Hearings on State of the Economy and Policies for Full Employment,* 87th Cong., 2nd Sess. (1962), p. 857.

12. Jessee W. Markham, "Is Kennedy Wielding a Bigger Stick?" *Challenge, 10* (March, 1962), pp. 10–13.

13. Ellis W. Hawley, *The New Deal and the Problem of Monopoly* (Princeton, N.J.: Princeton University Press, 1966), Chs. 20–24; and Gene M. Gressley, "Thurman Arnold, Antitrust, and the New Deal," *Business History Review, 38* (Summer, 1964), pp. 214–231. The historian Frank Friedel has written: "There are some indications . . . that the antimonopoly program that [Roosevelt] launched in the Department of Justice through the urbane Thurman Arnold was intended less to bust trusts than to forestall drastic legislation in the Congress." *The New Deal in Historical Perspective* (Washington, 1959), pp. 18–19. Quoted in Gressley, *op. cit.*

14. Louis M. Kohlmeier, "Antitrust Slowdown," *Wall Street Journal, 169*

(February 10, 1967), pp. i, 15; and "Gentle Trustbusters," *Wall Street Journal, 169* (March 7, 1967), p. 18.

15. Senate Select Committee on Small Business, *Hearing on Planning, Regulation, and Competition,* 90th Cong., 1st Sess. (1967), p. 28. Turner's reference is to a book he wrote with Carl Kaysen, *Antitrust Policy* (Cambridge, Mass.: Harvard University Press, 1959).

16. See Matthew Holden, Jr., "Imperialism in Bureaucracy," *American Political Science Review, 60* (December, 1966), pp. 943–951.

17. Earl Latham, *The Group Basis of Politics* (Ithaca, N.Y.: Cornell University Press, 1952), pp. 169–174.

18. Illustrative is the testimony by Paul Rand Dixon, Chairman of the Federal Trade Commission, in House Select Committee on Small Business, *Hearings on Activities of Regulatory and Enforcement Agencies Relating to Small Business,* 89th Cong., 1st Sess. (1965), pp. 56–67.

19. In fiscal year 1964 the FTC issued 136 cease-and-desist orders in restraint of trade (anticompetitive) cases. Of these 104 were based on Section 2 of the Clayton Act. House Appropriations Committee, *Hearings on Independent Offices Appropriations,* 89th Cong., 1st Sess. (1965), p. 454.

20. Corwin Edwards states that, through 1957, the FTC had completed 430 cases and issued 311 cease-and-desist orders. *The Price Discrimination Law* (Washington: The Brookings Institution, 1959), p. 66.

21. House Select Committee on Small Business, *Hearings . . ., op. cit.,* p. 37.

22. Lee Loevinger, "The Department of Justice and the Antitrust Laws," in Jerrold G. Van Cise, *Understanding the Antitrust Laws,* (New York: Practicing Law Institute, 1963), pp. 191–210.

23. Quoted in Daniel Jay Baum, *The Robinson–Patman Act* (Syracuse, N.Y.: Syracuse University Press, 1964), p. 112.

24. Mark S. Massel, *Competition and Monopoly* (New York: Doubleday, Anchor Books, 1964), pp. 84–85.

25. *Ibid.,* pp. 54–60. Included, among others, are the Atomic Energy Commission, Interstate Commerce Commission, Civil Aeronautics Board, Federal Power Commission, Comptroller of the Currency, Federal Reserve Board, and General Services Administration.

26. *U. S. v. El Paso Natural Gas Co.,* 376 U. S. 651 (1964); *U. S. v. Philadelphia National Bank,* 374 U. S. 321 (1963); and *U. S. v. First National Bank & Trust Company of Lexington,* 376 U. S. 665 (1964).

27. Quoted in Homer S. Cummings and Carl McFarland, *Federal Justice* (New York: Macmillan, 1937), pp. 322–323.

28. William Letwin, *Law and Economic Policy in America* (New York: Random House, 1965), pp. 117–137.

29. Richard Austin Smith, "What Antitrust Means under Mr. Bicks," *Fortune, 61* (March, 1960), pp. 120–123, 256ff.

30. *The New York Times,* December 10, 1965, p. 31; June 29, 1965, pp. 61, 65.

31. E. Pendleton Herring, *Public Administration and the Public Interest* (New York: McGraw-Hill, 1936).

32. See House Appropriations Committee, *Hearings on Independent Offices Appropriations for 1960,* 86th Cong., 1st Sess. (1959), p. 118; and *idem, Hearings on Independent Offices Appropriations for 1964,* 88th Cong., 1st Sess. (1963), p. 113.

33. See the articles by Lewis in *The New York Times,* May 3, 1964, pp. F1, 9; and May 17, 1964, p. 12E.

34. Corwin D. Edwards, *Maintaining Competition* (New York: McGraw-Hill, 1949), pp. 293–294.

35. Cf. Arthur W. Macmahon, "Congressional Oversight of Administration: The Power of the Purse," *Political Science Quarterly, 58* (June and September, 1943), pp. 169–190, 380–414; and Richard F. Fenno, Jr., *The Power of the Purse: Appropriations Politics in Congress* (Boston: Little, Brown, 1966).

36. House Appropriations Committee, *Hearings on Departments of State, Justice, and Commerce, the Judiciary, and Related Agencies Appropriations for 1967,* 89th Cong., 2nd Sess. (1966), p. 202. Hereafter cited as *Hearings on Antitrust Appropriation.*

37. House Appropriations Committee, *Hearings on Antitrust Appropriation for 1965,* 88th Cong., 2nd Sess. (1964), pp. 217–218.

38. Paul Rand Dixon, "Significant New Commission Developments," *Kentucky Law Journal, 51* (Spring, 1963), p. 412.

39. House Appropriations Committee, *Departments of State, Justice, and Commerce, the Judiciary, and Related Agencies Appropriation Bill, Fiscal Year 1963,* House Report 1966, 87th Cong., 2nd Sess. (1962), p. 9.

40. *Annual Report of the Attorney General of the United States for 1963* (Washington: Government Printing Office, 1963), pp. 99–100.

41. House Appropriations Committee, *Hearings on Antitrust Appropriation for 1964,* 88th Cong., 1st Sess. (1963), p. 204.

42. House Appropriations Committee, *Hearings on Independent Offices Appropriations for 1967,* 89th Cong., 2nd Sess., (1967), pp. 385–386.

43. House Appropriations Committee, *Hearings on Independent Offices Appropriations for 1965,* 88th Cong., 2nd Sess. (1964), p. 946.

44. House Appropriations Committee, *Hearings on Independent Offices Appropriations for 1964,* 88th Cong., 1st Sess. (1963), pp. 84–96.

45. House Appropriations Committee, *Independent Offices Appropriation Bill for 1964,* House Report 824, 88th Cong., 1st Sess. (1963), p. 9.

46. House Appropriations Committee, *Hearings on Independent Offices Appropriations for 1965,* 88th Cong., 2nd Sess. (1964), p. 950.

47. The following discussion is based on House Committee on Interstate and Foreign Commerce, *Budget Bureau Censorship and Control of Independent Agency Fiscal and Other Matters,* 86th Cong., 2nd Sess. (1960), pp. 3–4.

48. On the last item see "The Superbowl and the Sherman Act: Professional Team Sports and the Antitrust Laws," *Harvard Law Review, 81* (December, 1967), pp. 418–434.

49. House Committee on the Judiciary, *Consent Decree Program of the Department of Justice.* Report of the Antitrust Subcommittee, 86th Cong., 1st Sess. (1959), p. ix.

50. House Select Committee on Small Business, *Hearings . . ., op. cit.,* pp. 3–4, 56–67.

51. Joint Economic Committee, *Hearings . . ., op. cit.,* p. 785.

52. E.g., Vernon A. Mund, *Government and Business* (New York: Harper and Row, 4th ed., 1965), p. 108.

53. Joseph C. Palamountain, Jr., "The Federal Trade Commission and the Indiana Standard Case," in Eugene A. Bock, ed., *Government Regulation of Business: A Casebook* (Englewood Cliffs, N. J.: Prentice-Hall, 1965), pp. 218–219.

54. Of related interest here is Chester A. Newland, "The Supreme Court and Legal Writings: Learned Journals as Vehicles of an Anti-Antitrust Lobby?" *The Georgetown Law Journal, 48* (Fall, 1959), pp. 105–143.

55. Herbert A. Simon, Donald W. Smithburg, and Victor A. Thompson, *Public Administration* (New York: Alfred A. Knopf, 1950), pp. 338–339.

56. The following discussion draws in part on Joe Bain, *Industrial Organization* (New York: John Wiley and Sons, 1959), pp. 489–494, 527–533.

57. Loevinger, *op. cit.,* p. 194.

58. John Kenneth Galbraith, quoted in *The New York Times,* November 29, 1966. See also his *The New Industrial State* (Boston: Houghton Mifflin, 1967), pp. 184–197.

INDEPENDENT COMMISSIONS
AND BUSINESS REGULATION
Grant McConnell

The commissions date from 1887, when the Interstate Commerce Commission was created. This was well before the advent of the Progressive Movement, but in some respects it was an almost typical Progressive reform. It was designed to bring monopoly power under popular control; it was intended to be expert; and it was built to be free of "politics." The ICC was followed by the Federal Reserve Board in 1913, the Federal Trade Commission in 1914, the U.S. Shipping Board (later variously renamed) in 1916, the Federal Power Commission in 1920, the Federal Radio Commission (later the Federal Communications Commission) in 1927, and, in New Deal days, the Securities and Exchange Commission, the National Labor Relations Board, and the Civil Aeronautics Board.[1] The forces that brought about the creation of these agencies were varied. One force behind establishment of the Shipping Board, for example, was the incipient American entry into World War I; once again war conditions had an important influence on the development of governmental institutions. Chaos on the radio waves led industry itself to demand regulation by a Federal Radio Commission. For the most part, however, popular desire for regulation in the public interest (as seen in Progressive terms) was the more important and the more consistent motivation. A number of reasons have been given for adoption of the independent commission form, but perhaps historical accident was as strong as any. The ICC was given this form, and under the first chairmanship of the very able Thomas M. Cooley achieved a prestige that made it the model for the commissions that followed. Certainly, it seems probable that Cooley's strong direction did much to create the aura of legalism that has surrounded these bodies, sometimes to their benefit, but often to their vexation. To the reasons commonly offered for the peculiar independent commission form might be added the advantage it offers of swift

From *Private Power and American Democracy* by Grant McConnell, pp. 281–292. Copyright © 1966 by Alfred A. Knopf, Inc. Reprinted by permission of the publisher. Footnotes have been renumbered.

relegation to decent obscurity of issues that have become overheated in the glare of public controversy—an advantage most politicians esteem highly.[2]

The independent commission long ago became established with that degree of solidity and seeming immortality known only to old-line government bureaus. The commissions have successfully passed the test of survival; nevertheless, they have drawn recurrent criticism—some trivial, some serious, some damning. The literature of investigation on these agencies has grown to great volume, perhaps out of proportion to their importance in relation to other parts of government. However, a few of these examinations stand out to the extent that they deserve comment. In 1937, the President's Committee on Administrative Management opened the issue of their structure as it had not been opened before. The Committee termed the independent commissions "a headless fourth branch of the Government, responsible to no one, and impossible of coordination with the general policies and work of the Government as determined by the people through their duly elected representatives."[3] This criticism appeared in the context of a discussion devoted to the difficulties faced by the President in controlling more than 100 different agencies. Retrospectively, the Committee at times seems to have been preoccupied with the problem of administrative tidiness. Nevertheless, it did have a fairly clear perception of the largest issue posed by the commissions, responsibility.

In the same era there was also a quite different approach to the independent commissions, again a critical one. This was made by the Attorney General's Committee on Administrative Procedure. This distinguished group focused, as the Committee's title suggests, upon the process by which administrative agencies operated, rather than upon their organization. Unlike some other studies of "administrative agencies," the Committee study covered a number of other governmental bodies as well as the independent commissions. The test of an administrative agency, in Committee eyes, was that it held the power to determine private rights and obligations.[4] With the particular concern indicated by this definition, it was understandable that the report of the group was attacked as being too legalistic and too little concerned for the achievement of the ends of public policy. Perhaps there was a lawyer's bias in the Committee's work and a tendency to measure the administrative process by the standards of the judicial process, particularly in dealing with the independent commissions, which bore some analogy to the courts. Nevertheless, the hostility aroused by the Committee was too intense. The hopes aroused by the culmination of its work, the Administrative Procedure Act of 1946, were also too high.

The differences of orientation toward the problem of the independent commissions in these two reports is interesting. The first sought solutions by reorganization. The second rejected "mere change in the administrative structure, and sought reforms of procedure."[5] These approaches to reform reflect two fundamentally different—although properly complementary—assessments of the underlying problem. As the problem has become clearer in the years since the New Deal, it has become evident that the first approach is political, the second legal. When Congress created the independent regulatory commissions it was reasonable to hope (whatever may have been in the minds of Congress) that in time the commissions would build a body of largely consistent precedents out of which general principles would gradually emerge. By such a process, criteria would develop and the problem of bias would be solved. This process would meet a major part of the problem of fairness to individuals and also provide the order which is essential to effective administration. To the extent that this process did not develop, however, it was also reasonable to look for means for referring the basic value choices to the people. Typically, this means would consist of legislation by Congress. With the commissions, however, it has been assumed that the subject matter is so involved and abstruse that Congress is largely unable to deal with policy choices in the forms in which they appear in these fields. Thus, the question, how responsible to the public are the Commissions? has become very relevant.

Except among scholars, there has been great reluctance to confront this fundamental question. Reorganization of the commissions and placement of their functions within the departmental structure, recommended by the Committee on Administrative Management, was rejected by Congress. In 1949 the Hoover Commission decided that "the independent regulatory commissions have a proper place in the machinery of our Government, a place very like that originally conceived," although a small number of relatively small reforms were desirable.[6] The Second Hoover Commission in 1955 did suggest establishment of an administrative court, but this proposal had no success.[7] Nevertheless, the problem remained and it briefly exploded in a seriocomedy of exposures by the Legislative Oversight Committee in 1958.[8] A number of students re-examined the problem and, as a result, the issue of the commissions is very much alive today.

Criticisms of the independent commissions contain some quite different implicit theories as to what is wrong. Perhaps the most obvious criticism is the seemingly simple protest against *any* governmental regulation. This, however, is very deceptive. In general, this criticism is not seriously made by the regulated industries themselves. Some industries, including the radio industry, the airlines, the railroad and trucking industries, and the oil companies, have actively sought regulation.[9] When, a few years after establishment of the Interstate Commerce Commission its abolition was proposed, a very prescient U.S. Attorney General wrote to a railroad president in a letter much quoted since then, "The Commission . . . is, or can be made, of great use to the railroads. It satisfies the popular clamor for a government supervision of railroads, at the same time that the supervision is almost entirely nominal. Further, the older such a commission gets to be, the more inclined it will be found to take the business and railroad view of things. . . ."[10] Industry organizations have indeed often proved staunch defenders of their respective regulatory agencies. Thus, in 1948 *Railway Age* asserted flatly that transportation "has a natural tendency to become monopolistic," and that the "only sensible policy for government is to recognize this [and] regulate accordingly." The vocal denunciations of regulation still heard from some industry spokesmen are, as Huntington has remarked, a part of maintaining the myth of regulation as something imposed on industry.[11] This, of course, is not to say that all members of any industry are agreed upon the substance of regulation, however monolithic the industry is made to appear by its appointed spokesmen.

A second group of criticisms relate to various details of organization and inefficiencies of operation; criticism of the large backlogs of work in the commissions is typical. These matters are seemingly most easy to deal with, for they appear superficial. Nevertheless, it is likely that delay, inefficiency, and indecision are all related to the more fundamental difficulties of the commissions.

A much more important charge is that the independent commissions have failed to "make law." A federal judge has recently stated the difficulty: the commissions have failed "to develop standards sufficiently definite to permit decisions to be fairly predictable and the reasons for them to be understood." [12] The case for this legal diagnosis of the problem is very strong. Thus, the Federal Communications Commission has been deeply involved in scandal in the award of licenses for broadcasting. Given only the "public convenience, interest, or necessity," as a guideline by Congress, the Commission has been confronted with the necessity of formulating its own criteria for choosing among applicants. This it has been unable to do, with the result that its decisions have appeared to be based on whim or, even worse, bribery. [13] Similarly, the Civil Aeronautics Board has been confronted with exercise of large-scale discretion with little guidance from Congress. One of the most important of its duties is the assignment of routes among various airlines. Judge Henry J. Friendly has asserted that in seventeen years of existence, the Board arrived at no understandable criteria on this activity. [14] Here he was saying in specific terms what an outraged ex-member of the Board itself had asserted, that the Board had "almost no general policies whatever," and that such policies as did appear changed "suddenly, without notice, and often with no explanation or any indication that the Board knows it has changed policy." [15] Even this severe criticism was not substantially different from a statement by a chairman of the CAB: ". . . the philosophy of the Civil Aeronautics Board changes from day to day. It depends who is on the Board as to what the philosophy is." [16] This was painfully close to a confession that the Board's decisions were wholly arbitrary. At this point, the whole issue had been reduced to a question of power, in this case the power to determine appointments to the Board.

When serious scholars and active participants in the decisions of the commissions have been able to make and support such statements, it is almost irrelevant to ask what the substance of the decisions and policies of the Commissions have been; the presumption of bias and, as has been seen, even the suspicion of outright corruption are ultimately unanswerable. Yet, it is worth noting that specific charges of favoritism have not been lacking. Thus, the Civil Aeronautics Board has been faced with charges of discrimination in that it has generally denied certificates to new airlines. It has favored scheduled passenger lines over all-cargo lines in rate structure. It has discriminated against surface lines seeking to enter air transportation.[17] Similarly, the Interstate Commerce Commission has generally favored the railroads over the trucking firms. In particular, it has interpreted identical regulations on rate structure differently for the railroads and for the motor carriers.[18] Examples could be added at some length.

So long as the problem of the commissions is viewed in these terms, the solution indicated by Judge Friendly is incontrovertible: a better definition of standards. If the operations of the commissions are to be anything other than the playthings of sheer political power, this is the only answer. Unfortunately, however, this may be tantamount to saying that if the problem is to be solved it must be solved. Two questions of great importance remain unanswered. The first is whether it is technically possible for the commissions to develop standards giving reasonably precise meaning to such Congressional guides as "public convenience and necessity," "just and reasonable rates," "undue preference or prejudice," or "unfair methods of competition." Judge Friendly has persuasively argued, particularly with the example of the long-and-short-haul clause of the Interstate Commerce Act, that solution is thus possible.[19] His judgment deserves respect.

If the question of technical feasibility of better standards can be solved, the already long record of the independent commissions nevertheless indicates that in many areas it has *not* been solved. The second question thus becomes highly important: is it *politically* possible to develop the needed standards? At this point, where the issues of procedure encounter the issue of structure, the problem of criteria and the problem of power meet.

The outstanding political fact about the independent regulatory commissions is that they have in general become promoters and protectors of the industries they have been established to regulate. Attorney General Olney's prophecy to the railroad president in 1892 has not only been fulfilled by the ICC; it has gained the stature of a general rule of independent regulatory commission development in most fields. This is easy to understand where regulation has been sought by the industries themselves. Here the analogy with the NRA is obvious; it is less obvious with industries in which regulation has been instituted as the result of external forces and by the Progressive impulse. Marver Bernstein explains the process thus: independent commissions have a characteristic life cycle. In the period of a commission's gestation, agitation develops for reform of a condition that is causing widespread distress. The agitation is denounced as "socialistic" and a heavily ideological struggle occurs. Ultimately, however, the fervor for reform reaches a peak and the regulatory agency is established with a very vague and general Congressional mandate. Such were the origins of the ICC and the SEC, for example.

In its youth the commission has a crusading spirit. It encounters, however, the by now well-organized resistance of the industry it has set forth to control. The industry has superior knowledge of matters relating to itself and is determined to defend itself day in and day out against the apparent threat. Moreover, the legal standing of the commission may be uncertain and serious action may have to await Court determination of its validity. Even more serious, public concern over the problem quickly wanes and the commission is left without the strong political support that had brought it into being. Congress is happy about the disappearance of agitation and conflict, and the President is presumably freed of responsibility. In its maturity devitalization characterizes the commission. It achieves acceptance and loses its reforming zeal. It settles down to routine operation of established policies and more and more assumes the role of manager of the industry, of course serving the interests of the industry. Changes in commission personnel will now have taken place and the new appointees will probably be wholly acceptable to, if not indeed the nominees of, the industry. Those permanent staff members who remain will have become wearied by struggle and more and more responsive to the suggestions of industry members that they should get along together and forget past strife. These appeals, combined with the attrition of the former struggles, become strong indeed. In old age debility sets in and the primary task of the commission degenerates into maintenance of the status quo in the regulated industry and the commission's own position as the industry's recognized protector.[20]

This process has been remarked upon in one way or another by many students of administration.[21] It is by no means confined to the independent commissions; it is also familiar to veterans of active administration in many long-established governmental bureaus. Why, then, has the process been so particularly associated with the commissions? First, it is probably somewhat more severe in the commissions than in most other agencies. This is somewhat uncertain, however, since the commissions have generally attracted more attention than have bureaus better hidden from public observation. Second, the independent commissions have very large discretionary power, which has not been tempered and restrained by the development of rules and standards of a firm character. Third, the commissions are formally and in reality more independent than many other agencies.

Their independence is probably the crucial political issue regarding the commissions. Originally, independence was conceived quite simply as a matter of independence from partisan politics. To different degrees it was enforced not merely by overlapping terms of commissioners and appointment of members of both major parties, but by independence from the presidency as well. The judicial model was influential, but freedom from "politics" was also an important motivation. Unfortunately, what was achieved was not freedom from all politics, but freedom only from party and popular politics. The politics of industry and administration remained. In terms of the present analysis, independence substituted a small constituency, that of the industry itself, for a large constituency, that of the whole nation. Thus, it is incorrect to charge that the commissions have been irresponsible. They quite obviously have been responsible—indeed, particularly responsive—to the industries with which they have been associated. The question of responsibility is always meaningless unless it is asked *to whom* the responsibility is paid.

The fallacy of the organization of the independent regulatory commissions thus has two faces. On the one side is the assumption that standards could and would be developed by the commissions. On the other side is the assumption that the commissions could and would be independent of all political influence. Neither assumption has been justified. Under the disguise of antiregulatory rhetoric, the fiction has been maintained that the commissions' formal responsibility to the general public is the responsibility actually paid. Perhaps the legalists' contention that better definition of standards is really possible is correct, insofar as the diverse claims *within* the regulated industries are concerned. But analysis of the character of private government indicates that standards for regulated industries that meet elementary tests of fairness to weak and strong alike are most unlikely to emerge from the existing organization of the commissions. At best, it would seem reasonable to hope only for more *certain* standards—which, however, may be expected to serve the interests dominant with the industries. Even this less sweeping improvement would be dependent on accentuation of existing tendencies toward domination of the regulated industries by a few elements within them. No standards adequately reflecting the array of interests other than the industries themselves that are affected by the regulations are likely to emerge from the political context of independent commissions. The actual constituencies of these commissions are no more than the industries regulated.

Much of the context of recent discussions on the independent commissions is directed to reform.[22] Accordingly, it is fair to pose a question similar to that raised earlier about the legalist solution of better definition of standards: Isn't suggesting the political solution of reorganizing the commissions to make them responsible to a larger constituency tantamount to saying that solving the problem would solve the problem? Unfortunately, the answer to this question is also probably affirmative. The web of relationships between the regulators and the regulated and the influential committees of Congress is so complex and strong that it is unrealistic to expect reform except after great effort and much determination. Solutions actually offered are likely to take the form of minor internal reorganization and the selection of better personnel for commission membership, as James Landis recommended to President Kennedy before the latter took office.[23] Nothing in such recommendations, however, will meet either of the basic problems of the commissions.

The most curious feature of the independent commissions' history is the degree to which these expressions of the Progressive drive have produced the same phenomena as the agencies that emerged out of the orthodoxy of group self-determination. The commissions have exhibited the same accommodation of governmental bureaus to the industries with which they deal, sometimes even to the point of virtual fusion of public and private bodies. They are characterized by the same uncertainty of standards, sometimes to the point where they appear hopelessly adrift. The independent committees practice the same informality of operation and relationships—in extreme cases to the degree that corruption is difficult to disprove. There is the same drive toward autonomy of the conjoint regulator-regulated political systems. Finally, these systems have followed the same development of narrow constituencies.

The Progressive impulse has waned and the slogans of self-regulation are perhaps heard less than they once were. Nevertheless, the ideas of self-regulation are probably more pervasive than ever. Certainly, the phenomena of self-determination and self-regulation in business are more widespread than when Herbert Hoover was Secretary of Commerce. The most striking recent evidence of the strong vitality of the ideas of self-regulation came out of a re-examination of the workings of the Securities and Exchange Commission. This agency is somewhat unlike its fellows in that self-regulation has been an explicit part of its doctrine from its very beginning. The essential part of this doctrine is that the securities business should police itself, with the SEC largely standing by and keeping its shotgun behind the door, as SEC Chairman William O. Douglas once put it.[24] Thus, although the Commission has issued some regulations of its own, most of the controls exercised over the trade in securities have been those of the exchanges, which are intrinsically private clubs.

By 1963 the securities market had grown substantially and the number of stockholders had increased vastly. Moreover, a number of scandals had enveloped the stock market and public feeling was rising. A sweeping investigation of the market followed. To no one's surprise, the SEC itself concluded, "Our firm conviction is that self-regulation, an essential ingredient in investor protection, must continue in a strong, forward movement."[25] Perhaps the most interesting novelty of the study was its examination of the internal governmental systems of the various private self-regulating bodies. Although this examination was less than penetrating, it was at least an acknowledgment that problems of government persist even where public authority has been abdicated. A more important element of the entire investigation, however, was the call for extension of self-regulation. Regarding the over-the-counter market, for example, a variety of small reforms were proposed, but the major thrust of the recommendations was that the National Association of Securities Dealers should undertake a more aggressive policy of regulation of this market.[26] Accordingly, when legislation was drafted to deal with the problem, one of its quite logical provisions was a requirement that all broker firms should be members of a registered securities association. This and the requirement that the associations should establish rules and regulations over their members had, as the Senate Banking and Currency Committee noted with satisfaction, the support of all the national and regional exchanges as well as the National Association of Securities Dealers and the Investment Bankers Association.[27]

Perhaps at this point the assimilation of Progressive reform into the orthodoxy was complete.

NOTES

1. The early history of these agencies is set forth in Robert E. Cushman, *The Independent Regulatory Commissions* (New York: Oxford University Press, 1941).

2. A summary of arguments for and against the Commission form appears in Marver H. Bernstein, *Regulating Business by Independent Commission* (Princeton, N.J.: Princeton University Press, 1955), pp. 24, 25.

3. *Report of the President's Committee on Administrative Management* (Washington, D.C., 1937), p. 32.

4. Committee on Administrative Procedure Appointed by the Attorney General, *Report on Administrative Procedure in Government Agencies* (Washington, D.C., 1941), p. 7. It is notable that the leading contemporary text on administrative law is much less restrictive: "The administrative process is the complex of methods by which Agencies carry out their tasks of adjudication, rule making, and related functions." Kenneth Culp Davis, *Administrative Law Text* (St. Paul, Minn.: West Publishing Co., 1959), p. 1.

5. *Report on Administrative Procedure*, p. 59.

6. Commission on Organization of the Executive Branch of the Government, *Regulatory Commissions* (Washington, D.C., 1949), pp. 3, 4.

7. Commission on Organization of the Executive Branch of the Government, *Legal Services and Procedure* (Washington, D.C., 1955), pp. 84–88.

8. See Chapter 1, McConnell, *Private Power and American Democracy.*

9. Davis, *op. cit.,* p. 6.

10. This quotation appears in almost all critical discussions of the commissions, e.g., Davis, *op. cit.,* p. 7; Bernstein, *op. cit.,* p. 265. The letter itself was written by Richard Olney in 1892 to the president of the Burlington Railroad.

11. Samuel P. Huntington, *Clientalism: A Study in Administrative Politics,* Ph.D. dissertation, Harvard University, 1950, pp. 391, 392, 397.

12. Henry J. Friendly, *The Federal Administrative Agencies* (Cambridge, Mass.: Harvard University Press, 1962), pp. viii, 6, 7.

13. *Ibid.,* pp. 53–73.

14. *Ibid.,* pp. 97.

15. Louis J. Hector, "Problems of the CAB and the Independent Regulatory Commissions," 69 *Yale Law Journal,* 939 (May 1960).

16. Quoted in Friendly, *op. cit.,* p. 97.

17. Huntington, *op. cit.,* pp. 32–35. Also Walton H. Hamilton, *The Politics of Industry* (New York: Alfred A. Knopf, Inc., 1957), pp. 61–62.

18. *Ibid.,* pp. 24–35, 94.

19. This example is termed by Friendly—with much justification—"a rather beautiful story." *Op. cit.,* pp. 27–35.

20. Bernstein, *op. cit.,* pp. 74–102.

21. Thus Davis, *loc. cit.;* Huntington, *op. cit.,* pp. 378–380; Emmette S. Redford, *Administration of National Economic Control* (New York: Macmillan, 1952), p. 386.

22. Thus, Emmette S. Redford, *The President and the Regulatory Commissions, Report Submitted to the President's Advisory Committee on Government Organization,* 1960; James M. Landis, *Report on Regulatory Agencies to the President-Elect* (Washington, D.C., 1960).

23. Landis, *op. cit.*

24. William O. Douglas, *Democracy and Finance* (New Haven, Conn.: Yale University Press, 1940), p. 82.

25. *Report of Special Study of Securities Market of the Securities and Exchange Commission,* part 4, U.S. House of Representatives, 88th Cong., 1st Sess. (1965), p. ix.

26. *Ibid.,* pp. 679–682.

27. *Securities and Exchange Commission Legislation, 1963, Report of the Committee on Banking and Currency,* U.S. Senate, 88th Cong., 1st Sess. (1963), pp. 41, 42.

THE MARASMUS OF THE ICC:
THE COMMISSION, THE RAILROAD,
AND THE PUBLIC INTEREST
Samuel P. Huntington

Among the myriad federal agencies concerned with transportation, the Interstate Commerce Commission has long been preeminent.* It is the oldest transportation regulatory commission, and with the exception of the Corps of Engineers it is the oldest federal agency of any type with major transportation responsibilities. It is the only federal agency immediately concerned with more than one type of carrier: its activities directly affect four of the five major forms of commercial transportation. It is one of the few significant transportation bodies which have not been absorbed by the Department of Commerce, and it is the only important transportation agency completely independent of the executive branch. It is the sole administrative agency to which Congress has delegated the responsibility for enforcing the National Transportation Policy. During its sixty-five years of existence the Commission developed an enviable reputation for honesty, impartial-

Reprinted by permission of the author, the Yale Law Journal Company and Fred B. Rothman and Company from *The Yale Law Journal*, LXI (April, 1952), 467–481, 492–499. Footnotes 1 and 18 of the original are reproduced here; the others have been omitted.

*The principal federal agencies with major transportation responsibilities may be classified as follows: (1) Agencies primarily engaged in the construction and maintenance of transportation facilities: Bureau of Public Roads and Civil Aeronautics Administration (Department of Commerce), Corps of Engineers and Panama Canal (Department of the Army), Alaska Roads Commission (Department of the Interior); (2) Agencies primarily engaged in the regulation of carriers: ICC (independent), Federal Maritime Board (Department of Commerce), Civil Aeronautics Board (Department of Commerce for housekeeping purposes only); (3) Agencies primarily engaged in the aid and operation of carriers: Inland Waterways Corporation and Maritime Administration (Department of Commerce), Alaska Railroad (Department of the Interior), Panama Railroad (Department of the Army); (4) Agencies primarily engaged in transportation research: National Advisory Committee for Aeronautics (independent); (5) Agencies primarily engaged in supervision and coordination: Office of the Undersecretary for Transportation (Department of Commerce), Air Coordinating Committee (interdepartmental); (6) Agencies

ity, and expertness. Its age, prestige, and scope combined to make it the premier federal agency in the transportation field.

Despite this impressive past, however, there are many indications that the ICC is now losing its position of leadership. New developments threaten to bring about the end of the agency or to reduce it to a secondary position. The level of its appropriations and the number of its employees have been either stationary or declining. Its decisions are more frequently reversed in the courts than previously. Its leadership and staff have manifestly deteriorated in quality. The general praise which it once received has been replaced by sharp criticism. And, most importantly, it is now challenged by the rise of a new agency, the Office of the Undersecretary of Commerce for Transportation, which appears to be assuming federal transportation leadership. It is the purpose of this Article to analyze the causes of the decline of the ICC and the probable and desirable future position of this agency.

Successful adaptation to changing environmental circumstances is the secret of health and longevity for administrative as well as biological organisms. Every government agency must reflect to some degree the "felt needs" of its time. In the realm of government, felt needs are expressed through political demands and political pressures. These demands and pressures may come from the president, other administrative agencies and officials, congressmen, political interest groups,

---

concerned with the defense aspects of transportation: Defense Transport Administration (affiliated with ICC), Defense Air Transportation Administration and National Shipping Authority (Department of Commerce); (7) Agencies primarily concerned with labor relations and employee matters: National Mediation Board (independent), Railroad Retirement Board (independent). In addition, other federal agencies with different primary concerns which perform functions significant to transportation are: (1) Military Air Transportation Service, Military Sea Transportation Service, private carriage for the armed forces; (2) Weather Bureau and Coast and Geodetic Survey (Department of Commerce), Coast Guard (Treasury), which perform valuable transportation service functions; (3) Federal Power Commission, regulation of interstate pipe line transportation of natural gas; (4) Tennessee Valley Authority, various transportation functions in its area; (5) General Services Administration, Post Office, and Department of Defense, which are the principal federal purchasers of transportation; (6) Department of State, international transportation activities.

and the general public. If an agency is to be viable it must adapt itself to the pressures from these sources so as to maintain a net preponderance of political support over political opposition. It must have sufficient support to maintain and, if necessary, expand its statutory authority, to protect it against attempts to abolish it or subordinate it to other agencies, and to secure for it necessary appropriations. Consequently, to remain viable over a period of time, an agency must adjust its sources of support so as to correspond with changes in the strength of their political pressures. If the agency fails to make this adjustment, its political support decreases relative to its political opposition, and it may be said to suffer from administrative marasmus. The decline of the ICC may be attributed to its susceptibility to this malady.

I. Historical Background

The history of the ICC in terms of its political support divides naturally into two fairly distinct periods. The Commission was created in 1887 after the Supreme Court invalidated state attempts to regulate the railroads' abuse of their monopoly power. The driving force behind these early state regulatory laws and commissions [was] the farmers, who had suffered severely from exorbitant rates and discriminatory practices. This group plus equally dissatisfied commercial shippers were the political force responsible for the Act to Regulate Commerce. In addition, general public indignation and disgust at railroad financial and business practices provided a favorable climate of opinion for the creation of the Commission. President Cleveland endorsed the legislation and enhanced the Commission's reputation by appointing Judge Cooley and other prominent figures as its first members.

From 1887 down to the First World War the support of the Commission came primarily from the groups responsible for its creation. Opposition came principally from the railroads and the courts. In its first two decades the Commission was severely hampered by the combined action of these two groups. Subsequently farmer and shipper interests with the vigorous support of President Roosevelt secured the passage of the Hepburn Act of 1906. This enlarged the Commission, extended its jurisdiction, gave it the power to prescribe future maximum rates, and prohibited railroads from owning the products they transported. The decade which followed the passage of this Act was the peak of the Commission's power and prestige while still dependent upon consumer, public and presidential support.

The end of the First World War marked a definite change in the nature of the transportation problem and in the attitudes of the various interests towards railroad regulation. The vigorous actions of the ICC in the period immediately prior to the war had eliminated the worst discriminatory practices and had convinced the railroads that the path of wisdom was to accept regulation and to learn to live with the Commission. This domestication of the carriers consequently reduced the interest and political activity of shipper groups. And increased urbanization reduced the power of farm groups which had been such a significant source of support to the Commission. Finally, "normalcy" had supplanted progressivism and Harding and Coolidge were significantly different from T. Roosevelt and Wilson. Consequently there was little likelihood that restrictive regulation would find much support from either the public or the White House.

All these factors dictated not only the shift in public policy which was made in the Transportation Act of 1920 but also a shift by the Commission in the sources to which it looked for support.* Continued reliance upon the old sources of support would have resulted in decreasing viability. Therefore the Commission turned more and more to the railroad industry itself, particularly the railroad management group. This development was aided by the expansion of the Commission's activities and the resulting increased dependence of the Commission upon the cooperation of regulated groups for the successful

---

*The Transportation Act of 1920 required the Commission to fix rates so that the railroad industry as a whole would earn a "fair return upon the aggregate value" of its invested capital. Other provisions (1) extended the power of the Commission over the issuance of railroad securities, new construction and abandonments, car service, and minimum rates, (2) permitted poolings subject to Commission approval, (3) directed the Commission to draw up a plan for the consolidation of the railroads into a limited number of systems, and (4) provided for the recapture of excess railroad profits and their use for the benefit of the weaker roads.

administration of its program. The support which the Commission received from the railroads sustained it down to World War II and enabled it both to expand its authority over other carrier groups and to defend itself against attempts to subject it to executive control.

The present marasmus of the ICC is due to continued dependence upon railroad support. The transportation industry is not only large, it is also dynamic. Technological changes and economic development are basically altering the nation's transportation pattern. The tremendous expansion of air and motor transport, the resulting increase in competition, the economic development of the South and West, the rise of private carriage, and the increased significance of defense considerations all make today's transportation system fundamentally different from that of twenty-five years ago. These technological and economic developments have given rise to new political demands and pressures, and have drastically altered the old balance of political forces in the transportation arena. A quarter of a century ago commercial transportation was railroad transportation. Today, railroads are a declining, although still major, segment of the transportation industry. Their economic decline has been matched by a decrease in political influence. The ICC, however, remains primarily a "railroad" agency. It has not responded to the demands of the new forces in transportation. It has not duplicated the successful adjustment of its sources of political support that it carried out after World War I. Consequently, it is losing its leadership to those agencies which are more responsive to the needs and demands of the times.

II. Railroad Support of the ICC

Railroad Praise of the ICC

The attitude of the railroads towards the Commission since 1935 can only be described as one of satisfaction, approbation, and confidence. At times the railroads have been almost effusive in their praise of the Commission. The ICC, one sub-committee of the Association of American Railroads has declared, "is eminently qualified by nearly sixty years of experience to handle transportation matters with a maximum of satisfaction to management, labor and the public." Another representative of the same association has similarly stated that "[w]hat is needed for the solution of the tremendously important problems of transport regulation is the impartiality, deliberation, expertness, and continuity of policy that have marked the history of the Interstate Commerce Commission." Railroad officials and lawyers have commended the Commission as a "conspicuous success," a "constructive force," and as a "veteran and generally respected tribunal." The American Short Line Railroad Association has commented upon the "fair, intelligent treatment" its members have been accorded by the Commission, and the Pennsylvania Railroad has been lavish in its praise of the latter's policies. The ICC is probably the only regulatory body in the federal government which can boast that a book has been written about it by counsel for a regulated interest in order to demonstrate "how well" the Commission has "performed its duty."

The railroads and the Commission have both praised their harmonious relations. "The railroad industry," it has been said, "in wide contrast to other industry, has learned to live under government regulation." The editors of *Railway Age* have similarly spoken highly of the "collaboration" which exists between the Commission and its regulated enterprises and have remarked that this "stands out in strong contrast to the animosity and distrust which now separates many regulatory bodies from the areas of industry which they supervise." The Commission itself has noted with pride the lack of criticism which its administration of the Interstate Commerce Act has received from the carriers and has pointed out that while some interests have urged the abandonment of regulation the "railroads have never joined in that suggestion."

Railroad Defense of Commission Independence

The railroads have vigorously defended the independence of the ICC from control by other governmental units and have opposed all attempts to subordinate it to other agencies or to transfer from the Commission any of its functions. This support for the Commission has taken three principal forms.

Opposition to ICC reorganization. The railroads have successfully opposed all reorganization proposals to subordinate the ICC or transfer any of its functions to the executive branch. In 1937 the President's Committee on Administrative Management recommended that the ICC along with all other regulatory commissions be divided into administrative and judicial sections and be placed in an executive department. The administrative section would be a regular bureau within the department; the judicial section would be in the department for "housekeeping" purposes only. These proposals raised a storm of protest from the ICC-railroad bloc and legislation to effect them was defeated in Congress. Over a decade later similar opposition was expressed by the railroads to legislation designed to create a Department of Transportation which would absorb the "executive" functions of the ICC. The Hoover Commission recommendations that the equipment inspection, safety, and car service functions of the Commission be transferred to the Department of Commerce were likewise opposed by the rail carriers. In general, the railroads have repeatedly emphasized the desirability of maintaining the independence of the Commission against all forms of executive encroachment.

The significance of railroad support for the Commission in this connection was perhaps best demonstrated by the fate of the presidential reorganization plan designed to centralize administrative authority within the Commission in a chairman appointed by the president. This plan was one of six, all submitted by the president at the same time, and devised to effectuate similar reforms in five other commissions as well as the ICC. Resolutions of disapproval of four of these plans were introduced in the Senate and referred to the Committee on Expenditures in Executive Departments. This committee reported three of the resolutions unfavorably; the fourth, that disapproving of the ICC reorganization, was reported favorably. The explanation of this obviously inconsistent action (since all four plans were virtually identical) can, in the words of the minority report, "easily be found by reading the roster of the regulated interests (and their lawyers) which appeared in opposition." The hearings on the plans had been largely monopolized by railroad and associated witnesses appearing to defend the "independence" of the ICC. In the debate on the floor of the Senate the railroads were given primary credit for the committee's peculiar action, and in the end the ICC resolution was approved by a substantial majority. Railroad support saved the ICC from a reorganized fate to which five other commissions succumbed.

Opposition to the creation of new agencies which might rival the ICC.
Within the last decade the railroads have generally opposed the establishment of new agencies which might in any way infringe upon or
limit the powers of the ICC. In 1938 the railroad Committee of Six did
recommend the creation of a new transportation authority which
would take over the Commission's powers in regard to finance, entry,
and abandonment, and the establishment of a special court to handle
railroad reorganizations. Both recommendations, however, were opposed by numerous rail carriers and officials. Typical of the usual
railroad attitude was the rejection in 1946 by one Association of American Railroads group of the proposal for a new transportation planning body because apparently this "would provide another agency
duplicating the work of the Interstate Commerce Commission, and
further complicate a situation now made difficult by the intervening
of various government departments." Representatives of the AAR
also opposed the creation of the new office of Undersecretary of Commerce for Transportation on the grounds that the ICC was the leading
federal agency concerned with transportation and that this new official could only duplicate its functions and challenge its authority.
Similarly, railroad opposition to the creation of a Department of
Transportation has in large part been based upon the fear that even if
this body did not initially absorb the ICC it would eventually en-
croach upon the Commission's functions. Railroads have frequently
urged the creation of a single regulatory commission for all forms of
transportation; the implicit or explicit assumption in all such proposals, however, is that this Commission would be an enlarged and
reorganized ICC.

Opposition to the interference of existing agencies with the Commission.
Attempts by existing agencies to influence or dictate ICC policy
through intervention in proceedings before the Commission, informal
pressure upon commissioners, or by other means, have been severely
attacked by the railroads. The argument is that the ICC has the
responsibility to act in the public interest, and other agencies, if they
interfere, must be doing so on behalf of some parochial interest. Appearances of the Secretary of Agriculture before the Commission have
frequently been objected to, and the intervention of price control
agencies in the general rate cases has likewise been attacked. The

heaviest criticism along this line has been directed at the Department of Justice for its frequent interventions before the ICC and attempts to influence Commission policy in cases raising antitrust issues. On a much broader level, the railroads and associated groups have been staunch defenders of the independence of the Commission from presidential and congressional interference.

Railroad Support for the Expansion of ICC Power

In addition to defending the ICC against intrusions upon its powers by other agencies the railroads have fairly consistently in recent decades advocated the expansion of the Commission's authority. There are four principal points in the railroad program as it has developed.

Transfer to the ICC of all existing regulatory functions affecting the railroads. In the words of the Pennsylvania Railroad:

All regulation of the railroads should be in the Interstate Commerce Commission and not part under that Commission and part under the Securities and Exchange Commission or other Commissions. In other words, the Interstate Commerce Commission should be the only governmental agency regulating the railroads.*

Since 1941 the principal activity of the railroads in this area has been the drive to get the enforcement of the antitrust laws as applied to common carriers transferred from the Department of Justice to the ICC. The railroads argued that they were subject to two conflicting types of regulation and that the Antitrust Division was unfamiliar with and unsympathetic to their problems. In the end, the carriers were successful and the Reed-Bulwinkle Act of 1948 gave the ICC power to exempt rate conferences and bureaus from the antitrust laws.

Expansion of ICC regulatory authority over unregulated railroad-competitive groups. During the 1930's the railroads consistently urged the extension of ICC authority over unregulated carriers, particularly motor and inland water carriers. Their efforts in regard to the former achieved success in the Motor Carrier Act of 1935, which was the

---

[*House Committee on Interstate and Foreign Commerce, Special Subcommittee on Transportation, National Transportation Inquiry, 31 (1946).]

culmination of a determined legislative push by the railroads and the ICC. The latter itself had recognized in 1932 that:

... there is substantially no demand for public regulation of the charges of motor trucks to protect shippers against exorbitant or discriminatory charges. The demand has been chiefly from the railroads, and for the prescription of minimum rather than maximum charges.*

Yet the Commission in that year endorsed the regulation of motor carriers, and in succeeding years regularly gave its support to measures designed to achieve that end. The recommendations of ICC Commissioner Eastman in his capacity as Federal Coordinator of Transportation gave additional impetus to the drive for regulation. The strongest political support, however, came from the railroads themselves, and representatives of the Association of Railroad Executives actively participated in the drafting of motor carrier legislation. The great bulk of the motor carriers initially opposed regulation. The approval of the American Trucking Associations was achieved only in the later stages after they had received assurances that enforcement of the new legislation would be placed in a separate ICC bureau completely divorced from the existing railroad-regulating bureaus. Motor carrier regulation was also strongly opposed by all the principal farm organizations and most of the industrial shipper groups.

A comparable pattern prevailed in the struggle over the regulation of inland water carriers. The ICC, the Federal Coordinator, and the railroads strongly supported regulation. The farm organizations, the shippers, and the bulk of the water carriers themselves were equally strongly opposed. The strength of this latter combination was sufficient to delay the enactment of regulatory legislation until 1940 when the Transportation Act of that year gave the ICC control over these carriers.

Since the achievement of these two major objectives of basic ICC control over water and motor carriers, the railroads have attempted to fill in the gaps left in the regulatory jurisdiction of the Commission. They have urged that the exemptions given motor carriers of agricultural commodities and water carriers of bulk commodities be re-

*Annual Report of the Interstate Commerce Commission, Vol. 46 (1932), p. 20.

moved, and that private carriage and contract carriers likewise be subjected to the authority of the ICC. The AAR has also urged in recent years that the Commission be given power to charge tolls for the use of the inland waterways.

Transfer of regulatory controls over railroad-competitive groups from other agencies to the ICC.   Where the railroads have been unsuccessful in preventing the assignment to other agencies of regulatory functions over competing carriers they have waged prolonged campaigns for the transfer of these functions to the ICC. In the debates over the Transportation Act of 1940 the AAR urged that ICC authority be extended over all forms of transportation subject to federal regulation. In particular, the Association wished to transfer authority over coastwise and intercoastal shipping from the Maritime Commission to the ICC and to have the ICC assume the functions of the Civil Aeronautics Authority. Legislation introduced at the instigation of the railroads contained these provisions. The railroads were successful in achieving only the first of their objectives. Rail groups have subsequently regularly attacked the independent position of the Civil Aeronautics Board, and urged either its abolition and the transfer of its functions to the ICC or, in more general terms, the centralization of all regulatory activities affecting transportation in one agency.

Concentration of all federal transportation activities in the ICC.   The culmination of these various railroad policies towards the expansion of ICC authority was reached in 1950 when the AAR advanced the position that all government activities—regulatory and promotional—affecting all forms of transportation should be placed in the ICC. The representative of the railroads testifying before the Senate Interstate and Foreign Commerce Committee was quite explicit in stating that such agencies as the Bureau of Public Roads should be under the Commission. He left some doubt, however, as to the extent to which this recommendation also included such transportation service agencies as the Coast Guard, Weather Bureau, and Coast and Geodetic Survey. In addition, the AAR advocated that the authority of the ICC be extended so that all projects for improving the inland waterways proposed by the Chief of Engineers, United States Army, be submitted to the ICC for approval before their transmission to Congress. Insofar as the scope of its authority is concerned, no stronger support could be asked by the ICC than that which the Association of American Railroads has given to the Commission.

Railroad support in all its forms has been the basis of the Interstate Commerce Commission's viability. Other interests have at times supported individual actions of the Commission or defended the Commission against specific attempts to curb its authority. But such action on the part of these interests has always been sporadic and balanced by severe criticism of the Commission and opposition to it in other lines of policy. The railroads are alone among the interests surrounding the Commission in their constant and comprehensive support of that body. By their continuous praise of the Commission, by their defense of its independence and by their efforts to protect and to extend its authority the railroads have made the Commission the beneficiary of what has been their not inconsiderable political power. But in the rough world of competitive politics nothing comes for free. Political support must be purchased, and the price which the ICC has paid for its railroad support may be traced through almost all important phases of its policy and behavior. . . .

III. Rail-Motor Competition

The affiliation of the ICC with the railroads has resulted in an ambiguous relationship between the Commission and the principal railroad-competitive group, the motor carriers. On the one hand, there is a close affiliation between the motor carrier industry and the ICC's Bureau of Motor Carriers, with the two cooperating in the enforcement of the Motor Carrier Act of 1935. The Bureau has consequently been praised by the motor carriers and criticized by the railroads. On the other hand, the relationship between the motor carrier industry and the Commission apart from the BMC has been cool and frequently antagonistic. The reason for this is Commission partiality towards the railroads in conflicts of interest between the two carrier groups. The price of railroad affiliation has been motor carrier alienation.

Because a large portion of railroad traffic is non-competitive and must move by rail, the Commission has been able to aid the railroads by permitting selective rate-cutting during periods of intense rail-motor competition such as that from 1935 through 1941. For three years from 1937 to 1940 the Commission required motor carriers to bear the burden of proof in making competitive rate cuts while at the same time not requiring the railroads to do so. This policy was continued after Congress in 1938 amended the Motor Carrier Act to make its provisions concerning burden of proof identical with those applicable to the railroads. During this same period the Commission put further barriers in the way of motor carrier competition by prescribing comprehensive minimum rate levels for motor carriers in the northeast and middle west. Although initially requested by the motor carriers, the subsequent effect of these orders was, as Commissioner Eastman pointed out in one dissent, to substitute a much more difficult procedure for motor carriers wishing to lower rates than for railroads. The Commission rejected, however, motor carrier petitions to remedy the situation. Throughout this period the Commission in a number of cases encouraged the railroads to exercise their managerial discretion by meeting motor carrier competition through various devices. The injurious effects of proposed railroad competitive rates upon motor carriers were not sufficient cause to invalidate the rates. Railroads were usually permitted to meet motor carrier competition by rate reductions, and to regain by this means traffic which had been lost to the truckers. Relief from the provisions of Section 4 of the Act prohibiting the charging of a higher rate for a short haul than for a longer one was frequently granted the railroads in this connection. Rate reductions on competitive traffic not accompanied by reductions upon similar noncompetitive traffic were held not to be prejudicial or discriminatory. On the other hand, attempts by the motor carriers to meet railroad competition or to undercut railroads were usually disapproved by the Commission.

ICC action in regard to the most heavily competitive commodities was almost invariably favorable to railroads. The most competitive traffic between the two types of carriers was that which had normally up to that time moved at railroad less-than-carload (LCL) ratings. It was openly admitted that railroad rates on this traffic did not cover costs. Despite this, the railroads vigorously attempted to keep this traffic from falling to the motor carriers, and in carrying out their program to this end they received the cooperation of the Commission. In 1936 the Commission permitted the railroads to introduce free pick-up and delivery services and in the following four years gave them further assistance. The climax of the railroad drive was reached in 1940 when the southern roads filed reduced ratings on some 3,500 commodities and the Commission permitted these changes to go into effect over the most vigorous motor carrier opposition without even suspending them for investigation. In the regulation of other highly competitive traffic, such as automobiles, petroleum, and meats ICC actions and policies likewise tended to favor the railroads. Typical of ICC decisions at this time was one important case dealing with naval stores in which the Commission refused to set minimums beyond which the railroads might not go in meeting motor carrier competition.

The railroads during this period were frequently permitted to quote competitive rates of a type denied to the motor carriers. The Commission required the truckers to base their rates upon the fully allocated cost (constant and variable costs) theory of rate-making while the railroads were permitted to establish rates upon an added cost basis (variable costs only). The railroads were permitted to introduce volume minimum rates (rates applicable only to a minimum volume larger than a carload or truckload); the same privilege was denied to motor carriers. Similarly, for six years motor carriers were not allowed to utilize all freight rates (rates applicable to carloads of mixed commodities regardless of the latter's classification ratings) while at the same time railroads were permitted to do so. Also, freight forwarders and motor carriers were not allowed to charge joint rates (single rates quoted by two or more participating carriers) nor were motor carriers allowed to charge proportional rates (lower rates on through traffic) on freight forwarder traffic.

The incidence of ICC policy during these years can be measured by the criticism from the motor carriers. During the war the situation eased somewhat as there was plenty of traffic for everyone. After the war when the motor carriers again began to cut into railroad business the latter, encouraged by the Commission, commenced a series of competitive rate reductions. Again they received the favor and indulgence of the ICC, and again the motor carriers felt called upon to protest the "tendency upon the part of the ICC to treat 'public interest' and 'railroad interest' as synonymous terms. . . ."

While competitive rate-making has been the single most important field of Commission behavior favoring railroads in their struggle with the motor carriers, other actions and policies of the Commission also deserve mention. In the discussion prior to the passage of the Motor Carrier Act the industry only consented to regulation by the "railroad-minded" ICC on the condition that a separate motor carrier bureau and division be established. These two bodies became the representatives of the industry within the Commission and as such anathemas to the railroads, who consistently urged the Commission to organize itself on a "functional" rather than an "industry" basis. In line with these desires the Commission has gradually emasculated the motor carrier units. The division has been stripped of its responsibilities in regard to rates, securities, consolidations, mergers, purchases, accounts, and penalties; the bureau has lost its Section of Traffic, its Section of Accounts, and its functions in connection with motor carrier securities. In other fields of activity, the Commission has narrowly interpreted the "grandfather clause" (statutory authorization of operating rights to carriers for bona fide operations on a given date) so as to deny certificates and permits to many operating truck lines. When it has approved such rights it has frequently severely restricted them as to the territory or classes of shippers which might be served or the commodities which might be transported. For almost a decade the Commission interpreted the acquisition, certificate, and affiliation clauses of the Interstate Commerce Act in such a manner as to facilitate railroad penetration into the motor carrier industry and to raise genuine fears in the motor carriers as to the extent to which the Commission really wished to preserve the independent trucker. Only recently the Commission announced a policy which would seem to indicate that motor carriers are to be barred from operating upon a transcontinental scale.

The cumulative result of these ICC policies has been the alienation of the motor carriers from the Commission. Motor carrier criticism of the ICC has been consistent and vigorous. At the end of the war, the truckers seriously considered initiating a drive to free themselves from ICC control. After much discussion and the consideration of alternative plans, the industry now supports the break-up of the ICC into separate regulatory commissions for each type of transportation with an appellate commission to have jurisdiction over controversies involving two or more classes of carriers, the transfer of the executive functions of the ICC to an executive agency, and the further development of a general control over transportation by the Undersecretary of Commerce.

THE RISE AND FALL
OF THE NONSKEDS
Robert Bendiner

From all indications the American sky is about to become the permanent and uncontested preserve of just about the most exclusive club in the world. The dozen airlines that make up its membership may compete with each other for profitable routes here and there, as they have in the past, but with newcomers in effect barred from the blessed circle they will otherwise be happily free of the pressures of free enterprise. Such is the consequence of the Supreme Court's refusal last month to hear the appeal of Trans American Airlines, now under sentence of extinction by order of the Civil Aeronautics Board (CAB).

The largest and most audacious of the irregulars, or "nonskeds," in the business and the only serious challenge that the so-called "grandfather lines" have ever had, the Trans American group will go out of business on June 5 for having flouted the Board's regulations. It is most unlikely that an outsider will again have the impudence or the wherewithal to contest the stratosphere with the Big Twelve.

In its long struggle for survival Trans American, or North American as it was known before North American Aviation forced it to change its name, has inevitably suggested David confronting Goliath. Unfortunately for those who like their choices simple, Davids have their Uriah episodes, in which they are more lusty than principled, and Goliaths sometimes have points in their favor. So it is in this case, and the result is a mixed tale of legislative good intentions soured by bureaucracy, of high-pressure maneuvering, and of plain cynicism— all adding up to the point that "regulation," the shibboleth of our New Deal days, is not the complete answer to sin.

Back in 1938 Congress passed the Civil Aeronautics Act, sponsored by Senator Pat McCarran and nursed through a subcommittee by an obscure first-termer named Truman. The purpose was to spare the

From *The Reporter,* XVI (May 30, 1957), 29–34. Copyright 1957 by The Reporter Magazine Company. Reprinted by permission of the author and publisher.

public, just then beginning to take to air travel, the long period of cutthroat competition that had marked the spread of rail travel in an earlier day. Protection of passengers from undue hazard, the need to stabilize an infant industry, and the requirement of a reserve transport fleet for national defense—all made it undesirable to leave the emergent airlines to the mercies of the Darwinian market place. At the same time, it was obvious that air transport was not a "natural monopoly" like gas or electricity and had to be allowed a measure of competition.

The Act therefore set up the CAB as a regulatory agency and provided for two types of carrier. Certificates were to be issued to the sixteen lines then flying passengers and mail, authorizing them to operate as regular "scheduled" airlines, and subsidies in the guise of flexible mail payments were to offset their deficits. In return they were obliged to meet standards of safety and convenience set up by the CAB and to fly routes that included marginal areas as well as the lush markets of big terminal cities. New lines were to be certified on a showing of "public convenience and necessity," provided the Board found them able and willing.

A second group, known as "fixed base operators," were to be granted exemptions from the regulations. They could make irregular trips, provide local taxi service, run charter flights, and perform other functions not related to regular public travel over a fixed route. Most of the trips were short ones in small planes, and at first the "fixed base operators" were of very little public significance. After the war, however, they suddenly became very significant indeed.

At a time when the demand for air service seemed unlimited, the government found itself with surplus transport planes on its hands while scores of trained pilots were pouring into civilian life eager to make use of their wartime experience. With the government's blessing—in fact with its financing— veterans and planes inevitably got together and nonsked air travel was launched.

If the CAB did not see that in the normal course of things some of these entrepreneurs hoped legitimately to develop into regular airlines, it was singularly lacking in imagination. It "must have realized," a Senate committee report was to state in 1953, "that these large transport-type aircraft would have to be used in some sort of common-carrier route-type service." They were hardly designed for crop dusting or for rushing Florida oranges to Boston.

Standard and Viking

Among those who took their own future as public carriers for granted were Stanley Weiss, an Army transport pilot who had flown sixty-four trips over the Hump, and James Fischgrund, a Navy lieutenant commander. For $15,000 down and an RFC loan they bought two DC-3s and in 1946 set up business as Standard Airlines. At about the same time Ross R. Hart and Jack B. Lewin, both employees of Douglas Aircraft, raised the small capital required to establish Viking Airlines, a similarly modest enterprise. Their plan was to tap the vast potential market of would-be air travelers who could not afford the luxury prices of the regular lines. Their formula was to eliminate the frills, especially free meals, to increase seating capacity, and to fly as steadily as possible between points of heavy traffic. Cut-rate coach flights were operated between Los Angeles and New York for as much as $50 below the standard price. By 1948 Standard was in the black and had a fleet of seven DC-3s. Together the two lines had sewn up the lion's share of cut-rate transcontinental traffic—$75 between Chicago and California and $99 coast to coast.

Between 1947 and 1949, as Standard and Viking hauled in the cash and the country in general enjoyed good times, the "grandfather lines," overexpanded and evidently overpriced, wallowed in their own exclusive depression. Inevitably they took a jaundiced view of the upstarts even though their own deficits were covered by the U.S. government. W. A. Patterson, president of United Air Lines, subsequently put the case in its now classic form to the Small Business Committee of the Senate:

The irregulars moved in to make the most of this [postwar] situation, to fly anywhere at any time that loads were available. Thus began a cream-skimming operation whereby they would tap only the major markets and leave the scheduled airlines to carry out their responsibility of serving all communities, large and small. Thus they began undercutting the scheduled airlines and each other. They had to file no tariffs; they had to meet no route qualifications; they could operate in and out of any airport without prior crew familiarization procedures. Theirs was a free and easy business in which they had to answer to practically no one but themselves. The regulated scheduled operators, with their obligations to the general public, to the Government, to stockholders, and to employees, looked on with some amazement. . . .

"Strangulation by Regulation"

They looked also to the Civil Aeronautics Board—and there they found comfort. By defenders of the nonskeds the CAB is regarded as the greatest drag on aviation since gravity, but there is no doubt that the cut-rate fliers confronted it with a real dilemma. On the one hand it was directed by the Act to foster a sound and efficient air service without "unfair or destructive competitive practices," and on the other hand to encourage "competition to the extent necessary to assure the sound development" of the system. By certifying the nonskeds it could divest them of the advantages cited by Patterson, subjecting them to the same conditions as other regular lines, or it could keep them in their special status and squeeze them with regulations. Looking at the shaky financial state of the certificated carriers, perhaps with an eye on the subsidies for which it rightly felt it had a responsibility, and having no more boldness of vision than government bureaus generally have, the CAB moved toward regulating the brashness, if not the life, out of the nonskeds.

The process described by Senator John Sparkman as "strangulation by regulation" began in 1947. Blanket exemptions were withdrawn, and the nonskeds were required to apply for individual Letters of Registration as irregular carriers. Full reporting on rates, mergers, and other operating details were called for, and specific restrictions were laid down on the number of flights that could be made in a given period. Two years later the screws were tightened some more. The irregulars were prohibited from making arrangements, among themselves or with ticket agents, for interchange of passengers, or from rotating flights in such a way as to constitute a "collective air transportation service."

"Living up to those regulations was 100 per cent impossible, and the Board knew it," counsel for North American told the House Antitrust subcommittee a year ago. "That is why the Board adopted the regulations." Senator Wayne Morse was even more specific: "A traveler must know in advance when a plane is going to depart, when it is going to arrive, where he can buy his ticket, and from what place he can collect his baggage. These things cannot be done if the operation is conducted on a tramp-steamer basis." In any case, both Standard and Viking treated the rules cavalierly. Both applied for certification and were turned down. The CAB was more intent on strengthening the existing lines than in adding to their headaches. By 1950 both lines had their Letters of Registration revoked for flying too frequently, and technically they went out of business.

Actually they merged, along with two other lines, into a complex corporate arrangement, and as North American Airlines proceeded to do business in a highly profitable circumvention of the CAB and its rules. Through a web of partnerships with an interlocking directorate, they brought together the functions of flying, leasing, ticket selling, and accounting. And by artful shuffling of schedules they managed to furnish regular service from Los Angeles to New York and New York to Miami without seriously transgressing the frequency limits for any one line.

If the regulars were irritated before, they were now outraged. "Interlopers," "pretenders," and "bogus specialists," the nonskeds were called by Eastern Air Lines' president Eddie Rickenbacker—and these were among the more endearing names reserved for them. The Air Transport Association instructed its legal department to get the CAB to forbid uncertificated operators even to use the word "airline" or "airway." When a passenger having to take two or more lines to complete a trip inquired about a North American connection, ticket clerks would frequently express shock. On occasion they were heard to murmur something about "safety," although North American had no fatal accidents in its seven years of operation. Stanley Weiss of North American testified before Representative Emanuel Celler's Antitrust subcommittee that travel agents were warned by the A.T.A. to stop selling tickets for the nonskeds altogether or give up their franchises from the major lines.

The Air-Coach Boom

In terms of revenue, North American was never remotely a threat to the certificated carriers, which did ninety-six per cent of the passenger trade. But it was a yardstick, and as such its influence has been as marked—and as unwelcome—in the business of air travel as TVA's in the field of electric power. Some trunk-line executives dispute the North American group's claim to have pioneered in air-coach travel. Alexander G. Hardy, fiery vice-president of National Airlines, told me that his company had applied for permission to run a reduced-fare service from New York to Miami and had ordered coach planes before North American was even in the picture. Turned down by the CAB, which didn't think the idea financially sound, National took the matter to the courts but without success. What is more, Hardy said, the nonskeds appeared before the Board to oppose the move and then when it had been turned down went out themselves and flew at reduced rates.

Far from being the public's white knight, according to Hardy, "the nonskeds were gouging the public during the peak seasons." In the immediate postwar period, when demand far outran supply, they exacted as much as $100 for the New York-Miami run as against the standard first-class fare of $56.

Nevertheless, it was the nonskeds, especially Standard and Viking, that made a go of coach service. They were the first to increase the seating capacity of standard aircraft and to offer coach fares, not just for flights at inconvenient hours but on the basis of greater passenger load. Eventually forced to follow suit, the trunk lines found themselves with a boom on their hands. In 1948, for example, Capital Airlines carried 1,002 passengers on its regular first-class run between Chicago and New York. In December of that year, the second month of its newly installed coach service, 3,072 made the trip at the reduced fare. Six years later, coaches accounted for fully a third of all domestic airline traffic and more than a half of the overseas. By 1960 all the big lines expect that more than half their passengers will travel by coach.

Yet as late as 1949 United called such service "unsound" and American said air-coach travel had no part in their plans.

While the coach trade played a large part in getting the trunk lines out of the red and, not so incidentally, off public subsidy, they found the "yardstick" no more tolerable on that account. The North American combine may have given the industry a shot in the arm, but if it was allowed to go on operating outside the regulations, as it patently was doing, what was the good of the CAB or the Act itself? If North American wanted to operate as an airline, let it apply for certification and abide by the rules of the game.

This attitude sounded reasonable, but there was one hitch. Since its creation in 1938, the CAB has yet to find a single applicant it considered worthy of certification as a regular passenger airline. Out of 164 applications, not one was deemed to have met the requirements of the Act. That 126 of these applications were withdrawn, or withered on the vine before a determination could be made, is in itself illuminating. Of the twenty-one nonskeds that applied in the combined Transcontinental Coach case, only four lasted to the end of the proceedings. "We are small businessmen," one of them complained midway to a Senate committee. "We cannot afford to pay the fabulous attorney fees to have a lawyer present at this hearing every day that it has been going on for six months now. . . . They are slowly chopping our heads off while that is going on." Incidentally, none of the surviving four made the grade. The net result is that with twenty times the traffic we have four fewer trunk lines (because of mergers) than we had when the Act was passed.

Ambidextrous Appeals

The best the North American group could reasonably hope for was to forestall revocation of their Letters, and to this end they worked hard in Washington, covering both political sides of the street and ringing all the changes. Knowing how they stood with a majority of the Board, they concentrated elsewhere. Along with the other nonskeds, all of which were much smaller and less ambitious, they repeatedly and cogently presented their case before sympathetic committees on Capitol Hill, employing at various times such effective spokesmen as former Senator Claude Pepper, Senator Joseph C. O'Mahoney (when he was out of office between terms), and Maurice Rosenblatt, better known as the kingpin of the National Committee for an Effective Congress.

The appeal was essentially that of "the little man" at the mercy of monopoly, and it went well before the Senate's Select Committee on Small Business and Congressman Celler's Antitrust subcommittee in the House, both of which, unfortunately, had only peripheral jurisdiction in the field.

At the same time, the home office in California worked the other side of the street. It mailed out model letters and telegrams for sympathetic businessmen to send to the President, with copies for Vice-President Nixon, appropriate congressmen, and Senators Knowland and Kuchel. A few excerpts will indicate an appeal somewhat different from that made by Senators Pepper and O'Mahoney:

When the Republicans were elected with your leadership, many of us felt there would be considerable improvement with respect to continued Government interference with certain segments of our economy. . . . The Civil Aeronautics Board, in my opinion, ever since it was organized under the New Deal Administration, has had a fairly shabby record.

The Board has a great file of charges against North American. These charges take the same form as the New Deal checkreins which were used to restrict supply and to hobble independent enterprise.

I am behind your administration 100 per cent and want to continue to be so but I think it is time that something should be done about the Civil Aeronautics Board and its obvious favoritism against free enterprise.

In Washington North American enlisted the public-relations services of Raimond Bowles, formerly patronage chief of the Republican National Committee and assistant to Sherman Adams when he was governor of New Hampshire. On the Pacific Coast it retained none other than Murray M. Chotiner, Nixon's well-known adviser, who not only called at least one Board member but wrote a letter to President Eisenhower expressing the conviction that only White House intercession would "remedy the present high-handed and arbitrary action of the CAB. The survival of the free enterprise system in this field requires immediate and aggressive action."

For all its vigor and political ambidextrousness, however, the nonskeds' campaign was no match for the quiet pressure of the regulars. In the first place, the regulars had a strong technical case against the North American group, which, in spite of enforcement proceedings pending against it, merrily pursued its illegal way. It advertised itself blandly as "the fourth greatest airline in the United States" and the "largest and oldest air coach system." Postcards were distributed at its ticket counters with the legend "Written aboard one of North American Airlines luxurious 4-engine Douglas DC-6B air liners," though at the time it was flying only DC-4s. Far from being reticent or indirect about scheduling flights contrary to regulations, it defiantly printed timetables, adding only in very fine print at the bottom that these "samples of flight times are not representation that flights are made every day or with any specified regularity."

The regulars were every bit as alert to sentiment on the Hill as the nonskeds and played up to it from the start. In a letter to the heads of the certificated lines in 1948, Admiral Emory S. Land, then president of the Air Transport Association, laid down a public-relations program for combating the nonskeds' effort to get air-freight business: "Finally, the most important part of this letter is that you personally contact one or more key men who, directly or indirectly, have this matter under consideration," his communication wound up. "The addresses of these key men are Capitol Hill and Commerce Building [where the CAB is located]. Nufced."

Another document produced at the Celler subcommittee hearings was a memorandum to the Public Relations Advisory Committee from John W. Thompson, an A.T.A. official. Airlines were advised in this note to "get in touch" with a group of senators who had signed a petition in favor of slowing down CAB action against the nonskeds. It was to be pointed out to these legislators that unless the nonskeds were checked, "the areas which sent these gentlemen to Congress will be affected adversely as far as air passenger service, airmail, air parcel post is concerned." Once again, nufced. With the big airlines operating in every state if not in every congressional district, with their directors scattered in most major cities and generally men of considerable local importance, the impact of the regulars is very much greater than any that can be directed at congressmen by an isolated and comparatively small independent.

Friends in Court

It is with the CAB itself, however, that the "grandfather lines" have the vital advantage. The tendency is strong for members to identify themselves with the interests of the existing carriers, and to promote their financial health, if for no other reason than to keep them off government subsidy. Many of them conceive it to be their duty to build up these lines by adding to their routes, and a good case can be made that it is to the public's advantage to deal with a dozen expanded lines rather than with a network of small ones requiring intricate routing and frequent changes of plane.

Be that as it may, the degree of co-operation between the CAB and the giants is striking, and few unco-operative board members have ever been reappointed. The classic case was that of James M. Landis, who fought Pan American and whose reappointment was taken for granted until three days before the expiration of his term. No reason was ever given for President Truman's apparently sudden change of heart.

Joseph P. Adams, who did his utmost to stimulate competition, who befriended the nonskeds, encouraged coach service, and dissented from the CAB's majority in something like thirty decisions, was denied reappointment by Mr. Eisenhower despite pleas on his behalf by the chairman of the Board and a former chairman, both Republicans. Colonel Adams's rejection was bluntly described by *Aviation Weekly* as a "personal favor" to Secretary of Commerce Weeks, a close friend of Samuel F. Pryor, former Republican National Committeeman and a vice-president of Pan American. Adams had played a major role in the drastic reduction of mail subsidies to Pan American. Joseph J. O'Connell, another former chairman with whom I talked, suggested that in all administrative agencies controversial figures are poor bets for reappointment. The reward goes to the man who doesn't alienate anyone.

Given the feeling of the CAB's majority and the obvious violations of North American, no one was surprised when the CAB put out a "cease and desist" order in 1953. The surprise was that, largely because of the work of exceptionally able counsel, the line managed to continue for two more years, even adding another carrier to the combine, before the Board in July, 1955, finally revoked its various Letters of Registration for "knowing and wilful" violation of the Act. Even after that blow, the group continued operations, though somewhat limpingly, pending final adjudication in the courts.

Sympathy for the Trans American group is neither easy nor relevant. Its stoutest defenders concede the violations. One, a senator, says bluntly that "it brought on its own demise," and another suggests that to have granted the certificate would have been "like giving a bootlegger a liquor license after Prohibition on the ground that he had proved his efficiency." Even Colonel Adams concurred in the CAB's findings. "As a sworn government employee," he says, "I couldn't acquiesce in violations"—though he held out against the penalty as too harsh in view of the line's performance and the blank wall against which it found itself.

In a financial way, moreover, the position of these particular "small businessmen," however wronged, will hardly draw tears. According to their counsel, each of the four partners drew $111,835 in 1954 and $101,726 in 1955, exclusive of their salaries of $2,000 a month. Net profit after taxes in the latter year amounted to $835,994. Even the pending collapse of their enterprise was used to turn a handsome profit. The line's five DC-6Bs have been leased for five years to Eastern for between $35,000 and $40,000 a month per plane, for a total of $12 million. Since they are reliably reported to have cost around $7.5 million, the partners can forget all about flying and still split a profit of $4.5 million, not counting depreciation, on this leasing coup alone.

The financial fortunes of the partners, however interesting, have no bearing of course on the larger issue. "This was the last effort to crack the CAB policy against letting new trunk lines into the business," I was told at Trans American, "and like 162 efforts before it, it failed." While this may be putting the case too strongly, the fact is that almost all the remaining nonskeds are concerned exclusively with military contracts and the few that are not are so small as to preclude ambition. There are fourteen certificated "feeder lines," which operate locally, but they are well subsidized even now and their expansion is not regarded as economically feasible. Yet except by operating profitably as a nonsked, how is any line to demonstrate the fitness and ability required for certification under the Act?

Is the door really closed to new lines? The CAB denies it, as it must, but one of its former chairmen says, "The answer probably is 'Yes.' " Nor does the prospect bother him. "Freedom of access in this field is ridiculous," he explains; "the Act never contemplated it." But the record of congressional debate seems to show otherwise. The Small Business Committee's report found it "filled with repeated assurances that the door would still be open to new companies."

It is true that the CAB has been steadily cutting the smaller trunk lines into routes hitherto reserved for the Big Four, and in this process there is still room for competition. It is a competition, let it be admitted, unknown to the giant lines of other countries, but nevertheless it is competition among a select few, each satisfied with the *status quo* as soon as he has an adequate piece of the pie. If the pie has been greatly enlarged by expanded coach service—all the domestic trunk lines are now off subsidy—the Big Twelve who will share it have North American to thank for prodding them into the low-fare market. In the nature of things, of course, they can no more be expected to shed a tear at the wake of the nonskeds than North American can be credited with high social purpose. A vice-president of National Airlines, a small regular that has to contend with the giants above it while fighting the nonskeds beneath it, pretty well summed up the code of the trade. "No one in any business favors monopoly," he remarked, "until he's got one."

chapter five

Agriculture

The American farmer, despite a reputation for individualism, has long successfully sought governmental assistance in dealing with his economic problems. Today, when the farm population constitutes roughly seven percent of the nation's population and farm production accounts for less than five percent of the gross national product, the national government still operates a substantial variety of farm programs costing several billion dollars yearly. The farmer's success in obtaining this largess has been frequently accounted for in terms of such factors as rural overrepresentation in legislative bodies, the acceptance of the myth of agricultural fundamentalism, and the activities of powerful farm pressure groups.

Farmers, however, obviously do not comprise a single, monolithic group. Rather, they differ greatly on the basis of such criteria as size of farm, income, region, commodities grown, efficiency of operation, and political inclinations. Some farmers benefit much more from government programs than do others, e.g., commercial farmers as compared to subsistence farmers, or cotton growers as compared to poultry producers. Thus the student of agricultural policy-making should be concerned not simply with why farmers receive government assistance but with which groups of farmers receive what kinds of assistance. To answer that query, one must focus on the operation of the policy-making process and the factors influencing policy-makers in the agricultural arena.

In this chapter the focus will be primarily on agricultural price support policy. Although a wide variety of programs to assist farmers are administered by the Department of Agriculture, it is the price support program which involves the greatest expenditure of money and arouses the most political controversy.

Theodore Lowi, in explaining "How the Farmers Get What They Want," takes the position that agricultural policy is really made by a series of self-governing subsystems within the broader political system. Each of these subsystems is essentially comprised of a farm agency (usually a bureau within the U. S. Department of Agriculture), a congressional committee or subcommittee, and a farm group (often based on a local farmer-elected committee system). The subsystems deal with such policy areas as price supports, farm credit, research, soil conservation, and extension services. The reader should consider whether Lowi has overstated his case, especially in the instance of agricultural price supports. Is his argument consistent with the findings reported in the next two selections? To the extent that Lowi's argument is valid, what are its implications for democratic politics?

Within Congress the primary centers of decision on agricultural policy are the House and Senate agriculture committees. Although their approval does not guarantee the enactment of farm legislation, little that is unacceptable to the interests represented on them is likely to come to the floor for consideration. The agriculture committees are clientele committees and, as Professor Charles Jones' useful study of the House Agriculture Committee helps to demonstrate, are dominated by Representatives and Senators from farm districts and states. Almost never does one find an urban congressman on these committees, despite their relevance to urban dwellers as consumers of agricultural products. The subcommittee organization and staffing of the House committee reflects the regional and commodity divisions within agriculture and helps to explain why growers of some commodities, especially those produced in the South (e.g., cotton, tobacco, rice), benefit more from price supports than others.

Congressional voting on price support legislation has been rather strongly partisan since the end of World War II, with the Democrats generally favoring high price supports and production controls and the Republicans advocating low or flexible price supports and minimal if any controls on production. The Congressional Quarterly's study provides little support, certainly, for the old notion that a bipartisan "farm bloc" shapes congressional action on price support legislation. When congressmen vote contrary to their party's position, their deviation can usually be accounted for in terms of their constituency interests. (Instructive here is Professor Jones' discussion of the interplay of party and constituency influences in congressmen's decision-making.) The conventional wisdom about "voting one's constituency" is well-known.

HOW THE FARMERS GET WHAT THEY WANT
Theodore Lowi

In his Farm Message of January 31 [1964], President Johnson proposed that Congress establish a bipartisan commission to investigate the concentration of power in the food industry. In the same message the President called for new legislation to strengthen farmer co-operatives, to encourage their expansion through merger and acquisition, and to provide them with further exemptions from the antitrust laws.

This was the beginning of the "Johnson round" in agriculture. It is part of a familiar pattern. An attack on the food industry's market power, coupled with proposals for expanded and stronger farm co-operatives, is obviously not an attack on concentration itself. Rather it is an attack on the intervention of nonagricultural groups into strictly agricultural affairs.

That agricultural affairs should be handled strictly within the agricultural community is a basic political principle established before the turn of the century and maintained since then without serious reexamination. As a result, agriculture has become neither public nor private enterprise. It is a system of self-government in which each leading farm interest controls a segment of agriculture through a delegation of national sovereignty. Agriculture has emerged as a largely self-governing federal estate within the Federal structure of the United States.

President Johnson recognized these facts within three weeks of his accession when he summoned a conference of agricultural leaders to formulate a program by which agriculture should be served and regulated. The most recent concession to agriculture's self-government was the wheat-cotton bill. Because cotton supports were too high, the cotton interests wrote a bill providing for a subsidy of six to eight cents a pound to mills in order to keep them competitive with foreign cotton and domestic rayon without touching the price supports. On

From *The Reporter*, XXX (May 21, 1964), 34–37. Copyright 1964 by The Reporter Magazine Company. Reprinted by permission of the author and publisher.

the other hand, wheat supports were too low because wheat farmers last year in referendum overwhelmingly rejected President Kennedy's plan to provide some Federal regulation along with supports. The wheat section of the new act calls for a program whereby wheat farmers may voluntarily comply with acreage reduction for subsidies of up to seventy cents a bushel but without the Federal supply regulations. The press called this a major legislative victory for Mr. Johnson, but the credit is not his. That the press could see this as a victory for anyone but organized cotton and wheat is a testimonial to the total acceptance by President, press, and public of the principle that private agricultural interests alone govern agriculture and should do so.

The reasons for agriculture's self-government are deep-rooted, and the lessons to be drawn are important to the future of American politics. For a century agriculture has been out of step with American economic development. Occasional fat years have only created unreal expectations, to be undercut by the more typical lean years.

Quite early, farmers discovered the value of politics as a counterweight to industry's growth and concentration. Land-grant and homesteading acts were followed by governmental services in research and education. Continuing distress led to bolder demands. First there were efforts to effect a redistribution of wealth in favor of agriculture. As a debtor class, farmers saw inflation as the solution, and Bryan was their spokesman for cheaper money and cheaper credit. The monopolies, the railroads, the grain merchants and other processors, the banks, and the brokers were to be deprived of power over the market by dissolution or by severe restraints. Next, farmers sought solutions by emulating the business system: the co-operative to restrain domestic trade and international dumping over high tariff walls to restrain international trade. Yet all these mechanisms either were not enacted or did not live up to expectations.

With the coming of the New Deal and with its help, organized agriculture turned to self-regulation. The system created during the 1930s has endured to this day, and with only a few marginal additions and alterations is accepted almost unanimously by farm leaders. Self-regulation might have taken several forms, the most likely one being a national system of farm-leader representation within a farmers' NRA. Instead, a more complicated system of highly decentralized and highly autonomous subgovernments developed, largely for Constitutional reasons. Agriculture was the most "local" of the manufacturing groups the Federal government was trying to reach. The appearance if not the reality of decentralizing Federal programs through farmer-elected local committees helped avoid strains on the interstate commerce clause of the Constitution. But this avoidance of Constitutional troubles created very special political difficulties.

The Local Committees

The Federal Extension Service shows how the system works. It is "cooperative" in that it shares the job of farm improvement with the states, the land-grant colleges, the county governments, and the local associations of farmers. The county agent is actually employed by the local associations. In the formative years, the aid of local chambers of commerce was enlisted, the local association being the "farm bureau" of the chamber. In order to coordinate local activities and to make more effective claims for additional outside assistance, these farm bureaus were organized into state farm bureau federations. The American Farm Bureau Federation, formed at the Agriculture College of Cornell University in 1919, was used as a further step toward amalgamation. To this day there is a close relationship between the farm bureaus, the land-grant colleges, and the Extension Service. This transformation of an administrative arrangement into a political system has been repeated in nearly all the agricultural programs during recent decades. The Extension Service exercises few controls from the top. There are cries of "Federal encroachment" at the mere suggestion in Washington that the Department of Agriculture should increase its supervision of the extension programs or coordinate them with other Federal activities.

As the financial stakes have grown larger, the pattern of local self-government remains the same. Price support—the "parity program"— is run by the thousands of farmer-elected county committees that function alongside but quite independently of the other local committees. Acreage allotments to bring supply down and prices up are apportioned among the states by the Agricultural Stabilization and

Conservation Service. State committees of farmers apportion the allotment among the counties. The farmer-elected county Stabilization and Conservation Committees receive the county allotment.

These committees made the original acreage allotments among individual farmers back in the 1930s; today, they make new allotments, work out adjustments and review complaints regarding allotments, determine whether quotas have been complied with, inspect and approve storage facilities and perform as the court of original jurisdiction on violations of price-support rules and on eligibility for parity payments. The committees are also vitally important in the campaigns for the two-thirds vote required to fix high price supports. Congress determines the general level of supports and the Secretary of Agriculture proclaims the national acreage quotas for adjusting the supply to the guaranteed price. But the locally elected committees stand between the farmer and Washington.

Most other agricultural programs have evolved similarly. Each is independent of the others, and any conflicts or overlapping mandates have been treated as nonexistent or beyond the jurisdiction of any one agency. The Soil Conservation Service operates through its independent soil-conservation districts, of which there were 2,936 in 1963, involving ninety-six per cent of the nation's farms. Each district's farmer-elected committee is considered a unit of local government. The Farmer Cooperative Service operates through the member-elected boards of directors of the farm co-ops. In agricultural credit, local self-government is found in even greater complexity. The Farm Credit Administration exists outside the Department of Agriculture and is made up of not one but three separate bodies politic, a triangular system mostly farmer-owned and totally farmer-controlled.

Ten Systems and Politics

The ten principal self-governing systems in agriculture, in fiscal 1962, disposed of $5.6 billion of the total of $6.7 billion in expenditures passing through the Department of Agriculture. During the calendar year 1962, $5.8 billion in loans was handled similarly. This combined amount represents a large portion of the total of Federal activity outside national defense.

Each of the ten systems has become a powerful political instrumentality. The self-governing local units become one important force in a system that administers a program and maintains the autonomy of that program against political forces emanating from other agricultural programs, from antagonistic farm and nonfarm interests, from Congress, from the Secretary of Agriculture, and from the President. To many a farmer, the local outpost of one or another of these systems *is* the government.

The politics within each system is built upon a triangular trading pattern involving the central agency, a Congressional committee or subcommittee, and the local district farmer committees (usually federated in some national or regional organization). Each side of the triangle complements and supports the other two.

The Extension Service, for example, is one side of the triangle completed by the long-tenure "farm bureau" members of the Agriculture Committees in Congress and, at the local level, the American Farm Bureau Federation with its local committees. Further group support is provided by two intimately related groups, the Association of Land Grant Colleges and Universities and the National Association of County Agricultural Agents.

Another such triangle unites the Soil Conservation Service, the Agriculture subcommittee of the House Appropriations Committee, and the local districts organized in the energetic National Association of Soil Conservation Districts. Further support comes from the Soil Conservation Society of America (mainly professionals) and the former Friends of the Land, now the Izaak Walton League of America.

Probably the most complex of the systems embraces the parity program. It connects the Agricultural Stabilization and Conservation Service with the eight (formerly ten) commodity subcommittees of the House Agriculture Committee and the dozens of separately organized groups representing the various commodities. (Examples: National Cotton Council, American Wool Growers Association, American Cranberry Growers Association.) These groups and congressmen draw support from the local price-support committees wherever a particular commodity is grown.

The Farmer Had His Way

These systems have a vigorous capacity to maintain themselves and to resist encroachment. They have such institutional legitimacy that they have become practically insulated from the three central sources of democratic political responsibility. Thus, within the Executive branch, they are autonomous. Secretaries of Agriculture have tried and failed to consolidate or even to coordinate related programs. Within Congress, they are sufficiently powerful to be able to exercise an effective veto or create a stalemate. And they are almost totally removed from the view, not to mention the control, of the general public. (Throughout the 1950s, Victor Anfuso of Brooklyn was the only member of the House Agriculture committee from a non-farm constituency.

Important cases illustrate their power:

In 1947, Secretary of Agriculture Clinton P. Anderson proposed a consolidation of all soil-conservation, price-support, and FHA programs into one committee system with a direct line from the committees to the Secretary. Bills were prepared providing for consolidation within the price-support committees. Contrary bills provided for consolidation under soil conservation districts. The result: stalemate. In 1948, a leading farm senator proposed consolidation of the programs under the local associations of the Extension Service. Immediately a House farm leader introduced a contrary bill. The result: continuing stalemate.

In Waco, Texas, on October 14, 1952, Presidential candidate Eisenhower said: "I would like to see in every county all Federal farm agencies under the same roof." Pursuant to this promise, Secretary Ezra Taft Benson issued a series of orders during early 1953 attempting to bring about consolidation of local units as well as unification at the top. Finally, amid cries of "sneak attack" and "agricrat," Benson proclaimed that "any work on the further consolidation of county and state offices . . . shall be suspended."

From the very beginning, Secretary Benson sought to abandon rigid price supports and bring actual supports closer to market prices. In 1954, as he was beginning to succeed, Congress enacted a "commodity set aside" by which $2.5 billion of surplus commodities already held by the government were declared to be a "frozen reserve" for national defense. Since the Secretary's power to cut price supports depends heavily upon the amount of government-owned surplus carried over from previous years, the commodity set aside was a way of freezing parity as well as reserves. Benson eventually succeeded in reducing supports on the few commodities over which he had authority. But thanks to the set-aside, Congress, between fiscal 1952 and 1957, helped increase the value of commodities held by the government from $1.1 billion to $5.3 billion. What appeared, therefore, to be a real Republican policy shift amounted to no more than giving back with one hand what had been taken away by the other.

President Eisenhower's first budget sought to abolish farm home-building and improvement loans by eliminating the budgetary request and by further requesting that the 1949 authorization law be allowed to expire. Congress overrode his request in 1953 and each succeeding year, and the President answered Congress with a year-by-year refusal to implement the farm housing program. In 1956, when the President asked again explicitly for elimination of the program, he was rebuffed. The Housing subcommittee of the House Banking and Currency Committee added to the President's omnibus housing bill a renewal of the farm housing program, plus an authorization for $500 million in loans over a five-year period, and the bill passed with a Congressional mandate to use the funds. They were used thereafter at a rate of about $75 million a year.

On March 16, 1961, President Kennedy produced a "radically different" farm program in a special message to Congress. For the first time in the history of price supports, the bill called for surplus control through quotas placed on bushels, tons, or other units, rather than on acreage. An acreage allotment allows the farmer to produce as much as he can on the reduced acreage in cultivation. For example, in the first ten years or so of acreage control, acreage under cultivation dropped by about four per cent, while actual production rose by fifteen per cent. The Kennedy proposal called for national committees of farmers to be elected to work out the actual program. This more stringent type of control was eliminated from the omnibus bill in the Agriculture Committees of both chambers and there were no attempts to restore them during floor debate. Last-minute efforts by Secretary Orville L. Freeman to up the ante, offering to raise wheat supports from $1.79 to $2.00, were useless. Persistence by the administration led eventually to rejection by wheat farmers in 1963 of all high price supports and acreage controls.

The politics of this rejected referendum is of general significance. Despite all the blandishments and inducements of administration, the farmer had his way. The local price-support committees usually campaign in these referendums for the Department of Agriculture, but this time they did not. And thousands of small farmers, eligible to vote for the first time, joined with the local leadership to help defeat the referendum. It is not so odd that wheat farmers would reject a proposal that aims to regulate them more strictly than before. What is odd is that only wheat farmers are allowed to decide the matter. It seems that in agriculture, as in many other fields, the regulators are powerless without the consent of the regulated.

Agriculture is the field where the distinction between public and private has been almost completely eliminated, not by public expropriation of private domain but by private expropriation of public domain. For more than a generation, Americans have succeeded in expanding the public sphere without giving thought to the essential democratic question of how each expansion is to be effected. The creation of private governments has profoundly limited the capacity of the public government to govern responsibly and flexibly.

REPRESENTATION IN CONGRESS: THE CASE OF THE HOUSE AGRICULTURE COMMITTEE

Charles O. Jones

Students of American politics are told that our political system is fundamentally a *representative* democracy. Concepts of representation, since Burke, have commonly employed his distinction between action taken in response to instructions from constituents and action based on an independent appraisal of the national interest.[1] A very recent analysis has offered a refinement of this, by distinguishing three types: "delegate," "trustee" and "politico."[2] Theory and history alike tell us, however, that a representative does not invariably act in only one of these roles. There have been a number of empirical studies of representatives, few of which concentrate on specific policy fields,[3] and studies also of the play of interests in the enactment of specific legislation, but without a systematic account of the legislative committee members involved, acting in their representative capacities as they saw them. How then can we tell when to expect a representative to view his role in one way rather than another? The aim of this article is to shed a little light on some aspects of this broad question by means of a case study.

The subjects of the study were the members of the House Agriculture Committee and their action on the omnibus farm legislation (H. R. 12954 and S. 4071) in 1958 (85th Congress, second session).[4] Most of the data were obtained from interviews[5] with thirty of the thirty-four Committee members but, in addition, the specific stands of members in subcommittees, the full committee, and on the House floor were traced, through the printed hearings and the *Congressional Record* of floor debates. Finally, other interested and knowledgeable people were interviewed, newspaper accounts were studied, and the characteristics of constituencies were examined.

For analytical purposes the most useful concept I developed, to account for the behavior of a representative, was one I shall call his "policy constituency". This may be defined as those interests within

Reprinted from *American Political Science Review*, LV (June, 1961) 358–367, by permission of the author and publisher.

his geographical or legal constituency which he perceives to be affected by the policy under consideration. When he regards these interests as actively and homogeneously concerned, they are ordinarily sufficient to determine his public stand. When he sees them as weak, indifferent or divided, other factors come into play. But he is affected too by the nature of the committee institution within which the policy is being formed.

I. The House Agriculture Committee and Its Work

Organization.   In 1958 a Republican President was again faced with a Democratic Congress in a congressional campaign year. The margin of control for Democrats in the House Agriculture Committee was a less-than-comfortable four votes; the split was 19 to 15. The margin in subcommittees was one vote in most cases.

Harold D. Cooley (D-North Carolina) was chairman in 1958, as he had been in every Democratic Congress since 1949. Members did not class him among the strong House committee chairmen, but respected him as fair and honest. W. R. Poage (D-Texas) was vice-chairman. The Agriculture Committee was the only House committee in 1958 to have a vice-chairman and one member suggested that this was due to the chairman's complete and admitted willingness to share the responsibility of leadership with the very forceful, knowledgeable, and capable "Bob" Poage.

The ranking minority member in 1958 was William S. Hill (R-Colorado). Like Cooley, he was not considered a strong leader and it became apparent that Charles Hoeven (R-Iowa) was recognized as the spokesman of the minority viewpoint. Hoeven has since become the ranking minority member.

The principal work units in the House Agriculture Committee are the subcommittees. In 1958 there were 18 subcommittees of two kinds—ten commodity subcommittees and eight special-action subcommittees. The former are more important since they consider legislation designed to solve the many crises for specific commodities. Usually a member is assigned to at least one commodity subcommittee of his choice. The chairman consults the ranking minority leader but has the last word on appointments. Actually few decisions have to be made, since most commodity subcommittees are permanent and their membership is continuing; only the new members need assignments. The size of subcommittees varies considerably (from 12 for tobacco to five for rice), giving the chairman some flexibility in case several members are interested in one commodity.

Finally, the House Agriculture Committee has been able to rely on a small expert staff consisting of a counsel, research director, majority and minority clerks, and five staff assistants.

Representing agriculture. As might be expected, congressmen from constituencies with significant interests in farm policy make up the membership of the House Agriculture Committee. In 1958 there was but one exception to this rule—Victor Anfuso, Democrat from Brooklyn. Thirteen of the 19 Democrats came from areas where tobacco, cotton, peanuts, and rice are the principal commodities. Republican Committee members came from areas producing corn, hogs, small grain, wheat, and areas where the farming is diversified. Table 1 shows the geographical distribution of members.

Table 1. Geographical representation on the House Agriculture Committee*

Land-use area	Democrats	Republicans	Totals
Northeast	1	3	4
Appalachian	5	—	5
Southeast	3	—	3
Mississippi Delta	2	—	2
Southern Plains	3	1	4
Corn Belt	2	3	5
Lake States	2	2	4
Northern Plains	—	3	3
Mountain	—	2	2
Pacific	1	1	2
Totals	19	15	34

*Based on the areas presented in Bureau of Census and Department of Agriculture, Bureau of Agricultural Economics, *Land Utilization, A Graphic Summary, 1950* (December, 1952), p. 5.

Committee members may be classified by commodities of greatest interest to their constituencies, as in Table 2. Commodities receiving price supports are grown in the constituencies of members of all six groups there listed. The *basic* commodities, so labeled by the Agricultural Adjustment Act of 1938, are corn, cotton, tobacco, rice, wheat, and peanuts; price supports have been mandatory for them. An increasing number of *non-basics* have also received price supports, *e.g.*, milk and wool. The "diversified" (mainly non-basics) group often find their interests conflicting with those of representatives in the other groups. They complain that their farmers are at a disadvantage since their non-basics either do not receive price supports or receive less support than the basics; the price supports for the few basics grown do not make up for the deprivation of profits attributable to acreage and marketing controls (the complaint of California cotton farmers); and they must pay higher prices for the basics as well as pay higher taxes.

Almost without exception the six groups show an alignment between commodity interests and party allegiance. The corn and livestock group has five Republicans and one Democrat; the cotton and rice group, seven Democrats; the dairy, livestock, small grains group, two Democrats and three Republicans; the diversified group, four Republicans and two Democrats; the tobacco group, seven Democrats; and the wheat group, three or four Republicans.[6] Consequently, different commodities will ordinarily be favored when different parties are in control. For example, cotton, rice, and tobacco usually receive more attention when the Democrats are a majority in the Committee.[7]

Committee organization has been strongly influenced by the commodity problems in agriculture. First, subcommittees are established to deal with currently critical commodity problems. Second, members are assigned to commodity subcommittees on the basis of their constituency interests. Table 3 shows the high correlation prevailing. Only one Democrat (Anfuso) was assigned to no commodity subcommittee representing producers in his constituency and he has no agricultural production at all in his Brooklyn district, though the poultry trade is important there.[8] Two Republicans (Harrison and Dixon) found themselves on subcommittees of little or no concern to their constituencies. Significantly both of these members were identified by other members as being supporters of Secretary Benson's recommendations.

Party considerations dictate that some members must be on sub-committees of no concern to their constituencies: there must be Republicans on the cotton subcommittee and Democrats on the wheat subcommittee. For the most part, members who have little interest in the proceedings are expected either to remain silent during hearings or not to attend.

Table 2. Committee members and their constituencies' commodities*

1. *Corn and Livestock*
   Harrison (R-Nebraska)
   Harvey (R-Indiana)
   Hill (R-Colorado)†
   Hoeven (R-Iowa)
   Polk (D-Ohio)
   Simpson (R-Illinois)†

2. *Cotton and Rice*
   Abernethy (D-Mississippi)
   Albert (D-Oklahoma)
   Gathings (D-Arkansas)
   Grant (D-Alabama)
   Jones (D-Missouri)
   Poage (D-Texas)
   Thompson (D-Texas)

3. *Dairy, Livestock, Small Grains*
   Johnson (D-Wisconsin)
   Knutson (D-Minnesota)
   Quie (R-Minnesota)
   Tewes (R-Wisconsin)
   Williams (R-New York)†

4. *Diversified (non-basics)*
   Anfuso (D-New York)
   Dague (R-Pennsylvania)
   Dixon (R-Utah)
   Hagen (D-California)
   McIntire (R-Maine)
   Teague (R-California)

5. *Tobacco*
   Abbitt (D-Virginia)
   Bass (D-Tennessee)
   Cooley (D-North Carolina)
   Jennings (D-Virginia)
   McMillan (D-South Carolina)
   Matthews (D-Florida)
   Watts (D-Kentucky)

6. *Wheat*
   Belcher (R-Oklahoma)
   Krueger (R-North Dakota)†
   Smith (R-Kansas)

*Members were classified on the basis of their constituencies' principal commodities, as listed in the *Census of Agriculture,* Vol. I, 1956, and interviews with the members.

†These members were not interviewed. Simpson, Williams and Krueger clearly belong to the groups to which they have been assigned. Hill might also have been included in the wheat group.

Table 3. Constituency interests and commodity subcommittee assignments*

Member†	Major agricultural interests in constituency	Commodity subcommittees
Democrats		
Poage	Cotton, Livestock, Peanuts	Cotton; Livestock & Feed Grains (C)
Grant	Cotton, Peanuts, Wood Products	Forests (C); Peanuts
Gathings	Cotton, Rice, Soybeans	Cotton (C); Rice; Soybeans-Oilseeds
McMillan	Cotton, Tobacco, Peanuts	Forests; Peanuts (C); Tobacco
Abernethy	Cotton	Cotton; Dairy Products (C); Soybeans-Oilseeds
Albert	Cotton, Livestock	Livestock and Feed Grains; Peanuts; Wheat (C)
Abbitt	Tobacco, Peanuts	Tobacco (C); Peanuts
Polk	Feed Grains, Livestock, Dairy	Dairy Products; Tobacco
Thompson	Rice, Cotton, Peanuts	Rice (C); Poultry-Eggs
Jones	Cotton, Livestock, Soybeans	Rice; Soybeans-Oilseeds (C); Wheat
Watts	Tobacco, Feed Grains, Seeds	Tobacco; Wheat
Hagen	Cotton, Alfalfa Seed, Potatoes, Fruit	Cotton; Soybeans-Oilseeds
Johnson	Dairy, Forests, Livestock	Dairy Products; Forests; Poultry-Eggs
Anfuso	None	Poultry-Eggs
Bass	Tobacco, Cotton	Tobacco; Wheat
Knutson	Wheat, Dairy, Feed Grains	Dairy Products
Jennings	Tobacco, Livestock	Livestock and Feed Grains; Tobacco; Wheat
Matthews	Tobacco, Peanuts, Vegetables	Livestock and Feed Grains; Tobacco

*The major interests were deduced from the *Census of Agriculture, 1954,* Vol. 1, 1956, and from interviews with members.

†Members listed according to committee rank. Chairman Cooley, whose principal interests were tobacco, cotton and poultry, and William Hill, whose principal interests were wheat, feed grains, and sugar beets, were *ex officio* members of all subcommittees by virtue of their positions as chairman and ranking minority member, respectively.   (Cont.)

Table 3. Continued

Member	Major agricultural interests in constituency	Commodity subcommittees
Republicans		
Hoeven	Feed Grains, Livestock	Livestock and Feed Grains; Soybeans-Oilseeds
Simpson	Feed Grains, Livestock	Cotton; Livestock and Feed Grains; Soybeans-Oilseeds; Tobacco
Dague	Tobacco, Truck Farming, Poultry, Dairy	Tobacco; Wheat
Harvey	Feed Grains, Livestock	Livestock and Feed Grains; Soybeans-Oilseeds
Belcher	Wheat	Cotton; Peanuts; Wheat
McIntire	Forests, Poultry, Potatoes	Forests; Poultry-Eggs; Tobacco
Williams	Dairy, Truck Farming	Dairy Products; Rice
Harrison	Feed Grains, Livestock	Peanuts; Poultry-Eggs
Dixon	Wheat, Potatoes, Small Grain, Sugar Beets	Forests; Poultry-Eggs
Smith	Wheat	Peanuts; Wheat
Krueger	Wheat, Small Grains	Rice; Wheat
Teague	Vegetables, Fruit, Small Grains, Cotton	Cotton; Forests
Tewes	Dairy, Tobacco, Livestock	Dairy Products; Tobacco
Quie	Dairy, Feed Grains, Livestock	Dairy Products; Tobacco

The work of the Committee—1958. In 1958 serious problems existed for cotton, rice, wheat, dairy products, and corn. These crises involved four of the six commodity groups shown in Table 2, leaving the tobacco and diversified groups with little direct and positive interest in the legislation. The Committee decided to employ the "omnibus" procedure so as to get as much backing for the bill as possible. Apparently the leadership on both sides agreed to this, though some Republicans complained about such obvious "logrolling."

The work of the Committee proceeded according to plan with the cotton, dairy products, livestock and feed grains, and wheat subcommittees holding extensive hearings. The result was a 62-page bill

(H. R. 12954) which included eight titles. In addition to titles designed to solve immediate crises, titles to extend certain popular programs were added so as to increase the bill's dubious chances of passage.[9]

The Committee voted on June 13 to report H. Res. 12954 favorably, but on June 25, the Rules Committee's motion to debate the bill (H. Res. 609) was lost in the House, thereby defeating the bill.[10] Shortly afterward, on June 27, the Senate passed its farm bill (S. 4071) and sent it to the House. The House Agriculture Committee amended S. 4071 to bring it into line with their previously defeated bill and reported it on August 4. On August 6, Chairman Cooley moved that the House suspend the rules and pass S. 4071 as amended. The motion received a simple majority, but not the two-thirds vote required for such a motion, and so S. 4071 was also defeated. The House Agriculture Committee made a final attempt to modify their amendments to S. 4071, and on August 14 Chairman Cooley once again moved that the House suspend the rules and pass the bill as amended. This time S. 4071 was accepted after a short debate by a voice vote, and on August 28 it was signed into law by the President (P.L. 85–835).

In general, H. R. 12954 solved the cotton, rice, and feed grain problems to the satisfaction of Committee representatives from those areas and they were apparently willing to trade their support. Their modifications of S. 4071 were attempts to bring that bill closer to the provisions of H. R. 12954 for these commodities. The wheat and dairy titles in H. R. 12954 had little support outside the groups representing those interests. Though the Secretary of Agriculture and the American Farm Bureau Federation had objections to all titles in H. R. 12954, their most serious protests were directed against the dairy and wheat titles. Cotton and rice representatives were willing to drop these objectionable titles when the bill reached the House floor in order to save the sections of the bill they wanted most. Neither wheat nor dairy was included in S. 4071.[11]

S. 4071 was more in line with the Secretary of Agriculture's recommendations for fewer controls and lower supports.[12] Its ultimate passage, even with the modifications to bring it closer to H. R. 12954, was generally conceded to have been a victory for the Eisenhower Administration.

II. Member Discussion and Evaluation

The vote on the rule to debate H. R. 12954 was split along party lines (Democrats for, Republicans against) with the major exception of urban Democrats. Of the 59 Democrats who indicated opposition (either by voting against, pairing against, or answering the *Congressional Quarterly* poll), 47 were from metropolitan or mid-urban districts. Several Committee members charged that the opponents of H. R. 12954 had tried to identify it as a "consumers' tax" bill in order to win the support of the urban representatives. The Committee vote, also split along party lines, is indicated in Table 4.

Opinion of the legislation. Members were asked in interviews for their opinions of the legislation, both H. R. 12954 and S. 4071. Two conclu-

Table 4. House Agriculture Committee vote on House Resolution 609*

Democrats			Republicans		
Yea	Nay	Not voting or Paired	Yea	Nay	Not voting or Paired
Cooley	Hagen	McMillan (paired for)	Harvey	Hill	McIntire (paired against)
Poage			Smith	Hoeven	Williams
Grant			Quie	Simpson	
Gathings				Dague	
Abernethy				Belcher	
Albert				Harrison	
Abbitt				Dixon	
Polk				Krueger	
Thompson				Teague	
Jones				Tewes	
Watts					
Johnson					
Anfuso					
Bass					
Knutson					
Jennings					
Matthews					

*Compiled from data in the *Congressional Quarterly Almanac*, 85th Cong., 2d sess., 1958, pp. 392–3. Members are listed according to committee rank.

Table 5. Member opinion of the Legislation, by Commodity Group*

Commodity Interest	H. R. 12954				S. 4071			
	Good	Mostly good	Equiv-ocal	Bad	Good	Mostly good	Equiv-ocal	Bad
Corn and Livestock								
Democrats†			1					
Republicans		1	1	1	1	2		
Cotton and Rice								
Democrats	3	2	2		1		6	
Dairy, Livestock, Small Grains								
Democrats			2					2
Republicans				2		2		
Diversified								
Democrats‡			1	1		1		
Republicans		1	2	1	2	1	1	
Tobacco								
Democrats		1	6			1	6	
Wheat								
Republicans				2		1	1	
Totals	3	5	15	7	4	8	14	2

*In answer to the question, "Did you consider H. R. 12954 (S. 4071) a good bill, a bad bill, something in between, or just what?"

†Polk not interviewed on S. 4071.

‡Anfuso not interviewed on S. 4071.

sions emerged. First, there was little unqualified opinion in support of either bill. Of the 30 members interviewed in regard to H. R. 12954, three considered it good, five said that most of it was good, fifteen were equivocal (some sections good, some sections bad); and seven considered it poor. Of the 28 who were interviewed in regard to S. 4071, four labeled it good, eight thought it "mostly good", fourteen were equivocal, and only two considered it bad. Table 5 distributes the opinions by commodity group.

Several comments are appropriate. The commodity groups can be classified into the principal beneficiaries of H. R. 12954 (corn and livestock, cotton and rice) who enjoyed broad support; the champions of controversial titles who were also directly and positively affected (dairy, wheat); and the onlookers who were not involved or only indirectly affected (diversified, tobacco). Examined in this way the most favorable opinions were offered by those most affected: six of the eight "good" or "mostly good" responses came from representatives of the main beneficiaries. The middle category, concerned with controversial titles, tended to be suspicious of the bill. Both dairy and wheat members suggested that their titles would be sacrificed once the bill got to the floor.

Though it might be expected that Democratic tobacco representatives would actively support a bill from a Democratic committee, they were equivocal about H. R. 12954. On the basis of such comments as, "Frankly, I didn't think it would help very much," indications were that the tobacco representatives did little more than vote for the rule to debate. Nothing in either bill was of primary concern to their constituencies.

The diversified group offered very little favorable comment on H. R. 12954 and only one of them, a Democrat, voted for the bill on the floor. Once again, the bill gave very little direct, positive benefit to the group's constituencies though, as will appear, it soon became evident that they did have a constituency interest in the bill.

Opinion on the second bill shows a party split. Though the Republicans had less direct constituency interest in the bill (except for the corn and livestock group which considered it "good" or "mostly good"), nine of eleven committee Republicans considered the bill "good" or "mostly good." The Democrats were more qualified, with many of the cotton and rice group stating, "It was the best we could get." The tobacco group was no more enthusiastic about S. 4071 than they had been about H. R. 12954. Republicans obviously considered this a better bill because it was not a clear-cut victory for Democratic commodities. Though Republican commodities had not fared too well, the Democrats were not able to write the legislation with a free hand. Republicans from diversified farming areas were much more satisfied with S. 4071 since it reduced controls and price supports.

Second, the members' opinions, not only of the bill as a whole but also of specific titles, were influenced by their constituencies' interests. When asked what they liked most and least about the bills, members whose constituencies were directly affected replied that they liked best those sections which were designed to solve commodity problems in their own constituencies. On H. R. 12954, four from the cotton and rice group mentioned those titles, one from corn and livestock, both members from wheat, and two from dairy. The same held true for S. 4071.

Members were reluctant to say what sections they liked least. Some spoke in general terms, mentioning the over-all cost, the politics involved, the issues not faced, etc. Only the dairy title drew much critical comment. Ten members (six Democrats and four Republicans) suggested that the dairy title was not good legislation and was harmful to the bill. The most numerous response for S. 4071 was that no sections were "least liked."

As a follow-up question, members were asked which sections had beneficial or adverse effects on their constituencies. Once again, the replies supported the conclusion. In discussing H. R. 12954 all groups directly affected by the bill mentioned most often, as being beneficial, those titles of greatest interest to their respective constituencies. The most frequent response from the two least affected groups (diversified, tobacco) was that no section was beneficial. For S. 4071, those most affected were the cotton and rice and corn and livestock members. They all mentioned the titles of interest to their constituencies as most beneficial. Other groups either chose some section which was of tangential importance or stated that none was beneficial. Hardly any member admitted that any sections adversely affected his constituency.

Concepts of representation.   Members were also asked to discuss what they relied on in their action on the first bill (H. R. 12954)—independent judgment, constituency wishes, a combination of factors, or something else. The results are summarized in the following conclusions.

First, a majority of members stated that in making up their minds they relied on independent judgment or a combination of factors (22

Table 6. Bases asserted for action on H. R. 12954*

Commodity groups	Independent judgment	Constituency wishes	Combination	Other (Party)
Corn and Livestock†				
Republicans	1		2	
Cotton and Rice				
Democrats	1	2	3	1
Dairy, Livestock, Small Grains				
Democrats			2	
Republicans	1		1	
Diversified‡				
Democrats	1			
Republicans	2		1	1§
*Tobacco***				
Democrats	4		2	
Wheat				
Republicans		1	1	
Totals	10	3	12	2

*In answer to the question, "What did you rely on in your action on H.R. 12954—(1) independent judgment, (2) the wishes of your constituency, (3) perhaps a combination of these, or (4) something else?"

†Polk not included.

‡Anfuso not included.

§Usually relied on independent judgment.

**Cooley not included.

of 27 interviewed on this question). There was no important difference between Republicans and Democrats on this question. (See Table 6.)

Second, analysis by commodity groups reveals that those groups least positively affected by the legislation most often responded that they relied on "independent judgment." But the record shows that the diversified group did act to benefit constituency interests.

The members' replies must be weighed after taking into consideration both the importance of the legislation to their constituencies and the effect of their action for their constituencies. Of the ten who said that they followed independent judgment, four were from the tobacco group and three from the diversified. One other member from the diversified group said he supported his party in this instance but usually relied on independent judgment.

Despite these replies, two observations are pertinent: (a) all tobacco representatives who relied on independent judgment nevertheless voted in support of their party[13] and (b) the voting action (against the bill) of the diversified group tended to favor the best interests of their farmers—as they themselves described these interests. As one member put it: "Benson is an asset to me. I agree with him and there is nothing political involved because his philosophy is good for my farmers." All of the diversified group who responded "independent judgment" indicated that a continued program of high supports and controls for *basic* commodities was bad for their farmers, who grow principally non-basics.

The other three members who mentioned independent judgment were from the corn and livestock group (an admitted Administration and American Farm Bureau Federation supporter—he thought their programs would be best for his constituency in the long run); the cotton and rice group (a generally inactive member who "didn't have too much information from my constituency"); and a dairy Republican who said, "I only had this chance to vote against the cotton deal."

Third, those groups most directly and positively affected by the legislation relied on a "combination" or on "constituency wishes." Replies of these members indicated they were well aware of the problems involved in representing *all* interests in their legal constituency on such a piece of legislation.

Nine of the twelve responses indicating a reliance on a combination of factors came from members whose constituency interests were directly affected by the legislation. Some of the most detailed analyses of the process of representation were offered by senior members who replied that representation on policy was not a simple choice between independent judgment on the one hand and constituency wishes on the other. Typical of the extended remarks are the following:

I understand the problems of that area [his district]. I know what is best for the farm section. And I think that the majority in my area reflect my views.

I am in close contact with them at all times. I meet with them, ask their opinions on all matters. I don't use polls. I know the people. I vote my convictions and hope that they [constituents] will follow these. They expect this—unless a real organized group is excited about something. They generally expect that you have more information than they do.

I am sent here as a representative of 600,000 people. They are supposed to be voting on all the legislation. I try to follow my constituents—to ignore them would be a breach of trust—but I use my judgment often because they are misinformed. I know that they would vote as I do if they had the facts that I have. A lot of people expect you to use your judgment.

Under our form of government you have to rely on a combination. If I know the views of the constituents I will vote these views—as a representative, I must—but when I don't know I substitute my best judgment. There is not one case in a hundred where I do know their views fully. I figure if they knew what I know ... they would understand my vote. Most of us vote what we believe is sound, based on the information and our judgment. This can be changed if the people express themselves clearly enough. This, however, is improbable and doesn't happen very often.

Even the junior members in these groups had definite ideas about how their constituencies were affected:

I thought that it was a good bill and then I thought that I could go ahead in view of the referendum and support the bill. If there weren't a referendum [included in the bill], I would have checked [with the constituency] but I felt I could go ahead. On some legislation I hear from the people and rely on their judgment ... [after probing for specifics]. On labor legislation I rely on groups in my area since I don't know too much about it.

I depend on a combination. I should educate them; they don't really care how you vote. I make up my mind and then temper it with what the people want. After all, I think as they do.

One member who relied on constituency wishes was frank in explaining his position:

I vote for what I think will be the best economic interests of my people. Throughout the years I have gained an idea of what those best interests are. This is the way representative government should work.

Fourth, an analysis of members' extended discussions coupled with an examination of their interest and activity on the legislation reveals the importance of a concept of "constituency" in the action of members.

Those who purported to rely on independent judgment were of three types: members who had no commodities to represent on the legislation but opposed the bill—an action evidently in the best interests of their constituencies; members in the tobacco group who supported their party but had no direct interest in the legislation (though some expressed indirect interest); and members who had a constituency interest in the bill but said they relied on independent judgment in their actions, though this did not seem the case in fact.

Those relying on a combination of factors argued that defining constituency interests was no simple, straightforward interpretation. In their subcommittee work on the bill, however, these members—the most active of all who worked on the bill—evinced a shrewd conception of their constituencies' commodity interests.

Clearly, more evidence than the self-explained motivation for voting is relevant in appraising a representative's action and in interpreting his conception of representation: his work in subcommittee on acceptable compromises, *e.g.,* or his interrogation of witnesses in hearings, or his part in the Committee's executive sessions. The data gathered here from such successive stages of action as these tend to confirm Eulau's typology of "delegates," "trustees" and "politicos," and his suggestion that a representative might act in more than one of these roles.[14]

Knowing the constituency.   In order to discover some of the relationships and means of communication between the representative and his constituency, members were asked how they knew their constituency wishes on H. R. 12954. Table 7 summarizes the responses. The most important method, members said, was a type of individual "sounding-board" procedure. Some of those mentioning "intuition" or "sixth sense" observed that their own identity with the culture or mood of the district made it natural that they would know their neighbors' wishes. Responses which typified the members' analyses were:

You are in a position to know, of course, on a lot of things. I live there—there are many things I just know. I don't have to ask anybody. There are very few bills where I have to guess. If I did, I wouldn't be here as the representative.

I am a native of ——. I get letters—though I don't get very much mail. I have sent out questionnaires but I don't now. It is just the fact that I know and I can judge their needs.

Some of the members pointed out that they were farmers and reasoned that this gave them a special ability to know the needs of fellow farmers. Others indicated that their familiarity with the district through campaigns or frequent visits made it possible for them to know. Either way, they were identifying a "policy constituency."

Though such responses suggest that the representative has a concept of his constituency interests on legislation, there is still no reliable evidence as to how he develops it. But whether he gets it by divination, intuition or instruction, it appears to dominate his behavior as a representative where its outline is sharp.

III. Conclusions

The conclusions suggested by this case study can be set forth somewhat more systematically as follows:

1. If a policy measure is seen to affect substantial interests in a representative's legal constituency, then he will rely on his perception of the interests affected (his "policy constituency") when he acts at the working level (usually the subcommittee) in regard to this measure.

a) Institutional arrangements affect his ability to represent his policy constituency. The House Agriculture Committee is organized to allow a maximum of constituency-oriented representation.

b) The representative has a "sense" of constituency interests drawn from first-hand experience in the "legal" constituency and this "sense" influences his perception of a policy constituency.

c) Party allegiance is an important modifying factor.

　1) The legislative majority party may demand a vote in support of its policies. The legislative minority party may demand a vote in opposition to the majority's policies. The Administration may press for support for its stands.

Table 7. Methods for determining constituency wishes*

Method	Democrats† mentioning	Republicans mentioning	Totals
Just know it (live there, sense it)	8	5	13
Meetings	6	3	9
Correspondence	4	3	7
Questionnaire	1	2	3
Newspaper	—	2	2
Testimony	1	1	2
Advisory Committee (to advise on agricultural policy)	—	1	1
Telephone calls	—	1	1
Visitors	1	—	1

*In answer to the questions, "How did you find out what your constituency wishes were on this bill?" and "Are there other ways you use to tap opinion and get information about your constituency's agricultural interests? What are these?"

†Does not include Cooley, Polk, or Anfuso.

2) Representatives, whether or not affected by the legislation, tend to support their party's position more as the action moves beyond the basic working level, and most at the final vote.

2. If a measure is seen to have little or no direct effect on interests in a representative's legal constituency, then he will tend more readily to look to his political party for a cue when he acts in regard to this measure.

a) The representative will tend the more to suggest that he relies on "independent judgment," the less his constituency's interests are seen to be directly or positively affected by a policy.

b) He will vote in support of his political party but will not actively support the policy in other ways if his constituency interests are not perceived to be affected.

A final comment suggests a further and more tentative generalization. In this case study it became necessary to reconcile actions of certain members who seemed motivated by different forces at different action points. Table 4 shows that 11 Republicans voted or paired against the rule to debate H. R. 12954. Of these, seven were from constituencies which had a direct, positive interest in the legislation. Four of the seven were particularly active in effecting compromises in titles of major concern to their constituencies. They were apparently satisfied with the respective titles, yet had no difficulty in rationalizing opposition to the entire bill on the House floor. Further, while members of the diversified group apparently did little to obstruct the work on H. R. 12954 at the subcommittee level (thereby following an apparent norm for Agriculture Committee members), it nevertheless became obvious that some of them worked actively to defeat the bill on the House floor.[15]

An adequate concept of representation should account for a total action pattern, not merely a final vote. The representative on the House Agriculture Committee can view his composite role retrospectively as one in which he has taken several separate actions to make up a total pattern in regard to the omnibus farm legislation. He also can recognize that on different occasions he felt differing demands upon him in his several capacities, as a member of a party, a representative of a constituency, a member of a committee, of a Congress, of interest groups, etc. He was able to reconcile, compromise or avoid some of the inherent conflicts in these demands, at least in part, because of the multiple action points. Examples of such reconciliations in this case study justify a final hypothesis which merits separate study:

3. If a representative has a multiplicity of conflicting demands upon him in any series of actions on policy, he can satisfy many of them, over a period of time, because of the multiplicity of action points at successive stages in the legislative process.

NOTES

1. Some of the most useful studies of representation are: Charles Beard and J. D. Lewis, "Representative Government in Evolution," *American Political Science Review,* Vol. 26 (April, 1932), pp. 223–40; Francis M. Carney, "Concepts of Political Representation in the United States Today," unpublished Ph.D. dissertation, University of California, Los Angeles, 1956; Alfred de

Grazia, *Public and Republic* (New York, 1951); John A. Fairlie, "The Nature of Political Representation," *American Political Science Review*, Vol. 34 (April and June, 1940), pp. 236–48 and 456–66; H. F. Gosnell, *Democracy, The Threshold of Freedom* (New York, 1948); James Hogan, *Election and Representation* (Oxford, 1945). For an extended bibliography see Charles O. Jones, "The Relationship of Congressional Committee Action to a Theory of Representation," unpublished Ph.D. dissertation, University of Wisconsin, 1960, pp. 413–28, from which materials for this article were drawn.

2.   Heinz Eulau *et al,* "The Role of the Representative: Some Empirical Observations on the Theory of Edmund Burke," *American Political Science Review*, Vol. 53 (Sept., 1959), pp. 742–756.

3.   Two studies which do concentrate on specific policies are: Lewis Dexter, "The Representative and His District," *Human Organization*, Vol. 16 (Spring, 1957), 2–13; and L. E. Gleeck, "96 Congressmen Make up Their Minds," *Public Opinion Quarterly*, Vol. 4 (March, 1940), 3–24.

4.   I selected a committee which is more likely than most to be constituency-oriented. Commonly, representatives from farm areas are anxious to get on this committee to represent their constituency interests, though interviews with Republican members indicate that this generalization would now need modification since recent farm policies have not been notably successful. See Nicholas A. Masters, "House Committee Assignments," *American Political Science Review*, Vol. 55 (June, 1961), pp. 345–347.

5.   Focused interviews were conducted in March, 1959. An interview guide was followed but it was kept flexible. I wrote as the respondents discussed the questions and typed the responses immediately after the interview. All respondents were guaranteed anonymity.

6.   Four, if Hill were also assigned to it. Anfuso is assigned to the diversified (non-basics) group because he does not fit elsewhere. The overlap between the corn and livestock, and the dairy, livestock, small grains group is explained by the fact that livestock production is important to both but corn is more important in one and dairy products in the other.

7.   Recent Democratic victories in the middle west have changed the pattern somewhat. There are more Democrats from corn, livestock, and dairy constituencies than previously.

8.   Anfuso almost monopolized the Committee hearings on the extension of the Agricultural Trade Development and Assistance Act, since many New York City firms were testifying. His activity in these hearings provided unexpected evidence of constituency-representative relationships.

9. The titles were: I—Foreign Trade; II—Rice; III—Cotton; IV—Wool; V—Wheat; VI—Milk; VII—Feed Grains; and VIII—Miscellaneous. Titles I and IV in particular were included because they were popular programs.

10. The reported vote in Committee was 21–10. The House vote on H. Res. 609 was 171–214.

11. The dairy situation illustrates the in-fighting. Evidently the cotton and rice Democrats were opposed to any dairy legislation. Hearings were held but only after long delays. The Secretary of Agriculture's objections to the "self-help" bill proposed by dairy representatives were given the spotlight of a full committee hearing rather than a less sensational subcommittee hearing. The title which resulted was developed at the last minute and had little support, even among the national dairy groups.

12. See *The Congressional Digest,* Vol. 37 (March, 1958), pp. 75–7, for details of the Administration's recommendations.

13. Some tobacco representatives noted the importance of the wheat and feed grain titles for their constituencies. They thought these might eventually affect their livestock farmers (using the slogan, "cheap feed means cheap livestock"). Many of their farmers relied on wheat as an alternative crop.

14. Above, note 2.

15. Minority party members are more likely to feel conflicting demands since the majority party's commodities will probably be favored. Some majority party members will find, however, that they are not as directly concerned with the legislation and so will be less actively involved at all stages of action.

THE POLITICS OF PRICE SUPPORTS
Congressional Quarterly, Inc.

A remarkably consistent regional and party pattern of voting emerged in postwar Congressional votes in both chambers on agricultural issues. Again and again, Congress split into the same two blocs, one favoring high price supports, a high level of assistance to agriculture all along the line, and on occasion, strict production controls to reduce over-production; the other favoring no supports, or a lower level of supports and assistance, and minimal or no production limitations.

The high-supports bloc consisted of a majority of Southern and Western Democrats, a small number of Republicans from heavy farm districts of the Lakes States (Minnesota, Wisconsin, Michigan), corn belt and Plains (Iowa, downstate Illinois, Indiana, Nebraska, Kansas, Dakotas), and a fluctuating number of Northern urban Democrats. In a typical House vote on high supports, Southern and Western Democrats usually produced some 100 or more votes in favor of high supports, the small group of Midwestern farm Republicans anywhere from a half dozen to 40 or 50 votes in favor, and the urban Democrats from 30–70, the fluctuations depending on the exact nature of the issue and the party pressures involved.

The low-supports bloc consisted of Northern urban and suburban Republicans, most of the Midwestern and Western rural Republicans, Republicans from feed-deficit farming districts, particularly in the Northeast, some of the urban Democrats, and a few Southern and Western Democrats, generally from feed-deficit areas. The Republican groups usually produced about 150 votes against high supports, urban Democrats from 20–50, and Southern and Western Democrats a handful, usually no more than a dozen.

While it is difficult to say with certainty why any individual Congressman voted for or against a particular measure, the voting patterns described above appear to have been influenced by three major factors: regional economic interests, the general philosophies of the Republican and Democratic parties on all matters—not just agri-

Reprinted by permission from Congressional Quarterly, Inc., *U.S. Agricultural Policy in the Postwar Years 1945–1963* (Washington: 1963), pp. 9–13.

culture—and the positions of farm organizations strong in particular areas. The probable effects of each of these three factors ... are given below.

Influence of Regional Economic Differences

Differences in types of farms and products grown or raised among different sections of the country undoubtedly played a major role in determining the composition of the high- and low-supports blocs.

High-supports bloc. At the heart of the high-supports bloc were the majority of Southern and Western Democrats, who voted consistently throughout the postwar period in favor of high support levels and made "90 percent of parity" their rallying cry. The impelling economic factors behind this stance were, for both groups, the heavy incidence of farmers in their constituencies (the South has more farmers than any other region), and the large number of relatively poor or small farmers with high costs of production, needing guaranteed high prices to protect their slender profit margins.

Additional reasons for Southern support were the great importance of farming in the region's total economy and the special prominence of cotton, tobacco, and peanuts in Southern agriculture. Sharp drops in prices for those three crops would have meant severe economic losses not only for small farmers, but also for big farmers and large plantations and the region as a whole.

Still another factor was the absence, through much of the postwar period, of fears that high price supports would mean reduced markets.

In the latter part of the 1950's, a number of factors began to erode the strength of high-supports sentiment in the South: loss of cotton and tobacco markets to cheaper synthetic fabrics or to lower-price cotton and tobacco grown in other nations; increasing industrialization and urbanization of some areas of the South, producing a "consumer" desire there for lower food prices; and attempts to build up poultry and dairy farming in other parts of the South, leading to a desire for cheap feeds. An additional factor in some Southern districts was antagonism toward "Big Government" stimulated desegregation: even though farm programs did not affect racial matters directly, farm programs requiring considerable federal regulation of individuals were seen as enhancing federal power generally and therefore were considered undesirable.

Despite these trends, the bulk of Southern Democratic Congressmen were still voting for high price supports as the 1960's began, but the percentage was lower than in earlier years.

High-supports sentiment from Plains Republicans stemmed, as an economic matter, from the special market situation of wheat, the area's major crop. Demand for most types of wheat grown in the Plains was relatively inelastic: people ate about as much bread and macaroni in the U.S. as they wished to, and would not increase their consumption much even if prices dropped sharply. (Sharp increases in exports were not possible either because of anti-dumping policies.) For this reason, proposals that wheat prices be lowered in order to increase sales usually met opposition in the Plains. Instead, some Congressmen favored high supports and were willing to accept sharp production controls as the best way to sustain the income of wheat farmers.

High-supports backing from a few of the Lakes States Republicans stemmed in large part from the heavy incidence of small and poor farms in that area, needing price guarantees to maintain small profit margins. The northern Lake areas, together with the South and parts of the Pacific Northwest, were the major areas of rural poverty in the nation.

Those corn-belt Republicans who backed high supports were a minority in the area; most corn-belt Republicans opposed high supports for a variety of reasons. (See below.) GOP corn-belt Congressmen who voted with the high-supports bloc often represented relatively small-farm districts, or districts where the majority of farmers sold their corn for cash on the market (rather than feeding it to cattle and hogs on the farm), and for whom the immediate income-protection afforded by high price supports outweighed fears (very strong in the corn belt) of loss of markets because of over-high corn prices and competition from other feed grains, like grain sorghums.

The third (and an inconstant) element of the high-supports bloc was the urban Democratic delegation from the large cities of the Northeast, Middle Atlantic areas, and Midwest. As representatives of constituents whose chief interest in agriculture was as consumers, urban Democrats tended to oppose high price supports as producing higher consumer food costs, and they frequently voted in accord with this point of view. On other occasions, however, a substantial portion of urban Democrats backed high price supports, partly from New Deal sentiment dictating aid to the "small farmer," and partly from the need to work in harness at least some of the time with their Southern Democratic colleagues who strongly favored high supports. Whether the bulk of urban Democrats went along with the South in backing high supports usually depended on the current condition of log-rolling between the two groups, and on the presence (or absence) of a Democratic President, striving for party unity, in the White House. The majority of urban House Democrats, for example, opposed Southern-sponsored, high-support wheat and feed grains bills in 1959 and 1960, but voted for a similar measure (the emergency feed grains bill) in 1961 at the behest of the new Democratic President, John F. Kennedy.

Low-supports bloc. Four different regional groups of Republican Congressmen were the major force in the Congressional bloc voting against high price supports. One group consisted of Republican Congressmen from urban and suburban areas whose constituents feared high price supports as likely to increase consumer costs. Urban and suburban Republicans voted with few exceptions against high supports throughout the postwar period.

A second group consisted of Republicans from feed-deficit areas, particularly in the Northeast, with heavy dairying, poultry- and egg-raising. The North Central States, particularly the section known as the corn belt, were the great feed-grain producing area of the nation. The rest of the country bought substantial amounts of corn-belt feeds in order to produce livestock, dairy, and poultry products. If a particular region was especially poor in locally grown feeds, and had at the same time especially heavy dairying, poultry, and egg production, then it had to buy very heavily of feeds from other areas; it naturally wanted to buy this feed at a low price in order to reduce its own costs. As a result, Northeastern rural Congressmen (nearly all Republicans) have tended to oppose high price supports for feeds in the postwar period. Lake state dairy farmers, in contrast with the Northeasterners, grew most of their own feeds and so had no special desire for cheap feeds.

GOP Congressmen from the cattle areas of the West, notably the Mountain States and Western Plains, also opposed high supports in part from the cheap-feed motive. However, this has not been a major factor in those cattle areas, because cattle there are primarily grazed rather than fed. In the cattle areas of the West, the fact that the bigger farmers tended to be Republicans was a greater factor in influencing this third regional group of Republican Congressmen to vote against high supports. More prosperous cattlemen, to avoid Government interference, were willing to take market losses now and then. Less prosperous, smaller cattlemen, operating on a year-to-year basis and with fewer resources against even a single bad year, tended to favor Government assistance. The big cattlemen tended to back the Republicans, smaller cattlemen the Democrats.

The fourth major Republican group that opposed high price supports consisted of Congressmen from the rural Midwest, particularly the corn belt. Although a small number of corn-belt Republicans often backed high supports (see above), the bulk of rural Midwestern Republicans opposed them. The corn belt is the great corn and feed-grain growing area, and also the great hog and cattle feeding area, of the nation. Opposition to high supports was usually explained in terms of what they might do to hurt the corn and meat market. Several different factors were mentioned: [for instance,] farmers feeding most of their corn on the farm to hogs and cattle which were then sold on the market feared high price supports would be accompanied by production limitations. In that case, the farmer would have less corn to feed, less livestock to sell, and consequently less income.

On the other hand, farmers selling most of their grain for cash feared high supports would stimulate other farmers in other sections of the country to start producing corn, or other feeds, in competition with the corn belt, eventually flooding the market and creating surpluses. This might lead to production controls, and the corn belt would then have to share national acreage allotments with the new producer areas. And an excess of feeds might also mean excess production of meats, and a break in the price of meat. All this could be avoided, it was usually argued, if corn prices were not pushed up so high as to encourage other areas to compete with the highly efficient, low-cost producers of the corn belt.

Another argument against high supports was that sales of meats could be expanded greatly if feed prices did not go up too much and force meat prices up very high. Farmers would end up with greater income from selling more meat at a moderate price over a period of years than from selling less at a high price, it was contended.

Corn producers also feared that corn, or some other feed, would be grown in competition with corn-belt products in wheat and cotton areas and in other sections if there were high supports for wheat and cotton. The argument ran: high supports for wheat and cotton would inevitably lead to overproduction of those crops in the Plains and South, and the result would be Government imposition of acreage allotments. On the land cut back from wheat or cotton, Plains and Southern farmers would plant corn, grain sorghums, or some other feed and create feed surpluses that would hurt the corn belt.

All these fears, of which the American Farm Bureau Federation was the chief spokesman, explain why the bulk of corn-belt Congressmen, mostly Republicans, usually opposed a high level of price supports for corn and for wheat, cotton, and other crops as well.

Two groups of Democrats also voted against high price supports at times: those from some areas where there was heavy livestock, dairying, and poultry production and a desire to buy cheap feeds, and urban Democrats voting the consumer interest against higher food prices. Some of the votes by Democrats in Florida, Maryland, and Virginia against high supports are explained by desire for low feed costs. As indicated above in discussion of the high-supports bloc, the urban Democrats switched back and forth in their position on high supports, sometimes voting for them, sometimes against, in accord with their current relations with the Southern Democrats.

Farmer-Processor Relationship

A factor with effects in all areas of the nation, not only in one region, was the relationship between farmers and processors (canners, packers, distribution organizations, chain stores, etc.). Processors and other agricultural "middlemen" buying raw farm goods from farmers generally sought lower prices in order to keep their costs low, and processor organizations, throughout the postwar period, usually opposed high price supports. (In 1961, farmer income from each retail dollar of food prices was only 37 cents; the remaining 63 cents went to packers, canners, shippers, chains, and retailers.)

Influence of Party Positions

From the description of the high- and low-supports blocs given above, it can be seen that the majority of the Democrats generally backed high price supports. On the whole, both postwar Democratic Presidents, Harry S Truman (1945–1953) and John F. Kennedy (1961–1963), adopted the general party position in favor of high-level support to farmers in their legislative requests. Mr. Truman favored transition from high, rigid supports at 90 percent of parity to a sliding scale with lower supports early in his first Administration, but he gave up this position after Clinton P. Anderson resigned as Secretary of Agriculture in 1948. Thereafter, Mr. Truman backed high supports.

The majority of Republicans, as indicated above, opposed high price supports and stringent production controls, stressing the need for agriculture to get along without too much Government assistance, by means of efficient operations. Many of the urban Republican Congressmen opposed price supports and production controls altogether as repugnant to a free economy, over-interference with the farmer, as the source of too-heavy federal spending and waste, and as a device tending to encourage "Big Government." Members of this group often called for conversion to a free market for agriculture.

Farm area Republicans favored assistance to farmers, including price supports, but, for some of the reasons indicated above in the discussion of feed-poor areas and the corn belt, preferred supports not too high—to be used chiefly as safety devices against precipitate drops in farm prices. This called for a sliding scale of price supports at lower levels than favored by most Democrats. The one Republican President of the postwar period, Dwight D. Eisenhower (1953–1961), proposed to move toward a free market while retaining low-level, sliding-scale price supports as a safety measure. Although most of the party voted against high supports most of the time, a small number of GOP Congressmen from farm areas of the Plains, Lake States, and corn belt frequently backed high supports, for the reasons indicated above.

Both party patterns of voting were influenced not only by the regional interests, but also by general party philosophy on all issues, not just agriculture. Republicans, in general, have championed free enterprise, opposed enlargement of the economic role of the Federal Government. Their opposition to a highly managed and controlled farm economy is consistent with this over-all position. On the other hand Democrats, particularly Northerners, have been associated since the New Deal period of the 1930's with federal economic activism, management of the economy, and greater federal responsibility, particularly for welfare. This has made them amenable to federal management of farm prices and production in order to aid "the small farmer" or "the family farmer." In the South, fears of enlargement of federal power were usually overridden by the pressing desire for federal economic assistance due to the importance of cotton and tobacco in the economy of the region and the large number of small and poor farmers.

Influence of Farm Organizations

Farm organizations in part have shaped, and in part have been shaped by, the economic point of view of the farmers whom they represented. The three big national farm organizations are the American Farm Bureau Federation, the National Farmers Union, and the National Grange.

The largest, the *American Farm Bureau Federation,* claiming 1.6 million farm families as members, has most of its membership in the Midwest, particularly the corn belt, and the South. Like the NFU, its chief ideological rival, the Bureau has won powerful institutional loyalties by its activities in local affairs and various services to farmers. The Bureau appears to be the spokesman for the more prosperous farmers of the Midwest and parts of the South. During the Great Depression it backed price-support policies and was a major influence in passage of the Agricultural Adjustment Acts under the Roosevelt Administration.

After the Second World War, with agriculture in a far more prosperous condition than formerly, the Bureau began to move away from its backing of relatively high price supports. This appeared to be in part a repercussion of its fight against agriculture price controls in World War II, in part because of corn-belt fears of feed competition from other areas, in part because of the violence of the fight over the Brannan plan, and in part because of a change of national leadership in 1947 when Allan Kline of Iowa took over from Ed O'Neal of Alabama.

From the late 1940's on, the Bureau moved steadily in the direction of a free-market philosophy, advocating progressive removal of production controls and reduction of price-support levels. The latter, the Bureau said in a recent statement, could be retained at a low level as a device to facilitate orderly marketing for some crops, but should not be used to jack up prices artificially and thus prevent the market mechanism from adjusting supply to demand through drops in prices. On other issues, like labor law, the Supreme Court's constitutional role, etc., the Bureau took a "conservative" position.

In the early years of its existence the Bureau was associated closely with the Agricultural Extension Service. The original local farm bureaus were associations of farmers formed privately to work with county agents and pay part of their salaries (the land-grant colleges and Federal Government paid the rest). This connection, its large membership, extensive services to farmers, and representation among active, prosperous farmers made the Bureau one of the most powerful forces in farm life in the Midwest and parts of the South; Congressional voting was influenced very heavily by the Farm Bureau's positions on issues and it was traditional for many years that whatever farm legislation the Bureau opposed was doomed. At times in the South, however, some of the state farm bureaus opposed the national leadership and pushed for high supports.

The *National Farmers Union*, which claims 250,000 farm families as members, has its greatest strength in Oklahoma, Montana, Colorado, Utah, Wisconsin, Minnesota, the Dakotas, and Nebraska. It has long supported "the family farmer" (one who owns his own farm and operates it himself with family labor and relatively little or no hired labor). It has consistently supported a high level of Government assistance to farmers, stringent production controls and rigid price supports when necessary, and the use of direct payments to farmers when necessary (it backed the Brannan plan). It has supported the cooperative movement and in general taken a "liberal" point of view.

Institutional rivalries between the Bureau and NFU have been bitter during the postwar period. A Farm Bureau position that became basic in the later postwar period was that U.S. agriculture had to survive as a viable economic entity on its own, by means of efficient production, rather than through subsidies and controls that hobbled the able farmer while reserving a portion of the market for inefficient producers, all at a tremendous loss to the Government and taxpayer.

The NFU position has been that the end of the current price-support system would mean the end of the family farmer, and capture of U.S. agriculture by commercial and processing interests. NFU spokesmen have often charged that the Bureau was influenced strongly by processor interests whose real aim was to drive farm prices down so their costs would be lowered.

The *National Grange,* the oldest farm organization, claimed membership of about 800,000 persons in 1963. It is strong in Ohio, Pennsylvania, the Northeast, and Northwest.

The Grange for many years was the champion of the two-price idea: supports or quotas should be used to keep prices high in the U.S. for a certain portion of farm goods, and the rest should be sold on the free market at world-market price.

In the postwar period the Grange has favored price supports (although not at as high a level as the NFU), and has moved in the 1950's toward a position in favor of high-level supports and strict production controls. As a pressure organization, the Grange in recent years has been more gentle in its approach than the militant AFBF and NFU.

A notable difference among the three organizations has been that the NFU, generally "liberal" in its approach, has tended to be pro-union and pro-Democratic, and at one time was considered one of the twin anchors of a potential liberal "farmer-labor" alliance. Both the AFBF and the Grange have tended to be more "conservative" and less sympathetic to unions.

chapter six

Labor-Management Relations

There are two broad categories of labor legislation: laws regulating relationships between organized labor and management and laws prescribing minimum labor standards, e.g., minimum wage, industrial safety, and child labor statutes. This chapter considers the formation of national policy in the first of these areas.

Whereas labor unions have existed in the United States from the 1790's onward, the national government, and also the states for that matter, did little of a positive import to regulate union-management relationships until the 1930's. Since then, several laws relating to the thrust and substance of national labor policy have been passed by Congress, including the Norris-La Guardia Act (1932), Wagner Act (1935), Taft-Hartley Act (1947), and Landrum-Griffin Act (1959). Although labor-management relations legislation does not directly distribute substantive benefits, by prescribing rules for the governance of labor-management interaction it has a substantial effect on "who gets what" from the organizing and bargaining processes.

Organized labor has fared best under the Democratic party, whose general pro-labor orientation contrasts with the more business-oriented Republican party. However, organized labor has never enjoyed the success in the policy-making process that one might expect, given its large number of members. Their country cousins, the farmers, while numerically far smaller, have done much better for themselves. Organized labor has been adversely affected by such factors as low status in the social system, internal divisions and conflicts, and strong opposition from business and conservative groups. Conflict over labor policy has often been sharply ideological in nature, and labor's opponents have often enjoyed the benefits of such potent symbols as "freedom of contract," "a man's right to run his business as he sees fit," and "right to work."

The Wagner Act was designed to promote unionization and collective bargaining by providing government protection for these rights. The National Labor Relations Board was established to administer the statute. The Bernstein selection picks up the story of the Wagner Act in 1935 and discusses its consideration in Congress, noting some of the political pressures, administrative cross-currents, and legislative tactics involved. The prime role that a single individual, in this case Senator Robert Wagner of New York, can play in the adoption of major legislation is indicated. Of course, the favorable "climate of opinion" created by depression discontent with business, and support from President Roosevelt at a propitious moment, were also quite important.

The importance which constitutional considerations once had in the formation of economic policy is also illustrated by the Bernstein selection. This is now more a matter of historical interest than practical importance, given the broad interpretation by the Supreme Court of national power under the Constitution after 1937. However, "constitutional habits" still exist and may influence the congressional exercise of power.

Criticisms of abuses of power by labor unions and demands for remedial legislation greatly intensified in the middle 1940's. The Republican majorities and their leaders in the Eightieth Congress (1947–1949) assumed that they had received a mandate from the voters to place some curbs on the power of organized labor. The ultimate result was the Taft-Hartley Act. Seymour Mann examines the efforts of the Truman Administration, after the 1946 congressional elections, to develop a policy on labor law revision with which to meet the demand for such action. Although several agencies, especially the National Labor Relations Board, Bureau of the Budget, and Department of Labor, worked on the problem, the Administration was never able to formulate and convey to Congress a clear position on the issue. Consequently, those opposed to severely restrictive legislation were handicapped by lack of a positive counterproposal. Mann's conclusion that this contributed to the adoption of the Taft-Hartley Act seems quite sound. (A similar argument can be made concerning organized labor's inability to develop a unified position on labor reform legislation in 1959, and the passage of the Landrum-Griffin Act.) Pluralism is an administrative as well as a social phenomenon and the formation of an administration policy position is often hampered by differing and conflicting viewpoints and interests on the part of agencies and officials.

Agencies and their personnel usually possess some discretion in the administration of legislation, and therefore the substance of policy is shaped partly by agency actions. The decisions of the National Labor Relations Board interpreting and applying the Wagner and Taft-Hartley Acts were often criticized by management and conservative spokesmen as "pro-labor." In 1953, with the advent of the Eisenhower Administration, they saw an opportunity to reverse the situation by "doing something" about the NLRB. Scher, in his "Regulatory Agency Control through Appointment," discusses the Eisenhower Administration's decision to secure a more management-oriented labor policy by appointing personnel with pro-management philosophies to the NLRB as vacancies occurred. The success of this effort was later attested to by statements lauding and criticizing the actions of the "Eisenhower Board" by management and labor spokesmen, respectively. After 1961 the thrust of policy was once again reversed as President Kennedy appointed labor-oriented members to the NLRB. How independent, really, is the NLRB of the executive?

CONGRESS PASSES THE WAGNER ACT
Irving Bernstein

In the deliberations of the Senate Labor Committee Chairman Walsh reversed his 1934 position, delegating full responsibility to Wagner without asserting his own views. As a result, Wagner was asked to prepare the report and was again assisted by Keyserling. They regarded this as a key opportunity to break with the 1934 report and, more important, to state congressional intent for the guidance of the board and the courts.

On May 2nd the committee without a dissenting voice reported S. 1958 with amendments, one of great importance. The committee accepted Biddle's suggestion of a fifth unfair practice on the obligation to bargain in the original language. In addition, the declaration of policy was rewritten without disturbing the basic ideas; unions when acting as employers were covered; the Department of Labor was protected against encroachment of an independent board upon its conciliation and statistical functions; the arbitration section was stricken out, the alternative procedure for enforcement in the district courts suffering the same fate; and the right of individuals and minorities to present grievances was strengthened by elimination of, "through representatives of their own choosing."

"The compelling force of . . . experience," the committee declared, "demonstrating that the government's promise in Section 7(a) stands largely unfulfilled, makes unacceptable any further temporizing measures." The first objective was to remove a basic cause of strikes, perhaps twenty-five per cent of the total, involving the right to bargain. "Prudence," however, "forbids any attempt by the government to remove all the causes of labor disputes." A second purpose was to encourage equality of bargaining power. The depression demonstrated a disparity between consumption and production and the necessity to bring them into equilibrium by stimulating higher wages through collective bargaining. The committee found 7(a) in a state of collapse, criticizing its ambiguity and generality, diffusion of administrative

Reprinted by permission of the publisher from *The New Deal and Collective Bargaining Policy* (Berkeley: University of California Press, 1950), pp. 112–128. Footnotes deleted.

responsibility, the disadvantages in linking enforcement to NRA, the helplessness of the NLRB in compliance, and the obstacles to elections. These defects were neither "intrinsic nor irremediable" and might be cured by S. 1958.

The bill did not make all company unions unlawful but merely prevented interference by employers in their formation or operation. A variety of practices fell within the proscription: employer participation in framing constitutions and by-laws, approval prior to organizational changes, intervention in internal management or elections, supervision of agenda or procedure of meetings, and financial support. The committee named propaganda "absolutely false" which declared that the measure gave special legal sanction to or imposed the closed shop. The proviso to 8(3) simply preserved the *status quo*. The Biddle amendment, 8(5), was accepted because "experience has proved that neither obedience to law nor respect for law is encouraged by holding forth a right unaccompanied by fulfillment." It did not, however, compel agreement nor permit governmental supervision of contract terms. "It must be stressed that the duty to bargain collectively does not carry with it the duty to reach an agreement, because the essence of collective bargaining is that either party shall be free to decide whether proposals made to it are satisfactory." The committee found need to "establish a single paramount administrative ... authority in connection with the development of the Federal American law regarding collective bargaining."

The committee could discover no sound reason to apply the unfair practices to employees. No showing was made of practical need to prevent interference by workers or unions. The courts, on the other hand, had construed the word "coercion" to prohibit: a threat to strike, refusal to work on material of nonunion manufacture, picketing, and peaceful persuasion. To prohibit employees to engage in "coercive" acts would "raise in Federal law the ghosts of many much-criticized injunctions issued by courts of equity ... which it was supposed Congress had laid low in the Norris-LaGuardia Act." Its introduction would overwhelm the board with countercharges and recriminations, preventing it from doing the job at hand.

The constitutional argument followed that Wagner advanced during the hearings. The due process theory was based on the railway clerks case. Evidence for the effect of disputes upon commerce appeared in the estimate that the cost of strikes approximated one billion dollars annually, a fact judicially recognized. Failure to accept collective bargaining was a major cause of many of these stoppages. Since the courts, moreover, observed that unsound economic practices affect the volume and stability of commerce, congressional authority to prevent unfair practices should be exercised even where the threat of strife was not imminent.

While this bill of course does not intend to go beyond the constitutional power of Congress, as that power may be marked out by the courts, it seeks the full limit of that power in preventing these unfair labor practices. It seeks to prevent them, whether they burden interstate commerce by causing strikes, or by occurring in the stream of interstate commerce, or by overturning the balance of economic forces upon which the full flow of commerce depends.

The committee report discouraged the NAM. Emery wrote privately on May 10th, "The Wagner bill situation is more desperate. . . . If it comes to a vote it will undoubtedly pass." He continued to feel that opposition strength was concentrated in the Senate and that the major stand should be made there. As it was impossible to defeat S. 1958 as a whole, an attempt should be made to "divert" it by an amendment, the familiar "coercion from any source." This device, he hoped, would appeal to many Senators who would vote for the bill in its entirety. The AFL would then object so strenuously, Emery predicted, as to prefer no legislation at all.

The idea of amendment appealed as well to the Department of Justice, which, through Senator Robinson, proposed a change in the board's litigation. Instead of NLRB attorneys handling enforcement proceedings in the courts, Sec. 4 would give the Attorney General authority "to appear for and represent the Board in any judicial proceeding to which the Board is a party." The purpose was twofold, to guard the department's jurisdiction over federal litigation and give it control over enforcement like that exercised under 7(a). The draftsmen opposed the change for these very reasons. "If authority to conduct the civil litigation of the Board were vested in the Attorney General and the district attorneys, . . . [they] would be the final arbiters as to when and how various civil proceedings should be prosecuted or defended, and whether they should be prosecuted or defended at all." The proposal would, in other words, promote the diffusion of responsibility, conflict of interpretation, and delay they sought to avoid. Other administrative tribunals, ICC, FTC, and SEC, retained this authority themselves. The Robinson amendments were vigorously opposed by Wagner and hence were not formally offered.

Robinson and Senator Pat Harrison, in fact, were cool to the bill in its entirety. They tried to defer consideration in hope that the session would terminate before it came to a vote. To this end they sought to enlist the support of the President; Wagner received a call to the White House. Urging Roosevelt not to intervene again, he asked that the Senators have the opportunity to be counted. Roosevelt, finding this request fair on its face, placed no impediment in the way of consideration. Wagner felt certain of passage once the bill reached the floor.

On May 15th he presented S. 1958 to the Senate in a formal address. The bill, he declared, "does not break with our traditions. It is the next step in the logical unfolding of man's eternal quest for freedom." . . .

On the following day the Senate commenced debate, Walsh presenting the committee revisions which were accepted without objection. Senator Tydings of Maryland then brought out the NAM amendment, proposing that Sec. 7 read [additions italicized], "Employees shall have the right to self-organization, to form, join, or assist labor organizations, to bargain collectively through representatives of their own choosing, and to engage in other concerted activities, for the purpose of collective bargaining or other mutual aid or protection, *free from coercion or intimidation from any source.*" A wrong, he declared, was equally bad whether the act of an employer or a union. The individual workman would gain genuine freedom of association only if all forms of intimidation were outlawed. By omitting such language Congress would encourage the use of force by unions. "Is not this still a country where a man can select, without coercion or intimidation, the kind of organization to which he shall belong?" Senator Couzens added that rivalries between unions led them to employ force upon workers and their families. Wagner replied that the Tydings amendment was sponsored by large employers and that workmen did not request or need such relief. State and municipal law already prohibited noxious activities, while "coercion" had been the subject of extreme judicial construction. "If we should adopt this amendment, it would practically nullify the Norris Anti-Injunction Act." Senator Barkley noted that the prime instrument of coercion, the right to fire, was in the hands of employers. Senator Norris declared that he would favor the amendment "if there did not recur to me what I have learned of the injunction question, . . . if I had not the ideas which are now back in my brain which were pounded into me during long and tedious debates." We are a nation governed by the judiciary. "One man sitting as a district judge can nullify, by a stroke of a pen, the acts of the President, the Senate, and the House of Representatives, even though their action be unanimous."

The Administration leaders would have preferred to avoid a roll call. Tydings, however, insisted upon it and the amendment was rejected, fifty to twenty-one, a majority so impressive as to prevent further delay. The Senate then passed S. 1958 by a vote of sixty-three to twelve. Forty-nine Democrats, eight Republicans, one Farmer-Laborite, and one Progressive voted for the measure, while only four Democrats and eight Republicans opposed it. Twenty-three Senators did not go on record. The Democrats supported the bill overwhelmingly including the majority from the South. The Republicans divided evenly in the voting.

The speed with which debate proceeded, the feebleness of the opposition, and the preponderance of the vote exceeded Wagner's expectations. There were two reasons for this. The bill was presented at the most favorable possible moment since 1935 was the apogee of the New Deal as a progressive domestic reform movement. The influence of labor was at its height and Senators who had little enthusiasm for S. 1958 feared to face the AFL at the polls with a negative vote on their records. The White House, moreover, no longer blocked the way. Second, many Senators, convinced that the bill was unconstitutional, shifted the onus of its defeat to the Supreme Court. While gaining labor's political support, they felt certain that the measure would not take effect since employers would withhold compliance until the court declared it void.

In view of the large issues at stake, the "debate" in the Senate was a disappointment. This was due, first, to the fact that the bill had been discussed for more than a year in Congress, in the press, and over the radio and had been the subject of a flood of congressional mail. When the Senators entered the chamber they already knew how they would vote. Since this was recognized by both sides, neither sought needless debate. The second factor was that the opposition lacked a champion. . . .

The hearings of the House Committee on Labor were only a pale reflection of those held by the Senate and the arguments were echoes. Chairman Connery, in fact, delayed action by his committee until after Senate passage on May 16th. Three days later House leaders called at the White House and, although the President declined to state his views publicly, the way was cleared for consideration.

Meanwhile, within the House Committee a storm was brewing. The AFL at the instance of Miss Perkins prevailed upon Connery to place the board in the department. Despite efforts by Wagner and the NLRB to undo this decision, Connery secured a majority to go along with him.

On May 20th the committee reported H.R. 7978 in the form passed by the Senate except for an amendment to Sec. 3(a). Instead of being established "as an independent agency in the executive branch of the Government," the board would be "created in the Department of Labor." Only Representative Vito Marcantonio dissented on this question. The majority gave no reason for the change beyond inclusion of a letter from the Secretary summarizing her viewpoint. The report did emphasize independence and dignity, hence eschewing any intention "to subject the Board to the jurisdiction of the Secretary of Labor in respect of its decisions, policies, budget, or personnel." Marcantonio, on the other hand, felt that control of the purse gave Miss Perkins full authority over operations and policies. This made an impartial independent quasi-judicial agency impossible, subjected the board to shifting political winds, contaminated it with conciliation, undermined its prestige and capacity to obtain high-level personnel, and deterred the department from its appointed task, promoting the welfare of wage earners.

These legislative events and the imminent Supreme Court decision in the NRA case pressed Roosevelt to take a position on S. 1958. If he failed to take a stand, he might later feel constrained to veto the measure in face of an overwhelming congressional majority or accept it reluctantly without having taken a hand in its formulation. Accordingly, Roosevelt called Wagner, Miss Perkins, Richberg, Assistant Attorney General Harold M. Stephens, Green, Hillman, and Lewis to the White House on May 24th. Despite continuing pressure by industry, Roosevelt agreed to back S. 1958 subject to the ironing out of differences between Stephens and Richberg on one hand and Wagner on the other. After the conference the press learned that Roosevelt, after fifteen months of consideration, had endorsed the National Labor Relations bill.

The differences at the conference were so sharp that Wagner could not have accepted the views of the Department of Justice and NRA without radical revision of his bill. Stephens, in fact, did no more than make comments—eschewing a "legal opinion"—in setting down his and Richberg's suggestions. He criticized the statement of the purchasing power theory as being of dubious reference to the commerce clause. He was particularly concerned about the prerogatives of the Department of Justice in litigation, feeling that the board invited criticism by acting as both prosecutor and judge and by retaining exclusive jurisdiction. The power to determine appropriate unit, Richberg warned, would evoke complications, since employees had heretofore selected their own units and an unsympathetic tribunal might use the authority discriminatorily. Stephens felt that exempting the board from the rules of evidence went too far since the courts, in any case, would grant such authority within a "proper" area and the parties might be deprived of rights in such matters as cross-examination. The language in which the obligation to bargain was cast appeared to force employers to make contracts, infringing the basic legal concept that persons cannot be compelled to agree. He asked that the duty also be imposed upon employees and be limited to making "reasonable efforts" and affording "proper opportunity for collective bargaining."

With only the week end intervening after the President's endorsement of the Wagner bill as well as NRA extension the Supreme Court delivered the Schechter decision on May 27th, knocking out Title I of the Recovery Act, including 7(a), and questioning the power of Congress to regulate commerce. A unanimous court through Chief Justice Hughes ruled that the Act was an invalid delegation of legislative power and an unconstitutional regulation of intrastate transactions with only an indirect effect upon interstate commerce. The first was unrelated to the Wagner bill since it entailed no surrender of congressional authority, but the ruling on commerce was of utmost significance. . . .

The immediate effect of the decision upon the New Deal as a whole was drastic. The comprehensive program of social and economic reform before Congress was held in abeyance as that body recessed; silence fell over the White House; and the AFL was fearful that legislation on the verge of enactment would be snatched away. On June 4th, however, Roosevelt announced his decision: the New Deal program including S. 1958 would proceed, if necessary, in defiance of the court.

No less than the President, Wagner was determined that his bill be enacted. He and his advisers, in fact, were convinced that the ruling on commerce did not fundamentally challenge its constitutionality. . . .

Wagner, however, felt that some changes were necessary and instructed Keyserling, Magruder, and Levy to prepare them. They submitted amendments to the declaration of policy to make a showing by explicit language of the direct relationship between industrial disputes and commerce, emphasizing this by reversing the order of paragraphs, and basing authority exclusively on the commerce clause by striking out reference to the "general welfare." In addition, they altered the definitions of "commerce" and "affecting commerce" to attain the same objectives. The President approved the revisions and instructed Connery to press for immediate enactment with their inclusion. On June 5th he gained permission of the House to recommit the bill for this purpose.

The committee on June 10th made its second report, incorporating the Senator's amendments. Sec. 1, now styled "findings and policy" rather than "declaration of policy," began,

The denial by employers of the right of employees to organize and the refusal by employers to accept the procedure of collective bargaining lead to strikes and other forms of industrial strife or unrest, which have the intent or the necessary effect of burdening or obstructing interstate and foreign commerce by (a) impairing the efficiency, safety, or operation of the instrumentalities of commerce; (b) occurring in the current of commerce; (c) materially affecting, restraining, or controlling the flow of raw materials or manufactured or processed goods from or into the channels of commerce, or the prices of such materials or goods in commerce; or (d) causing diminution of employment and wages in such volume as substantially to impair or disrupt the market for goods flowing from or into the channels of commerce.

The provision went on to the subject of inequality of bargaining power and demonstrated its relationship to commerce. By removing sources of unrest, fostering friendly adjustment of disputes, and restoring equality of bargaining power commerce would be safeguarded from injury. The policy of the United States therefore was to encourage collective bargaining and freedom of association. Sec. 3 was amended to permit the President to remove NLRB members after notice and hearing for neglect of duty or malfeasance but for no other reason. The committee did not change its previous determination to place the board in the Department of Labor.

Connery, anxious for immediate consideration, sought a special rule from the Rules Committee, where he encountered Republican resistance and coolness on the part of many Democrats. Nevertheless, with apparent White House assistance, he won a rule on June 18th providing for three hours of debate and unrestricted amendments.

On June 19th, the House opposition struck at the bill on the grounds of constitutionality. The federal government, they charged, sought to destroy the distinction the Supreme Court had always made between production and commerce. "I know the difference," Representative R. F. Rich of Pennsylvania declared, "between regulating the relations between employer and employee in carrying on interstate communication on a railroad or a telephone company or a ship, and undertaking to regulate the employment relations of the parties who are engaged in building engines or making telephones or putting a ship together." They described the committee amendments as "circumventing" the Constitution as read by the court in the Schechter case. Law-abiding citizens, Representative Howard Smith of Virginia warned, would live with an invalid statute for two years before the tribunal could issue a ruling. Honest sponsors would withhold this bill until they had obtained a constitutional amendment granting Congress authority to act. Smith joined Eugene Cox of Georgia in denouncing the measure for stripping the states of residual police powers and subverting state sovereignty.

"Surely," Rich warned, "no Member of this House who has regard for the oath which he took to support the Constitution can fail to have a doubt as to the validity of this legislation. If he does have such a doubt, then he ought to resolve it before he acts." Congress could not in good faith pass the question to the courts. "We are agents with limited powers, and the Court gives every reasonable presumption to the constitutionality of what we do, because it believes that we have settled our own doubts."

Representative C. V. Truax of Ohio replied, "We see the same old faces that oppose all progressive humanitarian legislation. . . . What are you going to do with this sacred old Constitution? You cannot eat it, you cannot wear it, and you cannot sleep in it." Connery advanced the familiar argument that labor disputes are subject to the commerce power of Congress. The statute itself, Marcantonio pointed out, would not be unconstitutional but each case would be examined on its merits. The court would ask, "Does the application of the law in this case violate the interstate commerce definition as handed down in the Schechter case?"

Rich then turned his fire on the bill itself: The AFL was favored; the closed shop was imposed; the fundamental American right to work or not to work was violated; Communist unions won protection; employers must hire incompetents and malcontents; union coercion was permitted but denied to employers. "We are faced with a condition and not a theory," Truax replied. With the Recovery Act invalid the need for the Wagner bill was even greater to abate the threat of strikes over the right to associate and bargain.

The House then considered the committee amendments, adopting the new findings and policy, the revised definitions, and the removal of board members without discussion. Two committee members, Ramspeck and Marcantonio, vigorously attacked the plan to place the agency in the Department of Labor. The former argued that independence was essential to the NLRB's effectiveness and that the validity of the statute hinged upon it. The Rathbun case demonstrated the court's recognition of the distinction between quasi-judicial and executive agencies, while the Schechter case showed that legislative powers could not be delegated to the President. Connery replied that Roosevelt had approved the amendment. The House then voted to make the NLRB an independent agency, 130 to 48.

The opposition thereupon presented amendments seeking objectives that Tydings strove for in the Senate. They prohibited favoring a particular union or form of employee organization, denied "coercion from any source," regulated union activities as a qualification for enjoying the benefits of the Act, eliminated the closed shop proviso, permitted employer contributions to labor organizations, and required board adherence to the rules of evidence. The House rejected them without a roll call. An amendment by Representative Biermann of Iowa, defining a strike in conflict with an agreement as a "violation of the spirit of this act," however, was approved, 115 to 109. Connery's insistence upon a recount after Administration stalwarts were summoned buried the proposal 140 to 107.

Marcantonio described the conditions among farm workers and asked that the definitions be amended to cover them. "If the industrial workers are entitled to protection, then by the same token the agricultural workers are entitled to the same protection." Connery, despite personal sympathy with the amendment, declared that "just now I believe in biting off one mouthful at a time." Representatives from rural districts who otherwise would vote for the bill were certain to oppose it in this form. The House consequently rejected the amendment.

Ramspeck then asked that a proviso be added to Sec. 9(b) to give the board authority to determine appropriate unit only on condition "that no unit shall include the employees of more than one employer." The amendment aimed directly at textiles, since representatives from North Carolina who otherwise would vote for the bill were concerned about the unit power in relation to that industry which was organized in the North and nonunion in the South. They feared that the board would declare the whole country an appropriate unit and compel southern employers to accept unions.

Neither the National Labor Board nor the National Labor Relations Board, in fact, had ever certified a unit larger than one employer, although the latter felt that such a contingency might arise in the future. Representative Wood of Missouri opposed the proviso, declaring that it would undermine established association bargaining in such industries as coal and construction. Ramspeck replied that employees might continue to agree to bargain on a multiemployer basis; only the board would be barred from ordering it. The House then adopted the proviso, 127 to 87.

Concern with appropriate unit was not confined to employers. The craft leaders of the AFL, harassed by emerging industrial unionism that was later to erupt into the CIO, were similarly distraught lest an unsympathetic board join these forces against them. The NLRB, for example, might decide that drivers working for a brewery were part of a unit comprising all its employees, hence presenting the Brewery Workers rather than the Teamsters with a majority. The drafting of Sec. 9(b), Wagner wrote, "gave us more trouble than any other," and neither he nor the board derived much satisfaction from it. Their defense, in fact, was of a necessary evil, Biddle stating, "to lodge the power . . . with the employer would invite abuse and gerrymandering. . . . If the employees themselves could make the decision . . . they could defeat the practical significance of the majority rule; and by breaking off into small groups, could make it impossible for the employer to run his plant." Even though giving the power to the NLRB entailed a similar danger of gerrymandering, "that is the risk you must run in all democratic governments."

On May 25th the *Brewery Worker* published an editorial declaring that industrial unions would be "the immediate beneficiaries" of the Wagner bill.

As far as the Brewery Workers are concerned, nothing better could happen than the Wagner bill becoming the law of the land. Of course the craft unions and A. F. of L. in working for its enactment do not yet realize that in sponsoring the bill they are saying goodbye to their prerogatives of attacking an industrial union whenever they see fit.

Dan Tobin, President of the Teamsters, circulated this editorial among the members of the Executive Council, all of whom, except Lewis, expressed grave concern. T. A. Rickert of the Garment Workers, for example, wrote Tobin that the bill will "injure organizations like your own and possibly mine." Hence on June 6th Wagner appeared before the council in Washington to assure the members that S. 1958 would not destroy craft organizations, that AFL jurisdictional conflicts would continue to be resolved by the unions themselves rather than by the NLRB, that the power to fix unit had to be lodged somewhere and there was no alternative but to leave it to the board, and that board members would not be labor-baiters because their appointments must be approved by the Senate. Although the council's fears were not stilled completely and were, in fact, to break forth into an assault upon the board several years later, the members were constrained to keep them under the surface at this time. As a result the AFL continued its undeviating public support for the bill without asking for changes in 9(b).

The Ramspeck proviso adopted, Connery proposed a new Sec. 14 to read, "Nothing in this act shall abridge the freedom of speech or the press as guaranteed in the first amendment of the Constitution." It originated in a desire by publishers to avoid recognition of the Newspaper Guild. They put pressure on the White House, Louis Howe asking Connery to insert new language. The change, drafted by attorneys at the NLRB, innocuously restated the First Amendment and the House adopted it in perfunctory fashion.

The bill then passed without a roll call, a Republican attempt to require a count being defeated. On the following day, June 20th, the Senate voted to disagree with the House amendments and S. 1958 went to conference. At this time industry sought to introduce amendments through Secretary of Commerce Roper. In the interest of "friendly and sympathetic businessmen," he informed the President that the bill directly conflicted with his auto settlement, adding, "It seems important that the President avoid the inconsistency of signing a bill which does not conform with his definitely stated principles of employer-employee relations." Hence, he asked Roosevelt to instruct the conference that "a clear-cut provision should be inserted to guarantee the employee protection against coercion or intimidation from any source whatsoever."

Roosevelt, however, did not intervene and the conference report of June 26th contained no such language. The House findings and policy and definitions were accepted with only verbal changes, while the amendment covering removal of board members was adopted without revision. On location the committee made the NLRB independent. Ramspeck achieved this by sacrificing his proviso to 9(b). As a compromise on the latter the conference replaced "other unit" with "or appropriate subdivision thereof," to read "employer unit, craft unit, plant unit, or appropriate subdivision thereof." Ramspeck felt that this achieved the same result since "employer unit" now became the largest segment in the series. The "free speech" amendment was stricken out on the counsel of Senator Borah who argued that it had no legal effect since the Constitution was supreme in any case. The Senate conferees, through Newspaper Guild instance, were concerned lest publishers use it to evade the Act. On June 27th the House accepted the conference report 132 to 42 and the Senate acted affirmatively the same day without a vote.

On July 5, 1935, the President signed the National Labor Relations Act, giving the pens used to Wagner and Green. In a statement prepared by the Department of Labor and approved by Wagner, Roosevelt set forth the purposes of the Act: it would foster the employment contract, remove a chief cause of economic strife, and assure every worker "within its scope" freedom of choice and action. The NLRB would not mediate, that function remaining with the Conciliation Service. "It is important that the judicial function and the mediation function should not be confused." Emphasizing the narrow purpose of the Act, he predicted that it "may eventually eliminate one major cause of labor disputes, but it will not stop all labor disputes." . . .

After two years of indecision the government had committed itself to a policy . . . as well as an enforcement machinery. The result was primarily the work of the Senator whose name it bore. He mobilized the draftsmen, devised the political strategy, and carried the brunt of the fight with the public, Congress, and the White House. His principal technical assistants were Keyserling, Magruder, and Levy. Although the Act was not an "Administration" measure, the depression and the New Deal combined to create a climate of opinion that made passage possible. This mood along with the fortuitous timing of the Schechter decision weakened the opposition in Congress. It has been said that the Act could have been passed at no other time. Roosevelt— little interested in details and subject to conflicting pressures— added his support at the penultimate moment. The growing cleavage between the New Deal and business in the spring of 1935 joined with the decline of NRA to remove old inhibitions. The court's action left the President little alternative since 7(a) and the code labor standards were wiped out and he felt the need for a substitute.

POLICY FORMULATION
IN THE EXECUTIVE BRANCH:
THE TAFT-HARTLEY EXPERIENCE
Seymour Z. Mann

Almost all the line departments and a number of the independent commissions and agencies participated in the legislative history of the Taft-Hartley Act. The principal participants were the National Labor Relations Board, the Department of Labor, the Bureau of the Budget, and individuals in the Executive Office of the President. Proposals were offered, rejected, or modified. Important in determining official policy, at both the executive and the congressional levels, were the activities of individuals who occupied influential positions in the network of communications. A case analysis of the complex interplay involved in formulating the executive policy on the Taft-Hartley Act seems to show that the decision-making process, while shaped in its general contours by the major institutions of government, takes on special characteristics peculiar to the particular policy problem, the individuals involved, and the consequent communications process that develops. Certainly one does not perceive a centralized deliberative activity.

The National Labor Relations Board

More than any other single agency the National Labor Relations Board had reason to anticipate—and fear—legislative developments in the Eightieth Congress. The labor policy expressed in the Wagner Act had been its most intimate concern and responsibility for twelve years. The Board had been the subject of bitter attack from many sides throughout these years. A portion of the divided labor movement had stood strongly against it for at least the first five years of its life. In 1946 and the early weeks of 1947 the Board was aware of the difficult defensive position it was in.

From *Western Political Quarterly,* XIII (September, 1960), 597–608. Reprinted by permission of the University of Utah, copyright owners.

The members of the Board were faced with several related problems. First, what position were they going to take on revision of the Wagner Act? Were they to announce publicly for change? If so, for how much revision? Secondly, what kind of case were they going to make against the decade-old and now renewed charges against them of bias and maladministration? Thirdly, in view of their position as an independent agency, how vigorous a stand could they take and how active and open a relationship could they establish with the Democratic administration and the Democratic minority in Congress? Fourthly, they were faced with the problem of orienting one completely new member of the Board at this critical time.[1]

Immediately after the 1946 election Chairman Herzog wrote the President a rather long letter advocating the adoption of a bipartisan technique for working out a long-run labor policy. He adverted to the President's success in establishing a bipartisan foreign policy and the receptivity of Republican Senator-elect Ives to bipartisanship on labor questions. Chairman Herzog won the informal support of Secretary of Labor Schwellenbach, and actively advised the President for a time; but the bipartisan approach never materialized. After his first weeks in the Senate Ives gave no support to such a program. It was clear that the Republican majority would not accept it, and Herzog and Ives were forced to follow different courses. Although they remained friends, they battled each other on the "hill."[2]

John M. Houston was the second member of the Board. James Reynolds replaced Gerard D. Reilly as third member late in 1946.[3] Reilly had come increasingly to disagree with the majority of the Board during the latter part of his term,[4] and there was doubt as to the point of view Mr. Reynolds might adopt. General Counsel Van Arkel felt that with Mr. Herzog relatively new and Mr. Reynolds brand-new it was essential for the Board to examine its record for consistencies and inconsistencies, and to agree on a position. He was anxious to confront Congress with a unanimous Board.[5] With the failure of the bipartisan approach, Chairman Herzog gave his approval to the "self-study" proposal. Supervision of the effort was given to Van Arkel. Herman Lazarus was brought in from the Philadelphia office to serve as his assistant; Lazarus had active charge of the group preparing the studies, and was to be responsible for the presentation of the materials to the Board members. Most actively associated with him was Morris Weisz, chief of the economics section of the Board, who assigned and supervised the personnel doing the research.

On December 5, 1946, Weisz sent a memorandum to Lazarus outlining the studies under way. They concerned: (1) strike data—here in particular the purpose was to compare the period after World War I with that after World War II, and also to compare the record of industries over which the Board had asserted jurisdiction with that of those where it had not; (2) the organization of foremen and related issues, particularly to assess the effect of the *Packard*[6] and *Jones and Laughlin*[7] decisions, and to estimate the consequences if the rules had been applied earlier; (3) agricultural amendments; (4) employers' petitions; (5) labor groups as monopolies; (6) minority union coercion of employers; (7) freedom of speech of employers; (8) the time elapsed between various stages of Board cases; (9) craft severance cases; (10) repeated violations of the act by the same employer; and (11) the Rutland Court cases[8]—to determine what the Board's rules in these cases had been, the effect of these rules upon stability of collective bargaining relationships, and the impact of the rules upon democratic procedures within unions. In addition, a series of files was set up on general topics. The regional offices were frequently canvassed for materials and experiences in these areas.

The areas studied were those in which the Board had been most frequently criticized and amendments most often proposed. The inquiry was directed at the trend of Board decisions, to determine whether a consistent and orderly policy could be discerned. The results of the studies were organized in a series of twenty memoranda which were presented to the Board, where they became a basis for discussion. Each memorandum covered: (1) an examination of previously proposed legislation on the topic; (2) previous reports and statements made on behalf of the Board; (3) a summary of Board positions on the matter, particularly case decisions when they existed; (4) whatever relevant statistical and economic materials were available.

After a really serious study the Board concluded that its past decisions and actions were coherent and consistent. The members unanimously concluded that the Wagner Act should not be changed;

the Board should defend both the Act and its own administration of the Act. This conclusion did not ignore, however, the possibility of improved administrative practices and changing lines of decisions that would ease pressure and remove criticism without impairing the consistency of Board policy. They also considered the tactical desirability of a limited program of amendment. Should the Board agree officially and openly on some course of amendments in the hope of tempering the kind of legislation that might otherwise occur? Or would a yielding on amendments indicate that there was more wrong than the Board itself was conceding? The legislators might use the limited program merely as a starting point rather than a terminal point for legislation.

The Board position was summed up in a memorandum signed by Herzog and sent to the President on December 11, 1946. This memorandum was made available at the same time to the group in the Bureau of the Budget working on the State of the Union message discussed below. The memorandum argued that the public interest required the maintenance of the rights of labor under the Wagner Act. Any other course "is not likely to prevent strikes [but] it may well reinstate old causes of strikes." [9] The Board considered that the public interest would be served by only one amendment, "legislation that would protect both employers and employees from the use of pressure by labor organizations to compel an employer to violate or ignore certification or order of the N.L.R.B."

Nevertheless the Board did not rule out other anticipatory proposals. "But the administration may conclude that for certain reasons of strategy and equity they should move first without waiting for counter proposals. We do not presume to prophesy whether initiating such action might not have the result of encouraging more extreme proposals from some other sources. Some of us think that probable." [10] If the President desired to follow such a course, limited amendment of the Act to allow employer petitions, to remove foremen from the coverage of the Act, to broaden free speech, and to impose upon unions the duty to bargain collectively might be included. The Board did not consider these changes necessary or useful. "We say merely that they would not destroy the fabric of the Act if ultimately enacted in the law. We do not consider it advisable for the President to go into any of the detailed suggestions in his Message on the State of the Union." [11]

The remainder of the memorandum reviewed other proposed amendments and indicated why it would be unwise to amend national labor policy on these points. It further made suggestions regarding settling of disputes outside the Wagner Act; these paralleled closely proposals considered by the Budget Bureau and discussed below which did find their way for the most part into the presidential recommendations. It further suggested some kind of careful and adequate study before concrete proposals were adopted, although the memorandum indicated that the Board was not in a position to decide whether the study procedure should follow the bipartisan lines recently suggested by the Chairman.

Officially, then, the Board was to stand almost completely on the Wagner Act. Unofficially it felt that a program of limited amendment had to be ready to counter the extreme legislation that would inevitably arise in 1947. This latter unofficial program, however, never took firm hold with the administration until quite late; some close to the situation would argue that it was never employed.

It was on the basis of this activity that the statements presented to the labor committees of the two houses were prepared and developed,[12] and to a great extent it was upon these materials and the conclusions reached therefrom that the Murray substitute, which was finally agreed upon by the minority as counterlegislation to the Taft bill in the Senate, was grounded.

It is important to note the manner in which the Board reacted to the situation in late 1946 and their prognostications concerning the Eightieth Congress. The Board undertook an organized approach to the determination of policy. The procedure was in itself important, as were the manifold objectives of their organized efforts. It gave them a sure footing on their own past. Despite conclusions based on the facts of their administrative life, there was a recognition of the practical political situation and eventually a decision as to the course of action it would be necessary to follow. The manner in which they went at their work and the unanimity on policy they achieved paved the way for the active role which the Board, through the Chairman and various Board personnel, was able to play in respect to the development of administration policy throughout the legislative development and the aid they were in a position to render the minority members in the legislative battle. The importance of this and the individuals concerned are discussed further in the final section of this paper.

One other question, one which was never fully answered to the satisfaction of the Board personnel closest to the development of Board policy during this period, was how strongly the Board should act on the policy they had agreed to adopt. Should they act vigorously and with great force in the defense of their past and the Wagner Act itself? Or should they make their case continuously and in all areas in a quiet, courteous, behind-the-scenes manner? Tied to this was the question of how active Board members and Board personnel should be in administration circles and in work with individual legislators. One school, which centered around the Chairman, felt that they had to work quietly and without offense, largely because the status of the Board as an independent agency had to be protected. Others felt that the Board was fighting for its life (a Democratic victory in 1948 was unforeseen) and it had to shout and shout loudly that as an agency it knew more than others about the nature of the Wagner Act and labor relations under it and without it. Actually a middle course was followed. Official contacts with the legislature were made in a fashion to protect the independent, nonpartisan character of the agency. Behind the scenes the Chairman was very active, particularly in administration circles, as the Taft-Hartley Act came closer and closer to passage. But he insisted that this was done only at the request of the President and was therefore not wrong or unusual. Board personnel were very active in working with the official Committee minorities in the Senate and House and were particularly active with individual legislators.

The Department of Labor

As an administrative agency the Department of Labor was not so concerned with the substantive content of the labor legislation to be formulated as was the NLRB. As a clientele agency serving labor, however, it was naturally concerned with the outcome of the Act. It was its function, moreover, to deal at the political level with the labor organizations and interests. The Secretary of the Department was an official member of the President's family. It should be expected, then, that the Department, particularly at the secretarial level, would be involved in the formulation of administration policy. There was some effort in this direction, but for many reasons the Secretary did not play a decisive role in influencing the President's policy until the veto stage in the history of the Act had been reached.

Actually two groups or levels in the Department were involved. The first was at the secretarial level and consisted of Schwellenbach, his special assistant Louis Sherman, Assistant Secretary David Morse, and Millard Cass, Morse's assistant.[13] The other group centered around the Solicitor of the Department; aside from the Solicitor, Mr. Tyson, those most actively concerned were Kenneth Roberts and Kenneth Mikeljohn. This group was most active in working with the NLRB people during the legislative battle itself.

The letter Herzog addressed to the President in early November of 1946 indicates that Schwellenbach agreed with him on the need for a specific legislative program. Given the temper the Republicans were bound to bring to the Congress after the 1946 elections, it was certain that they would insist on the passage of some legislation. An administration that was going to pursue a nonpartisan policy on labor problems would have to go along at least part way on the question of amendatory labor legislation. While the Secretary and those about him undoubtedly wished to protect the essentials and the principles of the Wagner Act, Schwellenbach did not then have the strong feeling that he displayed at the time of the veto. His earlier position was probably based solely on an assessment of the political situation. The administration, facing a hostile Congress over which it had lost even nominal control, was in no position to adopt a standpat attitude on the matter of revised labor legislation. In fact the Secretary was informally active during the whole period in attempting to bring the unions to the same point of view.

Those working on the problem in the Solicitor's office did not see eye to eye with the group at the secretarial level at any time. The former group, in fact, was strongly opposed to giving in at all on the Wagner act. The Act was still needed. Its principles were still sound; and opening it up at all threatened to bring a flood that would sweep aside more moderate amendments in favor of extreme proposals.

In the Department as in the Board, a study group was set up in the late months of 1946. David Morse was in charge; he was to examine the stand of the Department and to begin the preparation of the statements which the Secretary would be called upon to give to the congressional committees. This same group prepared tentative drafts of a proposed labor section for the forthcoming State of the Union message. Schwellenbach did not have great influence with some of those close to the President at this early stage, and the Department's suggestions were not so closely heeded as were those of the NLRB in the preparation of the message.

The official stand of the Department came to be resistance to any legislation that would amend the Wagner Act except in rather minor instances. At all times, however, the Secretary tacitly encouraged those around him continually to be thinking and working on the problem of counterlegislation. Officially he supported what came to be accepted as administration policy of no amendment; but informally he began early to sound out former senatorial colleagues on the possibility of support for some kind of administration legislative proposals. Until the Department actually began active participation in what came to be the Murray substitute, the Secretary and the Solicitor were at variance with regard to the desirability of an administration legislative program. It may be because he did not make adequate contact with people in the Department, or it may be from a lack of accessible documentary materials; but this writer came to the opinion that there was never the intensive institutional or collective examination of the issues that occurred in the NLRB. This was, perhaps, partially a result of the conflict just noted, and most certainly it related in some ways to the kind of man the Secretary himself was. While Labor Department people would say otherwise, except at the last stages of the veto period the Department of Labor never commanded the influence in the formulation of administration policy that the NLRB and the Bureau of the Budget personnel discussed below did.

The Bureau of the Budget and the Executive Office of the President

Primarily the consideration here is with the Bureau of the Budget and its activities in the preparation of the 1947 administration policy as embodied in the State of the Union message to the Eightieth Congress. Since the Bureau seldom deals directly with the President on other substantive legislative questions than the budget, the question involves the relation of the Bureau to others in the Executive Office of the President. More narrowly, the participation of the Budget Bureau was almost entirely confined to the G7 (labor estimates) section of the Estimates Division.[14] This group became quite active again at the veto stage and was principally responsible for the form and content of the President's Taft-Hartley veto message. It is important to note as well that this was one of the first instances in the administration of President Truman that Bureau people were used as staff aides on substantive legislative questions other than budget matters and routine and advisory functions at the enrolled bill stage. Groups within the Bureau were later used frequently in this capacity by the President.[15]

At this time, the Bureau group worked most closely with Clark Clifford, then Special Counsel to the President, and Charles Murphy, who later succeeded to Clifford's position and at that time acted for the most part as an assistant to Clifford. Clifford actively supervised the work on, and was most responsible for, the labor section of the State of the Union message. It is to be recalled that this time there was a kind of split in the President's immediate family along "conservative-liberal" lines. It was largely a question whether the President was going to follow the advice of Clifford and those around him or the more conservative views of Secretary of the Treasury Snyder and his following. It ought also to be recalled that policy in this controversial area had to be fashioned at a time when the President was at the nadir of his political life prestige-wise. With November 1946 elections Harry S Truman was already widely described as the "defeated 1948 Presidential candidate."

While the G7 people were essentially technicians, it is obvious that they were aware as early as 1945 that some kind of amendatory labor legislation was inevitable. They were not blind nor could they ignore the activities of the second session of the Seventy-ninth Congress. They were, of course, during this early period most concerned with the settlement of dispute problems. They were preparing official memoranda on the subject; and a number of them were informally at work with some NLRB people in the preparation of legislation on this problem at the request of individual legislators. The earlier McMahon bill was a product of such a group, although the version finally introduced was considerably changed and emasculated in comparison with the earlier drafts.

But even in this area the proposals of the people in the Bureau would not undermine or substantially change the protection and practice of collective bargaining under the Wagner Act. Such a position was expressed in a 1945 memorandum which read in part: "Any scheme designed for the promotion or settlement of disputes or facilitation of collective bargaining should be based as much as possible on (1) the philosophy of voluntarism on the part of the parties and the government and (2) the availability of trained government personnel and clearcut procedures which can be invoked by disputants." [16] The section was not responsible for the President's message and actions during the 1945 railway strikes and it seems quite certain that Clifford too had counseled against action of the sort taken. By 1947 the G7 section position might be summed up as follows: "There were some definite abuses existent insofar as industrial relations and labor union activities were concerned. Limited amounts of legislation might be supported within the limits of the President's broad program or what the President's broad program ought to be." [17]

Accordingly the Bureau people set out to make a thorough assessment of the current situation and to prepare a series of memoranda that would suggest proposed courses of action for the administration. In the early weeks of December these were sent to the Director of the Bureau. The first memorandum reviewed all the proposals and suggestions that were then current. These included a review of scholarly and academic approaches as well as of bills introduced in the national and state legislatures. In another memorandum in early December the G7 group had begun to outline what should be included in legislation that might be proposed by the President. Included would have been a provision to place upon both parties the duty to bargain collectively (embracing a four-point definition of collective bargaining) and a proposal for the redesigning of the federal machinery in the settling of disputes (including status quo provisions, arbitration without compulsion, a Federal Mediation Board within the Labor Department, a Federal Arbitration Commission, and Boards of Inquiry, purely informative, to be appointed by the Secretary of Labor in cases of national significance). The sum total of the suggested legislation had begun to revolve around the four points which were contained in the 1947 presidential message, but the proposals were elaborated in more detail and with more specific suggestions than appeared there.[18]

About December 9, David Bell of G7 had prepared a tentative draft of what could be included on labor in the 1947 message. At this point the Bureau was asking for specific recommendations from NLRB and the Labor Department on the proposed items that most concerned those two agencies. It is not necessary to examine the early drafts in detail, but some of the text of this one draft may profitably be compared to the message finally delivered.

I feel now that we can take another long step forward by expanding the Wagner Act to require unions to bargain, to prohibit unions from certain specific unfair labor practices—such as violence, occupation of private property and interference with free choice of individuals to work or not to work—and to require unions to accept settlement of jurisdictional disputes by impartial government decisions under careful legislative standards. (This to be revised when NLRB recommendations are available.) I recommend that by law there be placed on both parties to collective bargaining the duty to exert every reasonable effort to make and maintain collective agreements.[19]

The message itself, of course, never mentioned the Wagner Act and did not use the phrase unfair labor practices. It proposed specific legislation in regard to union activities for only three matters: jurisdictional strikes; unjustifiable secondary boycotts; and the use of economic force, by either labor or management, to decide issues arising out of the interpretation of existing contracts. Other matters were to wait upon the report of the proposed investigating commission. In many other ways the message finally took on a more general tone than the Bureau drafts.

Sometime shortly after the preparation of this December 9 draft Clifford was informed of the work the G7 group was doing. He then asked for their materials and a conference with Stowe (and possibly others) to review their work and suggestions. Shortly afterward the group was detailed to the White House staff to work with Clifford. Clifford later described his feelings in pretty much the following manner:

I realized in 1947 after the elections that there was a tremendous amount of confusion and a good deal of viciousness in the air concerning labor relations and reconversion problems. I tried to give it an objective, sensible and unemotional consideration. We could see that our problem was to forestall the movement toward an unstable labor law. By that time I had been on the job about a year and the lines were clearly drawn between Clifford and Snyder. Here was an issue on which I was going to win out.[20]

Clifford used the G7 section to make the kind of appraisal of the situation which he thought necessary. On December 24 it submitted an extensive final memorandum to him. This was divided into four parts: first, the problems in terms of sources or causes of unrest; second, the group's reactions to proposed courses of action, including the suggestion that Congress create a Commission to study the problem (the make-up and activities of the Commission were outlined); third, a description of the disputes machinery which would constitute a part of the process; fourth, the identification of certain practices of labor and management which should be ended, along with the proposals for eliminating these abuses. Draft legislation for points three and four was supplied.

In this outline of the December 24 memorandum the labor section of the 1947 State of the Union message is clearly seen. In the days immediately following the message was written, but in considerably more general language than was proposed originally by the G7 group, with no reference to the submission of proposed legislation, and with the question left open as to whether any of the proposed action would actually amend the Wagner Act or not. The Bureau people as technicians felt quite definitely that legislation on these matters should have been submitted. They were not completely aware of—perhaps not greatly concerned over—the political dangers that might be incurred if Congress used a specific bill or bills submitted by the President merely as starting points.

It is not clear why a legislative program was not endorsed. Clifford seemed to indicate that he was in favor of an early administration bill or at least a counterproposal after the majority legislation was ready or close to ready. The President was deferred to here, and while the story does not completely jibe from the legislative side, it seems that the President was following the recommendations of advisors on the "hill" who said the President ought not to take the risk of what the Congress would do to such a bill. It was believed, and Clifford shared this opinion, that no counterlegislative action was possible until the public support of the labor groups could be won. Although this might have been true, minority legislators keenly felt the lack of Presidential leadership during the legislative struggle. The general statements of January did not suffice. Such leadership did come at the veto stage—but then it was too late.

Summary and Implications

Summing up, it is pertinent to point out that this Bureau group, while believing that the Wagner Act could work, felt more disposed on technical and professional grounds than those in the other agencies to suggest the need for amendatory legislation. Even on disputes machinery they were certainly prepared to go further than even the Labor Department. But they were not so aware of the political problems to be faced in the new Congress. Their education on this matter progressed rapidly under the tutelage of Clifford when close relations were established. This relationship proved of even greater importance during the veto stage, when Clifford assumed more the upper hand in the President's intimate official family.

We must call attention to the individuals from these agencies who were concerned in the effort. Representatives of the Board and the Solicitor's group in Labor became active in working for the minority, and supplied much of the committees' staff help as the legislative battle proceeded. Van Arkel from the NLRB was particularly active—sometimes with and sometimes without the knowledge of the NLRB Chairman. People close to the Secretary of Labor as well as NLRB personnel worked behind the scenes to attempt agreement on an administration counterlegislative program. Clifford later became active here and at one stage tried to get the national party organization to take some action in this direction.

At no stage of the legislative battle, however, was there any kind of effort to co-ordinate and direct the work of these groups and individuals. Congressmen, even those of the President's party close to him, were for the most part unaware of the early administration effort that went into the formulation of the President's policy. Certainly they were totally unaware of the kind of effort made in preparing the labor section of the 1947 State of the Union message. Neither the President nor those around him undertook to communicate this.

At every point these individuals and groups entered into the communicative relationships that were part of the process that led to individual decisions by a number of congressmen. Out of the Eightieth Congress, however, came an act establishing a national labor policy repugnant to the President and to most of the men herein discussed who had striven in some way to influence what the administration's stand on labor policy in 1947 was to be. It is very possible that this might not have been the case had the President, or a clearly designated emissary, earlier supplied a clear and unwavering co-ordinating effort in the consideration of basic policy issues.

Few pieces of legislation either in the ten years before or in the thirteen years since the Taft-Hartley Act have assumed such controversial proportions. It is still in many ways a live issue, and even today persons who played some active role in the legislative struggle preceding its ultimate passage speak or write about the experience with feeling and with vigor. Many of the practices, strategies, and tactics that Truman and many of the executive branch agencies displayed or practiced during this period were new or unusual reactions to the special nature of the policy proposals at hand. Presidential and agency activities during this period, however, fully illustrate the extensive formal and informal network of roles in the executive branch that operate to establish or influence basic public policy decisions.

NOTES

1. The writer is much indebted to former NLRB Chairman Paul Herzog for generously affording time for interviews and for permission to view his personal Board files on the subject of this paper. The writer's first conversations with Mr. Herzog occurred while he was still Chairman of the Board in 1950. Access to his files was also gained at that time. Most helpful also in giving extensively of their time and information and/or opening their files were former General Counsel Van Arkel and former Assistant General Counsel Herman Lazarus.

2. The idea of a bipartisan approach followed a meeting of the NLRB Chairman with Senator Ives in mid-November. It is Mr. Herzog's recollection

that President Truman and other members of the Board were apprised of this visit shortly thereafter. Non-Board personnel, however, were probably not aware of this meeting nor of the communications with the President until sometime later.

3.   Reilly's term expired August 27, 1946.

4.   Harry A. Millis and Emily Clark Brown, *From the Wagner Act to the Taft-Hartley Act* (Chicago: University of Chicago Press, 1950), chaps. 4–6, documents in detail the trend of the Board's decisions through the years and of Reilly's increasing dissents.

5.   While this was the attitude and objective of Van Arkel and other Board personnel, it is doubtful that the Chairman agreed to this study procedure with the "winning over" of Mr. Reynolds as a primary objective. In a later exchange of correspondence, after reading a draft of this article, Mr. Herzog indicated that he would not have accepted as a purpose of the "self-study" period the influencing of Mr. Reynolds. Mr. Herzog wrote in part: "I certainly would not have countenanced that, as my personal relationships with Mr. Reynolds were extremely close, despite our disagreements on policy questions, and the best way to bring him about to supporting a later unanimous viewpoint was to give him the facts directly and then appeal to the team spirit of an ex-Columbia football star. That this was successful and did him great credit is shown by the fact . . . that he stood with Houston and me in taking a unanimous position before the outside world later, whenever he was 'outvoted' at executive sessions."

6.   See 64 N.L.R.B. 1212 (1945); *Packard Motor Car Co.* v. *N.L.R.B.,* 330 U.S. 485 (1947).

7.   See 53 N.L.R.B. 1046 (1943); *N.L.R.B.* v. *Jones and Laughlin Steel Corporation,* 331 U.S. 416 (1947).

8.   See Rutland Court Owners, 44 N.L.R.B. 587 (1942); 46 N.L.R.B. 1040 (1943).

9.   December 11, 1946 N.L.R.B. memorandum to President Truman, from the files of Paul Herzog.

10.   *Ibid.*

11.   *Ibid.*

12.   The official Board position was summed up in the statement prepared for the Senate Labor and Public Welfare Committee. "However, as trustees who speak from 12 years' detailed experience, we declare our conviction that the congressional policy we have been administering is a wise one, and that changes in that fundamental policy would have the most unhappy conse-

quences." U.S. Senate Committee on Labor and Public Welfare, *Hearings, Labor Relations Program,* 80th Cong., 1st Sess., pt. 4, p. 1901, (1947). In the same statement two affirmative suggestions were made. The first was to do something about strikes against Board certifications; the second pertained to discharges under a closed-shop contract for dual unionism (Rutland Court rules). But in respect to both of these it was vague as to whether the Board was going to act on its own or whether it wanted a specific mandate from Congress.

13. It should be noted that David Morse had been the NLRB General Counsel in 1945–46. It was natural for the Secretary to turn to him on such questions.

14. The persons who did the work in this area in 1945 and 1946 were David Bell, David Stowe, Ross Shearer, and Harold Enerson. For this whole section of the study, the writer is most indebted to Ross Shearer, who gave generously of his time and interceded with Mr. Stowe (later on the White House staff) for access to the latter's files in the White House and consulted Stowe on questions when the writer was unable personally to see him. The Bureau of the Budget was reorganized in 1952 and the Estimate Division as such no longer exists.

15. It is interesting to note that Stowe and Bell later went from this group to the President's White House staff.

16. This represented the kind of thinking the G7 section was using and depending upon. Bureau people probably worked on this memorandum but G7 files show that for the most part it was prepared by some NLRB people in co-operation with William Leiserson.

17. From the transcript of tape-recorded notes made after a conference with Ross Shearer.

18. Compare the final version of the message, *New York Times,* January 7, 1947, p. 16.

19. From a copy found in the Stowe files.

20. An almost literal report extracted from a transcription from the recorded tape made shortly after the Clifford interview. The writer later learned that Clifford's first introduction to labor questions of this kind occurred at several evening meetings at the White House in December of 1946. Present at these sessions were David Morse, General Counsel Van Arkel and NLRB Chairman Herzog. These meetings had been arranged by Van Arkel. At these meetings it appears that it was necessary for Van Arkel and Herzog to argue strongly against recommending changes in the Wagner Act. Several persons

close to the situation remarked to this writer that Clifford during this whole episode had shown the effects of having been subjected to "education" on labor policy matters. These remarks reflect the expectation that because of his legal background his attitude toward labor-management relations would be more conservative than it ultimately proved to be.

REGULATORY AGENCY CONTROL THROUGH APPOINTMENT: THE CASE OF THE EISENHOWER ADMINISTRATION AND THE NLRB

Seymour Scher

Whatever the expectations of the early supporters of independent commissions as governmental devices, these agencies have not been divorced from politics. Continuing activity of all kinds by those whose vital interests are affected by agency action has been as characteristic of the lives of the so-called "independent" regulatory commissions as it has been of executive, presumably "non-independent" agencies. Regulated interests use whatever means they find available and consider useful to affect, first, the character of the regulatory legislation itself and then the direction of the agency that applies it. Judicialized procedures, the separation of agency functions, intercessions by Congressmen with agency officials, Congressional investigations, *ex parte* contacts by the regulated with administrators are important methods of influencing the course of regulatory action.

It is not surprising, then, that the appointive process, formally involving the President and the Senate, is also seen as a crucial, direct means of getting the agency to read the law as the regulated parties themselves would. Since it is the President and the Senate who finally decide who fills agency positions, they naturally become the focus of vigorous clientele activity to influence these selections. For Presidents who want to fix their stamp on the policies developed by the independent commissions, the opportunity to appoint their members is used with no reluctance. And it probably can be said that in the last analysis it is at this stage that the vigor or drift that will characterize these agencies is determined.

This paper focuses on efforts of the regulated clientele of one independent commission, the National Labor Relations Board, to invoke in their own behalf the Presidential appointive power in the Eisenhower years. As with all case studies dealing with limited, and in many respects unique situations, any general inferences that are

Reprinted from *The Journal of Politics*, XXIII (November, 1961), 667–676, 682–688, by permission of author and publisher. Footnotes renumbered.

drawn must be considered suggestive rather than conclusive. But what emerges from this discussion is additional evidence, if any is still needed, that if independence in the regulatory commissions means removal from direct Presidential influence, such independence does not exist.[1]

Attempts of the regulated parties to influence appointments to the NLRB are as old as the agency itself. These efforts have been founded on the belief that it is, after all, the people who administer the statute through case by case decision who determine the law's effect on the regulated; the interpretation of the Congressional standards, then, becomes more important than the standards themselves.

Both organized labor and management have relied heavily on the appointive process as a means of affecting the agency's application of the National Labor Relations Act and its amended version, the 1947 Taft-Hartley Act. From the passage of the Wagner Act in 1935 until 1953, labor had had few serious complaints about those appointed by two Democratic Presidents to administer the Acts. In the Wagner Act period the general and warranted feeling that the law was intended as a shield for organized labor meant that as a matter of course appointments to the agency would go to people who sympathized with the need to protect labor in its organizing and collective bargaining efforts.[2] Although much of the agency's employer clientele in this early period protested that the Board members were allied with labor against management, employers' support for this charge often betrayed their deeper feeling that the very existence of the Wagner Act, itself, denoted an unfair alliance of government and labor. So long as the White House was occupied by a Democratic President, however, organized management had to resort to other devices to win for itself more favorable consideration in the application of the national labor-management regulatory policy. The recurrent attempts to confine the Wagner Act agency within court-like procedures and the efforts, successful in 1947, to rewrite the substance of the Act and diffuse the powers of the NLRB, were devices that could be used by employers, with the help of a willing Congress, to ease the effects of the law on them.

Organized labor, on the other hand, stood with a good deal of confidence under the cloak of a protective Wagner Act administered by a sympathetic Board (even though at one point the American

Federation of Labor felt compelled to urge President Roosevelt to refuse reappointment to Board members who allegedly opposed craft unionism). Even when the Act became more restrictive and the Board divided in 1947, the two labor federations took some comfort from the knowledge that a President whom they considered their friend would make the necessary appointments.

This picture changed radically in 1952 with the election of a Republican President. The general dissatisfaction on the part of organized management with the course of the agency's application of the Taft-Hartley Act[3] could find an outlet in either of two channels. One involved abolishing the agency and placing the Act's adjudication in the courts; the other required reliance on Eisenhower appointments to the agency to change the direction of its decisions. The choice between them split management for a time into two factions and separated the Eisenhower Administration from its own labor spokesmen in the House.

I. A "Good" Board or the Courts—The NAM Debate[4]

Both the Chamber of Commerce and the NAM had undertaken a review of their labor policies in the light of the election of a Republican President in 1952. This review led the Chamber to propose frankly a complete overhaul of the agency through new Eisenhower appointments.[5] But the NAM's proposals to the Congress in 1953 to "reorganize" the NLRB[6] were not then given more specific content because of the Association's failure, until the following year, to obtain firm agreement among its own members on the fate of the agency. The controversy in the NAM in 1953 on "what to do with the Board" corresponded closely to the dispute within the new Republican Administration on a labor program to be submitted to Congress.[7]

The NAM was split into two factions on whether Eisenhower appointments to the NLRB or a wholly new decentralized administrative apparatus would be the preferred solution. One group, composed generally of small manufacturers with businesses typically located in a single area, felt that its interests would be best served by ending Federal pre-emption of the subjects covered by the Taft-Hartley Act. This would allow greater opportunity for state regulation and the adjudication of an abbreviated Federal act by the district courts. This group's approach was the same as that of the House committee members[8] from relatively unindustrialized constituencies and that of a Commerce Department group which for a time included the Secretary of Commerce himself. On the other side was a faction made up generally of large manufacturers, with operations spread over many states, who preferred a uniform statutory policy and interpretation by a single Federal agency to the varying policies of different states and the interpretations of many Federal district courts. This group, with little support in the small business-oriented House committee but powerful allies in the Commerce Department and in the White House staff, saw its interests best served by preserving the Board but changing the agency's policy direction through the appointment of new members.

The small business group in the NAM contended that the Eisenhower appointment of NLRB members and the General Counsel would have no effect on the agency's regional personnel so that "no number of appointments to the national board, regardless of calibre, can change the attitudes or end the 'hand-in-glove' relationship which exists between NLRB staff personnel and trade-union organizers."[9] It noted, on the other hand, that the NAM's adoption of the district court proposal in lieu of retaining the agency "would, of necessity, require additional Federal District judges and additional personnel for United States District Attorneys [who, in place of the NLRB General Counsel, would investigate charges and prosecute complaints]. These additional judges would be appointed by President Eisenhower."[10]

To reinforce its rejection of any plan that would save the NLRB, the NAM small business group criticized the performance of Guy Farmer, President Eisenhower's first appointment to a Board chairmanship. So far as this management group was concerned Farmer showed evidence of being little different from former Board members in his apparent belief in union organization and collective bargaining.[11]

The contrasting view, generally reflecting the sentiments of the NAM's large multi-plant manufacturers and the position that ultimately prevailed within the Eisenhower Administration, was contained in a memorandum written by Gerard Reilly and Theodore Iserman.[12] Indicating a preference for Presidential appointments to change the "pro-union bias of the old N.L.R.B. and its staff," the Reilly-Iserman memorandum expressed little confidence in more favorable treatment for employers from Federal district courts because of the "pro-labor bias of the District judges appointed by [former President] Truman for life. . . ." Reilly and Iserman recognized, on the other hand, a "start" in the direction of "curing the NLRB" that had been made by October 1953 through the Eisenhower appointments of Guy Farmer and Philip R. Rodgers. Thus, "if the President makes a wise choice [in filling a third vacancy] it will be possible within the next few months for the new Board to accomplish a thoroughgoing reform." [13]

It was substantially the Reilly-Iserman view that prevailed in the NAM's official policy. The Association ultimately proposed to replace the Board with a labor-management court and the General Counsel with a totally separate Administrator but otherwise retain a centralized administration of the Act.

II. The Eisenhower Administration Settles for a "Good" Board

The Administration's formulation of a labor program for submission to the Republican 83d Congress came after the House and Senate labor committees had already conducted extensive hearings on Labor Act revision. The House committee had shown a strong disposition to place the Act's adjudication functions in the Federal courts. The Senate committee, on the other hand, had before it Senator Taft's proposal [14] to separate the Board completely from the General Counsel, expand the Board to seven members, and make it bipartisan. The Taft plan would have allowed for Presidential appointment of a new Administrator in place of the Truman-appointed General Counsel and of two members to new posts on the Board. The filling of these positions and of the openings occurring in the Board in 1953 would have resulted in Republican control of both parts of the Act's administrative apparatus.

In deciding between the Republican House and Senate approaches, the Administration in the Spring of 1953 faced much the same kind of internal division as occurred within the NAM. The

Labor Department, headed by former AFL member Martin Durkin, wanted no changes in the agency's structure and vigorously resisted abolishing the agency for court adjudication of the Act.[15] This attitude reflected the two labor federations' general wariness of any tampering with the NLRB by a Republican administration.[16] This approach was in sharp conflict with both of the contending positions being fought out within the Department of Commerce in May and June 1953.

Early in the Eisenhower Administration's consideration of Taft-Hartley revision, Secretary of Commerce Sinclair Weeks had been favorably disposed toward abolishing the NLRB and placing the Act's adjudication in the Federal district courts. As with the same proposal before the NAM, the major impetus in the Commerce Department for the court plan came from small business groups. Their most important supporter within the Department was its General Counsel, Stephen F. Dunn.[17] Dunn's support of the proposed adjudication by Federal courts of unfair practice cases was instrumental in winning the Secretary of Commerce initially to the small business point of view.[18] The Department's official attitude changed later with its support shifting to the plan for a single labor court to be appointed by President Eisenhower. This change has been credited widely to the influence brought to bear on the Secretary of Commerce by large nation-wide employers. Thus the Reilly-Iserman view that prevailed in the NAM also won out in the Commerce Department.

At a high-level White House conference of Administration advisors on labor legislation,[19] Reilly and Iserman, expressing the dominant organized management and Commerce Department position, recommended a labor-management tribunal to replace the Board. This plan had the virtue of maintaining a centralized administration of the Act while providing for appointment by the Republican President of an entire new nine-member panel plus a new Administrator to investigate and prosecute unfair practice cases. The AFL's rejection of this approach left the Administration deadlocked on proposals for change in the administrative machinery of the Act. But the stalemate at this later stage in the Administration's formulation of its labor program was between the large employer approach favoring a single labor court and organized labor's resistance to any change at all in the

NLRB. The small employer-Dunn proposals for broader state jurisdiction and decentralized administration of Taft-Hartley through the
district courts had been shunted aside.

The final form of President Eisenhower's message to Congress in
January 1954 in which he offered his program for Taft-Hartley revision contained no recommendations at all dealing with the NLRB.[20]
Although this seemed to suggest the inability of the President's labor
advisors to reach agreement on changes in the machinery for the Act's
administration, it did not mean an absence of Administration policy
toward the Board. The Reilly-Iserman analysis for the NAM indicating that the management association and industry generally could
place secure reliance on Administration appointments to the Board in
the absence of further structural changes represented the dominant
approach to the NLRB of the Eisenhower Administration.

III. Appointment for Control: A Process of Compromise

A combination of resignations and expired terms in 1953 gave the
Eisenhower Administration an unusual opportunity to effect a rapid
change in the NLRB's composition.[21] But at least three different and
in part conflicting circumstances confronted the Administration in
determining who would fill the agency vacancies; two involved Congress, one concerned the Cabinet. The interplay of these factors suggests some of the difficulties inherent in making appointments to
achieve policy control of an agency that deals with a politically powerful clientele.

On the one hand the Eisenhower Administration, having rejected
the small business preference for centralized administration of the
Taft-Hartley Act, needed to make appointments to the NLRB that
could convince the small business-oriented House labor committee
members that their sentiments were not being entirely overlooked. But
the nominations also needed to be of a kind that could win, if possible, the agreement of the Secretaries of Commerce and Labor who
served typically opposing interests. Finally, the Administration had to
take into account the need to get confirmation of its appointments
from the Senate labor committee and then the full Senate; both were

almost evenly divided in the 83d and 84th Congresses between Administration-supporting Republicans and Democrats generally friendly to labor. . . .

Senate confirmation. The Senate labor committee, unlike its House counterpart, has the dual function of clearing for action by the parent body both labor legislation and Presidential appointments to the administering agency. While the opposition of House members to Presidential appointments can be registered indirectly (witness the urging of the NLRB's abolition by a stable majority of the House labor committee in the 83d and 84th Congresses), the Senate stands as a direct roadblock to appointments that do not satisfy that body. The Chief Executive will ordinarily hesitate in sending nominations to the Senate that are likely to be returned to him without approval. When the Senate is almost evenly divided between Administration supporters and opponents, as it was through most of the Eisenhower years, the President (or, more likely, his labor aides) will be expected to look several times before plunging into a Senate fight for an appointment in which he is likely to lose.

If the Democrats of the Senate labor committee were aware of an Executive intention from 1953 to 1955 to appoint NLRB members who accorded with the Morgan-Reilly-Iserman view of labor-management regulation, the committee members did not use all of the review power available to them.[22] For example, the Senate appraisal of the qualifications and attitudes of Philip R. Rodgers was little more than perfunctory.[23] Courtesy of the Democratic minority to a nominee who had been a labor committee staff director for Republican Senator Taft may account for their failure to question this particular nomination more seriously.[24]

The nomination of Albert Beeson in November 1953 for a ten month unexpired term was a test both for the Administration and the Senate labor committee. On the face of it, President Eisenhower's first two appointments to the Board left little room for objection from the opposition. Neither Guy Farmer nor Rodgers had had the kind of professional association with management that raised questions concerning their fitness in filling quasi-judicial positions on a labor-management regulatory agency.[25] Albert Beeson, on the other hand, had had a professional career in business. As an industrial relations director he had negotiated union contracts from the management side of the table, had been involved in union strikes against personnel policies for which he bore major responsibility, and had represented management in cases before the NLRB. At the time of his nomination, the Board was split evenly on some basic policy issues[26] between two Truman and two Eisenhower appointees. Beeson, then, represented the third Eisenhower appointment which would convert the Board to a Republican majority.

In contrast to their handling of the two earlier Eisenhower nominations to the Board, the Democratic members of the Senate committee conducted an exhaustive three-week review of Beeson's background and then pursued their objections to his appointment in debate on the Senate floor.[27] They characterized his experience in management as the kind that would not be best suited for the position of a presumably impartial adjudicator of cases involving labor and management. They expressed concern over Beeson's suggestions that he would join the other Eisenhower appointees to the Board in redressing what he termed an imbalance in the old Board which he believed had favored labor. The Democratic Senators also protested indications that the nominee had not severed ties with his former employers following his nomination. The Democrats' position was that these business connections would affect Beeson's judicial determinations in administering the statute. Beeson narrowly won Senate confirmation on a vote of 45 to 42 in which the Senate divided almost entirely along party lines.

The Senate Democrats, although willing to allow two earlier Eisenhower appointments to the Board to pass without serious question, saw the Beeson nomination as one that too evidently bore earmarks of the dominant NAM-Chamber of Commerce insistence that the Republican President "cleanse" the NLRB of its alleged pro-labor sympathies. In the fight over the nomination the Senate committee Democrats pitched their opposition on a distinction they sought to draw between appointments to an ostensibly independent agency like the NLRB and others to Executive departments which are expected to be more directly subject to Presidential influence. Whether the committee

Democrats' reference to this distinction was more a matter of their own partisan strategy—in seeking to maintain the character of the old Board which they had considered friendly to labor—than of conviction of a need to insure the presumed independent character of the NLRB is, of course, problematical. In either case, the contest over the Beeson nomination gave them a good opportunity to convey the latter. It suggested to outside observers that the kind of Senatorial scrutiny an opposition party could be expected to direct at nominations to an independent regulatory agency demanded a more positive function than the typically generous confirmation of appointments to Executive departments avowedly committed to the implementation of a Presidential program. The formal distinction between the two kinds of appointments are expressed by Senate labor committee member (and later Eisenhower's successor as President) John F. Kennedy in stating the reasons for his opposition to the Beeson nomination:

> Members of the Senate, regardless of party, recognize that their responsibility with respect to Presidential nominations is a unique one. The President is entitled to have his policies carried out by those whom he feels represent his philosophy. The President is entitled to appoint to the various posts in his administration those whose capabilities meet the standards he demands. But today we are speaking of a nomination to the National Labor Relations Board. It is not a policymaking branch of the administration which should be filled by one whose philosophy of labor relations is in keeping with the views of the political party in power. It is not a tripartite body, to which representatives of labor and management should be appointed. Its members do not serve at the pleasure of the President, nor for a term of years concurrent with the Presidential tenure. . . .
>
> The National Labor Relations Board is instead a quasi-judicial agency, whose primary function is to interpret and apply the basic labor relations law of the land . . . Board members are, in effect, judges; and their decisions are of tremendous importance in the determination of the legal rights of labor and management.
>
> Thus, Members of Congress have a special obligation to review with care the nominations to this quasi-judicial agency.[28]

Whether or not those in the Eisenhower Administration's inner councils accepted this distinction between the NLRB and so-called Executive agencies, or whether they simply were reluctant to face again the kind of bitter contest to win Senate confirmation that followed the Beeson nomination, subsequent nominations to the Board, superficially at least, were of a different character.[29] The arousal of the Senate Democrats in 1954 to a vigorous review of Presidential nominations to the agency can be credited for controlling to some degree the character of these appointments.

It is beyond the purpose of this study to evaluate the performance of a regulatory commission under any particular President's administration. Whether or not the presence of the first Republican national administration in the life of the NLRB had a discernible impact on that agency can best be determined through an analysis of the policy direction of the General Counsel and the Board since 1954 when a majority of the Board were Eisenhower appointees.[30] What has been presented here is evidence of an intent, at least, on the part of employer-oriented Eisenhower advisors to appoint a more "friendly" Board; and if the attitudes of the two clientele groups affected by the agency's operations indicate a changed direction in the NLRB during the Eisenhower years, this evidence is abundant.

Organized labor, until the advent of the new majority in 1954, had generally attributed the Board decisions that it found unfavorable to the requirements of what it considered an anti-labor statute. Labor spokesmen believed that since that Act required an unfriendly disposition toward unions, the agency from 1947 until a series of decisions by the "Eisenhower Board" could not be greatly blamed for acceding to this legislative intent.[31] This disposition toward the agency changed drastically, however, after 1954 with the decisions of the new Board. A new kind of anti-union direction that exceeded the requirements of an already union-restrictive statute was found in reversals[32] of a group of old Board doctrines. The new Board, labor thought, was pursuing a course determined by the members' understanding of the Republican Administration's labor policies rather than by the intent of the law.[33]

Conversely, the typical employer assertion that the agency was pro-labor changed abruptly with the new Board majority in 1954. The National Association of Manufacturers saw for the first time in the trend of decisions by the new Board an adherence to the legislative intent and the statutory language. By the end of 1954, the NAM was able to state:

As an over-all appraisal it can fairly be said that the Board, with a few exceptions, has followed a course of administration designed to give full faith and credit to the intent of Congress when the Taft-Hartley Act was put on the statute books.[34]

Though the language of Taft-Hartley has remained unchanged, its interpretation by the Labor Board has not. On numerous and important issues the new Board, a majority of whose members have been appointed by President Eisenhower, has overturned long established rulings, and given the Act a new, and almost always anti-labor meaning. Indeed the Eisenhower appointees seem to have taken office with that end consciously in mind. . . . They seem to have proceeded on the assumption that since they were appointed by a new administration, they had a license to overhaul any or all of the Board's policies. They have proceeded to imbue the Board with the employer-oriented interests of the new Administration.

Proposals that had been made within the Association for further separating Board and General Counsel, or for abolishing the agency and placing the Act's administration in the courts faded into the background.

Summary—Conclusions

However one reads the decisions of the Eisenhower-appointed Board members after 1954, an intention of the dominant employer elements in the Administration's labor advisory group to have the Board approximate the new regime's labor and political philosophy is apparent. The multiplant employer sentiment that predominated in the Eisenhower Administration's counsels succeeded in winning the major employer associations' support for relying on new appointments to bring about a more favorable administration of the Taft-Hartley Act. The appointment of "good" members to the agency was expected, too, to achieve a lessening of small-employer pressure in and out of Congress to decentralize the Act's administration. The restraining influence exerted by the Department of Labor and a Senate closely divided between the two parties served, to some extent, to prevent a series of too frankly employer-oriented appointments to the agency.

Too many general inferences cannot, of course, be drawn from the experience of one regulatory commission with one President's administration. Yet, whatever meaning we attach to terms like "quasi-judicial" and "independent" as applied to the regulatory commissions, there is good reason to expect that, as with so-called "executive" agencies, Presidential appointments will be used, unless inhibited by powerful counter influences, to fix an administration outlook on the commissions. The more powerful the clientele of an agency, whether "independent" or "executive," the greater the likelihood that Presidential action will be invoked, particularly through the appointive process, as a means of assuring favorable treatment from the agency. In the case of the NLRB, organized labor and management, in keeping with their past behavior, can be expected to press future Presidents to appoint people to the agency who will read the basic labor legislation as the regulated do themselves. The success of one group rather than another will depend largely on the extent of agreement of that group with the administration's own view of the course the agency should follow. How those appointees then behave is, of course, another matter.

NOTES

1. See, e.g., Marver H. Bernstein, *Regulating Business by Independent Commission* (Princeton, 1955), pp. 51f., 106f., 109–13, 148; Robert E. Cushman, *The Independent Regulatory Commissions* (New York, 1941) pp. 680–85; Emmette S. Redford, *Administration of National Economic Control* (New York, 1952), pp. 277–83.

2. This did not mean, necessarily, that appointments would be made from the ranks of labor itself. In fact, none of the Roosevelt appointees to the Board had had prior labor affiliations. However, Edwin S. Smith, appointed to the NLRB in 1935 had had experience in management as a personnel director, but had served as Massachusetts Commissioner of Labor immediately prior to his appointment to the national Board. As it developed, it was Smith who was most severely criticized by management for his allegedly pro-labor bias while a Board member.

3. This dissatisfaction was expressed initially in the Eisenhower era in a two-pronged attack aimed at the NLRB before the Congressional labor committees. First there was an appraisal by the National Association of Manufacturers and the Chamber of Commerce of important Board decisions that were considered unjust followed by a coordinated presentation by a large number

of employers—parties to NLRB action—who protested unfavorable decisions and alleged abuse by agency personnel. The Chamber of Commerce spokesman at the Senate labor committee hearings in the first months of the Eisenhower Administration conveyed a general employer attitude toward the Truman-appointed Board's implementation of the Act:

> Certainly, management has cause to doubt seriously whether the Board as presently constituted, is able with intellectual honesty to administer the Taft-Hartley Act as Congress wrote it and intended it to be. As long as any Board members and key staff members apply the one-sided philosophy of the Wagner Act, we cannot have the balanced labor-relations policy sought by the Congress in that act.
>
> A dispassionate review of the decisions of the Board seems to disclose a studied attempt to evade the clear-cut intent of Congress, as expressed in the Taft-Hartley Act, and to revert to the principles established under the Wagner Act.

In U.S. Senate, *Labor Act Revisions,* Hearings before the Committee on Labor and Public Welfare, 83d Congress, 1st Sess. (Washington, 1953), p. 155f; hereafter cited as *Senate Labor Committee Hearings,* 1953.

4. This section relies heavily on conversations between the writer and NAM legislative representatives, as well as on various NAM internal memoranda.

5. This was the Chamber's view:

> Now, we think that there should be a clean sweep and an opportunity for the new administration; if there are any present members of the Board or their staff that are good, they can be reappointed, but if they are not good then they can be eliminated as they should have been if they are no good. This new administration should have an opportunity for a clean sweep and to appoint the type of men ... that should have been appointed in the first instance.

In *Senate Labor Committee Hearings,* 1953, pp. 157, 159.

6. In U.S. House of Representatives, *Labor-Management Relations,* Hearings before the Committee on Education and Labor, 83d Cong., 1st Sess. (Washington, 1953), p. 571, hereafter cited as *House Labor Committee Hearings,* 1953.

7. The Congressional labor committees nonetheless proceeded in February 1953 to hold hearings on labor act revision, but they did so without recommendations from the President. The Administration proposals were not submitted to Congress until the following year. The NAM was likewise unable to

reach agreement, at least on its disposition toward the NLRB, until after the extensive labor committee hearings had been concluded.

8.   E.g., Republicans Gwinn, Smith, Velde, Hoffman, and Democrats Barden, Lucas, and Landrum in the 83d Congress.

9.   For this NAM group the Civil Service Commission's refusal early in 1953 to place some thirty NLRB policy-forming positions in Schedule C (which allowed personnel replacement without reference to Civil Service) underlined the "impossibility of curing the bias of the NLRB by means of new personnel."

10.   In an unpublished NAM memorandum titled *Labor Legislation—Comments on Memorandum of Opposition to Current Proposals for States Rights-Decentralization Amendments to Taft-Hartley,* dated November 6, 1953. This memorandum was circulated among the NAM's Industrial Relations Committee membership in the course of a poll to determine the Committee's sentiment on the questions of increased state jurisdiction and district court adjudication of the LMRA, or continued federal preemption of the field and adjudication by the NLRB.

11.   Referring to a speech by Farmer in which he posed three questions intended as tests of whether a businessman accepted what he considered essential principles of employee organization and collective bargaining, this NAM group observed:

> But the great majority of American business is not organized; the majority of NAM members are not organized. To them Farmer's questions indicate clearly and unmistakably that if they don't have a union, the new chairman of the NLRB from whom so much is anticipated by management, thinks they should have a union. It is doubtful if the unorganized NAM member looks with any feeling of security to the "new look" on the part of the NLRB.

12.   In an unpublished memorandum circulated to the members of the Industrial Relations Committee of the NAM, titled *Memorandum of Legislative Questions Being Considered by the Industrial Relations Committee of the N.A.M.,* dated October 28, 1953. Reilly, a former NLRB member, had been legislative counsel to General Motors and to General Electric. Iserman had been counsel to the Chrysler Corporation. Both played important roles as advisers to the Republican Congressional majorities that passed the Taft-Hartley Act in 1947.

13.   This third vacancy was filled with the appointment of Albert C. Beeson in February 1954. See U. S. Senate, *Nomination of Albert Cummins Beeson to*

be a Member of the National Labor Relations Board, Hearings before the Committee on Labor and Public Welfare, 83d Cong., 2nd Sess. (Washington, 1954), hereafter cited as *Beeson Nomination Hearings,* 1954.

14. S.659, 83d Congress, 1st Session.

15. In *Department of Labor Report to the President on Taft-Hartley Amendments,* an unpublished report, May 25, 1953, p. 8.

16. See the CIO General Counsel's statement rejecting Taft's S.659 and other proposals for increasing the number of Board members in *House Labor Committee Hearings,* 1953, pp. 2696, 2721; and AFL President George Meany's similar statement in *Senate Labor Committee Hearings,* 1953, p. 2078.

17. Dunn had come to his job in the Republican Administration from a position as counsel and legislative representative for the Furniture Manufacturers Association of Grand Rapids, Michigan, a group of employers in an industry that he described as "highly decentralized . . . composed of a large number of relatively small producers." In 1953, the Association urged Congress to cede jurisdiction to the states in several areas of labor relations regulation and to place remaining Federal labor regulatory administration in the Federal district courts. See also Dunn's testimony for the Furniture Manufacturers' Association in 1947, U. S. Senate, *Labor Relations Program,* Hearings before the Committee on Labor and Public Welfare, 80th Cong., 1st Sess. (Washington, 1947), pp. 1690f., 1698. On that occasion, incidentally, Dunn proposed that Congress ban industry-wide bargaining and convert the NLRB into a labor tribunal within the Department of Justice. By 1953, however, support for the latter proposal had shifted to preference for state regulation and/or Federal court adjudication of the Taft-Hartley Act. See *House Labor Committee Hearings,* 1953, pp. 1874, 1879f. But the furniture association proposed alternately in 1953 that Congress abolish the NLRB and establish a "new Board . . . with entirely new, impartial personnel who are not predisposed to the destruction of a congressional statute by administrative malpractices and preconceived bias."

18. In an early draft of Commerce Department recommendations to President Eisenhower on Taft-Hartley revision, the Department stated:

> Proposals to give to the Federal courts power to decide unfair labor practice cases have a great deal of merit. If Congress does not do this, we recommend that it abolish the present board and establish a Labor Court, functioning with rules of practice, procedure, and evidence that apply in District Courts, and with only deciding powers.

In an unpublished Commerce Department report, *Comment of Department of*

Commerce on Revised Material Submitted by the Department of Labor Concerning Amendments to the Taft-Hartley Act, May 27, 1953, p. 32f.

19. Including Gerard Reilly, Theodore Iserman, White House legal counsel Gerald Morgan, Senate labor committee counsel Michael Bernstein, former Taft aide Thomas Shroyer, and AFL counsels Herbert Thatcher and Albert Woll.

20. The President's labor message of January 11, 1954 is quoted in U. S. Senate, *Taft-Hartley Act Revisions,* Hearings before the Committee on Labor and Public Welfare, 83d Cong., 2nd Sess. (Washington, 1954) pp. 2961–63.

21. Guy Farmer, a former trial examiner and Associate General Counsel was confirmed by the Senate on July 10, 1953 to fill two years of Chairman Paul Herzog's unexpired term. Philip R. Rodgers, former chief clerk of the Senate Labor and Public Welfare Committee, was confirmed for a full five year term on July 30, 1953 replacing John M. Houston. Albert C. Beeson, former Industrial Relations Director of the Food Machinery and Chemical Corporation of San Jose, California, was nominated in November 1953 but was not confirmed until February 18, 1954 to fill ten months of the unexpired term of Paul L. Styles. After Senate confirmation on February 28, 1955 Boyd Leedom, a former Judge of the South Dakota Supreme Court, replaced Beeson. Leedom later replaced Farmer as Chairman on November 18, 1955; Stephen Sibley Bean, a former NLRB trial examiner, was appointed at the same time for a full term to fill the vacancy left by Farmer. From 1953 until 1955, then, three Eisenhower appointees joined two Truman holdovers, Abe Murdock and Ivar Peterson, on the Board. The Republican President in January 1955 filled the expired term of General Counsel George Bott, a Truman appointee, by appointing Chicago attorney Theophil C. Kammholz to the position. In terms of the origin of the appointments, at least, the NLRB by 1955 could be called an Eisenhower agency.

22. The Democratic members of the Committee in the Republican 83d Congress were James E. Murray (Mont.), Lister Hill (Ala.), Matthew M. Neely (W. Va.), Paul H. Douglas (Ill.), Herbert H. Lehman (N. Y.), and John F. Kennedy (Mass). Pat McNamara (Mich.) joined this group when the Democrats became the majority party in the 84th Congress.

23. See U. S. Senate, *Nomination of Philip Ray Rodgers to be a Member of the National Labor Relations Board,* Hearing before the Committee on Labor and Public Welfare, 83d Cong., 1st Sess. (Washington, 1953); hereafter cited as *Rodgers Nomination Hearings,* 1953.

24. But positions Rodgers was to take in applying the Act following appointment made several Democrats, and certainly organized labor, wish they had

taken a closer look before his easy confirmation. Rodgers had become convinced that a pro-union Board until 1953 had subverted the Taft-Hartley Act. After his appointment to the Board he expressed the belief that the new Eisenhower majority ought to have overturned all the old Board precedents and started anew in order to correct what he saw as the traditional imbalance favoring labor. The old NLRB personnel at the lower levels, Rodgers thought, also needed to be replaced to remove any opportunity for continued "perversion" of the Act. Rodgers, nonetheless, easily won confirmation from a Democratic Senate for a second term on the Board. See U. S. Senate, *Nomination of Philip Ray Rodgers to be a Member of the National Labor Relations Board,* Hearing before the Committee on Labor and Public Welfare, 85th Cong., 2nd Sess. (Washington, 1958).

25. Prior to his appointment as Board chairman, Farmer had been an NLRB trial examiner and later an Associate General Counsel. Although he had left the agency to take up a legal practice, specializing in labor relations with a primarily management clientele, this course was one frequently followed by former NLRB personnel who, on leaving the agency, had generally empty financial coffers to replenish and few alternatives from which to choose. Rodgers had had a career in university teaching of political science and for six years thereafter had been on the Senate labor committee staff before his appointment to the Board. See U. S. Senate, *Nomination of Guy Farmer to be a Member of the National Labor Relations Board,* Hearing before the Committee on Labor and Public Welfare, 83d Cong., 1st Sess. (Washington, 1953); and *Rodgers Nomination Hearings,* 1953.

26. These involved reappraisal of the old Board's jurisdictional standards, its position on employer interference in representation elections, its stand on the validity of "hot cargo" clauses in contracts between employers and unions to keep employers from handling struck goods, and its definition of the subject matter considered compulsory in good faith bargaining. The terms "old" and "new" Board are used here to conveniently distinguish the Truman-appointed majority led by Chairman Herzog which ended in 1953, from the Eisenhower majority which became effective with Beeson's confirmation in February 1954.

27. See *Beeson Nomination Hearings,* 1954; and 100 *Congressional Record ¢,* 1970–2005 (1954).

28. In 100 *Congressional Record ¢,* 2004 (1954).

29. For example, Boyd Leedom, a former state court judge, and Stephen Bean, a former NLRB trial examiner, came to the Board with some prior judicial experience rather than a primarily business or labor background.

What practical difference this made in their ability and willingness to remain aloof from what they might have found to be Eisenhower Administration policy on enforcing the Taft-Hartley Act is a question that will not be examined here.

30. Some such analyses are: "NLRB Under Republican Administration: Recent Trends and Their Political Implications," *Columbia Law Review* LV, 905 (1955); W. Willard Wirtz, "Board Policy and Labor-Management Relations: Employer Persuasion," New York University Seventh Annual *Conference on Labor,* pp. 79–118; W. Willard Wirtz, "Two Years of the New NLRB," American Bar Association, Section of Labor Relations Law, *Proceedings,* 1955, pp. 4–15; Mozart G. Ratner, "Policy-Making by the New 'Quasi-Judicial' NLRB," *University of Chicago Law Review* XXIII, 12 (1955); Joseph E. Finley, *"Labor Act Upside Down—NLRB: Now an Employer Agency?",* Public Affairs Institute (Washington, 1958).

31. Said former CIO President Walter Reuther about the pre-Eisenhower Board: "I think that out of the kind of total climate that gave birth to the Taft-Hartley Act there were certain pressures which have intimidated the National Labor Relations Board. I think they are trying to administer the act in what they think was the spirit of the people who adopted the act. . . . We think that they got involved in this climate that was created at that time by the Congress that got Taft-Hartley and they are trying to translate that climate into administrative decisions." In *House Labor Committee Hearings,* 1953, p. 1049; cf. also pp. 971f., 979f., as well as a statement by then AFL President George Meany in a similar vein, pp. 555f.

32. See espec., *Denver Building and Construction Trades Council,* 108 NLRB No. 66 (1954); *McCallister Transfer, Inc.,* 110 NLRB No. 224 (1954), *Breeding Transfer Company,* 110 NLRB No. 64 (1954); *Pacific Intermountain Express Co.,* 107 NLRB 837 (1954); *Special Machine and Engineering Company.* 108 NLRB No. 125 (1954); Turner Construction Co., 110 NLRB No. 237 (1954); and *Blue Flash Express, Inc.,* 109 NLRB No. 85 (1954).

33. See e.g. the resolution on the Taft-Hartley Act of the founding convention in December 1955 of the merged AFL-CIO, in American Federation of Labor-Congress of Industrial Organizations, Report of Proceedings, First Constitutional Convention, December 1955, p. 61f.

34. In *N.A.M. Law Digest,* December 1954, p. 1; cf. also Chamber of Commerce of the United States, *Labor Relations Letter,* September 1954, in which the Chamber defended the new Board against attack by the AFL Executive Council.

chapter seven

Conservation of Natural Resources

Conservation is a term which can have many meanings. Initially, in the late nineteenth and early twentieth centuries when conservation first became a significant public issue, the emphasis was on maintaining renewable resources and preventing waste in the use of nonrenewable resources, such as mineral ores. Since then conservation has been expanded to include the preservation of natural beauties and curiosities (e.g., wilderness areas and natural waterfalls), the maintenance of recreational areas, and control of pollution of the natural environment.

The formation of conservation policy involves efforts to balance the present and future needs of society, and the interests of the various users of natural resources—mining and lumber companies, stock raisers, sportsmen, vacationers, commercial recreation interests, and naturalists, among others. Conflict between material interests and aesthetic values characterizes the formation and implementation of conservation policy. The major question confronting policy-makers in this area is not that of use or nonuse of resources but, rather, whose values or interests shall be given effect in resource policy. The natural environment is not adequate to meet all of the demands made upon it.

In some instances, however, the primary conflict in resource policy development may take place among government resource agencies rather than private interest groups. Professor Robert Morgan's case study of the Salt-Wahoo flood control project in Nebraska and the Watershed Protection Act of 1954 is illustrative of this. General agreement apparently existed among the private parties involved on the need for action; the problem was to secure action from "the government," more particularly the Army Corps of Engineers and the Soil Conservation Service. Morgan shows how the complex web of agency, group, and congressional committee relationships in a policy area may constitute a barrier to action and how organized local pressure can play a positive role in overcoming such obstacles to policy formation. In this instance most persons would probably agree that the resultant policy is beneficent in nature. Is there a national interest in such situations? If there is, how does one alter the policy milieu so as to give effect to it?

The national government currently owns more than two hundred million acres of forest lands, with their management being assigned to the Forest Service (national forests), National Park Service (national parks and monuments), and Bureau of Land Management (public lands such as grazing lands which also include some forests). These agencies have been delegated broad powers to regulate the use of the forests and, through administrative action, fashion most of the national policy on forests. In essence, Congress has delegated to them the task of resolving conflicts over the use of national forests. Charles Reich examines the policy-making procedures employed by the agencies and concludes that they provide too little opportunity for meaningful public participation. He would assign a greater role to the "public" and a lesser role to professionals in the formation of forest policy, especially as this involves choice among alternative uses of forest resources. What is the proper role of experts in policy-making?

In the past two decades much attention has been devoted to the problem of controlling or preventing air and water pollution and protecting the quality of our natural environment. Population growth, increasing industrialization, urbanization, and the consumption habits of an affluent society have all contributed to the development of public concern with pollution. Both the national and state governments are active participants in this area, sometimes in cooperation, sometimes in conflict. Professor Matthew Holden, in his essay on state water pollution control activity, provides much insight into the process and problems of this type of policy-making, explicitly treating it as a bargaining process, both as regards the formation of pollution control standards and the effort to promote compliance with them. Pollution control agencies, he contends, must bargain in order to reach agreement with the contending parties and to secure compliance with standards once set. This bargaining process is affected by such factors as the technological nature of the problem, the social myths and values, the desire of pollution control agencies to prevent "appeals" to other decision-making bodies, and the agencies' need to maintain working relationships with the regulated parties.

PRESSURE POLITICS
AND RESOURCES ADMINISTRATION
Robert J. Morgan

Writing in the tenth and fifty-first essays of *The Federalist,* Madison concluded that the great virtue of the federal union and the separation of powers was that the variety of interests and territory embraced by the United States would render a majority of the whole either incapable or indisposed to invade the rights and interests of other members of the community. Even, however, if a majority were to discover its common motive and power, he thought that it would be difficult for it to act in unison. As a deterrent to democratic government in the eighteenth century, the effectiveness of Madison's proposition does not seem open to serious challenge. The real question is whether, in the twentieth century, it ought to be materially revised to take into account the prolific growth of pressure groups and their special relationships with legislative committees and administrative agencies. Would it not be more accurate to say that at present, because of the variety of sentiments growing out of the diversity of geographic, cultural, economic, ethnic, and other factors in the United States, particular interests are actually forced to discover their strength and to pursue their objectives, often with little serious regard for a majority or national interest?

Among the current problems awaiting rational public decision, the orderly conservation of water and land resources is caught up in this web. While much of the recent discussion concerning the failure to develop a comprehensive policy has centered in devising workable administrative machinery, one may ask whether the difficulty does not lie much deeper in a constitutional system which was deliberately intended to frustrate majority action.

Many of the obstacles to be overcome in framing legislative and administrative decisions regarding this matter are illustrated by the history of the Salt-Wahoo flood control project in southeastern Nebraska and its relation with the Watershed Protection and Flood

Reprinted from *The Journal of Politics,* XVIII (February, 1956), 39–60, with permission of the author and publisher.

Prevention Act of 1954. Hailed initially as an example of true co-ordination between federal agencies and a local interest group in re-sources development and later damned as an instance of "coordina-tion gone sour," the labored effort of four years finally produced agreement on the level of the field services and a local organization seeking to frame a program satisfactory to local interests.[1] The proj-ect's history is more than another dreary tale of inter-agency suspi-cion, jealousy, and acquisitiveness. It is, rather, an illustration of the powerful and perhaps indispensable rôle of pressure politics on all levels of government. Or equal importance, it is again indicative of the interlocking trinity of pressure group, administrative agency, and Congressional committee which has wrought a constitutional revolu-tion not wholly anticipated by Madison.

The innocent central party to this controversy which swirled back and forth between Lincoln, Nebraska, and Washington for more than four years is a normally muddy trickle of a stream called Salt Creek and its principal tributary known as Wahoo Creek. Together they drain over 1,000,000 acres of rich, undulating farm land embracing parts of six southeastern counties. They have periodically flooded the watershed, including the city of Lincoln, during the past fifty years; and a particularly heavy flood in May, 1950, cost an estimated $53,000,000 in damages and twenty-two lives in the six counties of southeastern Nebraska.[2] Although this flood and the less extensive ones which damaged Lincoln in May and again in June, 1951, were not as spectacular as the sort which occurs on the mainstream of the Missouri, their destructiveness was real enough to stimulate demands for preventive action.

Capitalizing on the dramatic news of the flood of May 9 to 11, 1950, Raymond A. McConnell, Jr., editor of the Lincoln *Evening Jour-nal*, unleashed a journalistic torrent of feature articles to demonstrate his conclusion that farms on which a high degree of approved soil conservation practices were completed had suffered little or no dam-age from the heavy rainfall. Judging the public to be especially receptive to his plan at this time, he asserted that if his readers wanted to avoid future loss of life and property, especially the soil, they would have to press "for consideration of the flood problem as one to be coped with properly only on a watershed-wide basis, beginning on the land and in the smaller tributaries."[3] McConnell was familiar with the Pick-Sloan plan authorized by the Flood Control Act of 1944, but he was convinced that it offered little prospect of solution to the flood problems affecting areas drained by the small tributaries of the mainstream. He was also aware that the Department of Agriculture had developed a comprehensive program for the Missouri Basin to include the construction of some types of flood control structures, not the least of which were small dams.[4] Whatever may have been the hidden wellspring of motive, a newspaper editor had turned raindrops into a public issue.

With a sure instinct for political realities, McConnell sponsored a meeting attended by 175 local and state civic leaders and office holders as well as representatives of the Soil Conservation Service and the Corps of Engineers. On this occasion E. A. Norton, then Assistant Chief, Soil Conservation Service (Washington), uttered a prophetic warning of coming events. "You'll need a strong organization to press for what you want. Federal agencies are not going to move any faster than you ask them to. Therefore, it is up to you to push this thing."[5] In the light of this warning it may be less than coincidental that those present at the meeting decided on two courses of action. They resolved to form a Salt Creek watershed organization. They also expressed approval of a program of flood control in which downstream flood works would be planned to supplement, and be integrated with, "the most widespread upstream application of water and soil conservation practices on all watershed lands of the tributaries." It was claimed that "experience and research have proved" such practices to be essential elements of flood control.[6] With these actions McConnell and his local supporters were caught up in a bitter struggle between the Department of Agriculture and the Corps of Engineers, centering in the question of proper techniques and administration of flood control.

So far as a mere layman can make out the issue, it amounts in essence to this: the most obvious and sensational sort of flood damage suffered in the Missouri Basin, as in much of the rest of the country, occurs when excessive rains or the melting heavy snows flood low-lying areas bounding major rivers and their tributaries. To reduce, or even prevent, the resulting destruction, large dams and levees have been built, channels have been dredged and straightened. This has been the work largely of the Corps of Engineers. In the western fringes and the upper basin of the Missouri, the need for irrigation water and the electric power to pump it to fields (and, in part, to pay for costly irrigation works) has stimulated construction projects by the Bureau of Reclamation. Differences in uses and consequent differences in construction techniques and payment of costs, not to mention institutional jealousies, led to a conflict between these two agencies with a resulting settlement of sorts in the Missouri Basin known as the Pick-Sloan Plan authorized by the Flood Control Act of 1944. Despite this uneasy truce, many of the flood control projects in the area are multi-purpose structures.[7]

This picture was further complicated when the Department of Agriculture framed its own comprehensive program of development for the Missouri Basin in 1949.[8] Of special relevance here is the portion dealing with flooding, especially as it causes sheet erosion of soil and the overflow of the small tributary streams draining croplands. According to Mr. Brannan, this program would "assure the safe disposal of water in small watersheds and the lesser tributary streams" and "contribute to flood control" by reducing sedimentation behind large dams and by protecting the destruction of lands through gully erosion, bank cutting, and stream sedimentation. The program "contemplates the construction of gully control structures, flood-ways, bank protection works and small retarding basins." This plan, which the Secretary termed "accelerated," would require thirty years for completion and would add "to flood control in all the major and minor valleys of the basin."[9] It would also, he claimed, place primary responsibility for results on the people of the area, provide a unified comprehensive and multi-purpose plan, and give a balance now lacking because the construction of "engineering works is outdistancing programs for the land." The Department's program would, he said, complement existing mainstream projects as well as any which might in the future be undertaken.[10] In short, stripped of its varnish, the Department of Agriculture's proposal was that it, too, would construct flood control works, including "small" dams, as a logical extension of its soil conservation work. Reduced to a slogan effective on the hustings, it was to "catch the raindrops where they fall." It was the Department's rejoinder to the claim that effective flood control measures must be limited generally to large dams on the mainstreams.[11] This program did, of course, call attention to the often unspectacular but real flood damage which occurs to our viable top soil both on the uplands and in the lesser floodplains of tributary streams.

Utilizing the initiative which was his, McConnell, with the assistance of other local leaders, set up a committee of twenty-five, including representatives of the three largest banks in Lincoln, several leading farmers from the two counties principally affected, editors of two rural newspapers, two soil conservation district supervisors, and other influential persons, including the mayor of Lincoln. Meeting on June 12, 1951, this committee secured a promise from Representatives Carl Curtis and Karl Stefan that the House Committee on Public Works would be requested to authorize the Department of Agriculture to make a survey and recommendations for flood works under the Flood Control Act of 1936. When this request was granted a month later, the Department of Agriculture was reported as saying that the survey would be completed within four to six months.[12] The watershed association was formally launched on its curious career at a mass meeting at the State Fair Grounds on July 21. On this occasion McConnell assured the public that he had promises of co-operation from every affected federal, state, and local agency. Pointedly, the major address of the evening was made by Bryce Browning of the Muskingum Conservancy District to stir public support for watershed management as a flood control.[13]

The first of much bad blood erupted out of the project when, on October 20, 1950, the Corps announced a plan for the Salt-Wahoo area to include structures to cost $14,000,000 (to be paid 90 per cent by the federal government) and to be built to withstand floods of an intensity likely to occur once every twenty-five years upstream from Lincoln, once in a hundred years around the city, and once in fifty years between Lincoln and the mouth of Salt Creek at Ashland on the Platte River. Professing complete consternation, the Salt-Wahoo Watershed Association responded by chastising the Engineers, calling the plan a piecemeal one which attacked the problem backwards by ignoring the possible benefits of the plan yet to be formulated by the Soil Conservation Service. Charging that the Corps had violated pledges given to the association, it admonished the Corps to reconsider its plans, co-ordinate its future work with the Soil Conservation Service, and present a genuinely integrated plan to the local interests.[14]

The following December, when Governor Peterson of Nebraska raised the issue of inter-agency co-operation before the Missouri Basin Inter-Agency Committee, he was assured by representatives of the two agencies that there was no dispute between them.[15] Since McConnell had raised the cry of non-co-operation in the Lincoln *Journal,* this profession of brotherhood had a counterfeit ring to it. On December 18, however, McConnell announced that the Soil Conservation Service had received an extension of time to complete its survey. Both agencies were now quoted as favoring co-operative effort of the sort which the "House . . . Public Works Committee instructed . . . and both agreed to . . . at the Washington level." [16] Assuring the association that orders had come down from Washington (from whom he did not say) to secure a co-ordinated plan, McConnell publicly exuded confidence when the two agencies made a report to the Nebraska Coordinating Committee in June, 1951. Although further studies were needed to complete the report for submission to Congress at its next session, the progress to date was "a milestone in federal flood control planning . . . meeting with great success." [17]

Despite the apparently bright prospects for a co-ordinated plan, the association adopted a wholly new approach to secure at least the soil conservation phase of the project, when in August, 1951, it was decided to act on the suggestion of Senator Kenneth Wherry to press for appropriations to make the Salt-Wahoo area a demonstration project, a model possibly to be copied nationally. Complaining that Secretary Brannan was unrealistic in insisting on the adoption of the agricultural program for the whole Missouri Basin, McConnell urged that it be broken down into small demonstrational watershed projects, saying prophetically, "that is the only way Congress is ever going to authorize it . . ." [18] Such a move was made in the agricultural appropriations sub-committee in the Senate, but when a request was also submitted to the House appropriations committee, it was rejected. McConnell lamented this failure, saying that one specific trouble was that with the death of Representative Karl Stefan, "Nebraska is without representation on the appropriations committee." [19]

Thrown back upon the original plan, the association awaited the project of the Soil Conservation Service which was revealed to its board of directors in January and March, 1952. There was private doubt that it would be received enthusiastically by the Corps, but McConnell gave assurances that the Engineers would not interfere with it. Thus, the association accepted the agricultural program at this time without any integration with the Corps. Early in July this plan was sent to Congress as a supplemental report to the Missouri Basin Agricultural Program. Significantly it was directed not to the Committee on Public Works which had authorized the Salt-Wahoo survey, but to the Committee on Agriculture.[20]

It was undoubtedly not without strong reason that this curious action was taken, for on March 27, 1952, a sub-committee (the Jones Committee) of the House Public Works Committee had commenced public hearings on a study of civil works, which included an extensive review of the relations between the Corps of Engineers and the Soil Conservation Service, making considerable use of the Salt-Wahoo project for illustrative purposes.[21] On May 8 Representative Curtis introduced Liebers, McConnell, and Byron Dunn of the Salt-Wahoo Watershed Association to testify before this committee. Dunn confined his testimony largely to a description of the enormous effort by the association to educate the Nebraska public in favor of the agricultural program. Liebers summarized the early efforts of his organization to secure co-ordination from the Corps and the Conservation Service, asserting that co-operation had continued until the final stages of program formulation. At this point, however, he averred, "disagreement at the top level of the two agencies caused delay in completion of the report. Seeing that the delay would forbid presentation of the joint report to this session of the Congress, the Salt-Wahoo Association requested the Department of Agriculture to complete its recommendations. . . .

"To date the Corps . . . has not submitted an alternative plan for the Salt-Wahoo Basin."[22] He added that while the organization was favorably impressed with the Department's program, the members were convinced that downstream works constructed by the Corps were necessary to complete an adequate program. For his part, McConnell expressed a fear that the monstrous floods on the Missouri in July, 1951, and April, 1952, would result in what he termed a permanent imbalance of programs frozen into the familiar form of the Pick-Sloan Plan. Moreover, a demonstration of the value of a co-ordinated plan of watershed management, such as in the Salt-Wahoo area, would be of inestimable use to the entire country. Such action, based on plans supported by locally affected interests, he claimed, would be the democratic way of shaping policy. He insisted that his organization stood not for two programs linked by a hyphen, but one genuinely integrated from the top to the bottom of the watershed. He concluded: "The Salt-Wahoo Watershed Association is not anti-Army Engineers. It is not anti anything—except piecemeal and incomplete planning and execution, or either of these that overlooks or brushes aside local problems and local needs." [23]

During the summer of 1952, the Jones Committee digested the evidence presented to it and in December released a devastating critique of the Department of Agriculture's attempt to participate in the flood control program. It found that co-operation in the Salt-Wahoo project had officially ended on January 22, 1952, when the Omaha District Engineer informed the Regional Director in Lincoln that joint planning was at an end because the Soil Conservation Service had continued its planning on an independent basis. The Regional Director had replied by saying that the Salt-Wahoo organization had urged both agencies to place their plans before the Eighty-second Congress, although the Corps had indicated its inability to ready its plan before May 15. At this time the Corps felt that questions of cost-benefits and standards of construction had not been resolved satisfactorily. On May 27, the District Engineer wrote the Regional Director, indicating his sympathy with the Soil Conservation Service's lack of funds for survey work and acknowledging its thesis that co-ordination could only follow Congressional authorization for the entire watershed program.

The Jones committee noted with apparent dismay that "at no time until late in May was the corps given any data on the Department's study to analyze and perhaps tie-in with the corps' report." [24] For some curious reason the committee did not mention the Corps' eagerness to act alone, when, in October 1950, it had submitted its plan for the area before the Soil Conservation Service could complete its plans. Amazed and chagrined, the Jones committee also observed that it had authorized the Department of Agriculture's survey for Salt-Wahoo only to have it referred to the Committee on Agriculture, citing the directives of the Public Works Committee merely as incidental authority for the action taken.[25] Denying a rumor that the Corps had deliberately sabotaged the joint approach in the summer of 1951 by claiming that it lacked funds, the committee concluded that the "responsibility for the breakdown rested with the Department of Agriculture's consideration of urgency as paramount."[26] This evident hostility to the Department's program was translated into recommendations which urged that the Department of Agriculture be denied further authority to make surveys under the flood control laws and that it be subordinated to the Corps of Engineers in future flood control planning and construction. The Jones committee emphatically rejected the Soil Conservation Service's watershed management program as "flood control in the accepted sense of keeping large flows of water from causing excessive damage."[27]

McConnell's response to this virtual death sentence for a joint solution to the Salt-Wahoo problem was a counter-charge that the Jones Committee report was "outdated" and that it had failed to account for "a series of meetings between the two agencies which began in October (1952)."[28] He further chided the committee for accepting what he called the "outmoded" idea that flood control should begin at the bottom of the stream. He admitted that joint planning had stopped late in 1951, but, he said, the new meetings had been called by the watershed association at the suggestion of the Engineers. Out of these contacts the association forged a four-point statement of principle, whereby the "enhancement of agricultural values" was to be the responsibility of the Department of Agriculture and the "protection of urban and industrial areas" was to be the primary responsibility of the Engineers, who were to recognize the contribution of the agricultural program; co-ordinated flood control works were to be built by the Engineers where watershed treatment would not afford adequate protection to urban property, but these structures should be so located as to minimize the impairment of agricultural values; such works were not to be duplicated by the Department of Agriculture.[29] Despite this apparent agreement in principle among the affected parties, the Soil Conservation Service in Washington reversed a decision reached by field technicians in regard to five dams which had been assigned to the Engineers, and the project again wallowed.[30]

One remaining strand of action proved essential to the success of the association. On February 2, 1951, McConnell met in Lincoln with several Kansans interested in the watershed movement. It was decided then, or shortly thereafter, that the Lincoln *Journal* should sponsor a meeting of interested groups to discuss ways and means of gaining Congressional authorization for the program of the Soil Conservation Service. The severe floods in Kansas during July stimulated a meeting which was held on August 11 and 12 in Lincoln and was attended by representatives of the watershed groups, the Soil Conservation Service, the Bureau of Reclamation, the Corps of Engineers, and members of Congress, including Senators Wherry of Nebraska and Schoeppel of Kansas. Representative Clifford Hope wrote to McConnell after the close of the conference, saying that the missing legislative element was specific legislation tying together the programs of the Department of Agriculture with those of the Corps of Engineers and the Bureau of Reclamation. He further expressed hope that a subcommittee of the House Committee on Agriculture would soon conduct hearings on the Missouri Basin program prepared by the Department of Agriculture.[31] On September 5 following, the Kansas-Nebraska Watershed Council was formed to propagandize newspaper editors in the two states through the use of a periodic newsletter and, ultimately, to pressure Congress in support of the Department of Agriculture's program. McConnell personally went beyond this step, however, as he moved in an ever widening circle to form a national pressure group in support of this legislation. He became special consultant on watershed management to the Capper Publications and wrote a series of articles evidencing enthusiasm for a flood control program to include the Department of Agriculture.[32] He arranged for a spokesman to address the National Association of Soil Conservation Districts, an obvious ally, in January, 1952. He personally addressed the Soil Conservation Society of America on November 6, 1953, and the National Association of Soil Conservation Districts on February 23, 1954. Meanwhile, in February, 1953, he was instrumental in forming the National Informal Citizens Committee on Watershed Conservation. This group of twenty-five members, of which McConnell was made chairman, consisted of individuals nationally active in the watershed movement.[33]

On May 15, 1952, even before the Jones sub-committee had completed its study, Representative W. R. Poage (D., Tex.), second ranking member of the House Committee on Agriculture, introduced H.R. 7868 to authorize the Secretary of Agriculture to co-operate with states and local agencies to plan and execute works for flood prevention. Referred to the agriculture committee and to Poage's sub-committee, this bill died in committee, although the sub-committee did report favorably, of course.[34]

For reasons not obvious on the record, Poage on June 17 introduced another bill, H.R. 8243, with the same stated purpose, and it was referred to the Committee on Agriculture. Two days later it was reported and placed on the Union Calendar, where it died.[35] According to a press report five months later, Poage said that he would again introduce such legislation in the Eighty-third Congress. His bill, he said, was "strongly opposed" by the Public Works Committee and the Rules Committee. A member of the Agriculture Committee's staff was quoted as saying that "we didn't have time to make a fight of it last time; it will be at the top of our agenda next year and we'll fight for it all the way." This "sweeping new flood control bill will involve two House Committees in a jealous fight for jurisdictional supremacy early next year."[36]

With the election of a Republican President and Congressional majority in 1952, the prospect for favorable action authorizing the Department of Agriculture's program brightened noticeably. The foresight by which McConnell had linked himself with the watershed interests in Kansas assured him that he would have the aid of one of the most vigorous Congressional supporters of the Soil Conservation Service, Representative Clifford Hope of Kansas, new chairman of the House Committee on Agriculture. Similar support was expected of Senator Frank Carlson of Kansas, one of the President's trusted advisers at the time. In addition, the inclusion of watershed advocates in Texas and North Carolina assured him of assistance from the minority in Representatives Poage and Cooley. Further entrée to the White House was available through ex-Senator Fred Seaton of Nebraska, who had been a very close campaign adviser to the President.[37] Immediate use was made of this propitious situation by McConnell's high command, the National Informal Citizens Committee on Watershed Conservation, which met with the President on February 23, 1953, to secure his support for the legislation which would authorize the watershed program. As a result the President urged this step in a special message to Congress on the following July 31.[38]

Meanwhile an old project was revived to achieve speed, and possibly finesse. Representative Hope was instrumental in adding an item of $5,000,000 to the Department of Agriculture's 1954 budget to start approximately sixty "pilot" watershed projects to demonstrate the value of watershed management as flood control. Although this amount was omitted by the Senate appropriations committee despite the efforts of Senator Carlson, it was restored in conference, as its friends confidently expected it would be. In cloakroom maneuvering Representative Hope and the members of the informal committee secured the pivotal allegiance of Representative Carl Andersen (R., Minn.) Chairman of the House agricultural appropriations sub-committee, who later engaged in the following exchange with J. C. Dykes, Deputy Chief of the Soil Conservation Service, regarding the Jones Committee's recommendations:

Mr. Andersen. Apparently you are not in agreement with that recommendation, then?

Mr. Dykes. I will say we are not in agreement with it if the Department of Agriculture will be taken out of the flood-prevention work.

Mr. Andersen. In the final analysis, the proposal by the House Public Works Committee would put this entire program under the domination of the Army engineers, would it not?

Mr. Dykes. It certainly would.

Mr. Andersen. I disagree with that proposal, and I thought it well to have something in the record on the subject.[39]

The members of the agricultural appropriations sub-committee were quite proud of the fact that the appropriation "happens to have been almost a piece of legislation on an appropriation bill, however, with the blessing of the legislative committee. So it came in a sort of left-handed way to the Department . . ." Representative Andersen, in fact, wanted credit where credit was due:

I want the record to show that when this subcommittee fought through its bill, putting the initial $5 million for the Andersen-Hope program into this bill in spring of 1953, that the Senate refused to agree to that item and struck it out in committee . . . If you will check the record, this subcommittee urged and fought for the retention of that item in conference and I am making this statement here, gentlemen, this morning to show where the credit belongs for actually bringing this thing into being. It was this subcommittee that started this particular program after having it called to our attention by Mr. Hope and Senator Carlson. They sat across the table from us and explained it to us. They had no hopes, however, of its even getting out of the Congress, and I reiterate, had it not been for these seven of us sitting here, that we would not today be already seeing the beginning of a program which I think is seizing the country with its popularity . . . even to the extent where the President . . . has . . . come out publicly in its behalf.[40]

Concurrent with the success in securing a one-year authorization by appropriation for the "pilot" projects, Representative Hope introduced H.R. 6788 which was intended to make the Department of Agriculture a "partner" with local interests (and with the Corps and the Bureau of Reclamation) in developing flood "prevention" through watershed management. It scarcely need be said that his bill was given a sympathetic ear by the House agriculture committee under Hope's chairmanship. Interested groups who supported the bill were invited to send their spokesmen and the "informal" committee, in particular, was given ample time again to present its case. Opposition forces were conspicuously absent (including the Corps) so that the bill was favorably reported and acted upon by the House.[41] The exponents of the Hope Watershed Bill expected that their measure would receive quick and friendly treatment in the Senate. At the request of the President, Senator Aiken (R., Vt.) introduced a companion bill, S. 2549. Senators Thye, Schoeppel, Anderson, Young, and Monroney joined him as sponsors of this bill which, like H.R. 6788, was intended to give the Department of Agriculture authority to survey and to construct flood control works, including dams with a capacity of 5,000 acre feet, independent of existing flood control laws.[42] To the alarm of some of the friends of the legislation Senator Aiken scheduled public hearings on his bill only to have the Corps of Engineers come out at long last with an emphatic public condemnation of the proposal. In his testimony General Sturgis said that the size of the dams authorized in the bill was too large (5,000 acre-feet); it would continue construction of purely federal and not state projects; local interests ought to share 50 per cent of the costs and should not rely on such federal largess as ACP and SCS payments to farmers in calculating them; and the bill would probably result not in more coordination, but less.[43] Senator Aiken turned the bill over to a subcommittee for study and possible amendment only to have it become lodged there on the objections of Senator Holland who later opposed the bill on the floor saying that Congress was unwise in hastening this legislation without waiting to observe the effects of the pilot projects. Immediately McConnell invited the proponents of the bill to meet in Lincoln on April 14–15, 1954, to generate pressure for it. As a result the fifty-odd persons who were gathered made use of the usual means of contact with all of their strategically located friends in Congress to force the subcommittee to report the bill. While the bill was in committee, it took McConnell another trip to Washington on May 4th and 5th and intensive, skillful maneuvering by the "informal" committee to fend off the determined counterattack of the Corps of Engineers. In fact, it was necessary to resort again to the White House to convince all concerned that the Engineers' version of the bill did not suit the President's views. With the support of Sherman Adams, who made some alterations embodying Presidential policy, it was passed ultimately in a form acceptable to its supporters. After five years the Department of Agriculture was made what its officers called a partner in assisting local interests in developing a "balanced" program of conservation and flood prevention independent of the Corps, the Bureau of Reclamation and, it might be added, of the public works committee of the House and Senate.[44]

This act incorporates the ingenious and disingenuous plea of its supporters, such as McConnell, that the initiative in planning and constructing works lie with "local organizations." The Secretary of Agriculture has blanket authority (subject to the support of appropriations) to commence a watershed management program in any area not exceeding 250,000 acres (though contiguous areas of this size may be in effect joined), provided that no funds for constructing a dam storing more than 2,500 acre feet of water shall be appropriated *without the consent of the House and Senate agriculture committees;* no dam may exceed 5,000 acre feet in capacity. The act provides no cost-sharing formula, but leaves this vital matter virtually to the discretion of the Secretary of Agriculture. The sole machinery for co-ordination provided in the act is the requirement that the Secretary of Agriculture submit any plan of works affecting irrigation or reclamation to the Secretary of the Interior, or affecting floodwater detention structures to the Secretary of the Army, for recommendations at least sixty days before any such plan is sent to Congress through the President. The lack of comments is no bar to the transmission of a plan. The President is authorized to issue regulations to effect co-ordination. The act also repeals the authority granted by the Flood Control Act of 1936 permitting the Secretary of Agriculture to make preliminary surveys for watershed management.[45]

With the funds appropriated for the "pilot watershed" program a start was made on the soil conservation phase of the Salt-Wahoo project with the construction of works on the Roca sub-watershed of Salt Creek and the Swedeburg branch of the Wahoo Creek in the late autumn of 1953. Three weeks after the President signed the Watershed Protection Act of 1954, the Salt-Wahoo Watershed Association met in Lincoln with the Corps and the Soil Conservation Service to resume discussion of a joint plan. With the Department of Agriculture's program now on a firm statutory basis (authorization before survey and planning) agreement was reached locally on the vexatious question of allocating structures to the two agencies and a co-ordinated plan was announced on November 28. Whether these terms of surrender will prove acceptable to all parties, Congressional and executive, remains yet to be seen. The only construction to date has been undertaken as part of the Soil Conservation phase of upstream development.

The history of the Salt-Wahoo project strikingly illustrates the price paid in our constitutional system for the fractionalization of power. It also demonstrates again need for instruments of co-ordination which can bridge the many gaps standing in the way of policy formulation. The machinery of government, moreover, does not supply sufficient initiative from within itself to foresee, much less to solve, many problems. Assuming at least for the moment, that both the Salt-Wahoo flood control project and the Watershed Protection Act of 1954 reflect desirable public policy, one may ask how they would have been put into being if adequate organized pressure had not been generated on their behalf by those directly interested in the outcome. The leaders of the Salt-Wahoo organization were told by a spokesman of the Soil Conservation Service that they would have to "push this thing" or they would not get what they wanted. The Soil Conservation Service offered a program which did not even have the hearty backing of the entire Department of Agriculture.[46]

It became one of the prime tasks of the Salt-Wahoo organization, and later of the informal citizens committee, to crusade with missionary zeal for the watershed program. Only the adroit maneuvering of organized opinion could have overcome the resistance of the Corps, the internal conflicts within the Department of Agriculture and the opposition of the public works committees in Congress. In the absence of satisfactory will or machinery for developing a program on the national level, the exponents of a relatively obscure project had to discover a similar interest elsewhere and amalgamate with it on a national basis. It may be presumed that the friends of the watershed movement belatedly have discovered what the members of the Rivers and Harbors Congress have long known, so that the National Watershed Congress which met in Washington in December, 1954, for its first annual meeting is now assured of a respectful and sympathetic Congressional audience. Moreover, its task has been simplified in so far as it may now deal only with the committees on agriculture.

In this instance the pressure group performed not only the representative function but an administrative one as well in seeking to coordinate the Corps and the Soil Conservation Service on the project level. Only when this effort failed because of reciprocal agency antagonism, did the Salt-Wahoo organization shift its rôle to the more common one of influencing legislation.[47]

The leaders of the Salt-Wahoo organization appeared to be guilty of duplicity in claiming that they were not anti-Engineers even though they were spokesmen for the SCS Program. Guilt in this instance may be more apparent than real. From the start of the project until after the passage of Watershed Protection Act of 1954 the Engineers claimed that small dams on the tributaries were unable to stop flooding after heavy rains. If there were any merit to the claims of SCS, there was need of proof by demonstration. Since the Corps would not build tributary dams, it was necessary for the exponents of the watershed movement to support SCS or no demonstration would ever be made. The transparency of the Corps position is made apparent by the fact that the Army construction portion of the Salt-Wahoo project announced in November, 1954, includes at least *five* dams of a capacity well under 5,000 acre feet. In other words, the Corps now sees the virtue of small dams—if they are built by the Corps! Unfortunately the friends of the watershed movement were not willing to rest on the "pilot" program as a demonstration of the claimed value of the watershed technique. Instead, they pushed the Watershed Protection Act of 1954 through Congress before they had any sound basis for advocating it as a major addition to the present water resources programs.

The Salt-Wahoo organization claimed that its action supplied a democratizing element in administration by insuring that the program fashioned at its insistence was satisfactory to the home folks. But if this is so, it was democracy bearing a price tag which eventually must be siphoned out of the federal treasury. If it is proper to believe that federal programs must suit local interests, it is equally proper to seek assurances that the people of the nation get both a beneficial and an economical program for the pain in their pocketbooks. The adoption of the Watershed Protection and Flood Prevention Act of 1954, together with existing programs such as Pick-Sloan, can only continue a situation in which the weak, the timid, the hesitant—and even on occasion the deserving—may well be trampled in the cynical rush of the aggressive and acquisitive to the federal cornucopia.[48]

In enacting the Watershed Protection and Flood Prevention Act of 1954 both Congress and the executive branch have once again demonstrated an apparent incapacity to deal with the problem of fashioning a comprehensive program of water resources conservation and development. It has been demonstrated that it is easier to yield to particular interests which are organized and articulate than it is to view a problem such as this from the standpoint of the entire nation.

As long as reliance is placed on local initiative and pressure politics of the sort demonstrated in this case study, there will be no consideration of the national interest. A program can be developed but only if the initiative does not come solely from the bottom. Leadership must come from the top, from a President who will demonstrate that in resources policy there is not only an administrative way, but also a political will. Congress, faced with a problem of administrative fratricide rooted in well organized pressures, found that in this dispute the easiest solution was a settlement by divorce (as in the case of the Pick-Sloan Plan authorized by the Flood Control Act of 1944). As matters now stand both the Soil Conservation Service and the Corps will build dams. The precise point at which raindrops become floods has not been decided.

NOTES

1. See *Missouri: Land and Water,* The Report of the Missouri Basin Survey Commission (Washington: U.S. Government Printing Office, 1953), pp. 216–227; and "The Flood Control Program of the Department of Agriculture," House Committee Print No. 22, 82d Cong., 2d Sess., p. 34; Lincoln (Neb.) *Sunday Journal and Star,* November 28, 1954.

2. *Missouri: Land and Water, op. cit.,* p. 132; Lincoln (Neb.) *Evening Journal,* May 11, 1950.

3. Lincoln *Evening Journal,* May 13, 1950.

4. *Missouri River Basin Agricultural Program,* House Document No. 373, 81st Cong., 1st Sess., 1949. Charles M. Hardin in *The Politics of Agriculture: Soil Conservation and The Struggle for Power in Rural America* (Glencoe, Ill.: The Free Press, 1952) indicates unflatteringly that this program was initiated on the eve of World War II at least in part to make work; p. 90. The watershed flood control program had already been started elsewhere in the country, especially in the Little Sioux watershed in Iowa, in the Arkansas—Red River watershed of Oklahoma, and on the Trinity River in Texas. The status of the program in 1952 is reviewed in House Committee Print No. 22, *op. cit.,* pp. 1–5.

5. Lincoln *Evening Journal,* June 1, 1950. In 1945 the Corps had surveyed the upper reaches of Salt Creek for flood control but had found no economically justifiable project.

6. *Ibid.*

7. 58 *Stat.* 665. A useful account of the programs proposed and authorized for the Missouri Basin can be found in Marvin Meade, *The Missouri Basin Proposals for Development* (Bureau of Government Research, University of Kansas, 1952), Citizen's Pamphlet Series Number 11. Three articles dealing with the general problem may be found in *Land Economics,* XXX, No. 4 (November, 1954): S. Blair Hutchison, "Fitting Big Dams Into Little Economies," pp. 329–332; Walter M. Kollmorgen, "And Deliver Us From Big Dams," pp. 333–346; Kris Kristjanson, "Institutional Arrangements in Water Resource Development," pp. 347–362.

8. House Document No. 373, *op. cit.,* Cf. *Missouri: Land and Water, op. cit.,* p. 220.

9. House Document No. 373, *op. cit.,* p. 25.

10. *Ibid.,* p. iii. Cf. House Committee Print No. 22, *op. cit.,* pp. 1–5.

11. The Department of the Interior greeted this program with a coolness evident in its half-dozen major objections. Curiously, however, the Corps of Engineers observed that the plan "includes provisions for *needed measures* to complement the coordinated plan for flood control . . . now being prosecuted by the Corps . . . and the Bureau of Reclamation. . . ." The Bureau of the Budget cleared the program as being in general accord with the President's policy but said that basic data to determine cost-benefit ratios would have to be developed before economic justification could be determined. House Document 373, *op. cit.,* pp. 1–2, 3–5, 6–7 (italics supplied). According to one view, both the Department of Interior and the Corps acting in the Missouri Basin Inter-Agency Committee requested such a program. It was said to have been received by the field representatives with approval which "bordered on the enthusiastic. Their superiors in Washington, however, found little to favor in the proposed plan. . . ." *Missouri: Land and Water, op. cit.,* p. 220.

12. Lincoln *Journal,* July 20, 1950.

13. *Ibid.,* July 21, 1950. The friends of the Muskingum District (at New Philadelphia, Ohio) have called it a model of local initiative and co-operation with federal agencies in providing flood control, but it does not lack critics who say that both initial and continued federal support has been necessary, and that it is not an example of watershed management as visualized by the Department of Agriculture. James Lawrence, editor of the Lincoln *Star* and chairman of the Missouri Basin Survey Commission, is one such critic. Cf. Meade, *op. cit.,* pp. 45–52. Cf. Arthur E. Morgan, *The Miami Conservancy District* (New York: McGraw-Hill Book Company, Inc., 1951).

14. *Missouri: Land and Water, op. cit.,* p. 216; Lincoln *Journal,* Oct. 20 and 31, 1950.

15. Missouri Basin Inter-Agency Committee, *Minutes of the Forty-Fifth Meeting,* Dec. 1, 1950, p. 3.

16. Lincoln *Journal,* Dec. 18, 1950. The Inter-Agency's cover-up of this dispute was not surprising in view of its previous record in such matters. See Arthur Maas, *Muddy Waters* (Cambridge: Harvard University Press, 1951), p. 114.

17. Lincoln *Journal,* June 11, 1951.

18. *Ibid.,* Aug. 20, 1951. McConnell's view was most interesting in light of the fact that Secretary Brannan had fought hard to overcome SCS objections to making his program a comprehensive one for the Missouri Basin. SCS preferred to limit the plan to erosion control and physical development. Hardin, *op. cit.,* p. 90.

19. Lincoln *Journal,* Oct. 11, 1951. The Department of Agriculture had asked for $1,475,000 for watershed projects in Nebraska and Kansas.

20. House Document No. 530, 82d Cong., 2d Sess. It should be noted that this program requiring ten years for completion included not only the Salt-Wahoo project, but also three others. Thus, in all probability the regional office in Lincoln was under some pressure from the Washington office to complete its plans regardless of whether co-ordination with the Corps had been achieved or not. For this and other reasons to be noted later, it appears that the desire for local integration of projects was not uppermost in the minds of the highest levels of the Soil Conservation Service. Cf. pp. 38, 45–78 for a description of the project. Cf. *Missouri: Land and Water, op. cit.,* pp. 132–136.

21. "Study of Civil Works," Hearings Before the Subcommittee to Study Civil Works, of the Committee on Public Works, House of Representatives, 82d Cong., 2d Sess., Parts 1 and 2.

22. *Ibid.,* part 2, p. 317.

23. *Ibid.,* p. 331. At this time Congress had no program before it, but it did receive the agriculture plan on the following July 3, just before the end of the session. On April 14, and on May 10, 1952, respectively, McConnell met separately with Secretary Brannan and General Pick (then Chief of Engineers) to iron out the differences on the Salt-Wahoo project, but apparently to no avail. He also attended a Presidential press conference, where he queried President Truman on his attitude toward the agricultural program. He said

that Truman approved this program as a supplement to the Pick-Sloan plan. Lincoln *Journal,* April 18, 19, May 11, 1952.

24. House Committee Print No. 22, *op. cit.,* p. 32.

25. *Ibid.,* pp. 34–35.

26. *Ibid.,* p. 33; *Missouri: Land and Water, op. cit.,* p. 216. One may speculate whether the Corps displayed interest in the Salt Creek area because Senator Wherry was a Vice-President of the Rivers and Harbors Congress and a member of the appropriations sub-committee for Engineer civil functions before his death. Mass, *op. cit.,* p. 46.

27. *Ibid.,* pp. 42–43. The Jones Committee actually wished a plague on both houses, calling the conduct of the two agencies "deserving of high censure for their uncompromising attitudes and actions which have unduly alarmed and confused the residents of many areas and have wastefully delayed efficient and economic prosecution of important programs. Both upstream and downstream works have their place in a balanced conservation program." House Committee Print No. 22, *op. cit.,* p. 40.

28. Lincoln *Journal,* Dec. 16, and Lincoln *Star,* December 17, 1952.

29. "Some Proposed Principles of National Policy," mimeographed, Lincoln, Neb., January 20, 1953. The Jones Committee had devoted much attention and criticism to the upstream-downstream controversy which had developed, the members thought, because the Department of Agriculture had encouraged farmers to expect greater flood protection from watershed management than the known facts warranted. See House Committee Print No. 22, *op. cit.,* pp. 12–13, 20. Rep. Jones (D., Ala.) appeared to be a friend of TVA and a critic of the Corps as well as the Department of Agriculture in this instance. See his trenchant questioning of Dwight Payton of the Kansas-Nebraska Watershed Council; "Study of Civil Works," *op. cit.,* part 2, pp. 366–367. Both Gladwin Young, "father" of the Agricultural plan, and Secretary Brannan testified that large downstream dams were necessary and that the controversy was one largely manufactured by those who had something to gain from it. *Ibid.,* pp. 206–207.

30. Lincoln *Journal* and *Star,* November 28, 1954. In November, 1952, the Salt-Wahoo association, suspicious of the Corps, received assurances from Governor Peterson and Governor-elect Crosby that neither would approve any Corps plan which did not meet with the association's approval. It is customary for Corps' plans to be cleared in each state by the Governor before they are submitted to Congress; see *Missouri: Land and Water, op. cit.,* pp. 250–251. Cf. Mass, *op. cit.,* pp. 23 ff.

31. Lincoln *Journal,* August 11, 12, 20, and 21, 1951.

32. *Capper's Farmer,* June, July and November, 1953.

33. The names of most of the members can be found in "Conservation and Watershed Programs," Hearings, House Committee on Agriculture, 83d Cong., 1st Sess., pp. 133 ff. The members came from such widely scattered farm states as Nebraska, Iowa, Kansas, Texas, South Carolina, North Carolina, Georgia, Oklahoma, and California. The committee had a journalistic outlet through the Capper Publications and the Curtis Publishing Company (*Country Gentleman*), both of which had members on the committee.

34. 98 *Cong. Rec.* 5292 (cf. Daily Digest, D315, D332), 82d Cong., 2d Sess.

35. *Ibid.,* pp. 7451, 7663; cf. House Report 2222, 82d Cong., 2d Sess.

36. Omaha *World Herald,* Nov. 2, 1952.

37. The watershed movement in Kansas had particularly attracted the attention of the Kansas delegation because of the bitter squabble over the Tuttle Creek Dam in Northeastern Kansas. Topeka *Capital,* August 9, 1952.

38. House Document No. 221, 83d Cong., 1st Sess.

39. "Department of Agriculture Appropriations for 1954," Hearings before the Subcommittee of the Committee on Appropriations, House of Representatives, 83d Cong., 1st Sess., Part 4, pp. 1902–1903. The appropriation was made by Public Law 156, 83d Cong., 1st Sess., 67 *Stat.* 214.

40. "Department of Agriculture Appropriations for 1955," Hearings before the Subcommittee of the Committee on Appropriations, House of Representatives, 83d Cong., 2d Sess., Part 3, pp. 1344–1345, 1315–1316. It is of interest to note that the initiative for this appropriation came from outside the Department of Agriculture—from Congress via the pressure groups.

41. See "Conservation and Watershed Programs," *op. cit.;* and 99 *Congressional Record* 10956. According to one observer, Rep. Hope has been an open proponent of the Soil Conservation Service in the power struggle within the Department of Agriculture and among farm organizations. Moreover, Senator Aiken has, according to Hardin, opposed the Service and this may account for his holding Senate hearings on the Hope Bill. See Hardin, *op. cit.,* pp. 26, 174 ff.

42. "Cooperative Soil Conservation and Flood Prevention Projects," Hearings on S. 2549, Committee on Agriculture and Forestry, Senate, 83d Cong., 2d Sess., esp. pp. 1–34. Legislation to authorize some phases of watershed management were not new to this Congress. At least fifteen bills were introduced in the House and three in the Senate during the Eightieth, Eighty-first,

and Eighty-second Congresses dealing with this matter; see Missouri Basin Survey Commission, *Bibliography of Congressional and Federal Documents on the Missouri River Basin* (1947–1952), Publication No. 1, mimeographed (Lincoln, Nebraska, 1952). In addition two other bills were introduced in the 83d Congress, S. 1916 and H.R. 4877.

43. "Cooperative Soil Conservation and Flood Prevention Projects," *op. cit.*, p. 95. Among the many groups now supporting this legislation were the American Farm Bureau (which also supported the 50 per cent federal-local cost feature), the National Grange, the National Council of Farmer Cooperatives, the National Association of Soil Conservation Districts, the National Farmers Union, the National Reclamation Association (with some amendments regarding state water laws), the National Wildlife Federation, the Chamber of Commerce (with amendments in regard to local cost features) and many others. The "informal" committee did not testify before Senator Aiken's committee—supposedly as a result of pre-determined strategy.

44. Actually the final bill enacted was H. R. 6788 with the Senate version substituted for the bill passed by the House. It became Public Law 566, 83d Cong., 2d Sess., 68 *Stat.* 666, the "Watershed Protection and Flood Prevention Act, 1954," and was approved by the President August 4. The limitations of space make it impossible to relate more of the history of the act. It may, however, be found in 100 *Congressional Record* 1168, 3128–3152, 3164, 8496, 8595, 8619–8625, 9888, 9930, 10831, 11060, 11480, 11495, 11405, 11763. Cf. House Report No. 1140, Feb. 2, 1954; Senate Report No. 1620, June 18, 1954; and Conference Report No. 2297, July 20, 1954, 83d Cong., 2d Sess. The bill passed the Senate without debate or a record vote. In the House the "debate" was heavy with the redolence of roses as the dozen or so members most sympathetic with the legislation spent the day tossing bouquets to each other with only Rep. Saylor of Pennsylvania opposing in the discussion. Oddly enough, even the Public Works Committee had apparently made its peace with the Committee on Agriculture after a series of conferences which included Rep. Jones, Rep. Poage, and Rep. Cooley—the price was not revealed on the floor of the House.

45. An account of the program contemplated under this act may be found in Gladwin E. Young, "Local Responsibilities for Watershed Protection Programs," *State Government*, XXVII, No. 12 (December, 1954), 255 ff. President Eisenhower issued regulations directing co-ordination in Executive Order 10584, December 18, 1954; *Federal Register*, Vol. 19, No. 246, pp. 8725–8726.

46. Certainly the Department did not pressure for appropriations to support its program. The initiative came from the pressure groups and the idea for

using the one year appropriation to start "pilot" projects came from Senator Wherry. The willingness of high Soil Conservation Service officers to gloss over their quarrel with the Corps has evoked snorts of disgust from the chief scribe of the watershed movement, Elmer T. Peterson, in his book, *Big Dam Foolishness: The Problem of Modern Flood Control and Water Storage* (New York: The Devin-Adair Company, 1954), pp. 37–49. Peterson has also frankly noted the implications of the watershed movement in regard to public power, pp. 101 ff.

47. It should be noted that the Salt-Wahoo organization attempted to formalize its co-ordinating rôle by securing a state enabling law in 1953 which permits the formation of watershed districts. Such a district is visualized as special unit or "local agency" of the sort mentioned in the Watershed Protection and Flood Prevention Act of 1954. For some details regarding the watershed district in Nebraska, see my article, "A New Voice in Government: The Watershed District," *State Government,* XXVI, No. 12 (December, 1953), 288 ff.

48. During the House "debate" on H.R. 6788 Rep. Hill (R., Colo.) quoted the conference report, saying: ". . . under the policies established by the bill, plans and projects will not be handed down from the top as part of some overall development plan, but can be initiated only by the people of the localities most intimately involved. . . ." 100 *Congressional Record* 3148. The Jones Committee observed that authorization overlaps permitted the Department of Agriculture to conduct its watershed projects under either flood control legislation or soil conservation legislation and thereby to co-ordinate with the Corps or not, as the Department saw fit, and to choose the committee which seemed to promise its blessing. House Committee Print No. 22, *op. cit.,* pp. 34–40. The "local initiative" authorized in the new law appears to be no different from that involved in projects which the Corps is invited to survey and construct.

BUREAUCRACY AND THE FORESTS
Charles A. Reich

The forests of our nation are a vast experiment in public ownership. The people of the United States hold in common a rich and splendid kingdom of timber, rivers, minerals, and mountains—well over two hundred million acres of land from New England to Alaska.

Ownership is easy. Effective ownership, including a voice in the planning and management of this vast acreage, is difficult. Managing the forests is no mere caretaker's job. There are fundamental choices to be made—choices that pit one portion of the public against another, and that can change irrevocably the character of the domain as a whole.

Forest land can be managed primarily for the exploitation of its material resources—its timber crop, grazing lands, minerals, water supply, and hydroelectric power. Or it can be given over to mass recreation—summer and winter sports, camping, picnicking, and resorts. Or it can be preserved for essentially spiritual values—a wilderness retreat from frantic city living, a sanctuary for the qualities of man that are "best when least in company."

Today's growing population tears insatiably at the forests. As people spread into every corner of the land the forests shrink. Armies of mechanized campers invade. Dam builders covet choice valleys. Sheep nibble the high pastures. The power saw turns beauty into board feet. Roads drive deep wounds into the solitudes.

Management must decide between the competing demands on the forests. When different uses clash, which shall be favored? How are local needs to be balanced against broader interests? Who is to have the benefit of the economic resources, and on what terms? How are the conflicting recreational demands of fishermen, skiers, hunters, motorboat enthusiasts, and automobile sight-seers to be satisfied? Should the requirements of the future outweigh the demands of today?

How to make such decisions—and similar decisions in every area of public ownership—is a major dilemma for democratic government. Government is now so complex that often it is impossible for the

Reprinted by permission of the Center for the Study of Democratic Institutions from *Bureaucracy and the Forests* (Occasional Paper, 1962), pp. 1–10.

people, or their elected representatives in Congress, even to be informed of the issues. Professional bureaucracies grow up to do the work of management and planning, and decisions touching the vital interests of the commonwealth are made in rooms insulated from the voice of the people.

In large measure, the power to create fundamental policy for the publicly owned forests has fallen to small professional groups. They make bitterly controversial decisions, choices between basic values, with little or no outside check. How this has come about, and whether there is any way the people can or should assume a voice in determining the future of their forest heritage, are questions that will be explored here.

Congress Delegates Its Responsibilities

In a democracy, laws and policies, including laws governing publicly owned resources, must theoretically be made in public by the people's elected representatives. But in today's overcomplicated world an overwhelmed Congress has been forced to delegate a large measure of legislative power to specialized executive and administrative agencies the officials of which are not elected or directly controlled by the people.

When congressional relinquishment of the law-making function first assumed major proportions, in the early days of the New Deal, the Supreme Court tried to halt the trend. The justices declared that legislative power cannot be delegated and that Congress can permit the executive agencies to make "regulations" only within the boundaries of carefully prescribed standards. But growing government soon broke through this retaining wall, and eventually the courts ceased to demand strict standards for delegation.

Congress has passed over the control of different portions of the nation's forest land to three not always cooperative executive agencies of the federal government: the Forest Service in the Department of Agriculture, and the National Park Service and the Bureau of Land Management in the Department of the Interior. The Forest Service has the largest share. It administers all public lands reserved as national forests. The National Park Service has jurisdiction over areas of special scenic or historic significance, including parks, monuments, battlefields, and other reservations. The Bureau of Land Management controls immense stretches of public land, much of it treeless but also including choice timber on the West Coast and other forests in Alaska. Congress has granted each of these agencies sweeping powers of legislation and policy-making.

The basic charter of the Forest Service is a statute passed in 1960[1] which declares:

It is the policy of Congress that the national forests are established and shall be administered for outdoor recreation, range, timber, watershed, and wildlife and fish purposes. ... The Secretary of Agriculture is authorized and directed to develop and administer the renewable surface resources of the national forests for multiple use and sustained yield of the several products and services obtained therefrom. In the administration of the national forests due consideration shall be given to the relative values of the various resources in particular areas. ...

The two crucial terms are defined as follows:

"Multiple use" means: The management of all the various renewable surface resources of the national forests so that they are utilized in the combination that will best meet the needs of the American people; making the most judicious use of the land for some or all of these resources or related services over areas large enough to provide sufficient latitude for periodic adjustments in use to conform to changing needs and conditions; that some land will be used for less than all of the resources; and harmonious and coordinated management of the various resources, each with the other, without impairment of the productivity of the land, with consideration being given to the relative values of the various resources, and not necessarily the combination of uses that will give the greatest dollar return or the greatest unit output.

"Sustained yield of the several products and services" means the achievement and maintenance in perpetuity of a high-level annual or regular periodic output of the various renewable resources of the national forests without impairment of the productivity of the land.

Earlier statutes giving the Secretary of Agriculture legislative authority were left standing as additional sources of power. A sampling of these shows the nature of the standards fixed as "guides" to the Secretary's action. He is authorized, on thirty days' notice, to sell timber in the national forests "for the purpose of preserving the living and growing timber and promoting the younger growth ..." to the extent "compatible with the utilization of the forests." He can set aside areas for town sites upon a "satisfactory showing of need therefor." He may permit the use of national forest land for hotels, resorts, facilities, summer homes, stores, or commercial, industrial, or public buildings, provided only that this does not "preclude the general public from full enjoyment of the natural, scenic, recreational, and other aspects of the national forests." When he finds that lands are "chiefly valuable for agriculture," and "may be occupied for agricultural purposes without injury to such national forests and . . . are not needed for public purposes," he may open them to homestead entry "in his discretion." He may permit the use of rights of way for electrical plants, power lines, radio and television, and other communication facilities "upon a finding . . . that the same is not incompatible with the public interest." He may permit roads and railroads, and in his discretion he may permit rights of way for dams, ditches, canals, and reservoirs.

The National Park Service in the Interior Department is required to preserve the special values of its lands; it cannot open them to multiple use. Nevertheless, it can make policy within wide statutory boundaries. The Secretary of the Interior is authorized to "make and publish such rules and regulations as he may deem necessary or proper for the use and management of the parks . . . sell or dispose of timber . . . where in his judgment the cutting of such timber is required in order to control the attacks of insects or diseases or otherwise conserve the scenery or the natural or historic objects in any such park . . . provide in his discretion for the destruction of such animals and of such plant life as may be detrimental to the use of any of said parks . . . grant privileges, leases and permits for the use of land for the accommodation of visitors . . . for periods not exceeding thirty years . . . grant the privilege to graze livestock . . . when in his judgment such use is not detrimental to the primary purpose for which such park . . . was created . . . grant said privileges, leases and permits and enter into contracts relative to the same . . . without advertising and without securing competitive bids . . ."

In addition, the Secretary may grant rights of way for power and communication facilities if these are not incompatible with the public interest; build airports in or in close proximity to the national parks if an airport is necessary to the proper performance of the Department's functions; build roads, bridges, and trails; and contract for services and accommodations for the public. He may also authorize timber sales, grazing, leases of land, and rights of way in specific parks; for example, in Sequoia and Yosemite Parks he may "sell and permit the removal of such matured or dead or down timber as he may deem necessary or advisable for the protection or improvement of the park . . ."

The miscellany of forest lands under the control of the Bureau of Land Management in the Interior Department is subject to no single pattern of statutory regulation. The lands forfeited under the Oregon and California Railroad and Coos Bay Wagon Road grants—among the nation's finest forests—are to be managed ". . . for permanent forest production, and the timber thereon shall be sold, cut, and removed in conformity with the principle of sustained yield for the purpose of providing a permanent source of timber supply, protecting watersheds, regulating stream flow, and contributing to the economic stability of local communities and industries, and providing recreational facilities."

Timber in Alaska may be sold by the Secretary of the Interior if necessary for consumption in Alaska; and he may sell "so much thereof as he may deem proper." In cases not otherwise governed by law, the Secretary may sell timber on the public lands if the sale "would not be detrimental to the public interest"; he may also allow public or non-profit bodies to take timber "in his discretion." He may also sell dead, down, or damaged timber and permit some residents to cut timber.

In general, lands under the jurisdiction of the Secretary of the Interior, not otherwise reserved, may be disposed of in small units to any governmental body or non-profit corporation for "public" or "recreational" purposes; small tracts may be sold or leased to private individuals for residence, recreation, business, or community sites unless this will impair the use of water for grazing or irrigation. And various types of rights of way may be granted. Many other statutes bear on these lands; they add up to the broadest sort of authority for the Bureau of Land Management.

The standards Congress has used to delegate authority over the forests are so general, so sweeping, and so vague as to represent a turnover of virtually all responsibility. "Multiple use" does establish that the forests cannot be used exclusively for one purpose, but beyond this it is little more than a phrase expressing the hope that all competing interests can somehow be satisfied and leaving the real decisions to others. The "relative values" of various resources are to be given "due consideration," but Congress has not indicated what those values are or what action shall be deemed "due consideration." Congress has directed "harmonious and coordinated management of the various resources," but it has left the Forest Service to deal with the problem that different uses of resources often clash rather than harmonize. Most significantly, Congress has told the Forest Service to "best meet the needs of the American people" but has left it entirely up to the Service to determine what those needs are.

What is the job of Congress if not to determine the needs of the people and how they should be met? The Forest Service has been given authority to decide whether the American people need the forests more for resources or for recreation or for wilderness or for dams and public power. And because Congress has offered no standards or policies of its own, almost any choice by the Forest Service would be within its delegated authority. Whether it cuts trees, builds dams, puts up hotels, or leaves the woods undeveloped, it would be hard indeed to hold the outcome to be legally in conflict with any congressional mandate.

The standards used for the areas under the Bureau of Land Management, and to a large extent those under the national parks, are equally vague. Words like "not incompatible with the public interest," "extent compatible with the utilization of the forests," "satisfactory showing of need therefor," are mere euphemisms that abdicate all real power; they are like the mumbled "drive carefully" employed by fathers when handing over the car keys.

The power granted by Congress is awesome. It is nothing less than the power to determine forever the character and use of the nation's forest heritage. For example, the authority to permit timber to be cut and sold, possessed to some extent by all three agencies, is the authority to make a permanent choice between wilderness and a forest busy with roads and bulldozers. The authority to permit the construction of permanent buildings, specifically granted to the Forest Service and the Park Service, is sufficient to allow the commercialization of recreation on a resort basis; parts of Yosemite and Glacier Parks are visible illustrations.

In view of this transfer of authority from Congress to three executive agencies, some very important questions arise. Are the decisions of the agencies made openly or in private? Are they made after deliberation and debate? Does the public have a chance to participate? Is there any check or review of what is decided? Answers to these questions are a measure of the degree to which the people retain control over the two hundred million acres of forest lands that they own.

The Agencies Make Policies

The forest agencies have adopted elaborate internal procedures in order to exercise their management, policy, and planning functions. Decisions are reviewed and rereviewed from field offices up to carpeted Washington chambers in stately administrative progression. But with only a few exceptions—important but limited—decisions are made wholly within the executive agencies, without notice to or participation by the public, and without effective check or review beyond the Secretary of Agriculture or of Interior.[2]

In the Forest Service, procedure begins with planning. National, regional, and sub-regional guides are prepared, with the assistance of Forest Service personnel on all levels. These tend to be very general. Specific decisions usually follow an upward route from local Forest Service officers, who make the proposals, through review at a regional level, to final approval in Washington. If the decision requires funds, it will also be considered by budget officials in the Department of Agriculture, by the Budget Bureau, and ultimately by Congress as part of the appropriation procedure.

Throughout this activity there are outside influences of varying importance. Local rangers are officially encouraged to participate in local civic activities, and to discuss the Service's plans on the local level. The Service appoints national and regional advisory councils which consult from time to time. On every level there are informal contacts with representatives of organizations, members of Congress, public officials, and interested persons who write in.

Procedures and influences in the National Park Service and the Bureau of Land Management are not dissimilar, but generally speaking they are less elaborate. All three agencies make "institutional" decisions—group decisions in which it is difficult to pinpoint individual responsibility.

In none of the three agencies do the over-all procedures provide an opportunity for the general public to participate. The agencies maintain close informal contacts with some outside persons and organizations, but these are not equivalent to the public. The agencies give no general notice of pending decisions and provide no general opportunity for the public to be heard. There is no procedure by which the public can initiate proposals. The post office is always available, but the influence of letters on official action is uncertain.

In short, there is a wealth of informal influence on the decision-making process, but virtually no formal public rights. The distinction is an important one, not only because the "informal public" is selective but because formal expressions of views must receive a degree of consideration and review that informal expressions cannot expect.

One exception to this practice occurs whenever some proposed action will interfere with the contractual rights or other legally protected interests of a particular individual. Then the person affected may seek to have the decision reconsidered. The Forest Service has detailed regulations governing the procedures in such situations.[3] The aggrieved person is permitted to file a written request for reconsideration, and may present evidence at a hearing, after which the agency renders a final decision based upon the record made at the hearing. The Bureau of Land Management has regulations for hearings on timber management units and rights of way in its northwest forests.

This special procedure is actually of very narrow effect. If confers no rights on the general public. And only in rare cases would any person have an individual legal grievance against the broader management or planning decisions of the agencies. Cancellation of a contract to sell timber could be reviewed at the instance of the buyer, but the underlying decision about the use of the land for lumbering, watershed, or recreation would usually not touch on any legal rights.

A far more important exception in terms of public participation is the so-called advisory hearing, which is sometimes held when an announced decision produces a loud enough clamor. This procedure is used on an *ad hoc* basis by the Park Service; the Forest Service has formally adopted it to assist them in their decisions about wilderness classifications. Although the advisory hearing method applies to only a tiny portion of the decisions concerning the forests, it reveals a great deal about the underlying problems of public participation in forest planning.

The Forest Service has recognized the desirability of preserving some forests in their natural state through regulations that provide for the classification of sections as wilderness areas or wild areas. Such areas are closed to lumbering, to roads, and to the more civilized forms of recreational use; they are to be preserved as much as possible in their primitive condition.[4]

Under Forest Service regulations wilderness and wild areas may be established, modified, or eliminated by order of the Secretary of Agriculture for wilderness areas or the Chief of the Forest Service for wild areas. Any such action may be preceded by an advisory hearing at which members of the public can appear and present their views. Notice of the contemplated action must be given at least ninety days before the effective date. Then, "if there is any demand for a public hearing" the regional forester is directed to hold one, and to make a report of it to the Chief of the Forest Service, who submits recommendations to the Secretary of Agriculture.

These regulations, which have the force of law, are supplemented by inter-office directives to Forest Service officials. Under the Forest Service Manual, action is begun by a district ranger, who prepares a report describing the area and assessing its "value for recreation versus value for other uses." The report then goes to the forest supervisor, who reviews it, amends it if necessary, and forwards it to the regional forester with recommendation for approval or disapproval. The latter can reject or forward it to the Chief. If the Chief tentatively approves, the regional forester posts notice of the proposed action and states that a hearing will be held if there is reasonable demand. The regional forester must also see that the notice is brought to the attention of groups known to be interested in wilderness and wild areas.

If the regional forester determines that there is demand for a hearing, it is his responsibility to call one. It is public and informal, and held before a presiding officer appointed by the regional forester. Ordinarily he is an attorney with the Department of Agriculture. The time and place of the hearing are apparently discretionary with the regional forester. At the hearing, a Forest Service representative outlines the proposal under consideration and then other persons are permitted to present their views. Cross-examination is not allowed, but questions for other speakers may be addressed to the presiding officer. After the hearing the presiding officer prepares a report containing a summary of the issues and the testimony, and this is submitted to the Chief to assist him in making his decision.

In any hearing procedure the crucial elements are notice to the public, opportunity to be heard, the method of decision, and the method of reviewing the decision. The advisory hearing procedure raises problems in each of these areas.

Forest Service regulations go to considerable lengths to provide adequate notice: publication in local newspapers, posting, and special notification of interested groups. The difficulty is that wilderness classification is of interest to the public as a whole, yet only local people, plus certain special interest groups, are likely to hear about any given proposal. Hence the hearing is likely to be a debate among local interests, rather than an assessment in terms of national goals. The people of eastern cities have a major stake in forest policy, yet they are unlikely to be represented at hearings. Perhaps there is no realistic way that notice could be given nationally. But the problem is real.

Opportunity to be heard is freely granted to all, but the difficulty is that the issues open for discussion at the hearing may be, as a practical matter, severely limited. It is likely to be a *pro* or *con* debate on the proposal itself without any practical way to consider alternatives. This is not necessarily the fault of the Forest Service procedures but may be inherent in the nature of the advisory hearing itself.

The process of decision, on the other hand, raises problems that flow very clearly from the specific hearing procedures. A proposal to establish or change a wilderness area is initiated by local Forest Service officials. These same officials are then responsible for the appointment of an officer to preside at the hearing. This officer performs only the very limited function of reporting the testimony. According to Forest Service practice, the real decision is that of the regional forester and the Chief, both of whom have been responsible, with their subordinates, for the original recommendation.

As a result, one group of persons holds the functions of advocate and judge. There is no provision for a detached judgment. The procedure thereby does violence to the well-established principle of separation of functions. Lawyers know from long experience that disinterested, well considered decisions are most frequently reached by a clear-cut separation between those who advocate and those who decide. The danger is not necessarily bias or unfairness, but simply the likelihood of a closed or made-up mind, a weakness to which all human beings are subject. Many agencies called upon to decide between competing interests have established a separate group of hearing officers who do not share in the day-to-day work. It is too much to expect that foresters who initiate and argue in support of a particular proposal can then adequately evaluate public criticism or counterproposals that often represent thinking they have earlier rejected.

Another problem with the advisory hearings is that the decision does not have to be supported by a statement of reasons. This can of course be a barren formality, but it can also have the effect of requiring someone to consider the testimony at the hearing and explain to himself (and therefore to others) why one point of view is to be accepted and another rejected. In a purely advisory hearing the public may talk, but there is no assurance that anyone will listen. Requiring an explanation for a decision might encourage listening. Furthermore, a statement of reasons gives some basis for a reviewing officer to determine whether a decision is well taken.

The final defect in the Forest Service advisory hearing procedure is the lack of any method for the public to participate in the review of a decision. If an initial decision is made after a hearing, and based upon reasons publicly stated, dissatisfied persons should have the opportunity to object and argue (at least in writing) before the Chief of the Forest Service or the Secretary of Agriculture makes his final decision. The present procedure has little provision for the correction of error, and little to ensure that final decisions are made only after genuine deliberation.

If public participation in forest agency planning is considered desirable, the advisory hearing procedure has serious shortcomings. It does not live up to the standards of the Administrative Procedure Act and the general law that has developed around the Act. At the same time it must also be said that advisory hearings, even though used for only one of the many types of forest decisions, are better than no hearings at all, and certainly better than relying solely on informal consultations with a few specially interested groups and individuals.

Public Rights Under the Law

Does the public have any rights that have been established by statutes or by the courts in these matters to do with public lands? In other words, does the general law offer any means by which members of the public can force an agency to heed their views?

In the few times when citizens have attempted to challenge the decisions of management concerning the public lands, they have been rebuffed by the courts. In 1961 the Superintendent of Yellowstone Park undertook an elk-slaughtering program that aroused intense controversy. Three men, all outfitters and guides, brought a suit in which they alleged that the Superintendent's action would drive them out of business; that it was a wanton, cruel, and needless slaughter; and that the Superintendent had shown a high-handed and autocratic attitude toward the complainants. Dismissing the suit, the court said that it could not "correct mistakes or wrongs allegedly resulting from abuse of discretion or from absence of necessity; [the courts] cannot assume a wisdom superior to that of the executive or legislative departments with respect to the disposition of animals in Yellowstone Park." Similarly, a land classification decision under the Taylor Grazing Act has been held to be non-reviewable, and so has a proclamation setting aside an area as a national monument. And when a citizen sought to challenge a Presidential proclamation prohibiting the hunting of wild geese, he was told that there was no judicial review because the action was "a proper exercise of the unlimited and unreviewable discretion vested and reposed by the [Migratory Bird Treaty] Act."

Congress seems to have intended these results. None of the statutes that confer powers over forest management on the Department of the Interior or the Department of Agriculture provides that the public must be allowed to participate in basic decisions of the National Park Service, the Forest Service, or the Bureau of Land Management. Congress, at least in those specific statutes, has vested sole policy-making authority in the agencies. There is, however, a general statute dealing with the procedures of all government agencies. This is the Administrative Procedure Act, passed in 1946, which lays down procedural requirements for two types of agency processes: "adjudication" and "rule-making." Of the two, most forest management decisions more nearly resemble "rule-making." About this the Act says: (1) notice of proposed rule-making must be published in the *Federal Register;* (2) interested persons must be allowed to submit their views orally or in writing; (3) the agency must incorporate in any rules adopted "a concise general statement of their basis and purpose."

If the forest agencies conformed to these requirements, there would be a substantial increase in public participation. They do not so conform, and it is far from certain that the Act really requires that they must.

In the first place, the rule-making provisions do not apply to "any matter relating . . . to public property." While it may be argued that this refers only to property in the narrow sense of buildings or street lamps, the exception can certainly be read to sweep in all forms of public ownership. In the second place, forest management decisions might be held not to come within the Act's vague and unpredictable definition of rule-making. In the third place, even in cases where the action is clearly rule-making, an agency is not required to observe the Act if it finds, for good cause, "that notice and public procedure are impracticable, unnecessary, or contrary to the public interest." Furthermore, the Act requires no procedures whatever for "interpretative rules, general statements of policy, rules of agency organization, procedure or practice. . . ."

The Act does state that interested persons may appear and present their views to "any agency" on "any issue" unless this would interfere with the orderly conduct of the public business. But this provision has rarely been employed in practice, and it is doubtful if it confers on the public any enforceable rights if an agency chooses to keep the door closed.

Unless the three forest management agencies voluntarily subject themselves to the Administrative Procedure Act, the question of its applicability to them can be settled only by court decision. But here another difficulty arises: the Act says that judicial review is barred on any agency action that is "by law committed to agency discretion." The issue has not been squarely decided, but it seems likely that building a road, classifying a forest area for lumbering or recreation—in fact, all management and planning actions—would be held to be within "agency discretion." In short, the public can look for little help from the Administrative Procedure Act.

Leaving aside the Act's vagaries and exceptions, are there any rules of *general law* under which the public may have a right to participate in forest planning? Here a highly technical but probably insurmountable legal obstacle bars the way. The courts have held that the public as such cannot complain of government action; only an individual with a specialized interest called "standing" can assert any rights.[5] In other words, a member of the public could complain of action concerning the forests only if he had an individual contractual or other special interest to distinguish him from other members of the public. A concessionaire with a contract to maintain a hotel on National Park land might have such a right; one whose favorite fishing spot in a national forest was threatened by bulldozers surely would not. It was on grounds of "lack of standing" that the courts held that a group of American citizens, citizens of Pacific islands, and other nationals could not challenge proposed nuclear testing. In view of the nature of forest management decisions, it would be rare for anyone to have "legal standing" under which he might participate or protest.

Behind this technical legal rule of "standing" lies a major question: Who is the "interested public" in terms of a planning decision? Clearly it is not just the special interests—the loggers or concessionaires—that are affected; it is the entire population that uses or might use the forests for any purpose. The problem of "interest" lurks under the surface of all discussions of "public rights" in the agency process.

In any event, although the law is always in a state of change, neither Congress nor the courts have yet recognized public legal rights in forest management beyond the point of voluntary invitation by the agencies themselves. And it should be added that it is far from certain that judicial review of a typical Forest Service or Park Service decision would have any important effect even if it could be obtained. Courts cannot review the wisdom of agency decisions but only the limited question of whether a given action was a proper exercise of the power granted by Congress. Given statutory authority as broad as the Multiple Use Act, it is hard to see how a court could overturn as "unauthorized" any imaginable decision concerning policy or planning for the forests.

The Professionals and the Public

Is a greater role for the general public in forest management possible or desirable? Before this can be answered, two prior questions must be asked. First, is forest management so technical and specialized that only professionals can intelligently contribute to it? Second, even if forest management is not unrelievedly technical, is unrestricted management by professionals desirable because it is most likely to achieve a balanced response to the public interest?

Virtually every forest management decision depends in part upon factual information of a technical nature. A knowledge of timber, soil, watershed, fire hazards, and recreation is essential to determine what uses can be made of a particular section, and under what circumstances. However, when the technical information is all in and fully evaluated, it will not necessarily dictate, in and of itself, the choices that management may make.

The Forest Service recognizes that management requires conscious planning because the national forests and their resources are not adequate fully to satisfy individual desires for space and other resources. In other words, after the possible uses have been ascertained, there must often be a choice between them. It is this choice that involves non-technical judgments, as well as a consideration of the choice in its relation to over-all planning for the future. The Forest

Service Handbook recognizes this when it says that, to merit classification as wilderness, an area must satisfy the following condition:

Its tangible and intangible values as a wilderness area must fully offset the value of all resources which would be rendered inaccessible or otherwise unavailable, both within and adjacent to the proposed boundaries, as a result of the classification.

And there must even be a choice among kinds of recreation:

The wilderness classification precludes many other types of use and it is necessary to consider all competing values. A majority of people who go to the forest for recreation do not have the ability or the desire to get away from the easy travel made possible by roads. They are interested in camping near their cars, picnicking, touring, and visiting summer homes or resorts. Many feel that the wilderness classification is discriminatory because it permanently excludes them from areas which might otherwise be developed for their enjoyment.

Wilderness classification clashes with many economic interests. It shuts off all revenues that would otherwise grow from the forests. And it directly hurts certain specific elements in the economy. Among these are the lumber industry, segments of the tourist recreation industry, and local school and road districts, which by law are entitled to 25 per cent of the receipts from timber sales from national forests within their county.

Can it be said that the issues in wilderness classification depend wholly upon specialized knowledge? Clearly the answer is no. On the contrary, the ultimate issue is essentially political—the choice between the desires of different segments of the community. And this is the kind of issue on which the public may have independent views. Thus, in New York State the entire forest preserve was set aside as wilderness through the political process, by virtue of a famous provision in the state constitution:

The lands of the state, now owned or hereafter acquired, constituting the forest preserve as now fixed by law, shall be forever kept as wild forest lands. They shall not be leased, sold or exchanged, or be taken by any corporation, public or private, nor shall the timber thereon be sold, removed or destroyed. . . .

Significantly, the constant proposals to amend this "forever wild" provision of the New York constitution in order to permit more civilized forms of recreation always produce widespread concern among the general public.

Wilderness classification is not the only decision demanding a choice between conflicting interests. For example, use of the forests for grazing may interfere with various other values, including recreation, as John Ise has pointed out in his book, *Our National Park Policy:* "The general rule is that *any* grazing of a forest is injurious, whether by domestic or wild animals, although there may be exceptions to this. . . . The problem of the Park and Forest Services often is: How much damage are we justified in inflicting on the land for the sake of promoting wool or meat production?"

As another example, building a dam for irrigation purposes creates a lake that may look scenic on a map but may actually be an eyesore because of changing water level. Ise says: "A dam usually raises the level of a lake reservoir in the spring of the year, killing trees along the shores; but this water is for irrigation use, and by the end of the summer the level of the lake is far down, perhaps to the point where there is scarcely any water left, and there is revealed a broad shore strip of dead trees, black stumps, trash, mud or dry earth. A dammed lake is usually damned scenically." The greatest disaster ever to occur to a national park was the drowning of Hetch Hetchy Valley in Yosemite, a magnificent canyon, to supply water to San Francisco via a dam on the Tuolumne River.

The major economic use of the forests is lumbering. A decision to lumber has consequences for all other potential uses. It affects grazing and watershed. It profoundly affects recreation, even mass recreation, since the appearance and availability of the woods are altered and the public is crowded into other areas. It permanently changes the character of the region, introduces roads and machinery, and intrudes an element of civilization virtually impossible to eradicate. Even such a seemingly technical question as whether to lumber a wind-damaged wilderness area to protect it against fire may involve major choices of policy, for wilderness values can be destroyed under the appearance of protecting them.

Choice between interests must also be made in such "managerial" decisions as whether to permit hotels, picnic grounds, ski jumps (with or without recorded yodels), or motorboats on forest lakes.

Such choices all require specialized information as a preliminary. How suitable is an area for grazing; how much damage will a given number of animals cause; how great would be the economic return; what are the alternatives? But after this information is in hand, the competition of interests still remains and a choice must still be made—a choice on which the public might have intelligent views.

Moreover, even after the choice is made, there are policies to be determined concerning each type of use. For example, it is decided to devote an area to recreation; judgments must then be made about the relative desirability of closed or open shelters, giant camp-grounds, concessions, paved paths to scenic attractions, and so forth. These are the things that will determine the character of the area. Here, again, the issues are understandable enough to make public participation possible. "Housekeeping" usually involves assumptions about what the public wants. Before concrete bridges for horses are built to keep riders' feet dry while crossing streams, before raucous gasoline-powered tote gotes are allowed to shatter the forest calm, before luxurious hotels are built, and before a man-made waterfall of fire is approved as a nightly tourist attraction in a valley famous for its natural waterfalls, the public might well be given an opportunity to express "non-technical" views.

Expert advice is indispensable. But in view of the general policy of Congress, expressed in the Administrative Procedure Act, that interested members of the public should have a chance to take part in formulating decisions of general and future effect, and in view of the fact that the forests and parks have such relevance to the lives of the American people, exclusion of the public from most decisions is difficult to justify on the ground that the decisions are "technical" only.

Naturally, the mere fact that many of these issues are non-technical ones of interest to the public does not demonstrate that the public should decide them. "The public" can be shortsighted and ill-informed and indifferent. Professional managers, on the other hand, can sometimes take a broader, more detached, and more knowledgeable view of the public interest, and thus give the people better service.

There are strong arguments in favor of leaving forest management to the experts. But the issue is not whether the public or the experts are to manage, but whether, and to what degree, the experts should be made aware of, and responsive to, public opinion. The answer to this question depends in part on whether the experts have shortcomings that public participation might remedy.

One problem common to many groups of professional managers in government is the tendency to lean heavily toward one of the various conflicting elements of the public that they serve. The Interstate Commerce Commission, for example, has often been charged with being "railroad-minded" although it also has responsibilities to the customers of railroads, to truckers, and to the public as a whole. The same charge of "one-sidedness" has been made about the Maritime Board, the Federal Power Commission, and others. The Forest Service is sometimes considered to be unduly sympathetic to the lumber industry, one of its "clients." It is said to emphasize the timber management and sales part of its function over other aspects of "multiple use." Another complaint sometimes heard is that the Service, which has an unusually decentralized administrative organization, is overly concerned with the immediate local needs of communities near the forests, and correspondingly less responsive to over-all national and long-range needs. Whether these particular complaints are justified is not important; they merely suggest a general administrative tendency that all agencies have to watch.

Another tendency of professional managers is to develop a definite point of view or mode of thinking that makes them less receptive to attitudes beyond their own perspective. Foresters tend to think about forests in certain ways. They tend to think in terms of productivity. A leading forester once spoke of the Adirondack wilderness preserve as an area condemned to "economic waste," "offset by no tangible public benefits." He argued that lumbering does not destroy scenic values. "Even clear cutting followed by fire affronts the eye only until nature heals the wounds with green."

A somewhat similar point of view is found in the Forest Service Handbook's directions to rangers when they are preparing recommendations on wilderness classification. They are asked to discuss "economic and social values, if any, which would be withdrawn from use if area were established but which might be realized from commodity use, if area were not established. Discuss particularly the effect of withdrawing commercial timber on the allowable cut of adjacent working circles." One Forest Service instruction showed that even a "professional" attitude about beauty in trees may differ from that of the public: "Many people like big timber and do not understand or appreciate vigor or thrift in a tree. To them, a large overmature, spiketopped, catfaced, conky old veteran is magnificent, has character and is much to be preferred to a thrifty intermediate tree. Annual growth and clear lumber are of little concern to people enjoying the area for recreation, hence a big branching wolf tree may be much more desirable than a clear-boled tree."

Many professional managers are also inclined to think of themselves as owners. Having devoted their lives to a particular job of management, they begin quite unconsciously to think of "their" post office, "their" television channels, or "their" forests. It is an easy step from here to the feeling that they alone know what is best, and without always realizing it they may close their ears to the "outsiders."

The profession of forestry has strong elements of solidarity. A vigorous esprit de corps, a proud history, and many common experiences bind foresters together. The same is true of Park Service officers. These experts sometimes come to believe that they can best perform their responsibilities without "interference" by those who are mere amateurs.

These tendencies of government managers are found in many different agencies. What makes them especially significant in the area of forest and park management is the degree to which the three agencies in this field engage in long-range planning and permanent choices based upon notions of the public interest. Planning of this sort peculiarly requires an openness to many points of view. Indeed, it can be argued that in a democracy the "public interest" has no objective meaning except insofar as the people have defined it; the question cannot be what is "best" for the people, but what the people, adequately informed, decide they want. Professional forest and recreation managers, no matter how dedicated, are not necessarily qualified to engage in this form of planning on their own.

NOTES

1.   Multiple Use Act, Public Law 86–517 §§ 1 and 2, 74 Stat. 215, 16 U.S.C. §§ 528, 529 (June 12, 1960).

2.   An excellent general description of policy formation and decision-making for the public lands is found in Clawson & Held, *The Federal Lands: Their Use and Management,* Chapter 3 (1957).

3.   36 C.F.R. § 211.2. There are actually two separate procedures. The first—§ 211.2 (a) (1)—applies to the following persons:

> Any person having a contractual relationship with the Forest Service (other than one relating to the construction, alteration or repair of public buildings or works, or to the purchase of administrative supplies, equipment, materials or services), including an application therefor, aggrieved by any administrative action or decision of an officer of the Forest Service relating thereto . . .

This is the class of persons entitled to hearings. A second class of persons, entitled only to file a written statement and to have a reviewing officer prepare a statement of review and explanation, is described as follows [§211.2(b)]:

> Any person aggrieved by any administrative action of an officer of the Forest Service other than those relating to contractual relationships . . .

The key word here is "aggrieved" which in its legal meaning is limited to persons suffering certain types of "legal injury."

4.   A wilderness or wild area is one in which "there shall be no roads or other provisions for motorized transportation, no commercial timber cutting, and no occupancy under special use permit for hotels, stores, resorts, summer homes, organization camps, hunting and fishing lodges, or similar uses." 36 C.F.R. § 251.20(a).

5.   "Standing" is an elusive term that defies translation into ordinary English. Even a lawyer as free from jargon as the late Judge Jerome Frank could only explain that *absent* a statute a citizen has no "standing" to complain in court about government action unless the action "invades or will invade a private substantive legally-protected interest of the plaintiff citizen; such invaded interest must be either of a 'recognized' character at 'common law,' or a substantive private legally-protected interest created by statute." *Associated Industries of New York* v. *Ickes,* 134F. 2d 694, 700 (2d Cir. 1943), vacated as moot, 320 U.S. 707.

POLITICAL BARGAINING
AND POLLUTION CONTROL
Matthew Holden, Jr.

The hypothesis that regulatory agencies tend to engage in some loose interchange (bargaining) with regulated parties until they find a settlement which is tolerable to them all is based largely upon the experience of federal economic agencies. In order to show its relevance to pollution control, we shall draw some illustrative material from state pollution control agencies. Characteristically, these agencies are inter-departmental committees with the addition of some persons designated by law as representatives of the "public" or of specified private interests, e.g., "agriculture," "mining," etc.[1]

In addressing themselves to their mission, they start with the difficult problem of defining what "pollution" is. In common speech, this seems rather easy, for it apparently means some "defilement" from a natural condition or a basic change induced by some human notion which is beyond the character of natural stream processes to rectify. But it may even occur that "natural pollution" has some of the same effects as human action. Hynes shows this by citing a Belgian study to the effect that spruce and red cedar in the Ardennes so shadowed trout streams that algae would not form. Moreover, some unidentified noxious substance appeared to emanate from the needles producing toxic effects in the streams. As a result, fishing was impaired many miles away in larger streams in whose headwaters regions the forests stood.[2]

The sensible *policy* conception is that pollution is simply whatever action produces a biological, chemical, or physical condition averse to those interests which it is the current business of policymakers to sustain.[3] No water use is wholly without consequences for some alternative use. For example, if the quantity of water is too small, in relation to the acreage to be irrigated, then as water is passed through one field into the stream and on into a second field, and so on, the re-

Reprinted from *Pollution Control as a Bargaining Process: An Essay on the Regulatory Process* (Ithaca, N.Y.: Cornell University Water Resources Center, 1966), pp. 11–40, by permission of the author. Some footnotes have been deleted and the others renumbered.

used water will pick up quantities of salt injurious to the crops of the later users. Now we may think of drinking water as a wholly innocent use, but if the volume of water withdrawn for city drinking increases, then it follows that the damage to downstream farmers will increase simply because there is that much less water for irrigation. Since all men use water, in short, the problem of regulation is to make decisions about alternative uses in such a way as to preclude those uses not desired, to sustain those uses desired, and to give priorities even among those desired uses.

So elusive a problem tends to evoke wide discretionary powers as may be illustrated from the recent (1961) Texas legislation which defines pollution as:

... any discharge or deposit of waste into or adjacent to the waters of the State, *or any act or omission* in connection therewith, that by itself, or in conjunction with any other act or omission or acts or omissions, causes or continues to cause or will cause such waters to be unclean, noxious, odorous, impure, contaminated, altered or otherwise affected to such an extent that they are rendered harmful, detrimental or injurious to public health, safety or welfare, or to terrestrial or aquatic life, or the growth or propagation thereof, or to the use of such waters for domestic, commercial, industrial, agricultural, recreational or other lawful reasonable use.[4]

The language of the cited statute makes clear that from the public point of view *pollution control* actually becomes the *control of the actions of the people* and, thus, a species of social regulation. The discretionary latitude permitted the agency (in this case, the Water Pollution Control Board) is substantially similar to the latitude permitted those bodies which we characteristically call "regulatory" agencies. Such legislation represents one further step in a long set of moves from the historic police power doctrine that the public official has the inherent power to abate nuisances, but its central feature remains the legal control over discharge practices. From the initial position where the major control act was to forbid particular persons to continue to discharge particular matter, the system has increasingly broadened to permit advance specification of kinds of permissible and impermissible discharges (effluent standards), to require advance permission for discharges, and to specify the particular characteristics to be maintained in bodies of water (quality standards).

In order to make clear the application of the basic hypothesis (regulation as bargaining) to the state experience, we shall wish to consider three major aspects: (1) the manifestations of bargaining, (2) the reasons for bargaining (or why bargaining occurs), and (3) the techniques of bargaining (or how bargaining occurs).

The Standard-Setting Process

As we have said already, pollution control systems have developed out of *ad hoc* exercises of the police power, and these exercises have been directed to the control of real or putative water-borne diseases.[5] As the visible threats to public health have receded, other quality considerations have come to be more important, and as these have also been more complicated, pollution control agencies have moved toward the general prescription of rules to govern action, rather than *ad hoc* controls. With a growing presumption that it would be "unreasonable" to impose *ad hoc* controls to sustain "inappropriate" uses, pollution control policies have been oriented toward rule-making or, as it is characteristically described, setting standards. The standard-setting process will be somewhat altered by the Water Quality Act of 1965, but even before that Act at least forty-five states had established some legal process for establishing some form of standard.[6]

One of the first clues to whether an agency is in a position to ordain results is how it actually utilizes the legal process for the establishment of standards. Such standards have two main forms. *The first form is the "quality standard." The quality standard is to water use substantially as the "master plan" is to urban land use.* That is, it broadly establishes the preferable uses either in qualitative terms[7] (such as saying that the water in a particular stream shall be of a quality suitable for food processing) or in quantitative terms (such as saying that "it shall not contain less than 5 parts per million of dissolved oxygen"); this, by implication, eliminates or controls all uses adverse to that standard and sustains all uses which require such a standard. Quality standards are, no more than master plans, self-executing and nothing changes about the watercourse simply because an agency has promulgated a quality standard. The significant indicator to what happens is the rate at which the substances discharged into the stream *consume oxygen* ("biochemical oxygen demand" or BOD), so the other form of standard is an *"effluent standard."* Such a standard might, for instance, specify that any sewage discharged into streams shall first have undergone "primary treatment," which is the stage at which up to forty percent (40%) BOD reduction may be achieved.[8]

No one could have a realistic appreciation of whether the results he desired were feasible or not without some appreciation of the natural-scientific and technological problems involved in promulgating and implementing either a quality standard or an effluent standard, and the level of knowledge is much less than the untutored layman might suggest. (It is at least as complicated as the question of the cigarette-cancer relationship.) But it would be an even grosser misunderstanding to suppose that the parties affected let the issues rest on wholly technical terms. If this were so, then the process would be primarily "analytic" in March and Simon's terms.[9] But the actual evidence indicates that, while the various parties utilize the analytic confusions, they are moved largely by recognition of the implications of any particular decision for the interests which they have in mind.[10]

As a first example of the process, we may cite an experience in the Buffalo area discussed by Martin. As part of a more inclusive program, the state agency proposed to assign the Buffalo River to a classification of "D." This would have meant legal authority and obligation to control all other uses so that the water might be used for agriculture and industrial cooling. This would have restricted significantly its use for sewage or industrial waste disposal in the sense that any discharges into the river would have had to be discharges consistent with other parties' making agricultural and coolant uses. Immediately, the agency was beset by two mutually exclusive sets of claims. At public hearings (October 21, 1953), the sportsmen's clubs were present to object that the stream should be assigned to class "C," which would have protected fishing as well (i.e., the agency would have assumed the obligation to control any use adverse to fish life).

The counterpoint was provided by five major national firms who had plants along the river. Their brief argued for class "E," which would have permitted sewage and industrial waste disposal, and one firm went further to argue that "it had already spent $2,000,000 'solely for the benefit of the community.'" It stated further that installation of the treatment works necessary to conform to class "D" standards would cost the company $5,500,000 plus $1,000,000 annually for operation, and all for the maintenance of the Buffalo River as a fishing stream, ". . . which is no longer an appropriate use of these waters." [11] In this instance the industrial claims were accepted, for one year later (October 18, 1954) the Executive Secretary of the Board recommended, and the Board approved, a classification of "E" for the Buffalo River.

The same problem arises when effluent regulations are under consideration, whether these are or are not preceded by some fairly clear set of quality standards. We may illustrate this from one of the states in which pulp-and-paper manufacturing is important. A waste product involved in pulp manufacture is sulphite, which has the effect of reducing the oxygen level of streams by a significant margin. In this state, there had been a long-standing controversy since the oysterers and fishermen claimed that their interests were damaged by the adverse effects of spent sulphite discharges. At one point, the executive officer of the pulp-and-paper trade association called an emergency session of his trustees to meet with the executive officer of the pollution control agency to discuss new regulations proposed by the agency. These regulations had three facets. (1) They forbade further concentrations of sulphite waste liquors, i.e., the quantities of such liquors going into the streams should not increase. (The practical implication would be important process changes within the mills, assuming that production of pulp continued to increase, with the costs being borne by the producers.) (2) All pulp and paper mills should be equipped, within three years, for "adequate treatment for recovery of settleable solids." This is a question of physical pollution as well as chemical and, thus, different from the waste liquor problem. (3) All sulphite pulp mills should be equipped, within the same three years, with full recovery facilities.

In calling the special meeting, the executive secretary said:

In talking with me and members of the industry, (Blank) has asked that we "not get excited" or "disturbed" over the proposal or language. He feels that the proposal will get the oyster growers and fisheries off his back. He says he doesn't intend to require "full" recovery (85 percent was in one recent draft), and he strongly intimates that a number of the sulfite mills might now qualify for either permanent or long-run temporary permits. Frankly, in spite of some rather long discussion, I do not know what he intends. I have told him that the sudden raising of the settleable solids and recovery proposals would certainly raise questions among the industry members. He has asked for a private and unpublicized session with management to discuss and explain his intentions and his interpretation of the proposed rules.

When we consider that the oyster question had long been debated in this state, and that the oyster spokesmen had carried their fight to the national level in support of new federal police powers, we may interpret the interchange here (even though we have not had all sides) somewhat as follows: (1) By raising new questions, beyond the simple question of how much sulphite wastes the oyster beds could tolerate, the administrator raised the ante enough to prevent his having to bargain over that issue alone. (2) He had sought to promulgate the new and more stringent rules as a placatory gesture to the oystermen. (3) He had recognized that the additional rules would excite or disturb the pulp-and-paper industry. (4) He had hastened to assure them that he did not really mean all that, on the face of it, step 2 seemed to mean. (5) He had indicated that, though subject to much pressure by the pulp-and-paper people, he knew that he had enough power, simply by raising the issue, to create enough of a disturbance that they could not wholly refuse to cooperate, at least to the extent of a settlement which guaranteed the first step.

The basic summation of the standard-setting process is that, like other forms of administrative rule-making, it is actually an exercise in legislation by an administrative body. Such legislation, having been adopted, requires implementation if its promises actually are to be brought to fruition. Essentially, we can describe the next phase as that of policing and adjudication.

Bargaining for Compliance

Just as the technical complexity of their task gives pollution control agencies pause in rule-making, so the breadth of their task makes it necessary for them to make very basic choices in seeking compliance. They are similar to the Internal Revenue people, and rather dissimilar to, say, the welfare administrators, in that every discharger every day commits some act which potentially brings him within their jurisdiction. Since it is a physical impossibility to control every discharger in all the relevant details, they have three basic decisions to make: (1) whom to regulate and whom to ignore, (2) how long to wait before imposing regulations, and (3) what to accept as compliance with the regulatory objective.

The necessity to choose whom to regulate means that tactical selectivity (or picking a victim) may be of great moment and is strongly influenced by the extent to which the decisions in seeking compliance will be *punitive* or *distributive*. Few decisions can be wholly one or the other, but there is certainly a dominant tendency. Punitive decisions are those compliance with which will require some party to accept an obligation he would not otherwise have had, without conferring upon him or anyone else easily visible benefits not otherwise available. Distributive decisions (such as allocating TV franchises)[12] may penalize some but they clearly give rewards to others. The greater the potential dispersion of punitive decisions, the more selective the regulatory agency will tend to be about its precise target at any moment. If the regulatory agency is careless, what it may provoke is a widespread reaction (as does the police chief who tries to enforce every personal morality statute). Hence, tactical selectivity requires it to "pick a victim" upon whom it seems to stand some reasonable chance of making the enforcement stick. This may involve two options. One option is [to select a victim in such a way] that other potential subjects of enforcement will read the signs and reform themselves enough, before their turn comes, that they will not need to be subjected to actual proceedings. This was the practice of the Wisconsin Committee on Water Pollution, in its early years, when it deliberately neglected "small fry" and chose to direct itself against major symbolic targets.[13] The other form of picking the victim involves choosing one "so bad" that the victim cannot secure allies; this serves the purpose of showing that "something" is being done, with the implicit promise that others less "bad" will be permitted indefinitely to continue operations if they do not become "bad enough" to be a visible embarrassment to the agency.

The experience of the states has never, so far as we know, been studied in any comprehensive or detailed manner, so we are being speculative at this point, but the apparent record indicates that most of the agencies have felt inhibited about seeking any serious compliance at all. One indicator is the absence of *any pending case at all* in about half the states (20 out of 42, to be exact) which replied to the House Committee survey in 1960. Unlike such matters as labor relations, pollution control problems are sufficiently difficult to specify and to correct that settlement by private negotiation—leading to actual change in the physical situation—is most improbable. If this is so, and considering that most of the cases formally entered in the record actually continue for long times without actual change in the physical situation, we may only guess that most of the regulators have not really felt free to move.

This brings us to the second problem: when does the regulatory agency feel free to act or how long shall it wait? One of the commonest sources of external criticism is that a particular agency acts as if the problem "will just go away" if the agency heads wait long enough. Such criticism may be well founded, but it may also ignore the possibility that the delay which the outsider regards as inefficient, inertial, or lazy may actually be a highly rational administrative strategy likely to produce better results (in terms of the decision-makers' policy preferences) than any more vigorous and overt course of action. It may be an application to regulation of the politician's much-vaunted sense of timing.[14] When so used, it permits the regulatory decision-maker gradually to discover, identify, or manufacture packets of ends-and-means which may eventually lead to results he can find tolerable.

Once a decision-maker takes an action, many results will be attributed to that action when they are, in fact, logically and factually independent of it. If those results are undesirable, it is a sound strategy for the regulator not to make himself a lightning rod by moving into a situation so soon that he does attract such attributions to himself. One major kind of delay, therefore, is that which simply permits an inevitable situation to develop so far that the decision-maker *does not get any of the blame* for it.

Murphy reports that at a point when the State Committee on Water Pollution "ought" to have been enforcing clean-up regulations energetically, there was an economic crisis in the cheese industry. Smaller producers were being forced out of business at a very rapid rate. To avoid the political ramifications of any supposition that its "clean-up" regulations were contributing to economic hardship for the smaller producers, the Committee decided not to intervene, but "to let nature take its course before (stepping) in with pollution requirements for the survivors." [15]

Delay may also be a rational strategy reflecting the decision-maker's need to feel some pressure in order to have guidance about what the relevant constituencies want[16] and, indeed, about what the relevant constituencies are.[17] Officials who see a particular course of action as desirable may actually wait until an atmosphere arises in which their critics will "force" them to do what they might have preferred anyway, but which might have been too risky had they themselves taken the initiative. This second relationship may be indicated in one major eastern state which had placed great stress on the installation of municipal sewage treatment plants. The agency made what its officials thought great progress, but after 20 years, it was still the case that about 20 percent of the population of one metropolitan area (which had a population of more than 2,000,000) still resided in municipalities without sewage treatment plants.

This meant that their wastes went untreated in the stream, to the great dissatisfaction of adjacent municipalities which had met the financial costs of installing treatment plants. However, the delinquent municipalities took the position that they simply could not afford to meet the state standard.[18] For a long time, the regulatory agency held its action in abeyance, while the clamor from the neighboring municipalities (and the conservationist lobby) grew apace. The agency eventually undertook an enforcement proceeding which elicited bitter criticism from the delinquent municipalities and some opposition from important legislators. The legislators were particularly able to point out that the agency was "picking on little people" but not on major industrial firms (which were allied with the state administration). Under normal circumstances, some farily routine compromise might have been reached without any clear sign that significant change would be expected.

This possibility was foreclosed by a new factor: the federal presence and the federal dollar. The availability of federal grants under the Act of 1956 offered some promise of aid to the local governments involved, so that the regulatory agency now had some realistic basis on which to decline to accept the contention that "we cannot afford it." Secondly, the Public Health Service—in an effort to offset Congressional pressure on itself—had now started an enforcement proceeding under the Act of 1956 and, to forestall that proceeding, some show of action by the state agency was required. Since the maintenance of good relations with PHS was also critical to the state agency, the contrary pressure from local officials and their legislative spokesmen was no longer adequate and, for the first time, the regulatory agency set a firm construction schedule for primary treatment in all the concerned towns.

By proceeding in this manner, the regulatory agency achieved two objectives. (1) It was able to increase its own pressure on the non-complying municipalities through itself "submitting" to "outside" pressure which it could not deflect. (2) At the same time, it escaped for itself most of the criticism which would otherwise have been visited had it seemed to make the same demands upon the non-complying municipalities without "having to do so."

The third kind of decision which has to be made in the compliance process is simply what to accept as compliance. It may be illustrated by the case of a major steel firm which (as of October, 1964) was operating without a permit to discharge certain wastes into an adjacent river. When critical legislators raised the issue in February, 1966, the regulatory agency took the position that the steel firm was not really at fault (tantamount to saying that the firm had done all reasonable in compliance). The firm had applied for a permit as of May, 1965 (all the while continuing its operation), but the application had never been processed because the pertinent field office was "too short of staff." In this case, the policy objective (changing the quality of the stream) had been wholly unaffected by either new legislation or new administrative regulations because the agency was in a position where it felt that it had to accept the filing of an application as a sign of good intentions and good intentions in that context had to be accepted as compliance.

In the pulp-and-paper case, it will be recalled that the regulatory administrator had privately informed the industry spokesman that he did not intend to require full recovery of the relevant wastes (despite the fact that such language appeared in his proposed draft). He had also apparently intimated a willingness to treat formal industry acceptance of his proposed rules as sufficient evidence of good intentions that a number of plants would get "permanent or long-run temporary permits" which would require little or no change in their actual practices.

What these cases, and many similar ones, suggest is that the accretion of many small exceptions in the policing process amounts often to a significant deviation from the policy norm from which the regulatory agency began. The more this is so, the more it must be clear that large amounts of regulatory action have little or nothing to do with the achievement of any over-all systemic result, and much more to do with achieving a tolerable day-to-day working arrangement. That is what a bargaining arrangement is largely about. Now we must be frank to assert that our examples do not prove that bargaining is the dominant mode of decision in the regulation of pollution. Hence, the argument is in the nature of hypothesis. However, we have searched with some diligence for materials which indicate its absence and find them very sparse. Even if, however, we should more rigorously search and prove the point, we should be about where most political scientists and administrative lawyers would expect us to be. Apart from demonstrating to those mainly interested in pollution—whom, we assert, normally deny the relevance of bargaining—that it really does exist, how should we explain the process and why might we suppose the explanation consequential?

Incentives and Limits to Regulatory Bargaining

Regulatory decision-makers do not bargain simply because they lack knowledge of the problem or because they are given to the values of compromise and friendly settlement or because they are lacking in ethical fealty to the policy norms (although these all may be relevant from one time to another). The essential incentive is that the agency has some mission to interpret and to accomplish in some reasonable degree. If this is to be done, the agency has to behave in a way which increases the likelihood that regulated parties will yield compliance, for if compliance is less than some difficult-to-determine "enough," then the agency itself is a "failure." Failure has adverse consequences for the organization, its program, and those individuals who are responsible for the agency and its program.[19] Why does this conduce to bargaining? Because bargaining is the only way to maneuver the agency successfully through the environing web of constituency[20] relations, and those relations shape up around the agency's jurisdiction and the possible human consequences from its decisions therein.

The bargains made or avoided reflect the decision-makers' level of awareness of these consequences, and the clues to these consequences may be derived from (1) the technological character of the problem, (2) the social values and myths associated with the problem, (3) the largeness or smallness of the alternative points of decision to which the regulated interest may repair in quest of a favorable decision, and (4) the extent to which the regulatory agency and the regulated party must have continuous relations in the future or may have one-time-only relationships.

If the regulatory decision-maker looks to the future, in an act of policy, he has in a sense to try to change something about the present which threatens that future. In designing the appropriate rules, he has to make two main cognitive decisions. (1) Who or what is responsible for the situation which has to be changed? (2) What would be the consequences (including the adverse consequences) of prescribing certain action to change that situation? The more complex the technological situation, the more difficulty the regulator has in laying down rules which he feels confident in enforcing or which are actually enforceable no matter how confident he feels.

The difficulty of attributing responsibility is exemplified by a well-known stream in southwestern Pennsylvania, Slippery Rock Creek, just above Pittsburgh. In that area, much public attention focuses on stream pollution due to drainage of mine acids. In 1964, Slippery Rock Creek was the scene of one of the country's most dramatic fish-kills (something above 2,000,000 fish). Yet an examination of the background shows how difficult it may be to say "who is responsible" with any certainty. Acid mine wastes were no novelty in this area and, for many years indeed, public policy had accepted the mine wastes as a necessary incident to industrial production. But it is also worth noting that there had been a limestone plant downstream from some of the points from which the most obvious mine discharges took place. The effect of the alkaline discharges from the limestone plant was to neutralize much of the acid, so that the stream remained supportive of fish life. Then, the limestone company shut down its plant, the alkaline contribution was withdrawn, and the fish-kill was one of several adverse results.

Imagine that you have the rule-making power in such a situation. What do you do? You certainly do not now require the mine owner to stop producing because his downstream neighbor has stopped producing. This is the more so because you also know that the mines will (by normal flow induced by gravity) continue to discharge wastes even if production stops. But imagine a further situation. Imagine that the basin contains not only the mines and the limestone plant, but petroleum refineries, a steel mill or two, some food processors, and a vast concentration of human beings whose wastes also go into the stream in one form or another.

The ordinary agency neither has, nor could have, sufficient time and energy and skill to know enough to attribute responsibility to each of these parties in any reasonably precise fashion. Moreover, even when it is possible (in simpler situations) to attribute responsibility, it is not easy to find ways to specify feasible remedies. Again, if we treat industrial pollution as the example, feasible remedies are not merely those which could change the physical situation, but those which could change the physical situation without inducing adverse consequences for the affected interests. To tell a firm to stop a certain discharge practice is to tell it to assume a cost which it has been able to pass on to someone else. Yet this cannot be done without reference to whether the firm can afford to do so. In general, only the firm or industry itself is likely to have the relevant information on such matters as the importance of the firm or industry in the political economy, the nature of product and process, and the related possibilities for technological adaptation. And the firm or industry is likely to be secretive, both because of uses which its competitors might make of the information and because of the uses which public officials might make of it.

If the regulatory agency had to deal with only one kind of producer, it would be intellectually feasible for the agency to develop a competence so that it would know as much about the industry as management itself would know. (The practical problem in this event would simply be that a one-industry situation is one in which all efforts are bent to sustain the industry, and such knowledge would not be used for control purposes.) If, as is more likely to be the case, there are several types of users, then it is intellectually impossible for the regulatory agency to have the relevant range of knowledge. Yet action cannot be wholly foregone, and the result is to try to find something which seems likely to make a "reasonable" impact and which also will be complied with by the discharger on terms which do not require great compulsion.

The second relevant constraint which is pertinent is the complex of social values and myths pertinent to the problem. Without trying to evaluate them precisely, let us note at least the following which are now pertinent to pollution control: (1) There is the image of pollution as a threat to health, a throwback to the period in which the main thrust was against bacterial pollution. But in the policy context, changes in water temperature (which can be a function of industrial use of water for cooling purposes) are also pollution and have virtually nothing to do with human health. (2) There is the image of pollution control as a costly process which inevitably will diminish productive investment by the firms which provide an employment base for the affected area or community. (3) There is an image of pollution represented in reactions to re-use proposals as proposals for "consuming our own filth." (4) There is an image of pollution as "exploitation" by "the spoilers" much in the vein of earlier criticism of the "robber barons." (5) There is an image of pollution as desecration of "nature" (although what "nature" means is itself hard to ascertain).

Some of these myths and values are broadly diffused through the population while others are sharply concentrated around particular social groups.[21] In pursuing an actual policy, the regulatory decision-makers have to come to terms with these myths and values which both push them toward bargaining and impose constraints on the kinds of bargains they can make and the ways in which they make them.

In this respect, the regulator's problem is the same as that of the politician who, as described by Tugwell, continuously "projects the consequences of proposed actions and tries them in the imagination to see whether the useful will outweigh the dangerous." To the degree that social myths and values demand "action" (because, say, pollution means "filth" plus "exploitation" by the powerful who do not care about the "little man")[22] the regulator will find himself in much the same position as the police commissioner who permits himself to be openly represented as bargaining about whether he will "enforce the law." The dangerous will decidedly outweigh the useful.

The importance of this constraint is not that it precludes bargaining, but only that public myths and values define the boundaries of the permissible and the impermissible in such a way as to structure the bargaining process which he may follow. Like the legislator he has much actual freedom in deciding which voices he will hear and which he will not, as he seeks the course which will most expediently combine his own preferences and the settled necessities of his operational world. The greater the tension between a mythology which demands "action" and a constituency resistance which makes it clear that compliance will come at high costs, the more important will become tacit bargaining[23] through manipulation of the technical issues. This is one of the features which makes the compliance process so important, for the more distant publics are able to see the broad statements of policy fairly clearly, but are unable to comprehend the low-visibility decisions involved in implementation or non-implementation. Thus, a regulatory agency which stipulates a policy but broadly interprets "good intentions" as evidence of compliance is, in effect, making a deal with the party whose compliance is necessary. That deal asserts that if the regulated party will take just enough action to permit the regulator to ward off public pressure, then the regulator will be understanding and sympathetic about the regulated party's difficulty in complying in the detail which would produce a drastic change in the environment.

A third order of constraint is the organizational system itself and the largeness or smallness of the alternative access points through which the regulated party may exert influence when unsatisfied with the manner in which the regulatory agency itself is proceeding. This is very well exemplified by the desire of those who advocate regulation to exclude judicial action on the same policy questions wherever possible. The values which judicial decision-makers emphasize, notably those of "reasonableness" and of consistency with prior decisions on similar matters, have often seemed to prevent rapid adaptation to new circumstances. (This would be particularly obvious in such a case as that cited in the Slippery Rock basin, where the liability of the mine owner suddenly was exaggerated by the withdrawal of an ecologically relevant limestone producer rather than by an action by the mine owner himself which was way out of line with that which he had previously been permitted to do.) Although the matter has most often been cited in terms of judicial inability to comprehend the technically relevant data, to have the time to make the pertinent inquiries, or to take the initiative rather than depending upon adversary proceedings, the problem is more generally pertinent to any other kind of decisional forum. The most obvious and commonly remarked feature is that different constituencies are likely to be differently represented in different decisional bodies. Even if it were possible to give the different bodies the same combination of constituencies, however, the fact that attitudes and alliances build up *over time* on the part of those who have actually been handling the matter is extremely relevant. Those who have been involved tend to acquire, as a result of this involvement, commitments which have a sort of emotional first-mortgage upon them. Others who have been not engaged are likely to be in a position to take a new look; this means that the entire decision of the first body may be revised substantially if it goes to a second body. The possibility of such revision is a constraint which may lead regulatory decision-makers to make such compromises as will give them a settled situation, thus excluding some of the opportunities for review by courts, legislatures, or political executives.

This leads to the fourth constraint. If the regulatory agency must expect to deal with the same discrete parties indefinitely into the future, then bargaining rather than ordaining increases in value because the good will of the regulated party increases in value. The finding of tolerable settlements depends upon the willingness of the regulated party to make some of the adjustments which will be necessary if the desired physical result is to be achieved. As one example, the municipal government which has been ordered to install a treatment plant may do so, under the severest compulsion (e.g., a threat to withhold all building permits), but the regulatory agency will undoubtedly have to go to that same municipality later on projects involving plant expansion, cooperation with adjacent municipalities in some joint plant, and so on. The price of rigid compulsion may be that the municipal authorities, who may have suffered political losses themselves because of the action they had to take (e.g., greater antagonism between themselves and local builders), will be much less cooperative simply because they feel abused. The same problem exists with respect to the industrial firm. If the agency has severely alienated the industrial user, it is quite possible for the user to generate severe pressure by throwing up obstacles to cooperation in the relevant adjustments. Such a problem is apparently what was involved in the pulp-and-paper regulation described above. Not only did the industrial representatives object to the particular measures, but even more they objected to the dislocation involved in the "sudden raising" of these issues, and we may speculate that one of the reasons the administrator found it so urgent to have a private and unpublicized meeting to explain the new regulations and his interpretation was his desire to create a new bargaining atmosphere more conducive to securing the future collaboration of industrial firms. In fine, one of the incentives to bargaining when an agency desires changes is that it cannot suddenly pull out the rug and still expect future relations to be sufficiently harmonious to produce "reasonable" compliance.[24]

It is within the bounds of these constraints that the regulators in pollution control have specific opportunity to ordain public policies and/or have necessity to engage in bargaining relationships. They suggest that, whatever the limits of bargaining in any specific instance, the process itself is ineluctable.

NOTES

1.   As illustrations see Roscoe C. Martin, *Water for New York,* Syracuse: Syracuse University Press, 1960, relative to the Water Pollution Control Board of that state; Earl Finbar Murphy, *Water Purity,* Madison: University of Wisconsin Press, 1961, relative to the State Committee on Water Pollution; William F. Schulz, Jr., *Conservation Law and Administration,* relative to the Pennsylvania Sanitary Water Board; and U.S. House of Representatives, Committee on Government Operations, Subcommittee on Natural Resources

and Power, *Hearings ... on Water Pollution Control and Abatement* (1963), Part 6, pp. 3580–3581, relative to Texas Water Pollution Control Board. (These hearings are hereinafter cited as *Jones Subcommittee Hearings.*)

2.   H. B. N. Hynes, *The Biology of Polluted Waters,* Liverpool: Liverpool University Press, 1963, p. 2. Some of the natural-scientific problems in defining pollution are discussed in Louis Klein, *River Pollution: II, Causes and Effects,* London: Butterworth, 1962, Chapter 2.

3.   Klein, *ibid.,* makes the point that this complicates the natural scientist's job for, in his view, pollution is best defined in terms of substances in the waterway.

4.   H. B. No. 24 of the 57th Legislature, First Called Session, Codified as Article 7621d, *Vernon's Annotated Civil Statutes,* Sec. 2(g) as reprinted in *Jones Subcommittee Hearings,* Part 6, p. 3580. Emphasis additional.

5.   We do not consider ourselves competent to get into the argument among the health specialists whether pollution control (control of what went into the streams) was actually more important than providing sanitary water supplies (providing adequate filtration of that water taken out of streams and piped to consumers), but to note the fact that control of discharges was believed to be relevant and that policy was predicated on this belief. Cf. Gaylord West Anderson, "Regulation of Public Health," in George A. Graham and Henry S. Reining, Jr., *Regulatory Administration* (New York: John Wiley and Sons, Inc., 1943), Ch. 3. For a contemporaneous study, the internal evidence of which clearly indicates that people thought control of discharges relevant, see Frank E. Wing, "Thirty-five Years of Typhoid," in Paul U. Kellogg (ed.), *The Pittsburgh District: Civic Frontage,* (Pittsburgh Survey, Vol. 6), New York: Survey Associates, Inc., 1914.

6.   *The Jones Hearings,* Part IB, p. 1512, used 1960 data from the House Committee on Public Works showing thirty-eight states with such a process. Independently, we were able to verify at least seven additional such states.

7.   For such a qualitative standard see Martin, *Water for New York,* pp. 184–185.

8.   Allen V. Kneese, *The Economics of Regional Water Quality Management,* Baltimore: Johns Hopkins Press, 1964, pp. 21–24, provides a useful, quick summation of the various stages of treatment now in common use.

9.   James G. March and Herbert A. Simon, *Organizations,* New York: John Wiley and Sons, Inc., 1958, pp. 129–131.

10. Cf. Robert A. Gilpin, *American Scientists and Nuclear Weapons Policy,* Princeton: Princeton University Press, 1962, Chapter 9; and Samuel P. Hun-

tington, *The Common Defense: Strategic Programs in National Politics,* New York: Columbia University Press, 1961, at p. 2891.

11. Martin, *op. cit.,* p. 187.

12. Most of the studies of regulatory politics refer to these distributive decisions. Cf., for example, Victor G. Rosenblum, "How to Get into TV: The Federal Communications Commission and Miami's Channel 10," in Alan F. Westin (ed.), *The Uses of Power: 7 Cases in American Politics,* New York: Harcourt, Brace and World, Inc., 1962, pp. 173–227.

13. Murphy, *op. cit.*

14. The emphasis placed on this point by those who have been closely associated with political decision-makers is so strong that one cannot ignore it. Cf. Theodore Sorensen, *Decision-Making in the White House,* New York: Columbia University Press, 1963, p. 29.

15. Murphy, *op. cit.,* p. 124.

16. Decision-makers' need for guidance in the form of constituency pressure is not a well-developed point in political theory although it is implicit (and sometimes explicit) in natural-history studies of decision-making such as Victor A. Thompson, *The Regulatory Process in OPA Rationing,* New York: King's Crown Press, 1950, Chapter 6.

17. The suggestion that decision-makers operating without pressure tend to behave quite irrationally is put forth in Matthew Holden, Jr., "Committee Politics under Primitive Uncertainty," *Midwest Journal of Political Science,* Vol. 9, No. 3 (August, 1965), pp. 251–253. One might even go further to say that political pressure performs some of the same functions which economists attribute to the price system and may even (normatively and empirically) be somewhat superior if one assumes democratic values, simply because votes are likely to be more evenly distributed than dollars.

18. For a similar case see Harold Herman, "The Metropolitan Sewage Treatment Plant," in Roscoe C. Martin and Frank J. Munger (eds.), *Decisions in Syracuse,* Bloomington: Indiana University Press, 1961, pp. 80–109.

19. For an example of an agency unable to strike the bargains which might have saved it see Harry D. Wolf, *The Railroad Labor Board,* Chicago: University of Chicago Press, 1927.

20. Definition: *"Constituency" means any group, body, or interest to which the decision-maker looks for aid and guidance, or which seeks to establish itself (in his judgment) as so important that he "had better" take account of their preferences even if (which would not often be the case) he were wholly averse to those preferences.*

21. Samuel P. Hays, *Conservation and the Gospel of Efficiency,* Cambridge: Harvard University Press, 1959, indicates that "conservation" is largely the spawn of a particular group with a scientific interest. (Since this means an *educated* group, it also means–particularly for the generation about which Hays wrote–an upper-middle or even upper-class group.) White comes to the same point in his assertion that "One striking fact is that a large number of environmental quality decisions are made by people who feel a strong professional identification. Their view of themselves as conservationists, economists, sanitary engineers, foresters, or another claimed vocation may be expected to shape their perceptions of the environment and their competence to handle it. In these roles they not only inherit customary ways of defining significant parts of the environment but they are disposed to distort or ignore phenomena that they regard as beyond their professional responsibility. Their perceptions and preferences become the implicit and usually unchallenged determinants of plans presented for public choice." Gilbert F. White, "Formation and Role of Public Attitudes in Environmental Quality Decisions." Paper presented at the 1966 Resources for the Future Forum on Quality of the Environment, Washington, March 8–9, 1966, p. 27.

22. The alienation literature is pertinent here. Cf. Marvin E. Olson, "Alienation and Political Opinions," *Public Opinion Quarterly,* Vol. 29, No. 2 (Summer, 1965), pp. 200–212; and Clarence N. Stone, "Local Referendums: An Alternative to the Alienated Voter Model," *ibid.,* pp. 213–222.

23. Thomas C. Schelling, *The Strategy of Conflict,* Cambridge: Harvard University Press, 1960, pp. 59–60.

24. Lionel Robbins has some wise words on this, addressing himself to his economist colleagues, observing that changes in policy cannot simply be done "rationally" but must depend on the accommodations of people. See his *Politics and Economics: Papers in Political Economy,* New York: St. Martin's Press, 1963, pp. 20–21.

ANNOTATED BIBLIOGRAPHY

The items in this bibliography are of two general sorts. Some are concerned primarily with theoretical and methodological considerations in the study and research of public policy formation. Others are studies dealing with policy formation in particular substantive areas or with particular participants, such as independent regulatory commissions, in the policy-making process. While the bibliography reflects the compiler's interests, it does not focus on any single approach to policy study and is intended to be suggestive and helpful rather than exhaustive in nature. Many useful items could not be included in a short listing.

Bailey, Stephen K., *Congress Makes a Law* (New York: Columbia University Press, 1950). A classic account of how the enactment of the Employment Act of 1946 was shaped by ideas, interests, individuals, and institutions.

Baldwin, Sidney, *Poverty and Politics: The Rise and Decline of the Farm Security Administration* (Chapel Hill: University of North Carolina Press, 1968). The best treatment of the Farm Security Administration and rural poverty policy during the New Deal.

Bauer, Raymond A., Ithiel de Sola Pool, and Lewis Anthony Dexter, *American Business and Public Policy* (New York: Atherton Press, 1963). An important, empirically-based study of reciprocal trade policy-making, focusing on communication and decision-making processes.

Bauer, Raymond A., and Kenneth J. Gergen, eds., *The Study of Policy Formation* (New York: The Free Press, 1968). A collection of empirically-oriented essays dealing with theoretical and methodological aspects of the study of policy formation.

Bernstein, Marver H., *Regulating Business by Independent Commission* (Princeton, N.J.: Princeton University Press, 1955). A useful critical study of the politics and process of commission regulation and policy development.

Bock, Edwin A., ed., *Government Regulation of Business: A Casebook* (Englewood Cliffs, N.J.: Prentice-Hall, 1965). Seven cases on administrative regulation and policy formation prepared for the Inter-University Case Program.

Cary, William L., *Politics and the Regulatory Agencies* (New York: McGraw-Hill, 1967). A former chairman of the Securities and Exchange Commission presents a lively discussion of regulatory commissions in their political context.

Dahl, Robert A., and Charles E. Lindblom, *Politics, Economics, and Welfare* (New York: Harper and Row, 1953). An important and indispensable contribution to the development of a theory of political economy.

Dawson, Richard E., and James A. Robinson, "Inter-Party Competition, Economic Variables, and Welfare Policies in the American States," *Journal of Politics*, XXV (May, 1963), 265–289. A seminal empirical study which concludes that the economic variables are more significant than political variables in the formation of state welfare policy.

Dye, Thomas R., *Politics, Economics, and the Public: Policy Outcomes in the American States* (Chicago: Rand McNally, 1966). A systematic, quantitative, and comparative study of several areas of state policy-making.

Edleman, Murray, "Governmental Organization and Public Policy," *Public Administration Review*, XII (Autumn, 1952), 276–283. Assessment of the effect of administrative structure on policy decisions, utilizing group theory.

———, "Symbols and Political Quiescence," *American Political Science Review*, LIV (September, 1960), 695–704. A psychological study of the role of symbols in policy formation and compliance.

Engler, Robert, *The Politics of Oil* (New York: Macmillan, 1961). An informative, normative-oriented examination of the petroleum industry and public policy.

Fainsod, Merle, Lincoln Gordon, and Joseph C. Palamountain, Jr., *Government and the American Economy* (New York: W. W. Norton, 1959). The leading textbook on American economic policies, their evolution, formation, and substance.

Foss, Phillip O., *Politics and Grass* (Seattle: University of Washington Press, 1960). A study of the formation and administration of policy for the public grazing lands of the United States.

Freeman, J. Leiper, *The Political Process*, 2nd ed. (New York: Random House, 1965). A short but valuable examination of executive bureau–congressional committee–interest group subsystems in policy formation.

Hadwiger, Don F., and Ross B. Talbot, *Pressures and Protests* (San Francisco: Chandler, 1965). A case study of agricultural price support policy-making during the Kennedy Administration along structural-descriptive lines.

Hardin, Charles M., *Food and Fiber in the Nation's Politics* (Washington: Government Printing Office, 1967). A survey of the politics of agricultural policy formation and administration.

————, *The Politics of Agriculture* (New York: The Free Press, 1952). Despite the title, the focus here is on conflict and struggle among administrative agencies in the formation of soil conservation policy.

Hawley, Ellis W., *The New Deal and the Problem of Monopoly* (Princeton, N.J.: Princeton University Press, 1966). Thorough treatment of antitrust policy and politics during the New Deal.

Herring, Pendleton, *The Politics of Democracy,* paperbound edition (New York: W. W. Norton, 1965). Originally published in 1940, this remains an insightful analysis of the American political process as a bargaining and compromise system.

Kroll, Morton, "Hypotheses and Designs for the Study of Public Policies in the United States," *Midwest Journal of Political Science,* VI (November, 1962), 363–383. Kroll discusses two sets of categories for policy study— environmental and internal process features.

Latham, Earl, *The Group Basis of Politics* (Ithaca, N.Y.: Cornell University Press, 1952). A group theory approach to the conflict over basing-point legislation during the Truman Administration.

Lawrence, Samuel A., *United States Merchant Shipping Policies and Politics* (Washington: Brookings Institution, 1966). A good institutional-descriptive treatment of policy formation and development in this area.

Lekachman, Robert, *The Age of Keynes* (New York: Random House, 1966). A broad effort to assess the impact of Keynes and Keynesian theory on American economic stability policy.

Lindblom, Charles E., *The Intelligence of Democracy* (New York: The Free Press, 1965). A discussion of bargaining and other types of mutual adjustment in policy formation, based on economic concepts.

————, *The Policy-Making Process* (Englewood Cliffs, N.J.: Prentice-Hall, 1968). An eclectic introduction to the policy-making process which points up its complexity.

————, "The Science of 'Muddling Through,' " *Public Administration Review,* XIX (Spring, 1959), 79–88. A comparison of the incremental and rational-comprehensive models of decision-making which finds the former more realistic.

Lowi, Theodore, "American Business, Public Policy, Case Studies, and Political Theory," *World Politics,* XVI (July, 1964), 677–715. An assessment of the condition of policy theory and an attempt to develop a framework for comparison and interpretation of case studies. Lowi suggests that there are distributive, regulatory, distinctive policy-making processes.

———, "The Public Philosophy: Interest Group Liberalism," *American Political Science Review,* LXI (March, 1965), 5–24. An argument that the traditional liberal-conservative framework is no longer adequate for understanding or rationalizing public policy in the United States.

Maass, Arthur, *Muddy Waters* (Cambridge, Mass.: Harvard University Press, 1951). A description and evaluation of the role of the Army Corps of Engineers in water resource policy.

McConnell, Grant, *Private Power and American Democracy* (New York: Alfred A. Knopf, 1966). An analysis of the role of private groups in policy formation. Decentralization and pluralism have often made them dominant.

Mitchell, William C., "The New Political Economy," *Social Research,* XXXV (Spring, 1968), 76–110. A useful summary of new trends in policy research utilizing economic concepts.

Monsen, R. Joseph, Jr., and Mark W. Connor, *The Makers of Public Policy* (New York: McGraw-Hill, 1965). A discussion of "power groups" and their ideologies.

Morgan, Robert J., *Governing Soil Conservation: Thirty Years of the New Decentralization* (Baltimore: Johns Hopkins Press, 1965). A comprehensive study of the administration, politics, and policy of soil conservation.

Moynihan, Daniel P., *Maximum Feasible Misunderstanding* (New York: Free Press, 1969). A study of the development and administration of the community action program established by the Economic Opportunity Act. Moynihan is quite critical of social scientists and professional reformers as policy-makers.

Ranney, Austin, ed., *Political Science and Public Policy* (Chicago: Markham, 1968). Essays on issues, problems, and methods in the analysis of policy and policy outcomes.

Redford, Emmette S., "Perspectives for the Study of Government Regulation," *Midwest Journal of Political Science,* VI (February, 1962), pp.1–18. Ecology, structure, and other factors are suggested as useful perspectives in a broad view of the topic.

————, ed., *Public Administration and Policy Formation* (Austin: University of Texas Press, 1956). Studies include oil, natural gas, trade regulation, banking, and water resources.

Rourke, Francis E., *Bureaucracy, Politics, and Public Policy* (Boston: Little, Brown, 1968). A short but substantial consideration of the policy-making activities of agencies from a political perspective.

Schattschneider, E. E., *The Semisovereign People* (New York: Holt, Rinehart and Winston, 1960). The author's ideas on group theory and political conflict are especially relevant.

Schneier, Edward V., ed., *Policy-Making in American Government* (New York: Basic Books, 1969). A useful collection of readings under the headings of policy formulation, articulation, mobilization, codification, application, and redefinition.

Shapiro, Martin, *Law and Politics in the Supreme Court* (New York: The Free Press, 1964). A political perspective on the Court as a policy-maker in several areas, including labor relations, taxation, and antitrust.

Smith, Frank E., *The Politics of Conservation* (New York: Pantheon Books, 1966). A stimulating political history of conservation by a former congressman who contends that most major conservation developments have been rooted in pork-barrel politics.

Steiner, Gilbert Y., *Social Insecurity: The Politics of Welfare* (Chicago: Rand McNally, 1966). An excellent analytical treatment of welfare policy-making which demonstrates the relationship between the nature of the policy-making process and policy substance.

Sundquist, James L., *Politics and Policy: The Eisenhower, Kennedy, and Johnson Years* (Washington: Brookings Institution, 1968). Case studies and analysis of several areas of domestic policy-making during 1953–1966.

Talbot, Ross B., and Don F. Hadwiger, *The Policy Process in American Agriculture* (San Francisco: Chandler, 1968). Concerned with all facets of agricultural policy formation, the substance of the volume compensates for any lacks in methodological rigor.

Truman, David B., *The Governmental Process* (New York: Alfred A. Knopf, 1951). The standard work on interest groups in the American political process.

Wildavsky, Aaron B., "The Analysis of Issue Contexts in the Study of Decision-Making," *Journal of Politics*, XXIV (November, 1962), 717–732. An argument that the context of policy issues helps shape the policy-making process and its outcomes, as in public power policy.

————, *The Politics of the Budgetary Process* (Boston: Little, Brown, 1964). An analysis of the national budgetary process, utilizing game theory insights, which indicates the relationship of the budgetary process to public policy.

Zeigler, Harmon, *Interest Groups in American Society* (Englewood Cliffs, N.J.: Prentice-Hall, 1964). A solid textbook on the nature and role of interest groups in the political process.

————, *The Politics of Small Business* (Washington: Public Affairs Press, 1961). A study of the political life of American small businessmen and the formation of national policy relating to small business.

ABCDE79876543210